Party Strategies in Western Europe

This book examines political party system change from a party-centric perspective and assesses how, and to what extent, established political parties in western Europe can maintain their dominant positions.

Parties are increasingly competing in a changeable environment and this book assesses the ways in which political parties have tried to adapt to these changes, by undertaking a study of the strategies employed by established parties since 1950. It features analysis of 17 western European countries, with eight case studies explored in greater depth, including France, Germany, Portugal, Greece, Denmark, Ireland, Switzerland and Luxembourg. The book assesses two groups of 'strategies': institutional strategies, by which parties aim for success through control of rules, regulations and laws; and strategies oriented towards the electorate, through which parties seek success by proving themselves responsive to voters. Offering a detailed empirical assessment of the frequency with which these strategies have been employed, this book assesses the impact on established political parties, and argues that parties can shape their own fate by strategic choices.

Party Strategies in Western Europe will be of interest to students and scholars of European politics, government and party politics.

Gemma Loomes is a teaching fellow in Comparative Politics at the University of Birmingham, UK.

Routledge advances in European politics

1 **Russian Messianism**
Third Rome, revolution,
Communism and after
Peter J.S. Duncan

2 **European Integration and the Postmodern Condition**
Governance, democracy, identity
Peter van Ham

3 **Nationalism in Italian Politics**
The stories of the Northern
League, 1980–2000
Damian Tambini

4 **International Intervention in the Balkans since 1995**
Edited by Peter Siani-Davies

5 **Widening the European Union**
The politics of institutional change
and reform
Edited by Bernard Steunenberg

6 **Institutional Challenges in the European Union**
*Edited by Madeleine Hosli,
Adrian van Deemen and
Mika Widgrén*

7 **Europe Unbound**
Enlarging and reshaping the
boundaries of the European Union
Edited by Jan Zielonka

8 **Ethnic Cleansing in the Balkans**
Nationalism and the destruction of
tradition
Cathie Carmichael

9 **Democracy and Enlargement in Post-Communist Europe**
The democratisation of the general
public in fifteen Central and
Eastern European countries,
1991–1998
Christian W. Haerpfer

10 **Private Sector Involvement in the Euro**
The power of ideas
*Stefan Collignon and
Daniela Schwarzer*

11 **Europe**
A Nietzschean perspective
Stefan Elbe

12 **European Union and e-Voting**
Addressing the European
Parliament's internet voting
challenge
*Edited by Alexander H. Trechsel
and Fernando Mendez*

13 **European Union Council Presidencies**
A comparative perspective
Edited by Ole Elgström

14 **European Governance and Supranational Institutions**
Making states comply
Jonas Tallberg

15 **European Union, NATO and Russia**
Martin Smith and Graham Timmins

16 **Business, the State and Economic Policy**
The case of Italy
G. Grant Amyot

17 **Europeanization and Transnational States**
Comparing Nordic central governments
Bengt Jacobsson, Per Lægreid and Ove K. Pedersen

18 **European Union Enlargement**
A comparative history
Edited by Wolfram Kaiser and Jürgen Elvert

19 **Gibraltar**
British or Spanish?
Peter Gold

20 **Gendering Spanish Democracy**
Monica Threlfall, Christine Cousins and Celia Valiente

21 **European Union Negotiations**
Processes, networks and negotiations
Edited by Ole Elgström and Christer Jönsson

22 **Evaluating Euro-Mediterranean Relations**
Stephen C. Calleya

23 **The Changing Face of European Identity**
A seven-nation study of (supra) national attachments
Edited by Richard Robyn

24 **Governing Europe**
Discourse, governmentality and European integration
William Walters and Jens Henrik Haahr

25 **Territory and Terror**
Conflicting nationalisms in the Basque country
Jan Mansvelt Beck

26 **Multilateralism, German Foreign Policy and Central Europe**
Claus Hofhansel

27 **Popular Protest in East Germany**
Gareth Dale

28 **Germany's Foreign Policy Towards Poland and the Czech Republic**
Ostpolitik revisited
Karl Cordell and Stefan Wolff

29 **Kosovo**
The politics of identity and space
Denisa Kostovicova

30 **The Politics of European Union Enlargement**
Theoretical approaches
Edited by Frank Schimmelfennig and Ulrich Sedelmeier

31 **Europeanizing Social Democracy?**
The rise of the party of European socialists
Simon Lightfoot

32 **Conflict and Change in EU Budgetary Politics**
Johannes Lindner

33 **Gibraltar, Identity and Empire**
E.G. Archer

34 **Governance Stories**
Mark Bevir and R.A.W Rhodes

35 **Britain and the Balkans**
1991 until the present
Carole Hodge

36 **The Eastern Enlargement of the European Union**
John O'Brennan

37 **Values and Principles in European Union Foreign Policy**
Edited by Sonia Lucarelli and Ian Manners

38 **European Union and the Making of a Wider Northern Europe**
Pami Aalto

39 **Democracy in the European Union**
Towards the emergence of a public sphere
Edited by Liana Giorgi, Ingmar Von Homeyer and Wayne Parsons

40 **European Union Peacebuilding and Policing**
Michael Merlingen with Rasa Ostrauskaite

41 **The Conservative Party and European Integration since 1945**
At the heart of Europe?
N.J. Crowson

42 **E-government in Europe**
Re-booting the state
Edited by Paul G. Nixon and Vassiliki N. Koutrakou

43 **EU Foreign and Interior Policies**
Cross-pillar politics and the social construction of sovereignty
Stephan Stetter

44 **Policy Transfer in European Union Governance**
Regulating the utilities
Simon Bulmer, David Dolowitz, Peter Humphreys and Stephen Padgett

45 **The Europeanization of National Political Parties**
Power and organizational adaptation
Edited by Thomas Poguntke, Nicholas Aylott, Elisabeth Carter, Robert Ladrech and Kurt Richard Luther

46 **Citizenship in Nordic Welfare States**
Dynamics of choice, duties and participation in a changing Europe
Edited by Bjørn Hvinden and Håkan Johansson

47 **National Parliaments within the Enlarged European Union**
From victims of integration to competitive actors?
Edited by John O'Brennan and Tapio Raunio

48 **Britain, Ireland and Northern Ireland since 1980**
The totality of relationships
Eamonn O'Kane

49 **The EU and the European Security Strategy**
Forging a global Europe
Edited by Sven Biscop and Jan Joel Andersson

50 **European Security and Defence Policy**
An implementation perspective
Edited by Michael Merlingen and Rasa Ostrauskaitė

51 **Women and British Party Politics**
Descriptive, substantive and symbolic representation
Sarah Childs

52 **The Selection of Ministers in Europe**
Hiring and firing
Edited by Keith Dowding and Patrick Dumont

53 **Energy Security**
Europe's new foreign policy challenge
Richard Youngs

54 **Institutional Challenges in Post-Constitutional Europe**
Governing change
Edited by Catherine Moury and Luís de Sousa

55 **The Struggle for the European Constitution**
A past and future history
Michael O'Neill

56 **Transnational Labour Solidarity**
Mechanisms of commitment to cooperation within the European trade union movement
Katarzyna Gajewska

57 **The Illusion of Accountability in the European Union**
Edited by Sverker Gustavsson, Christer Karlsson and Thomas Persson

58 **The European Union and Global Social Change**
A critical geopolitical-economic analysis
József Böröcz

59 **Citizenship and Collective Identity in Europe**
Ireneusz Pawel Karolewski

60 **EU Enlargement and Socialization**
Turkey and Cyprus
Stefan Engert

61 **The Politics of EU Accession**
Turkish challenges and Central European experiences
Edited by Lucie Tunkrová and Pavel Šaradín

62 **The Political History of European Integration**
The hypocrisy of democracy-through-market
Hagen Schulz-Forberg and Bo Stråth

63 **The Spatialities of Europeanization**
Power, governance and territory in Europe
Alun Jones and Julian Clark

64 **European Union Sanctions and Foreign Policy**
When and why do they work?
Clara Portela

65 **The EU's Role in World Politics**
A retreat from liberal
internationalism
Richard Youngs

66 **Social Democracy and European
Integration**
The politics of preference formation
*Edited by
Dionyssis Dimitrakopoulos*

67 **The EU Presence in
International Organizations**
*Edited by Spyros Blavoukos and
Dimitris Bourantonis*

68 **Sustainability in European
Environmental Policy**
Challenge of governance and
knowledge
*Edited by Rob Atkinson,
Georgios Terizakis and
Karsten Zimmermann*

69 **Fifty Years of EU–Turkey
Relations**
A Sisyphean story
Edited by Armagan Emre Çakir

70 **Europeanization and Foreign
Policy**
State diversity in Finland and
Britain
Juha Jokela

71 **EU Foreign Policy and
Post-Soviet Conflicts**
Stealth intervention
Nicu Popescu

72 **Switzerland in Europe**
Continuity and change in the
Swiss political economy
*Edited by Christine Trampusch
and André Mach*

73 **The Political Economy of
Noncompliance**
Adjusting to the single European
market
Scott Nicholas Siegel

74 **National and European Foreign
Policy**
Towards Europeanization
*Edited by Reuben Wong and
Christopher Hill*

75 **The European Union Diplomatic
Service**
Ideas, preferences and identities
Caterina Carta

76 **Poland within the European
Union**
New awkward partner or new
heart of Europe?
Aleks Szczerbiak

77 **A Political Theory of Identity in
European Integration**
Memory and policies
Catherine Guisan

78 **EU Foreign Policy and the
Europeanization of Neutral
States**
Comparing Irish and Austrian
foreign policy
Nicole Alecu de Flers

79 **Party Strategies in Western
Europe**
Party competition and electoral
outcomes
Gemma Loomes

Party Strategies in Western Europe

Party competition and electoral outcomes

Gemma Loomes

Routledge
Taylor & Francis Group

LONDON AND NEW YORK

First published 2012
by Routledge
2 Park Square, Milton Park, Abingdon, Oxfordshire OX14 4RN

Simultaneously published in the USA and Canada
by Routledge
711 Third Avenue, New York, NY 10017

First issued in paperback 2014

Routledge is an imprint of the Taylor & Francis Group, an informa business

British Library Cataloguing in Publication Data
A catalogue record for this book is available from the British Library

Library of Congress Cataloging-in-Publication Data
Loomes, Gemma, 1982–
    Party system change in Western Europe : party competition and
    electoral outcomes / Gemma Loomes.
    p. cm. – (Routledge advances in European politics ; 79)
    Includes bibliographical references and index.
    1. Political parties–Europe, Western. 2. Europe, Western–Politics and
    government. I. Title.
    JN94.A979L64 2011
    324.2094–dc23
                                                              2011018935

ISBN 978-0-415-60160-3 (hbk)
ISBN 978-1-138-80239-1 (pbk)
ISBN 978-0-203-18245-1 (ebk)

Typeset in Times
by Wearset Ltd, Boldon, Tyne and Wear

Contents

List of illustrations   xi
Acknowledgements   xiv

1 A party-centric approach to party system change   1
   1.1 The impact of social change on modern-day party systems 2
   1.2 Parties as dependent and independent actors 5
   1.3 Measurements and definitions: party strategies and party
      systems 7
   1.4 The impact of party strategies on party system change 14

2 Electorate-orientated strategies   16
   2.1 Ideological change 16
   2.2 Electoral responsiveness 26
   2.3 Relations with anti-political establishment parties 30
   2.4 Pre-electoral coalition agreements 34
   2.5 Length of coalition agreements 37
   2.6 Conclusion 40

3 Institutional strategies   42
   3.1 Electoral laws 43
   3.2 Electoral systems 54
   3.3 Television campaigning airtime 66
   3.4 State subsidies 74
   3.5 Conclusion 87

4 Selection of cases and measurements   89
   4.1 Electorate-orientated strategies 89
   4.2 Institutional strategies 94
   4.3 The Mair typology and party system change 98
   4.4 Assessing the fate of established parties 106
   4.5 Conclusion 111

5 The use of electorate-orientated strategies   112

5.1 Portugal 112

5.2 Germany 119

*5.3 The frequent use of electorate-orientated strategies and
      established parties' centrality 125*

5.4 Switzerland 129

5.5 Luxembourg 136

*5.6 The infrequent use of electorate-orientated strategies and
      established parties' centrality 141*

5.7 Conclusion 145

6 The use of institutional strategies   148

6.1 France 148

6.2 Greece 155

*6.3 The frequent use of institutional strategies and established
      parties' centrality 160*

6.4 Denmark 164

6.5 Ireland 171

*6.6 The infrequent use of institutional strategies and established
      parties' centrality 177*

6.7 Conclusion 181

**7 Party strategies in western Europe: party competition and
    electoral outcomes**   183

7.1 The impact of party strategies 183

7.2 The chain of causality 190

7.3 Electoral change and party system change 193

7.4 Conclusion 195

Appendix 1: established parties in western Europe, 1950–2009   197

**Appendix 2: anti-political establishment parties in western
Europe, 1950–2009**   201

**Appendix 3: centrality data for countries not the subject of
case studies, 1950–2009**   205

Notes   228

Bibliography   232

Index   250

Illustrations

Figure

7.1   Levels of electoral centrality in Greece, Spain and Portugal,
1976–2009   192

Tables

1.1   Defining established and non-established parties, illustrated by
the German example   9

2.1   Ideological change (left–right) in western European governing
parties, 1950–2003   20

2.2   Average ideological change (left–right) and party incumbency,
1950–2003   24

2.3   Ideological change and government status (within-country)   26

2.4   Ideological change and government status (across-country)   26

2.5   Electoral responsiveness of western European governing parties,
1950–2009   29

2.6   Established parties' strategies towards anti-political establishment
party system entrants, 1950–2009   33

2.7   Coalition governments based on pre-electoral coalition agreements,
1950–2009   36

2.8   Average length of coalition agreements in western Europe,
1950–2009   38

3.1   Coding categories for electoral laws   47

3.2   Electoral laws and non-established parties in western Europe,
1950–2009   48

3.3   Electoral systems and non-established parties in western Europe,
1950–2009   58

3.4   Coding categories for political television advertising   69

3.5   Television advertising regimes and non-established parties in
western Europe, 1950–2009   70

3.6   Coding categories for state subsidies   77

3.7   State subsidies and non-established parties in western Europe,
1950–2009   78

4.1	The use of electorate-orientated strategies by country, 1950–2009	91
4.2	The use of institutional strategies by country, 1950–2009	95
4.3	The Mair typology	99
4.4	The revised Mair typology	103
4.5	Introducing the numerical factor into the Mair typology	104
4.6	Measuring the centrality of established parties in western Europe	110
5.1	Established and non-established parties in Portugal, 1976–2009	113
5.2	Centrality of established parties in the Portuguese party system, 1976–2009	114
5.3	Party system change in Portugal, 1976–2009	117
5.4	Established and non-established parties in Germany, 1953–2009	120
5.5	Centrality of established parties in the German party system, 1953–2009	121
5.6	Party system change in Germany, 1953–2009	124
5.7	Established and non-established parties in Switzerland, 1951–2007	130
5.8	Centrality of established parties in the Swiss party system, 1951–2007	131
5.9	Party system change in Switzerland, 1951–2007	135
5.10	Established and non-established parties in Luxembourg, 1951–2009	136
5.11	Centrality of established parties in the Luxembourgish party system, 1951–2009	138
5.12	Party system change in Luxembourg, 1951–2009	140
6.1	Established and non-established parties in France, 1958–2007	150
6.2	Centrality of established parties in the French party system, 1958–2007	152
6.3	Party system change in France, 1958–2007	154
6.4	Established and non-established parties in Greece, 1975–2009	156
6.5	Centrality of established parties in the Greek party system, 1975–2009	158
6.6	Party system change in Greece, 1975–2009	160
6.7	Established and non-established parties in Denmark, 1950–2007	165
6.8	Centrality of established parties in the Danish party system, 1950–2007	167
6.9	Party system change in Denmark, 1950–2007	170
6.10	Established and non-established parties in Ireland, 1951–2007	172
6.11	Centrality of established parties in the Irish party system, 1951–2007	174
6.12	Party system change in Ireland, 1951–2007	176
7.1	Criteria to determine levels of centrality for established parties, 1950–2009	184
7.2	Levels of systemic centrality in 17 western European countries, 1950–2009, ranked by electorate-orientated strategies	185
7.3	Levels of systemic centrality in 17 western European countries, 1950–2009, ranked by institutional strategies	187

7.4   Levels of engagement in strategies in Greece, Spain and Portugal,
       1975–2009   191
7.5   Levels of electoral, parliamentary and governmental centrality for
       established parties in Greece, Spain and Portugal, 1975–2006   193
7.6   Electoral change and party system change in western Europe,
       1950–2009   194

Acknowledgements

Throughout the process of completing this book, I have received invaluable advice and support from a great number of people. Primarily, I would like to thank Richard Luther for providing me with encouragement and constructive criticism throughout the entirety of this project. His advice has always been sound and his enthusiasm unwavering, and I am indebted to him for his guidance in completing this study. I am also grateful to a number of other members of staff at Keele University, both past and present. Elisabeth Carter always provided useful suggestions for improvements and has assisted me in many respects far more than I could have reasonably expected. Thomas Poguntke also provided valuable guidance and assistance at the beginning of the project. I am also grateful to Rosemary O'Kane, for encouraging me to undertake a study of this magnitude in terms of geographical and temporal scale; her encouragement and constant faith in my ability to complete the study were invaluable throughout. The entire School of Politics, International Relations and Philosophy (SPIRE) at Keele, and in particular the Keele European Parties Research Unit (KEPRU), has been a valuable source of support in creating a positive and productive environment in which to complete this research, and I am grateful for all the support I have received.

I am also indebted to the Economic and Social Research Council (ESRC) for their generous funding of the project. Further afield, Richard Katz, Steve Wolinetz and Jörgen Elklit have provided useful comments on papers presented at conferences based on chapters of the book. Primarily, I would also like to thank Peter Mair for his encouraging feedback, and for the interest that he has shown in the study. The support of my colleagues at Leicester University, Philip Lynch and Richard Whitaker, has also been invaluable.

I like to thank Routledge for their willingness to publish this book and for their assistance in preparing the manuscript for publication; any errors in the data are entirely my own responsibility.

Finally, I would like to thank my family, who have been a constant source of support and encouragement throughout the project. I dedicate this work to them.

1 A party-centric approach to party system change

Political parties are central actors within western European political systems, and the choices they make in terms of electoral, parliamentary and governing strategies can significantly influence their success or failure as political actors. It may be a truism that parties compete for 'policy, office and/or votes' (Müller and Strøm 1999b), but exactly *how* political parties compete and, more specifically, what impact the competitive choices made by political parties have on their own fate, and the party systems in which they compete, remains an understudied area of research. The significance of party strategies has been highlighted in the work of Müller and Strøm (1999b) among others, and the role that political parties can play in the process of party system change has also been highlighted, most notably by Peter Mair (1997, 2002). However, the work of Müller and Strøm does not consider the systemic impact of a party's strategic choice and the impact that these choices can have on party competition. In contrast, the work of Mair focuses on the role of political parties in the process of party system change, but does not consider in detail the strategic decisions and actions that influence party behaviour, ultimately influencing the shape of the party system. This book seeks to fill a gap in the literature by developing the work of Mair, and Müller and Strøm to combine these approaches and to address specifically how established political parties may seek to influence the process of party system change, and with what impact.

The importance of party strategies has become an increasingly pertinent research question since the 1970s, when the dawning of the 'post-industrial' age (Bell 1973) substantially changed the political landscape in which political parties acted and competed. Sustained peace in western Europe, unparalleled prosperity, a vast expansion in higher education and increased travel and communication between countries (Crewe 1985: 5) led to changes at the societal level that significantly altered electoral behaviour. The votes of parties' core supporters were no longer assured, and the erosion of societal cleavages facilitated the process of party system fragmentation. Indeed, since the 1970s, there has been an increase in the fragmentation of party systems (Wolinetz 1979), electoral volatility (Pedersen 1979), partisan dealignment (Dalton *et al.* 1984), decreasing electoral turnout (Franklin 2004) and declining party membership (Mair and Van Biezen 2001) across western Europe. However, this is not to say that political parties have acted solely as passive victims of the process of radical change.

It is the contention of this book that political parties have adjusted and adapted to the unquestionably changed political and social landscape since the 1970s. Although the environment in which they compete has changed significantly, continuity remains a significant feature of many western European party systems, with core political parties still shaping and structuring party system dynamics as they have throughout the post-war period.[1] This book examines why there appears to be a dichotomy between levels of social and electoral change on the one hand, and levels of party system change on the other, and will explore a party-centred response to this problem. The relationship between social change, electoral change and party system change is not deterministic; instead, the strategies of political parties can act as intervening factors in these processes. Political parties can act strategically to attempt to consolidate or improve their systemic position, and the purpose of this book is to assess the ways in which political parties can restrict or facilitate the process of party system change, and to assess the outcomes of these strategic decisions.

1.1 The impact of social change on modern-day party systems

The 1970s marked the start of a period of electoral turmoil for many established political parties in western Europe. New parties on both the left and the right of the political spectrum challenged previously dominant parties and stable party systems were thrown into disarray. Perhaps the best and most often cited example of the radical electoral changes experienced in the 1970s is the Danish 'earthquake' election of 1973, where electoral volatility amounted to 29 per cent[2] and the number of parties represented in parliament doubled overnight. The changing western European electoral landscape appeared to suggest that the era of stability and absence of change was ending.

From a socio-structuralist perspective, social cleavages structured stable party systems. Most electors did not vote as autonomous individuals, but instead voted as members of organised communities based on their class or religion, or occasionally based on language, race, national origin or region (Crewe 1985: 2). Seymour Martin Lipset and Stein Rokkan's (1967) work best exemplifies this approach, arguing that that 'the party systems of the 1960s reflect, with few but significant exceptions, the cleavage structures of the 1920s … the party alternatives and in remarkably many cases, the party organisations, are older than the majority of the national electorates' (1967: 50). The electoral volatility of the 1970s challenged this view.

The changed electoral landscape of the 1970s in many western democracies appeared to suggest that the influence of social cleavages on electoral behaviour was waning. The 'social change' literature (see Crewe and Denver 1985, Franklin *et al.* 1992) had begun to challenge the 'freezing hypothesis' of Lipset and Rokkan (1967). Mark Franklin *et al.* (1992: 3) argue that 'since the late 1960s … the world of electoral politics has changed dramatically and in all countries voters have shown increasing unpredictability in their choice between parties, often to the extent of voting for parties that are new to the political scene'.

The changing electoral and social backdrop suggests that traditional cleavages are waning. Russell Dalton *et al.* (1984: 19) argue that advanced industrialisation has undermined the stable bases of western European party systems. Political party alignments are fragmenting, socio-psychological bonds between voters and parties are weakening and party systems have experienced increasing levels of electoral volatility (1984: 19). Dalton and Martin Wattenberg (2000a: 264) echo these sentiments and argue that dealignment within the electorate and falling turnout indicate a broad-based weakening of party systems throughout western Europe.

The social changes of the 1970s not only created a dealigned electorate where social cleavages no longer securely structured voting behaviour, but realignment was also taking place (Inglehart 1977). Social change produced a set of 'post-materialist' values in the younger generation, leading to Ivor Crewe's conclusion that 'a new political cleavage, based on cultural rather than economic or religion divisions, on conflicts of values not interests or communities, was slowly spreading across the Western democracies' (1985: 5).

The socio-structuralist literature emphasises the importance of social change for patterns of party competition, with a common assumption that social cleavages structure voting behaviour and party systems. Where cleavages are stable, voting behaviour is predictable and party systems are stable. Where these cleavages break down, electoral volatility and party system flux occurs. The picture painted of change, volatility and instability is an attractive one and implies that high levels of renewal and dynamism are present in western European party systems, but is this really an accurate picture?

Three of the authors that have produced the most significant challenges to the assumed causality of the relationship between social change, electoral change and party system change are Gordon Smith, Peter Mair and Wolfgang Müller (1989a) argues against the assumption that social change leads to party system change. Instead, he suggests that the weakening of cleavages does not necessarily mean the deconstruction of traditional patterns of competition in party systems. Smith argues that cleavages do not have inherently systemic qualities; cleavage structure relates to the social make-up of party support and not to the party system per se. If a party system is viewed as the sum of interactions between parties, then cleavages become just one set of factors shaping electoral alignments, with cleavage change being registered through other dimensions such as the number and size of parties, polarisation and volatility (Smith 1989a: 351).

In a similar vein, Mair challenges the assumption that 'one can only speak of ... party system change if and when electoral change is seen to occur' (1989a: 271), proposing an interpretation of party system change 'which may owe its origin to factors other than simply flux in voter preferences' (1997: 215). For Mair, electoral change produces changes in the environment in which parties operate, but the terms 'electoral change' and 'party system change' should not necessarily be viewed synonymously (2002: 101). Mair uses the Danish example cited previously to support his argument. He argues that although Denmark witnessed a 'massive shift' in 1973, 'it is certainly possible to question whether this change had any substantial impact on the workings of the Danish party system' (2002: 101–2).

Another interesting perspective on the relationship between electoral change and party system change is provided by Müller (1993, 2002), who argues that the institutions of the state can act as a vital intervening factor in the relationship between electoral and party system change. According to Müller, 'the institutions and regulations of the state or their alteration are favourable to ... party system change' and the state can prevent or 'limit' natural party system change (1993: 420). The study of electoral systems is one area of the institutional architecture that has received the most comprehensive scholarly attention, as electoral systems can ' "structure" party systems by keeping only those parties in the business that can meet the system's viability test and removing those that cannot' (Müller 2002: 265). The institutional arrangements in a particular country can play a vital role in the process of party system change, with institutions able to act as a barrier potentially suppressing party system change.

These contributions challenge what some regard as overly deterministic assumptions about the relationship between social change, electoral change and party system change, with the contributions of Mair, Smith and Müller constituting a 'party-centric' approach to party system change. This approach challenges the socially deterministic approach to party system change of the social change literature. The socially deterministic and party-centric approaches to party system change both acknowledge the changed environment in which political parties must operate since the 1970s and that the environment can affect the fate of parties and the party system. However, whilst the social change literature is deterministic, the party-centric approach offers an alternative perspective.

The party-centric approach to party system change suggests that in the process of party system change, political parties and institutions are important intervening factors. Mair, Smith and Müller view political parties as potentially independent actors, able to influence their own fate and shape the party system and institutional environment in which they operate. Smith argues that within the process of party system change, 'the parties occupy the key position' (1989a: 355) and must be regarded as independent forces. Parties are strategic actors able to initiate change, as well as alter its direction to their own advantage. Moreover, parties are adaptive actors, able to cope with changing circumstances (Smith 1989a: 355–6). From this perspective, Smith highlights the crucial role of political parties by arguing that 'party interaction and party responses to electoral movements are at least of equal importance to the structural changes in society for an understanding of how and why systems change' (1989a: 356).

Mair echoes the sentiments of Smith and argues that parties are adaptive organisations that can respond to changed circumstances. He maintains that '[p] arties ... are ... independent actors, capable, at least in part, of moulding the environments in which they compete. Thus while the social bases of party support change ... parties adapt and modify their appeals and their methods of mobilising support' (1993a: 130–1). Indeed, Mair's typology of party system change (2002) reflects the position that parties can influence their own fate to the extent that party system change may originate from the actions of parties themselves and not solely from the electorate, and provides the foundation of the definition of party system change adopted in this study.

Müller argues that political parties are important in influencing party system change, in particular, focusing on their interplay with the institutional architecture. He argues 'institutions rule out some types of behaviour and make others more or less likely by influencing the costs and benefits that a party can expect when following a certain course of action' (2002: 252). Institutions act as a strong restraint or facilitating influence on party behaviour. Yet 'institutions are no more than rules and rules themselves the product of social decisions' (Riker 1980: 444–5). Accordingly, although institutions limit or permit certain party behaviours, governing (or established) political parties ultimately determine the institutional system in which they operate. Müller convincingly argues that political parties are a strong influence on the institutional framework, arguing that institutional engineering, that is, the manipulation of institutions for the benefit of certain political parties, is a 'relevant, but much understudied strategy of political parties' (2002: 292).

This approach challenges the socially deterministic approach to party system change of the social change literature, offering an alternative perspective, acknowledging the presence of intervening factors in this relationship. Unlike the socially deterministic literature, which sees party system change as emerging above all from shifts at the level of society and the electorate, the contributions to the literature by Smith, Mair and Müller embody a party-centric approach. Their work provides a more comprehensive understanding of party system change by acknowledging the importance of factors other than the electorate, most notably political parties and institutions, in the process of party system change.

Both the literatures reflect a much broader theoretical debate concerning the role of political parties in democratic systems. Cleavage-focused, or socio-structuralist, interpretations of party system change assume that changes at the electoral level ultimately lead to party system change. Political parties are subject to the whims of the electorate and are largely dependent on voters for their survival; parties have only a minimal independent role to play and therefore play a dependent role in the process of party system change. In contrast, the party-centric literature argues that political parties can act as independent actors.

1.2 Parties as dependent and independent actors

Parties can thus be viewed as either dependent or independent actors in the process of party system change. According to the first perspective, political parties should act as agents of the electorate and are dependent actors in the process of party system change. Parties should play a predominantly passive role, mainly as structures through which electoral and social change are transmitted to the party system. The electorate determines the fate of political parties and parties should not actively attempt to moderate the impact of electoral change.

This interpretation of the role of political parties shares many similarities with one of the normative definitions of a political party contained in the work of Richard Katz (2002). Katz argues that one of three definitions is that of a political arm of one of the classes, ethnic groups or economic interests that make up society. Parties are viewed as agents of a specific segment of society and although parties are autonomous with respect to the state, they are firmly rooted in society (2002: 89–90). The 'parties as dependent actors' model has much in common with cleavage-based interpretations of party system change, reflecting the dependence of political parties on social and electoral changes.

The second perspective on the role of political parties posits that they are able to control their own fate. By engaging in certain behaviours, political parties can attempt to control party system dynamics and moderate the impact of electoral change upon the party system. According to this view, parties have agency and although the electorate is an important influence shaping the behaviour of political parties, ultimately, parties are independent actors, able to take certain steps in order to preserve or improve their positions in party systems. This interpretation of the role of political parties has much in common with the final two definitions of a political party noted by Katz (2002). The first of these two definitions suggests that political parties are teams of politicians engaged in competition for political power through elections, with parties understood to be autonomous from society (Katz 2002: 89). According to Katz, 'democracy results from popular choice among competing parties' and '[p]opular control results from the parties anticipating the reactions of the electorate at the ballot box and acting to increase or maintain their electoral score' (2002: 89).

This interpretation has much in common with the work of Anthony Downs, who specifically argues against aspects of the 'parties as dependent actor model', by declaring that 'political parties are not agents of specific social groups or classes; rather they are autonomous actors seeking office per se and using group support to attain that end' (1957: 97). His work acknowledges the importance of vote-seeking as a major role of political parties, and ultimately argues that political parties are independent actors seeking to influence their own fate by obtaining as many votes as possible.

Furthermore, Downs' approach to the functions of the electorate and parties in political systems is highly significant, as his rational choice approach argues that the rational party's principal aim is to maximise its share of the vote and that it seeks to change ideologically and organisationally in order to do so (1957: 34). This view supports the argument that parties are not merely passive actors in the process of party system change. Rather, they can shape their own fate by actively changing in order to increase their share of the vote. In Downs' model, parties are the ultimate utility maximisers and even in coalition systems, individual parties continue to place their own priorities above those of the coalition as a whole (1957: 159). Downs argues that all parties seek to maximise their own utility and that a party's primary purpose in all situations (especially when the party system is limited to two parties) is to accumulate as many votes as possible.[3]

Although Downs emphasises the importance of both the electorate and parties in his rational interpretation of democracy, the key feature of his model is its emphasis on the primacy of competition between parties for votes. In terms of the role of political parties in the process of party system change, Downs' model assumes that parties try to influence the electorate in order to secure a higher percentage of the vote come the next election. Political parties and party leaders thus play a vital role in maintaining systemic stability, or encouraging party system change.

The final definition given by Katz also implies that political parties are independent actors, able to dictate their own fate, but instead of seeking to maintain or improve their positions through improving their electoral score, political parties seek refuge in the institutions of the state. This view sees parties regulated as if they were part of the machinery of elections, rather than organisations that contest elections (2002: 90). Parties are able to become part of the state machinery and enjoy a privileged institutional position. Katz and Mair (1995) develop this view, and argue that the emergence of the 'cartel' party represents the dawning of a fundamentally altered relationship between the state and political parties.

The underlying basis of this book is that parties act as independent actors, with Katz's perspectives shaping how parties can act as independent actors. Building on Katz's models, parties may engage in two more or less distinct types of 'strategies'. On the one hand, parties may engage in strategies that are responsive to voters. Parties should attempt to influence the views of the electorate at election time, acting as vote-seeking utility maximisers (Downs 1957), with these strategies referred to as 'electorate-orientated strategies'. On the other hand, parties may seek to pursue their office-seeking goals through the utilisation of state institutions, referred to as 'institutional strategies'. The extent to which established political parties engage in these strategies and the impact this has on their fate, and the party system as a whole, constitutes the principal research question this book seeks to explore.

1.3 Measurements and definitions: party strategies and party systems

The study assesses the impact of strategies used by established parties in 17 western European countries between 1950 and 2009.[4] Although this study aims to assess the impact of party strategies on party system change, not all parties have the resources available to them to be able to act as independent actors within the process of party system change. Instead, it is only the core, 'established' parties that are able to engage in strategies to influence their own fate.

Established parties

The concept of an 'established' party builds upon the work in particular of three key contributions to the literature. The first of these is Smith's concept of the 'core' of western European party systems. He argues that this core comprises:

the party or parties that over a substantial period have been in leading positions; those parties that have been especially influential for the functioning of the system and the particular pattern of party alignments, especially the coalitional line-ups, that has evolved.

(Smith 1989b: 161)

Smith considers that parties can be deemed part of the 'core' of their respective party systems if they have been central to patterns of competition over time in western European party systems, particularly with respect to the governing arena. According to the definition of party system change and competition developed later in this section, competition for government lies at the heart of competitive relations in any party system. Only those parties that have crossed the governing threshold are established parties. Although other parties can be 'relevant' (see Sartori 1976: 300–4), parties that have governed have been the major influence on patterns of governmental competition and have the opportunity to affect patterns of governmental formation from within government.

The second contribution is to be found in the work of Mair, who argues that 'traditional' parties can be defined as those that had already begun to contest elections by the early 1960s (1993a: 126). The early 1960s represents a rather limited time period, therefore the early 1970s is the cut-off point instead used to determine whether parties have achieved established status, as this represents the approximate period where volatility began to increase in western Europe and party systems began to show increasing signs of fragmentation. Established parties thus only include those parties that had been competing in elections by the early 1970s and had become important actors in the governmental arena by this time.

The concept of established parties used throughout this book takes its lead from Smith's concept of 'core' parties and Mair's 'traditional' parties. Parties can only be considered established parties if they have crossed the governing threshold, but this does not mean that all parties that cross the governing threshold become established parties, as they must have been active in government between 1950 and the early 1970s to be considered an established party. This definition directs the understanding of established parties throughout this book, and Appendix 1 provides the full list of established parties.

A third contribution to this debate constitutes the literature regarding the 'cartel party'. Katz and Mair's (1995) concept of the 'cartel party' sees some parties seeking refuge in the institutions of the state in order to secure their systemic and particularly governmental position. This perspective clearly shares much in common with the definition developed of an established party, especially due to the focus of both concepts on governmental competition. The concept of what constitutes a cartel party is further developed by Karin Bottom (2003), who argues that the cartel is a layered concept, featuring majoritarian and coalitionist parties within the cartel and non-cooptable challenger and non-cartel parties outside the cartel. The definition of what constitutes an established party for the purposes of this book differs slightly from Bottom's in terminology and substance, and instead sees two distinct groups (each comprising two sub-groups) of parties competing in western European elections. Table 1.1 illustrates these groups with reference to the German party system.

'Core' and 'other' established parties comprise the group of established parties, whereas 'non-established political establishment' and 'anti-political establishment' parties comprise the 'non-established' group. Parties may of course move between groups over time. In Germany, the Greens began their time in parliament as an anti-political establishment party, but have now progressed to become a non-established party, as the party has reduced its radical ideological rhetoric and has become part of the mainstream in German politics. At present, the German Left remains an anti-political establishment party, but may eventually follow the lead of the Greens and become non-established.[5] Developing an understanding of which parties are the established parties in each country is important, as generally only established parties are able to engage in strategies to protect their own systemic position.

Party strategies

In order to understand the strategies in which established parties engage, the concept of 'strategies' must be explored. It is a fundamental assumption of this book that political parties are rational actors and engage in certain behaviours or

Table 1.1 Defining established and non-established parties, illustrated by the German example

Established parties	Non-established parties
'Core' established parties	*Non-established political establishment parties*
These parties have been in the leading positions in party systems and specifically government before the early 1970s (see Smith 1989b). Examples include the SPD (Social Democratic Party of Germany) and the CDU/CSU (Christian Democratic Union/Christian Social Union).	These parties have yet to constitute regular governmental actors, but they pursue a mainstream ideology and may have (prospective) episodic governmental participation. Any governmental participation is limited to the period after the early 1970s. Examples include the German Green party.
Other established parties	*Anti-political establishment parties*
These parties have not dominated governments, but have been loyal coalition allies to core, established parties before the early 1970s. Examples include the FDP (Free Democrat Party)	These parties reject the party system of which they are part and, unless a major ideological shift occurs, do not become established parties, but may have been included in government briefly for strategic reasons. Examples include the Die Linke (the German Left).

Note
See section 2.3 for a more detailed discussion of the definition of an anti-political establishment party.

'strategies' in order to maximise their utility in a given party system. The first important issue is why political parties engage in strategies. The work of Downs, as already stated, views parties as engaging strategies in order to achieve the highest number of votes possible, and Müller and Kaare Strøm (1999b) further this rational choice approach to provide a more complete understanding of why parties engage in strategies.

The work of Müller and Strøm (1999b) shares Downs' rational choice perspective, but does not view all parties as solely vote-seeking organisations and instead proposes other reasons why parties may engage in strategies. Instead, Müller and Strøm conceive of three models, which all assume that 'parties have a small and well-defined set of objectives' (1999c: 5) and that they engage in certain utility maximising strategies that are tailored to their goals. The vote-seeking model is developed from the work of Downs, but instead of viewing votes as an end in themselves, the model of Müller and Strøm views votes as an instrumental goal, as 'it makes little sense to assume that parties value votes for their own sake' (1999c: 9). The office-seeking party (1999c: 5–6) counters the arguments of Downs and instead of seeking to maximise votes, seeks 'to maximise [votes] only up to the point of subjective certainty of winning' (Riker 1962: 33). Votes are an instrumental goal according to the office-seeking model where parties seek to gain enough votes to enter and control government. The policy-seeking model suggests that parties seek to maximise their impact on public policy and assumes that 'citizens of democracies become politically engaged because [public policy] choices matter and they support certain political parties over others because these parties make a difference' (Müller and Strøm 1999c: 8). As the focus of this book is on established parties, the prime motivation for engaging in strategies is office-seeking, where parties value votes and policy as instrumental goals intended to facilitate the ultimate goal of governmental representation and control.

Additionally, it is also important to consider the strategies in which political parties engage. Section 1.2 drew on the work of Katz (2002) and suggested two types of strategies in which political parties might engage. Political parties could seek to engage in strategies relating to the electorate (electorate-orientated) or strategies related to the state (institutional).

Parties may engage in electorate-orientated strategies along the lines of the rational choice argument outlined by Downs. According to a Downsian perspective, parties seek to maximise their utility by developing political ideologies that they believe will attract voters, but equally that shape the way that voters perceive the party and the system in which it operates. Parties are not merely acting in a dependent manner; they are not only reflecting the views of the electorate, but also helping to shape the views of the voters. Downs convincingly argues that 'parties seek as their final ends the power, income and prestige that go with office' (1957: 111). For Downs, 'vote-maximising is still the basic motive underlying the behaviour of parties' (1957: 159); thus in the Downsian model of party competition, political parties engage in strategies in order to achieve the highest number of votes possible. Electorate-orientated strategies relate to the interaction of parties with the electorate, trying to mould the views and preferences of the

electorate, and the relations of parties to each other, as the nature of the interaction and competition between parties will affect the way that the electorate
view parties. Chapter 2 provides an assessment of the extent to which parties
engage in these strategies.

In addition to electorate-orientated strategies that imply the pursuit of vote-
seeking goals by political parties, parties may also engage in institutional strategies. Katz and Mair, and Müller have addressed the ways that political parties
can manipulate the institutional arena in which they operate. Müller (1993)
argues that the relevance of the state for party and party system change is a neglected topic in the literature and outlines how party law, electoral law, party
finance, mass media, interest groups, the economy and the institutions of the
state can influence party system change (1993: 420). Müller argues that although
the decline of the importance of traditional cleavages and the emergence of new
lines of division have been important factors in party system change in western
Europe, the institutions of the state have also played a major role. According to
Müller, institutions are not fixed and 'parties can ... win the political game by
two strategies. They can play according to the existing rules of the game, or they
can change the rules of the game' (2002: 251). This approach raises the possibility of partisan institutional manipulation by parties seeking to benefit their own
cause. From this perspective, political institutions can play a vital role in influencing the process of party system change, with political parties often being the
guiding forces behind institutional changes in the pursuit of office-seeking goals.

Several specific ways in which political parties can manipulate the institutional set-up feature in the work of Katz and Mair (1995). Katz and Mair argue
that some political parties have now become part of the state bureaucracy and
hence political parties can more effectively manipulate state institutions. Their
cartel thesis argues that environmental change is far from exogenous to the parties as it is parties who are ultimately responsible the rules regarding state subventions as well as the amounts of money and resources that are made available
(1995: 15). Katz and Mair similarly cite the electronic media as another area that
is subject to a large degree of state control with political parties able to manipulate rules in their own interests (1995: 15). In sum, Katz and Mair argue that the
state is an important determinant of party system change, along the lines of
Müller, but equally, they see political parties as part of the state in their cartel
model of party competition. Thus:

> the state, which is invaded by political parties and the rules of which are
> determined by the parties, becomes a fount of resources through which these
> parties not only help to ensure their own survival, but through which they
> can also enhance their own capacity to resist challenges from newly mobi-
> lised alternatives
>
> (Katz and Mair 1995: 16)

The work of Katz and Mair, and Müller highlights the importance of the institutional arrangement for the process of party system change, with political parties

able to influence the environment in which they compete. Furthermore, relations with the electorate and other parties also provide significant strategic opportunities for political parties, reflecting the work of Downs. Chapters 2 and 3 will explore the extent to which parties engage in these two groups of strategies, with the systemic impact of these strategies explored in Chapters 5 and 6.

If parties can act as independent actors in the process of party system change, then the term 'strategies' can be applied to the tactics and devices that parties would use in an attempt to enhance or consolidate their systemic positions. The term implies the pursuit by political parties of a conscious, well-defined and organised set of tactics. One tactic is insufficient; a strategy is an organised and thought through collection of tactics, aimed at the achievement of desired goals, be they vote-seeking or office-seeking goals in this instance. Parties may engage in well-defined strategies, but these strategies may not always achieve their desired outcomes. However, the work of George Tsebelis suggests why parties may not necessarily engage in optimal behaviours for the desired outcomes.

Tsebelis' seminal text *Nested Games: rational choice in comparative politics* (1990) seeks to answer the question why actors do not always choose apparently optimal behaviour. Tsebelis concludes that actors are involved in 'nested games' and that a behaviour that appears to be sub-optimal in one context may be better understood from the perspective of the 'nested games' in which the actor is the participant (1990: 11). He argues that 'in games in multiple arenas, events or strategies in one arena influence the way the game is played in another arena' (1990: 248), suggesting that party strategies should not be viewed in isolation. Instead, multiple strategies interact with each other, raising the importance of considering the interaction between electorate-oriented and institutional strategies. Tsebelis also highlights the possibility that parties may appear to engage in strategies that do not benefit themselves. In order to understand these decisions from a rational choice perspective, it is important to consider the wider context of these decisions.

In order to understand the role of parties within the process of party system change, it is important to consider the strategies in which parties can engage, but also to consider the impact of these strategies. This study explores the impact of the strategies in which parties engage on the party systems in which they compete, as engagement in differing strategies should produce different systemic outcomes.

Party systems and party system change

The classic definition of a party system as 'a system of interactions resulting from inter-party competition' (Sartori, 1976: 43) is widely accepted. This definition from Giovanni Sartori highlights the importance of examining parties from a systemic perspective and not as individual entities. He argues that 'the system in question bears on the relatedness of parties to each other, on how each party is a function of the other parties and reacts, competitively or otherwise, to the other parties' (1976: 44). Although this definition of what constitutes a party system is relatively uncontested, the issue of what constitutes party system change is somewhat more problematic. Most commentators agree that a party system has changed when the defining properties of the system change, but this definition naturally relies largely on what the author determines the defining properties of the system to be. For Dalton *et al.* (1984) it is electoral behaviour; for Smith (1989b) it is the 'core' of the party system; for Otto Kirchheimer (1966) it is how effectively parties fulfil their functions; for Mair (1997, 2002) it is governmental relations; for Müller (1993, 2002) institutions have a large role to play and for Michael Laver (1989) the defining properties of party systems are to be found in the interaction between the legislative and electoral arenas.

Sartori creates a typology of party systems based on two distinct elements: 'format' and 'mechanics'. The format of the party system is the number of parties and the size of parties in a party system. The mechanics relates to actual relations between parties and incorporates aspects such as ideological distance, the direction of competition in the system (either centripetal or centrifugal) and the number of poles (whether the system is unipolar, bipolar or multipolar) (Sartori 1976: 128, 293, 315–16). The relationship between format and mechanics is crucial for Sartori's interpretation of party systems. The format contains mechanical predispositions (1976: 128) so the number and size of parties in a party system has a direct impact on the relations between parties. When the format of a party system changes, the mechanics of a system are also pressurised to change.

Sartori's work also implicitly acknowledges the role that intervening factors, such as parties, institutions or historical context, can play in this relationship. He argues that the relationship between format and mechanics is not a law, but instead is a 'statement of mechanical tendencies' (1966: 173). Although a change in format offers different options for parties, as a change in the number and relative size of parties in a system alters the range of options available for political parties when forming parliamentary and governmental alliances, the relationship between format and mechanics may not always be deterministic. These arguments clearly relate to the earlier discussion regarding the deterministic relationship between electoral and party system change, with the work of Sartori supporting the argument that a change in the number and size of parties in the party system does not necessarily lead to change in the party system, due to the intermediate role of political parties.

Sartori uses his concepts of format and mechanics to produce a typology of party systems, which determines when party system change has occurred. According to Sartori, a party system has changed when it moves from one type to another. A change in type can occur when the ideological distance in the party system changes or when there is a substantial shift in the number of parties in the system.

Mair argues that Sartori's typology is the most comprehensive typology available, has yielded an exceptional degree of insight into the functioning of party systems and, crucially, underlines the influence exerted by systemic properties and by the party system, on electoral behaviour and electoral outcomes (Mair

2002: 91). However, Mair draws attention to the overloaded category of moderate pluralism in Sartori's typology and also highlights the increasingly few examples of polarised pluralism and two-partism present in western European nations over recent decades (2002: 92). Based on these criticisms, but using the Sartori typology as a starting point, Mair constructs his own party system typology, to be considered in detail in section 4.3. Mair argues that whether the structure of competition is closed or open defines party systems. Alternation in office, familiarity of governing formulae and access to government are the features considered when placing a country's party system in either the open or the closed category. The Mair typology allows the classification of a party system as open or closed, with a change occurring when a system changes from open to closed or vice versa. Where the structure of competition changes from open to closed or vice versa, party system change has occurred. The principal advantage of the Mair typology is that is allows for party system change to occur *without any preceding electoral change*, that is, it explicitly acknowledges the agency of political parties.

Like Sartori's typology, the Mair typology considers party systems as independent variables, constraining or even directing electoral preferences. This is clearly a view in line with the assumptions made in this chapter concerning the relationship between political parties and the electorate and furthermore, the focus on the governmental arena as the crucial area of competition sits well with the assumptions that parties are essentially office-seeking organisations. For these reasons, this study uses the Mair typology as an analytical framework. Chapter 4 provides a full discussion of the Mair typology and the strengths and weaknesses of the typology as an analytical tool.

The Mair typology is of particular value because it focuses on the governmental arena as the decisive 'site' for political competition (Dahl 1966). These ideas owe much to the work of Kurt Richard Luther (1989), who argues that party systems operate in different arenas. Luther argues that his approach 'permits insights into the significance for party system change of factors endogenous to the party system. In particular, we have sought to demonstrate the importance for party system change and resilience of parties and their strategies' (1989: 25). This thinking is clearly in line with the assumptions behind this book and presents a useful framework for an assessment of systemic change. In particular, these ideas shape the definition, development and measurement of the concept of 'systemic centrality' to be discussed in Chapter 4.

1.4 The impact of party strategies on party system change

This book assesses the extent to which established parties engage in strategies and examines the impact of these strategies on their fate and that of the party systems in which they operate. The study is strongly influenced by the contributions that Smith, Mair and Müller have made to the party literature and is underpinned by the rational choice perspective of Downs, in addition to the cartel thesis of Katz and Mair (1995). In order to understand to what extent political parties are able to influence the process of party system change, the first half of this book seeks to understand the behaviours in which political parties engage in order to improve or maintain their positions within their respective national party systems. As such, this section of the book is guided by the 'parties as independent actors' model. The second half of the book analyses the extent to which the established parties' behaviours and strategies have influenced their own fate and the party system as a whole.

This introductory chapter has placed the book into context and addressed some of the definitional issues relevant to the study. Chapter 2 assesses the extent to which established parties engage in electorate-orientated strategies, with data collected to show the countries where parties have engaged in the lowest and highest levels of electorate-orientated strategies. Chapter 3 progresses in much the same way as Chapter 2, but addresses institutional strategies to highlight countries demonstrating the highest and lowest use of institutional strategies.

Chapter 4 marks the division between the two sections of the book and moves to consider and measure the impact of electorate-orientated and institutional strategies on the fate of established parties and on the party system as a whole. Based on the findings of Chapters 2 and 3, Chapter 4 presents the eight countries that are analysed as case studies in Chapters 5 and 6. Chapter 5 assesses the impact of the low and high use of electorate-orientated strategies on the fate of established parties and party systems within four selected countries, while Chapter 6 examines the effect of institutional strategies. Chapter 7 summarises the empirical findings of the book and provides an overall assessment of whether and to what extent established parties may control their own fate. As will become clear in the course of this study, there is considerable evidence to suggest parties have much to gain by employing various strategies that safeguard their future and shape the party systems in which they operate. The study begins with an assessment of the extent to which established political parties in western Europe engage in electorate-oriented strategies.

2 Electorate-orientated strategies

Established political parties can engage in a range of behaviours to attempt to improve or maintain their position within their national party systems. In line with rational choice assumptions, political parties seek to maximise their utility. According to Katz (2002) and Downs (1957), parties can attempt to do this by engaging in strategies that are responsive to voters' existing preferences, but equally by seeking to mould their views before election time. This chapter explores the electorate-orientated strategies that established parties might engage in, and assesses the extent to which established parties engage in strategies that are responsive and open towards the electorate. A number of different strategy dimensions can indicate responsiveness towards the electorate, and intent to shape the views of the electorate. As established parties are primarily office-seeking, the focus will be on strategies that pertain to the ways in which parties can respond to, or shape voter preferences, through the coalitions in which they choose to engage.[1]

This chapter engages in consecutive discussion of five electorate-orientated dimensions chosen to illustrate the extent to which established parties engage in strategies towards the electorate: ideological change; electoral responsiveness; relations with anti-political establishment parties; pre-electoral coalition agreements; and length of coalition agreements. This chapter discusses these five areas derived from the literature that seek to capture established parties' relations with the electorate. Data produced from the study of 17 countries generates hypotheses concerning the expected systemic impact of engagement in these electorate-orientated strategies. The analysis weights all dimensions equally when considering the countries in which established parties engage in the highest and lowest levels of electorate-orientated strategies in Chapter 4.

2.1 Ideological change

The first strategy under discussion is ideological change. Ideology is 'a verbal image of the good society and of the chief means of constructing such a society' (Downs 1957: 96). Ideologies are a vehicle to power and enable voters to differentiate between competing political parties. According to a Downsian interpretation of party competition, parties mainly increase their vote by changing their policies and ensuring that their ideological location maximises voter potential within a two-party system. However, because of the uncertainty under which parties and the electorate operate, parties have the opportunity to persuade voters to revise their beliefs (Downs 1957: 82–3). Equally, parties cannot be sure to which social groups it would be most electorally profitable to appeal and, due to the dynamism of society, the right combination of social groups in one election may be the wrong combination at the next (1957: 101).

Parties seeking the highest share of the vote possible are expected to change ideologically in line with the 'median voter' (1957: 114–41), in order to capture the highest number of votes. Data relating to the position of the median voter relative to the policy positions of established parties is unavailable for all countries over the period covered, but data is available to measure the extent to which ideological change is prevalent within established parties. High levels of ideological change indicate responsiveness to the needs of the electorate and equally that parties are seeking to be ideologically flexible in order to attract votes. Conversely, low levels of ideological change may indicate that parties are unresponsive to the needs of the electorate and do not try to influence electoral behaviour.

Underlying these hypotheses is the assumption that parties are responsive if they change ideologically, with higher levels of change indicating higher levels of responsiveness. This is a problematic argument in several ways. First, responsiveness does not necessarily require change as, if the position of the median voter does not change, a lack of movement indicates responsiveness. Second, if parties do move, they may not move in the same direction as the electorate; therefore the direction of the ideological change is significant. Third, the argument assumes that parties move only in response to ideological changes within the electorate. Parties, of course, may change ideologically for a variety of other reasons, such as a change in internal party dynamics (Panebianco 1988), or as a response to external shocks (Harmel and Janda 1994). Janda (1990: 5) argues that electoral defeat is 'the mother of all party change', so following an electoral defeat, parties should change ideologically in order to try to improve their electoral share.

Time diminishes the significance of these arguments. If the focus was limited to a short period of time, only two elections, or a particular decade, the ideological positions of the electorate may not have changed dramatically. However, over the 60-year period covered, the positions of voters *have changed*. Adopting a long-term perspective thus involves the assumption that electoral change has occurred during this period, allowing the measurement of the responsiveness of established parties. It is widely acknowledged that the behaviour of the electorate has become more volatile since the 1970s. Electoral volatility (Pedersen 1979), a decline in partisanship (Dalton and Wattenberg 2000b) and a decline in party membership (Mair and Van Biezen 2001) have created challenges for established political parties. Bartolini and Mair (1990) examine electoral availability and study the enduring importance of cleavages structuring the preferences of the electorate, developing the pioneering work of Lipset and Rokkan (1967). Although they conclude that 'in the long-term, the bonds which tie the electorate into a set of political identities and alignments have demonstrated their resilience', they do accept that 'to say that nothing has changed across this century of mass politics ... would be clearly indefensible' (Bartolini and Mair 1990: 287), acknowledging that changes have occurred in the availability of the electorate over time. This changed environment suggests that the ideological positions of the voters has changed during the past 60 years, and that parties have necessarily had to respond to these changes by demonstrating ideological flexibility to cater to a changing electorate.

Content analysis, and more specifically, party manifesto analysis, is the approach used to assess levels of ideological change within party systems across western Europe. Party manifestos represent the only clear and direct statements of party policy available to the electorate and directly attributable to the party (Volkens 2001: 93). Parties publish manifestos before every election, showing changes in ideology, and are representative statements for the whole party and as such are the principal authoritative statement of party policies, as party conventions ratify party programmes (Budge *et al.* 2001: 216).

The data produced by the Comparative Manifesto Project (CMP) has been the most widely used data in the field of content analysis. Although other methods of content analysis are available (see, for example, Franzmann and Kaiser 2006), the CMP stands out in terms of the number of countries covered, the intuitive nature of the findings and the consistency of the data produced. The CMP embarked on content analysis of 24 OECD party programmes[2] in order to show ideological trends. The data produced has proved to be invaluable for political scientists seeking to conduct research concerning the relative ideology of parties, the decline of the left-right division, coalition theory and ideological change (Budge and Bara 2001: 1–2) and is a suitable set of data through which ideological changes within established parties can be seen over time.[3]

The CMP data measures the ideological change for individual parties, but HeeMin Kim and Richard Fording (2001) provide an alternative measure to capture the ideological change of a group of parties and measure the ideology of governments. Although this dimension assesses the ideological change found within *established* parties, the close link between established party status and government status should ensure that the measurement for assessing the ideological change of governments is also an indication of ideological change within established parties.

The Kim and Fording measure incorporates information concerning the relative share of power held by each of the governing parties and takes into account the ideology of the governing parties as measured on a left-right scale (Kim and Fording 2001: 166). By calculating the ideological position of a government at time t, the ideological change that has occurred in the governing parties between points $t-1$ and t can also be calculated. This provides a figure that, given certain caveats, captures the amount of ideological change in established parties and is an indicator of the change in ideology that parties experience when they enter government, or when they have retained or lost their governing status. The Kim and Fording formula for calculating the ideology of governments is as follows:

$\Sigma(\text{ideology}_i * (\text{\#posts}_i/\text{total posts}))$

The measurement for change in government ideology is:

$\Sigma\{(\text{ideology}_i\, t - \text{ideology}_i\, t - 1) * (\text{\#seats}_i/\text{total seats})\}$

Where: $\text{ideology}_i\, t$ = the ideology of party i at time t; $\text{ideology}_i\, t-1$ = the ideology of party i at time $t-1$; $\text{\#seats}_i$ = the total number of seats in parliament held by party i and total seats = the total number of seats in parliament held by the government.

Instead of measuring a single point in time by using a single ideological value, the difference between the ideological position of the governing party at election t and at election $t-1$ captures ideological change. The measure changes to reflect the proportion of seats instead of posts in cabinets, more accurately reflecting the strength of established parties. Each governing party's ideological change between t and $t-1$ is calculated, before calculating the proportion of 'influence' the party has, which under the revised measure, reflects parliamentary strength. The figure produced provides an indication of the ideological change governing parties have undergone between t and $t-1$. The figures weigh heavily in favour of the larger parties, as in a hypothetical government where one party receives 100 seats and another ten, the larger party exerts ten times the influence on the overall figure obtained than the smaller party. This argument to a certain extent counteracts the problem that by measuring the ideological change of governments, the ideological change of some non-established parties is also included. As established parties are generally larger parties, the weighted nature of the measure in favour of the larger parties should ensure that the measure adequately captures the ideological change of established parties.

This measure of ideological change seeks to measure only the extent and not the direction of change. Parties record positive or negative scores depending on whether they have moved to the left or the right on the ideological scale, but for the purposes of this dimension, the positive or negative nature of the move is disregarded and the value is simply viewed as indicating the extent of change.

Incumbency effects represent a further interesting issue that emerges when assessing ideological change. The literature shows that parties in western Europe who enter government lose votes at the next election. For example, Müller and Strøm have collected data on the electoral performance of 277 governments. Of these, only 92 (33 per cent) have been able to improve their electoral strength, whereas 179 (65 per cent) suffered losses (2000c: 588). Parties who were in government at both times t and $t-1$ may therefore make different ideological choices compared to those parties who were not in government at point $t-1$. This measure explores the relationship between ideological change and the movement of parties into or out of government, and may generate interesting findings relating to incumbency effects.

Table 2.1 Ideological change (left–right) in western European governing parties, 1950–2003[a]

	1950s	1960s	1970s	1980s	1990s	2000s	Overall
Finland	22.9 (n=3)	24.4 (n=2)	19.9 (n=4)	48.6 (n=2)	16.5 (n=3)	16.2 (n=1)	24.0 (n=15)
Germany	30.2 (n=2)	18.0 (n=3)	10.3 (n=2)	9.1 (n=3)	21.9 (n=3)	5.2 (n=1)	16.7 (n=14)
Ireland	10.0 (n=3)	23.9 (n=3)	34.2 (n=2)	13.1 (n=5)	8.0 (n=2)	12.8 (n=1)	16.5 (n=16)
Austria	7.7 (n=3)	6.6 (n=2)	24.3 (n=4)	18.5 (n=2)	15.5 (n=3)[b]	22.2 (n=2)	16.3 (n=16)
Sweden	12.8 (n=3)	24.6 (n=3)	15.2 (n=4)	2.9 (n=3)	21.5 (n=3)	14.8 (n=1)	15.4 (n=17)
Portugal	–[c]	–	13.0 (n=1)	21.1 (n=4)	13.5 (n=3)	0.0 (n=1)	15.3 (n=9)
Denmark	10.6 (n=4)	10.5 (n=4)	14.2 (n=5)	15.7 (n=4)	21.3 (n=3)	6.3 (n=1)	13.7 (n=21)
Switzerland	16.1 (n=3)	10.5 (n=2)	9.0 (n=3)	18.4 (n=2)	10.9 (n=3)	14.2 (n=1)	12.9 (n=14)
Greece	–	–	35.9 (n=1)	12.7 (n=4)	6.6 (n=3)	3.4 (n=1)	12.2 (n=9)
Luxembourg	14.6 (n=3)	9.5 (n=2)	11.6 (n=2)	9.4 (n=2)	14.0 (n=2)	–	12.1 (n=11)
United Kingdom	10.3 (n=4)	5.9 (n=2)	18.3 (n=4)	3.1 (n=2)	20.5 (n=2)	5.5 (n=2)[d]	11.5 (n=16)
France	–	9.4 (n=3)[e]	14.5 (n=2)	10.0 (n=3)	12.2 (n=2)	11.6 (n=1)	11.2 (n=11)
The Netherlands	9.4 (n=3)	10.6 (n=2)	13.5 (n=3)[f]	8.2 (n=4)	15.3 (n=2)	5.7 (n=2)	10.3 (n=16)
Italy	11.4 (n=2)	4.4 (n=2)	7.9 (n=3)	8.2 (n=2)	9.2 (n=2)[g]	28.3 (n=1)	9.9 (n=12)
Belgium	8.7 (n=3)	10.2 (n=3)	11.4 (n=4)	9.0 (n=3)	7.4 (n=3)	0.0 (n=1)	8.9 (n=17)
Norway	3.2 (n=2)	7.6 (n=3)	3.5 (n=2)	11.3 (n=3)	10.8 (n=2)	10.1 (n=1)	7.8 (n=13)
Spain	–	–	0.9 (n=1)	3.9 (n=3)	9.9 (n=2)	0.0 (n=1)	4.6 (n=7)
Overall	12.6 (n=38)	13.0 (n=36)	15.2 (n=47)	12.7 (n=51)	14.1 (n=43)	10.0 (n=19)	13.3 (n=234)

Sources: Based on own calculations using the Kim and Fording (2001) index applied to the CMP data (Budge et al. 2001 and Klingemann et al. 2006).

Notes

a The data can only be presented for this period as this is the period covered by the CMP data. Additionally, missing data is a significant problem when attempting to measure party ideology, and although the CMP data attempts to plot the ideologies of all significant parties over time, on occasions, data for parties is missing and some parties featured in coalitions do not appear in the CMP's dataset. Where this occurs, the calculation excludes the parties that do not feature in the dataset.

b There are problems with treating parties as continuous entities ideologically and organisationally, as parties often split for ideological reasons. For example, the FPÖ (Freedom Party) in Austria split in the early 1990s into the LF (Liberal Forum) and the remainder of the FPÖ, and split further between the FPÖ and the BZÖ in 2005. Ideological conflict was at the root of the splits. However, the issue of considering the parties as continuous entities is only problematic for one election. At the 1994 election, the first election after the split, the ideological position of the FPÖ in 1990 is compared with the average weighted ideological score of the FPÖ and the LF following the split. Yet in 1995, the FPÖ's position is compared with the party's position of 1994 and the same methodology is applied to the LF, with the same methodology applied to the subsequent split in 2005.

c Blank cells indicate a lack of data present for this particular decade in this country. As has already been stated in section 1.3, the periods of democratic rule in Spain, France, Greece and Portugal begin from 1978, 1958, 1975 and 1976 respectively; therefore, no data is available before these years. A gap is also present in the 2000s for Luxembourg, as the first election of the decade took place in 2004, following the last update of the CMP data.

d Figure includes the 2005 election.

e Where a party has changed name, the analysis treats the party the same before and after the change. A change in name does not necessarily affect the organisation or ideology of the party, so the party will be analysed as a continuous entity following a name change. With regard to the French data, the parties of the centre-right have changed their names regularly, but for analytical purposes, the analysis treats them as the same party. Equally, where parties have split, the analysis considers the party to be the same party before and after the split and not completely new entities. For example, in the calculation of ideological change for Belgium, where the established parties split into separate Walloon and Flemish camps, the difference in ideological change compares the ideological position of the unified party with the average weighted ideological score of the two parties following the split.

f For parties that merge, the analysis treats parties as the same entity before and after the merge, with perhaps the best example being the CDA (Christian Democratic Appeal) in the Netherlands. In the 1970s, the KVP (Catholic People's Party), ARP (Anti-Revolution Party) and CHU (Christian Historic Union) merged to become the CDA. To measure ideological change for these parties, ideological values for the three individual parties are calculated for the election before the merger, a weighted average calculated and the value compared to the value obtained for the CDA after the merger. The figure produced represents the amount of ideological change in the Christian parties in the Netherlands before and after the merger.

g This value does not include the 1994 Italian election, as figures for this election were unobtainable due to the transformation of the Italian party system between 1992 and 1994 and the lack of continuity in parties present within the party system.

Table 2.1 shows the change in ideological positions of governing parties between consecutive elections. Figures represent the average amount of change of all governing parties between elections, averaged out over a decade to assess long-term trends. High values reveal that governing parties have made substantial changes to their party programmes since the previous election, suggesting that governing parties in countries with high values have engaged in high levels of ideological change. Conversely, low values indicate that governing parties have made only minor or no changes to their party programmes since the previous election and have engaged in low levels of ideological change. Table 2.1 shows countries ranked from the highest overall levels of ideological change to the lowest. Where two countries have the same value, the country with the higher number of cases ranks the higher.

Table 2.1 shows that the countries in which the highest levels of ideological change occur are Finland, Germany and Ireland, whereas the lowest levels of ideological change were found in Belgium, Norway and Spain. Established parties engage in widely differing levels of ideological change, but the values over time are relatively consistent, although the 1970s stands out as the decade in which established parties engaged in the highest levels of ideological change, perhaps reflect the economic turbulence of the time across western Europe, in addition to the social changes outlined in Chapter 1.

Chapter 1 argued that political parties engage in strategies in order to maintain or improve their systemic position and to obtain the rewards of office. Parties that engage in high levels of ideological change are attempting to meet the needs of a changing electorate by supplying voters with dynamic and flexible party programmes, but also to influence the policy preferences of the voters. This argument is in line with the Downsian (1957) argument that political parties change ideologically in order to meet the needs of the median voter and capture the largest share of the electoral market possible. Parties that engage in low levels of change are behaving in a less responsive manner towards the electorate, making only minor or no changes to their party programmes and not attempting to mould the views of the voters. These findings generate two hypotheses. First, established parties in Finland, Germany and Ireland should achieve high levels of systemic centrality within their party systems because of their high levels of engagement in ideological change. Second, established parties in Belgium, Norway and Spain should achieve low levels of systemic centrality because of their low levels of engagement in ideological change. Chapter 5 tests these hypotheses, when the impact of the high and low use of electorate-orientated strategies on the fate of established parties is analysed.

Incumbency effects are another interesting area to examine in relation to ideological change and established parties. Table 2.2 shows the average amount of ideological change in parties that moved into office, retained office, or left office. Unlike in Table 2.1 where the units analysed were governments, Table 2.2 illustrates individual parties' ideological change and arranges figures according to whether a party moved into government, out of government or stayed in government. The table can show if an incumbency effect exists; that is, if the levels of ideological change that occur in parties that remain in government differ from the levels of ideological change found in parties that enter or are removed from government. Table 2.2 also illustrates how much ideological change corresponds most frequently with parties entering government or retaining their governing status. The table arranges countries in the same order as Table 2.1 to allow comparison.

The data in Table 2.2 appears to show that no incumbency effect exists. Indeed, by examining the average figures over time for all countries, the amount of ideological change experienced by parties is almost the same, varying from 12.9 to 13.9, regardless of whether parties moved into, out of, or remained in government. According to Table 2.2, high, low or moderate levels of ideological change appear to have virtually no impact on whether parties remain in government, enter or leave government. Further analysis of the data may shed more light on this issue. In Table 2.2, each country obtained three average values for parties that move into government, move out or retain their governing status. These values can be ranked in order from lowest to highest to show whether a relatively low or high amount of ideological change produces governing retention or a move into government. These results are summarised in Table 2.3.

Table 2.3 reveals no clear difference between the categories, although there are some interesting patterns. For parties wishing to maintain governing status, the table shows that a strategy of a low or high amount of ideological change is preferable to a moderate level of ideological change. Parties when in government should endeavour to change their party's ideology significantly or minimally if they wish to continue in government, although high levels of ideological change are equally associated with removal from office in seven countries. A moderate amount of ideological change is the least optimal strategy to employ for established parties wishing to retain governing status, but the most optimal strategy for gaining governing status; in over half the countries studied, moderate ideological change was the strategy that was associated with the movement of a party into office. High levels of ideological change were equally likely to be associated with movement out of office and retaining governing status, suggesting only a weak incumbency effect.

These findings reflect within-country trends, but an across-country study may not produce the same findings. A 'moderate' amount of change in one country, that is, the middle category, might be at a much higher or lower level than in another country. In order to interpret cross-country trends, the study can be repeated to determine the relationship between minimal, moderate or high levels of ideological change and government status.

Table 2.4 produces some interesting results although, again, no significant incumbency effect or clear pattern is obvious. Where the lowest levels of ideological change are present, parties are equally likely to retain governing status, move into office or leave office. Moderate and high levels of ideological change are more positively associated with governing retention and moving into government, although they are also most likely to be associated with removal from office, suggesting that no clear pattern emerges. Based on the findings from

Table 2.2 Average ideological change (left–right) and party incumbency, 1950–2003

		1950s	1960s	1970s	1980s	1990s	2000s	Average
Finland	Move in	13.3 (n=4)	28.7 (n=2)	27.7 (n=6)	22.0 (n=2)	15.7 (n=5)	6.6 (n=1)	20.3 (n=20)
	Retain	26.5 (n=7)	21.6 (n=5)	16.7 (n=9)	59.0 (n=6)	16.9 (n=9)	28.9 (n=2)	26.5 (n=38)
	Removed	–	14.8 (n=4)	26.4 (n=5)	37.8 (n=2)	32.1 (n=4)	18.3 (n=3)	25.0 (n=18)
Germany	Move in	–	7.4 (n=2)	–	8.7 (n=1)	9.9 (n=2)	–	8.7 (n=5)
	Retain	29.6 (n=4)	24.9 (n=4)	10.2 (n=4)	9.3 (n=5)	16.5 (n=4)	4.6 (n=2)	17.1 (n=24)
	Removed	1.1 (n=1)	3.5 (n=1)	–	13.2 (n=1)	1.4 (n=2)	–	4.1 (n=5)
Ireland	Move in	10.1 (n=5)	–	36.1 (n=3)	14.6 (n=7)	7.5 (n=2)	–	16.2 (n=17)
	Retain	–	24.3 (n=3)	–	5.5 (n=1)	6.6 (n=2)	20.4 (n=2)	15.3 (n=6)
	Removed	28.7 (n=7)	–	–	14.2 (n=6)	15.4 (n=2)	–	19.9 (n=18)
Austria	Move in	–	–	38.5 (n=1)	26.8 (n=2)	–	30.7 (n=1)	30.7 (n=4)
	Retain	7.8 (n=6)	7.0 (n=3)	19.6 (n=3)	14.8 (n=2)	15.4 (n=6)	20.0 (n=3)	13.4 (n=23)
	Removed	–	2.3 (n=1)	12.6 (n=1)	21.0 (n=3)	–	40.1 (n=1)	19.7 (n=6)
Sweden	Move in	–	–	10.3 (n=3)	3.2 (n=1)	14.8 (n=4)	–	11.7 (n=8)
	Retain	11.9 (n=5)	24.6 (n=3)	16.7 (n=5)	2.7 (n=2)	27.3 (n=1)	14.8 (n=1)	15.5 (n=17)
	Removed	–	–	3.8 (n=1)	5.4 (n=3)	14.3 (n=5)	–	10.2 (n=9)
Portugal	Move in	–	–	13.0 (n=1)	16.7 (n=1)	4.9 (n=1)	0.0 (n=2)	6.9 (n=5)
	Retain	–	–	13.1 (n=1)	19.4 (n=5)	17.8 (n=2)	–	18.2 (n=8)
	Removed	–	–	24.7 (n=1)	26.1 (n=2)	4.6 (n=1)	–	16.3 (n=5)
Denmark	Move in	8.9 (n=5)	9.9 (n=3)	20.4 (n=3)	13.1 (n=5)	18.4 (n=3)	0.0 (n=1)	12.6 (n=21)
	Retain	12.5 (n=2)	10.3 (n=4)	2.3 (n=2)	16.4 (n=7)	16.4 (n=4)	4.5 (n=2)	13.2 (n=19)
	Removed	5.9 (n=3)	6.6 (n=3)	22.8 (n=5)	16.6 (n=3)	25.0 (n=4)	10.8 (n=2)	16.1 (n=20)
Switzerland	Move in	35.4 (n=1)	–	–	–	–		35.4 (n=1)
	Retain	12.8 (n=10)	10.4 (n=8)	9.1 (n=12)	18.3 (n=8)	10.9 (n=12)	14.2 (n=4)	12.1 (n=54)
	Removed	33.4 (n=1)	–	–	–	–		33.4 (n=1)
Greece	Move in	–	–	–	13.8 (n=4)	10.9 (n=1)		13.2 (n=5)
	Retain	–	–	–	7.0 (n=3)	4.5 (n=2)	3.4 (n=1)	5.6 (n=6)
	Removed	–	–	–	8.0 (n=2)	17.1 (n=3)		13.5 (n=5)

							Average
Luxembourg	Move in	13.7 (n=2)	1.1 (n=2)	11.2 (n=2)	1.8 (n=1)	17.44 (n=1)	—	8.9 (n=8)
	Retain	16.1 (n=4)	17.5 (n=2)	11.2 (n=2)	11.1 (n=3)	11.3 (n=3)	—	13.5 (n=14)
	Removed	2.9 (n=2)	7.0 (n=2)	7.7 (n=2)	28.7 (n=1)	0.6 (n=1)	—	8.1 (n=8)
United Kingdom	Move in	1.6 (n=1)	2.8 (n=1)	16.8 (n=3)	—	38.5 (n=1)	—	15.6 (n=6)
	Retain	13.4 (n=3)	9.0 (n=1)	21.0 (n=1)	3.1 (n=2)	2.6 (n=1)	5.5 (n=2)	9.0 (n=10)
	Removed	7.1 (n=1)	15.5 (n=1)	4.7 (n=3)	—	2.2 (n=1)	—	6.5 (n=6)
France	Move in	—	—	—	10.2 (n=4)	0.9 (n=2)	8.0 (n=2)	7.2 (n=9)
	Retain	—	5.9 (n=1)	14.1 (n=4)	—	—	—	12.3 (n=9)
	Removed	—	10.8 (n=5)	—	—	—	—	—
The Netherlands*	Move in	5.4 (n=2)	0.0 (n=1)	—	8.1 (n=3)	12.7 (n=6)	10.8 (n=3)	11.1 (n=12)
	Retain	10.1 (n=10)	14.5 (n=10)	—	5.7 (n=2)	9.1 (n=4)	10.1 (n=2)	7.2 (n=11)
	Removed	6.1 (n=2)	0.0 (n=1)	—	17.2 (n=4)	7.8 (n=5)	6.9 (n=3)	11.5 (n=40)
Italy	Move in	0.9 (n=1)	7.0 (n=4)	—	6.2 (n=1)	3.9 (n=2)	11.7 (n=3)	7.1 (n=11)
	Retain	11.3 (n=2)	8.5 (n=3)	4.4 (n=2)	13.8 (n=5)	8.9 (n=8)	11.0 (n=16)	11.0 (n=16)
	Removed	1.6 (n=1)	5.0 (n=2)	5.4 (n=1)	7.5 (n=4)	—	17.6 (n=4)	8.3 (n=19)
Belgium	Move in	12.9 (n=3)	13.8 (n=5)	0.0 (n=1)	11.0 (n=4)	10.0 (n=5)	19.2 (n=4)	11.5 (n=12)
	Retain	0.8 (n=1)	10.4 (n=12)	8.4 (n=8)	6.7 (n=4)	8.4 (n=8)	0.0 (n=4)	11.3 (n=14)
	Removed	9.7 (n=4)	12.3 (n=4)	11.8 (n=6)	8.1 (n=10)	14.0 (n=5)	0.0 (n=2)	9.1 (n=35)
Norway	Move in	—	2.0 (n=1)	11.6 (n=4)	2.6 (n=3)	13.2 (n=3)	6.1 (n=1)	11.4 (n=14)
	Retain	3.1 (n=2)	5.0 (n=1)	5.6 (n=5)	7.1 (n=4)	9.4 (n=4)	10.8 (n=2)	9.5 (n=13)
	Removed	—	11.3 (n=4)	12.1 (n=1)	—	8.9 (n=1)	16.7 (n=1)	7.0 (n=14)
Spain	Move in	—	—	—	12.7 (n=4)	8.9 (n=1)	—	12.2 (n=11)
	Retain	—	0.9 (n=1)	—	19.0 (n=1)	0.3 (n=1)	—	9.7 (n=2)
	Removed	—	—	—	0.9 (n=1)	5.6 (n=2)	0.0 (n=1)	2.6 (n=5)
Average	Move in	10.0 (n=16)	17.9 (n=33)	12.2 (n=43)	12.0 (n=38)	10.6 (n=15)	—	12.9 (n=165) (n=151)
	Retain	13.4 (n=59)	12.3 (n=70)	15.3 (n=71)	12.6 (n=64)	11.0 (n=27)	—	13.4 (n=348)
	Removed	9.4 (n=14)	14.4 (n=32)	14.7 (n=40)	14.0 (n=39)	13.9 (n=20)	—	13.9 (n=167)

Sources: Based on own calculations using the Kim and Fording (2001) index applied to the CMP data (Budge *et al.* 2001 and Klingemann *et al.* 2006).

Note

* Figures for the Netherlands in the 2000s exclude List Pim Fortuyn (LPF), as no data is available for the party before 2002.

Table 2.3 Ideological change and government status (within-country)

Government status after ideological change	Number of countries where the amount of ideological change was the lowest, middle or highest value		
	Lowest value	*Middle value*	*Highest value*
Move in	4	10	3
Retain	8	2	7
Removed	5	5	7

Tables 2.2, 2.3 and 2.4, no clear incumbency effect appears to exist, and additionally, no one strategy appears to be optimal in relation to parties moving into government, retaining governing status, or leaving government.

To summarise this section, Table 2.1 shows the countries in which high and low levels of ideological change has taken place, generating two hypotheses. In countries where established parties engaged in the highest levels of ideological change, these parties should achieve high levels of centrality within their national party systems. Conversely, where established parties engaged in low levels of ideological change, established parties should not be able to dominate their party systems to the same extent as those parties that engaged in high levels of ideological change. Tables 2.2, 2.3 and 2.4 explored the relationship between incumbency and ideological change, although the data presented appeared to show no significant association. Chapter 5 will explore the extent to which ideological change influences established parties' systemic positions.

2.2 Electoral responsiveness

The relationship between votes cast and the 'political complexion' (Blondel 1968: 191) of government is the second electorate-orientated strategy under consideration. The work of Strøm (1990) most clearly expresses this concept of electoral responsiveness. He argues that electoral responsiveness is a component of the decisiveness of elections and occurs when parties form governments that have gained rather than lost seats in the election (1990: 72). The presence of responsiveness is vital to ensure that parties perform responsibly in government

Table 2.4 Ideological change and government status (across-country)

Government status after ideological change	Number of countries where levels of ideological change were minimal, moderate or high		
	Minimal (0–8)	*Moderate (8–16)*	*High (16+)*
Move in	3	10	4
Retain	3	11	3
Removed	3	8	6

and are aware of the potential costs of incumbency (1990: 47). In a situation of perfect electoral responsiveness, winners must emerge through the electoral process and must be rewarded. In a scenario where parties that repeatedly lose votes continue to govern, the costs of incumbency are not a threat to their dominant position. Strøm concludes that electoral responsiveness is a vital measure for capturing the relationship between government formations and electoral verdicts and has important implications for the democratic legitimacy of the system (1990: 72).

A weak relationship between vote share and coalition make-up may call into question the legitimacy of the government and the democratic nature of the system. Therefore, electoral responsiveness, that is, a close relationship between votes cast and the political complexion of government, is a further way in which established parties can prove themselves responsive to the needs of the electorate. By acting in a responsive manner, political parties are not only responding to the desires of the electorate, but are also acting proactively in order to attract an increased number of votes at the next election. Conversely, according to the cartel thesis of Katz and Mair (1995), some governments should be unresponsive to electoral pressures, as the creation of cartels necessarily reduces electoral responsiveness.

Parties that engage in high levels of responsiveness are attempting to be responsive to the needs of the voters and to mould their views, whereas parties that engage in low levels of electoral responsiveness are less responsive to the needs of the electorate and less willing to attempt to shape the views of the electorate. Strøm (1990) rates each government according to the proportion of electoral gainers among its constituent parties. For example, where both parties in a coalition have increased their share of the vote since the previous election, the figure would be 1.0 or 100 per cent. If one had increased its share and one decreased, the value would be 0.5 or 50 per cent. This methodology produces somewhat limited results, producing many discrete scores of 0.0, 0.5 or 1.0, whereas amendments to the methodology could produce data that is more discriminating.

Instead of measuring the proportion of electoral gainers within a government, a more useful measure is to calculate the average amount of responsiveness of all parties in government. By adding together the responsiveness values of all the governing parties and noting the overall level of electoral responsiveness of a government as a positive or negative value, values are more detailed and discriminating. For example, where each party in a coalition has gained 0.3 per cent and 0.4 per cent of the vote respectively since the previous election, the responsiveness value is 0.7. If one party had gained 25 per cent and the other 27 per cent, the figure recorded would be 52. The revised measure captures far more detail concerning the responsiveness of the coalition partners to electoral trends than using Strøm's measure, which would have stated a figure of 1.0 for both of the examples. The revised measure is also far more useful for viewing comparative trends, as coalition parties in the first example have proven to be less responsive than the parties in the second example, permitting comparisons between countries and over time.

If all parties in government have increased their share of the vote since the previous election, then the government produced has been responsive to electoral trends. However, if none of the parties increased their share of the vote, then the government is categorised as unresponsive. The measure partly captures the electoral responsiveness of non-established parties, as with the previous dimension. However, this problem is less important here. This dimension measures the strategies of established parties and determines the relationship between electoral trends and the political complexion of government. Established parties, predominantly, make decisions regarding government formation and make choices concerning which parties enter government, therefore the electoral responsiveness of governments is a substitute for the electoral responsiveness of established parties. Established parties have been the most influential in determining the make-up of the government and can determine the closeness of the relationship between electoral trends and government formation.

Table 2.5 shows that the countries in which established parties have proven to be the most responsive are Portugal, France and Spain, whereas the countries in which established parties are least responsive are Austria, Switzerland, Sweden and Belgium. In general, established parties have proven to be relatively responsive to the electorate in terms of the relationship between electoral scores and governmental composition, recording an overall value of 1.3, suggesting that the average government in western Europe over the period covered is comprised of parties that have gained 1.3 per cent of the vote since the previous election. The pattern over time is relatively consistent, although there is an interesting trend towards greater responsiveness, with the 1990s and 2000s recording the highest decade averages. This trend may relate to increasing levels of electoral volatility over recent decades, and in particular, a substantial number of 'earthquake' elections that have occurred in the 1990s and 2000s. The Netherlands is one of the countries that contributed significantly to this increase in responsiveness over the past two decades, with parties such as List Pim Fortuyn (LPF) appearing on the electoral scene in 2002, entering government in the same year, before the collapse of the party's vote in 2003. This electoral 'shock' to the Dutch party system resulted in high levels of responsiveness in both 2002 when LPF received 17.0 per cent of the vote and entered government and also in 2003, when the party left government after receiving just 5.7 per cent of the vote.

Another interesting feature is the high level of electoral responsiveness found within the 'newer' western European democracies. Portugal, Spain and Greece rank as three of the six countries in which established parties engaged in the highest levels of electoral responsiveness and are the three countries in the study that have democratised most recently. This finding may suggest that in new democracies, parties are more eager to be responsive to the electorate than in more established democracies, where perhaps the priority is to remain in office at all costs instead of acting in a responsive manner towards the electorate.

Table 2.5 shows that established parties within Portugal, France and Spain have engaged in the highest levels of electoral responsiveness, demonstrating their responsiveness to the electorate and equally, willingness to attempt to

Table 2.5 Electoral responsiveness of western European governing parties, 1950–2009

	Percentage of governments where all parties were responsive	Percentage of governments where all parties were unresponsive	1950s	1960s	1970s	1980s	1990s	2000s	Overall responsiveness
Portugal	75.0 (n=9)	16.7 (n=2)	–	–	3.2 (n=2)	8.4 (n=4)	5.1 (n=3)	2.2 (n=3)	5.2 (n=12)
France	41.7 (n=5)	0.0 (n=0)	–	1.5 (n=3)	2.5 (n=2)	6.0 (n=3)	3.8 (n=2)	9.8 (n=2)	4.6 (n=12)
Spain	66.7 (n=6)	33.3 (n=3)	–	–	0.4 (n=1)	3.1 (n=3)	1.6 (n=2)	6.8 (n=3)	3.7 (n=9)
Italy	13.3 (n=2)	13.3 (n=2)	-3.1 (n=2)	-1.7 (n=2)	-0.6 (n=3)	0.3 (n=2)	13.0 (n=3)	1.5 (n=3)	2.2 (n=15)
Luxembourg	23.1 (n=3)	15.4 (n=2)	1.0 (n=3)	3.6 (n=2)	4.3 (n=2)	0.1 (n=2)	0.8 (n=2)	3.3 (n=2)	2.1 (n=13)
Greece	58.3 (n=7)	25.0 (n=3)	–	–	-12.5 (n=1)	6.7 (n=4)	1.2 (n=3)	1.8 (n=4)	2.1 (n=12)
The Netherlands	6.3 (n=1)	0.0 (n=0)	2.1 (n=3)	-3.4 (n=2)	0.0 (n=3)	0.6 (n=4)	4.2 (n=2)	7.6 (n=3)	1.9 (n=17)
Ireland	41.2 (n=7)	17.6 (n=3)	5.5 (n=3)	-0.9 (n=3)	1.1 (n=2)	0.2 (n=5)	2.5 (n=2)	0.6 (n=2)	1.4 (n=17)
Germany	18.8 (n=3)	18.8 (n=3)	11.1 (n=2)	-0.4 (n=3)	1.0 (n=2)	0.4 (n=3)	-0.4 (n=3)	-1.6 (n=3)	1.1 (n=16)
United Kingdom	50.0 (n=8)	50.0 (n=8)	1.1 (n=4)	2.1 (n=2)	2.2 (n=4)	-0.8 (n=2)	4.2 (n=2)	-4.0 (n=2)	1.0 (n=16)
Denmark	30.4 (n=7)	26.1 (n=6)	0.2 (n=4)	0.5 (n=4)	2.5 (n=5)	-2.0 (n=4)	1.8 (n=3)	1.3 (n=3)	0.7 (n=23)
Finland	43.8 (n=7)	37.5 (n=6)	-1.5 (n=3)	2.3 (n=2)	-3.2 (n=4)	2.3 (n=2)	2.4 (n=3)	3.0 (n=2)	0.3 (n=16)
Norway	40.0 (n=6)	20.0 (n=3)	1.3 (n=2)	-0.2 (n=3)	-2.2 (n=2)	-1.3 (n=3)	0.2 (n=2)	3.5 (n=3)	0.3 (n=15)
Belgium	27.8 (n=5)	22.2 (n=4)	4.4 (n=3)	-7.7 (n=3)	-0.8 (n=4)	-0.4 (n=3)	2.1 (n=3)	5.9 (n=2)	0.2 (n=18)
Sweden	35.3 (n=6)	41.2 (n=7)	-1.0 (n=3)	1.3 (n=3)	-1.8 (n=4)	0.0 (n=3)	0.9 (n=3)	3.9 (n=2)	0.2 (n=18)
Switzerland	6.7 (n=1)	20.0 (n=3)	0.6 (n=3)	-2.6 (n=2)	0.9 (n=3)	-4.8 (n=2)	4.4 (n=3)	-1.0 (n=2)	0.1 (n=15)
Austria	38.9 (n=7)	38.9 (n=7)	2.1 (n=3)	1.7 (n=2)	2.1 (n=4)	-5.7 (n=2)	-6.0 (n=3)	-5.4 (n=4)	-1.8 (n=18)
Overall	34.4 (n=90)	23.7 (n=62)	1.7 (n=38)	-0.4 (n=36)	0.3 (n=48)	1.3 (n=51)	2.5 (n=44)	2.1 (n=45)	1.3 (n=262)

Sources: All figures based on own calculations using the revised electoral responsiveness measure of Strøm (1990).

Note
A negative value shows that, in sum, governing parties have lost votes since the previous election, whereas a positive value indicates an increase in the total share of the vote.

mould its views. These parties should achieve high levels of centrality within their respective national party systems. Conversely, established parties in Austria, Switzerland, Sweden and Belgium have engaged in the lowest levels of electoral responsiveness and appear to be less responsive to the electorate and less willing to mould its views, compared with parties in Portugal, France and Spain.

A perverse argument may hold for this dimension, based on the cartel thesis. If, as the cartel thesis suggests, parties are detaching themselves from civil society in order to gain access to state resources by becoming part of the state machinery (Katz and Mair 1995), low levels of electoral responsiveness may indicate high levels of engagement in cartel strategies. Engagement in cartel strategies should ensure that parties achieve high levels of centrality within their party systems, due to their status as part of the state machinery and the closure of competition that results from the dominance of a cartel. A relationship may therefore exist between electoral and institutional strategies, with parties engaging in high levels of one strategy and low levels of another to reap the greatest benefits. The issue of perverse effects is considered again in the conclusion of this chapter and examined in more detail in Chapter 5, where the impact of the high and low levels of the use of electorate-orientated strategies on the fate of western European established parties is examined.

2.3   Relations with anti-political establishment parties

The competitive relations between existing political parties are not rigidly defined and the introduction of new actors into the political fray can significantly affect these relations. Often, these new actors fall into the category of 'anti-political establishment parties' and can affect the existing balance of the party system and cause a strategic dilemma for the established parties. Established parties can seek to 'normalise' these parties by incorporating them into the party system and potentially government, undermining their anti-political establishment credentials (a strategy of inclusion). The second option available to established parties is to reject these parties and treat them as 'pariahs' within the party system, denying the anti-political establishment parties systemic legitimacy and access to government, but equally reinforcing their raison d'être (a strategy of exclusion). Established parties seeking to engage in a responsive relationship with the electorate should engage in a strategy of inclusion; by embracing anti-political establishment parties within the party system and considering these parties as potential coalition allies, established parties are responding to the section of the electorate who have voted for these parties. A strategy of exclusion indicates an unresponsive strategy by established parties, disregarding the votes cast by a portion of the electorate.

Andreas Schedler (1996) uses the term anti-political establishment party and argues that these parties share resentment against the establishment, the elite, the 'power block', but more specifically, 'anti-political establishment actors declare war on the political class' (1996: 292–3). Schedler argues that anti-political establishment parties employ two concurrent strategies, emphasising the cleavage between established parties and citizens and between established parties and themselves (1996: 291). It is this emphasis on the specific attack on established parties that makes the term 'anti-political establishment party' more intuitively useful for the purposes of this discussion than other terms applied to similar parties.[4]

One of the most recent contributions to the debate concerning precisely what constitutes an anti-political establishment party comes from the work of Amir Abedi (2004). He shares Schedler's (1996) terminology and argues that these parties should not be described as new politics, libertarian left, populist or right-wing extremist parties; parties which reject the system within which they operate can be grouped together under the name of anti-political establishment parties (Abedi 2004: 12). Abedi produces a classification of political parties and constructs a list of parties that he considers to belong to the group of anti-political establishment parties.[5] The criteria are as follows: a party that challenges the status quo in terms of major policy issues and political system issues; a party that perceives itself as a challenger to the parties that make up the political establishment; and a party that asserts that there exists a fundamental divide between the political establishment and the people. It thereby implies that all establishment parties, be they in government or in opposition, are essentially the same (Abedi 2004: 12).

The list of anti-political establishment parties constructed by Abedi can assist the study of the strategies employed by established parties towards these parties. Parties can engage in strategies of inclusion or exclusion, or they can engage in a mixed strategy as if a system contains multiple anti-political establishment parties, established parties may incorporate one into the party system and potentially government, but reject others. A strategy of inclusion occurs when a party listed as an anti-political establishment party enters government and a strategy of exclusion occurs when anti-political establishment parties are rejected within the party system and do not enter government. A mixed strategy occurs when an anti-political establishment party governs, but established parties reject others. According to these criteria, strategies can be categorised as inclusive, exclusive or mixed.

A significant problem occurs when a party moves from anti-political establishment status to non-established status as if a party enters government, it is not opposing the system in which it operates, as it has become part of the system itself. However, the purpose of this dimension is to assess the treatment of anti-political establishment parties by established parties. Established parties develop a strategy towards these parties from the start of the anti-political establishment party's time in parliament. The exact dimension is therefore the treatment of parties that *enter the party system* as anti-political establishment parties.

A further problem emerges when considering the size of anti-political establishment parties considered relevant. All countries contain anti-political establishment parties, ranging from minor parties with no parliamentary representation, to parties that obtain a substantial share of the vote. A share of five per cent of the vote or more is a sensible threshold over which anti-political establishment parties are considered to have systemic relevance, thus only parties receiving more than five per cent of the vote are included in the study.

Table 2.6 shows that the predominant strategy found in the relationship between established parties and anti-political establishment parties is that of exclusion, as in 71 per cent of the decades in which an anti-political establishment party was present, a strategy of exclusion was present. The data is relatively consistent over time, although the 1980s–2000s demonstrate a lower level of exclusion than the 1950s–1970s, reflecting the increase in support for anti-establishment parties during this time. The countries in which the strategy employed has been the most inclusive are Finland, the Netherlands and Belgium, whereas in eight countries, the strategy employed has been exclusive throughout, with no anti-political establishment party achieving government status.

In Finland, the Netherlands and Belgium, established parties should achieve high levels of centrality within their party systems. The established parties in these countries have engaged in inclusive strategies towards the anti-political establishment parties active within their party systems and have demonstrated a high level of responsiveness towards the electorate. By including almost all relevant parties in government, established parties are demonstrating a desire to incorporate a wide range of parties into government, indicating to the electorate that 'every vote counts' and no party is excluded from government. This responsive strategy employed towards anti-political establishment parties should have a positive effect on the levels of party system centrality achieved by the established parties in Finland, the Netherlands and Belgium.

Conversely, in Ireland, Spain, Portugal, Denmark, Switzerland, Norway, Sweden and Luxembourg, established parties should achieve low levels of centrality. In these eight countries, established parties exclude anti-political establishment parties from government. This strategy towards anti-political establishment parties indicates a lack of responsiveness towards the electorate, as a portion of the electorate that cast its votes for anti-political establishment parties will feel that the established parties, effectively, are ignoring their votes. This unresponsive strategy towards the electorate and anti-political establishment parties should have a negative impact on the levels of party system centrality achieved by the established parties in these countries. Chapter 5 will test these hypotheses and assesses the impact of the high and low use of electorate-orientated strategies on the fate of established parties.

There may be a possibility of perverse effects concerning this dimension, as the established parties in the eight countries that have excluded anti-political establishment parties from government may achieve high levels of centrality due to their engagement in cartel-like behaviours. According to Katz and Mair (1995), cartel parties should act to keep other parties from entering the system and the cartel. The exclusion of anti-political establishment parties from government is evidence of cartel strategies by established political parties seeking to maintain their dominant positions within their national party systems.

Table 2.6 Established parties' strategies towards anti-political establishment party system entrants, 1950–2009

	1950s	1960s	1970s	1980s	1990s	2000s	Overall
Finland	Exclusion	Inclusion	Mixed	Mixed	Inclusion	Inclusion	3/6 Inclusion (50%)
The Netherlands	Exclusion	N/A[a]	Inclusion	Inclusion	Mixed	Mixed	2/5 Inclusion (40%)
Belgium	N/A	Exclusion	Inclusion	Inclusion	Mixed	Exclusion	2/5 Inclusion (40%)
Italy	Exclusion	Exclusion	Exclusion	Exclusion	Inclusion	Inclusion	2/6 Inclusion (33%)
Greece	–	–	Exclusion	Inclusion	Exclusion	Exclusion	1/4 Inclusion (25%)
Austria	Exclusion	Exclusion	Exclusion	Inclusion	Exclusion	Mixed	1/6 Inclusion (17%)
Germany	N/A	N/A	N/A	Exclusion	Mixed	Mixed	2/3 Mixed (67%)
France	Exclusion	Exclusion	Exclusion	Mixed	Mixed	Mixed	2/6 Mixed (33%)
Ireland	N/A	N/A	N/A	N/A	N/A	Exclusion[b]	1/1 Exclusion (100%)
Spain	–	–	Exclusion	Exclusion	Exclusion	N/A	3/3 Exclusion (100%)
Portugal	–	–	Exclusion	Exclusion	Exclusion	Exclusion	4/4 Exclusion (100%)
Denmark	N/A	Exclusion	Exclusion	Exclusion	Exclusion	Exclusion	5/5 Exclusion (100%)
Switzerland	Exclusion	Exclusion	Exclusion	N/A	Exclusion	Exclusion	5/5 Exclusion (100%)
Norway	Exclusion	N/A	Exclusion	Exclusion	Exclusion	Exclusion	5/5 Exclusion (100%)
Sweden	Exclusion	Exclusion	Exclusion	Exclusion	Exclusion	Exclusion	6/6 Exclusion (100%)
Luxembourg	Exclusion	Exclusion	Exclusion	Exclusion	Exclusion	Exclusion	6/6 Exclusion (100%)
United Kingdom	N/A	N/A	N/A	N/A	N/A	N/A	N/A
Overall	10/10 Exclusion (100%)	7/8 Exclusion (88%)	11/14 Exclusion (79%)	9/15 Exclusion (60%)	9/15 Exclusion (60%)	9/15 Exclusion (60%)	55/77 Exclusion (71%)

Sources: Abedi (2004), Parties and Election in Europe (2010) and own judgements.

Notes

a A decade receives the notation N/A when no anti-political-establishment party of sufficient size is present within the party system in that particular decade.

b Although the Green Party entered government in 2007, the party received only 4.7 per cent of the vote, and is therefore not considered a significant anti-political establishment party.

2.4 Pre-electoral coalition agreements

Most of the countries in this study, with the exception of Spain and the United Kingdom, have experienced coalition governments at some point since 1950.[6] The operation of coalitions represents an opportunity for parties to show that they are responsive to the needs of the electorate, and established parties can use pre-electoral coalition agreements in order to demonstrate their responsiveness. These are arrangements made before elections take place, committing parties to govern together after the election and can provide established parties with an opportunity to inform the voters about the composition of potential coalition governments.

Pre-election coalition agreements are an understudied way in which parties can influence their own fate and maintain their position within party systems. Sona Golder (2006: 193–4) outlines three reasons why pre-electoral coalition agreements are important and warrant further study. The first is that parties that choose to cooperate before an election are simply more likely to win the election if they can pool resources and choose to field a common candidate in each district. Second, pre-electoral agreements can allow voters to identify governing alternatives at election time, increasing democratic transparency and providing coalition governments with increased legitimacy and stronger policy mandates. Finally, pre-electoral coalition agreements occur frequently, as pre-electoral agreements form the basis of approximately a quarter of all governments formed in Golders's study. In line with Golder's arguments, pre-electoral agreements are an important tool available for established parties seeking to be open and responsive towards the needs of the electorate. Yet, they also provide an ideal opportunity to influence the way that the electorate votes by encouraging the electorate to vote for a coalition as opposed to a single party. This may prove to be a particularly useful strategy in countries where the electoral system provides the opportunity for voters to cast votes for more than one party, for example, in Germany.

Müller and Strøm (2000a: 18) define a coalition agreement as 'the most binding written statement joined by all parties, that is, the most authoritative document which constrains party behaviour'. Two issues arise from this definition. The first is the binding nature of the agreements. Pre-electoral agreements commit parties to a particular alliance and sometimes contain information regarding policies and the formal rules concerning coalition governance. The second important feature to note is that 'all parties' make pre-electoral agreements. If a pre-electoral agreement is agreed upon by two parties and the government is formed by these parties and a third, the government is not counted as one that has been formed following a pre-electoral agreement, as not all parties participated in the pre-electoral agreement.

Golder defines pre-electoral coalitions as occurring 'when multiple parties choose to co-ordinate their electoral strategies rather than run for office alone' (2006: 195), with the prevalence of pre-electoral coalitions measured by examining the number of times that a government is formed based on a pre-electoral coalition agreement, although the nature of the pre-electoral agreement can produce differing data. For the purposes of this dimension, only pre-electoral *written* agreements are considered. Verbal agreements often occur before an election, but it is difficult to determine when a verbal agreement occurs and the data would rely on qualitative judgments; therefore only written agreements are included. By limiting the study to written agreements only, the data is easier to obtain and will be more comparable for the purposes of this cross-national study over time. Due to the focus on written agreements and agreements made by all subsequent governing parties only, the data should reveal fewer pre-electoral agreements than the Golder data.

Table 2.7 shows that pre-electoral coalition agreements occur far less widely than in Golder's study, in line with expectations due to the more restrictive definition adopted. Just 6.6 per cent of all coalitions formed in western Europe between 1950 and 2009 were based on a pre-electoral coalition agreement and in ten out of the 15 countries with a history of coalitions, no coalition has ever been formed which was based on a written, pre-electoral agreement made by all governing parties. Indeed, it is only in Norway that written, pre-electoral agreements form the basis for the majority of coalition governments. However, the trend over recent decades does appear to point towards increasing use of these agreements. Since the start of the 1980s, pre-electoral agreements have formed the basis of 10 per cent of coalition governments. In the previous section, the trend towards increasingly levels of electoral responsiveness was also noted, potentially suggesting a growth in electoral accountability and responsiveness since the 1980s.

Another important issue is why the overall figures for the use of pre-electoral agreements are so much lower than Golder's figures (2006), which state that approximately a quarter of coalitions were formed following a pre-electoral agreement, compared to the figure of 6.6 per cent for this study. From a rational choice perspective, it should not be surprising that established parties are somewhat reluctant to declare their hand before the election and bind themselves to certain policies, allocation of offices and procedures (Müller and Strøm 2000a: 19), before the election result is known, due to the uncertainty of the election result. A rational party seeks to minimise uncertainty and waits until after the election, where coalition negotiations can take place between parties that know their legislative weights and are in a better position to judge their bargaining power.

Methodological considerations are also important, as this dimension adopted a rigorous measure. Only written agreements agreed by all parties that went on to govern were included in the study, so the criteria were somewhat restrictive. For example, in countries such as Austria and Germany, potential coalition partners often agree upon informal and unwritten agreements, but these agreements do not feature in Table 2.7. Thomas Saalfeld (2000: 39) highlights the 'regular' use of informal pre-election coalition pacts as one of the principal features of the German coalition system and argues that these pacts are perfectly rational as they reduce the level of electoral competition between the governing parties.

The data shows that the countries in which written, pre-electoral coalition agreements occur with the greatest frequency are Norway, Portugal and France. Ten countries have never used these agreements but Italy, Finland and Switzerland stand out as systems where coalition governments dominate, but pre-electoral agreements

Table 2.7 Coalition governments based on pre-electoral coalition agreements, 1950–2009

	1950s (%)	1960s (%)	1970s (%)	1980s (%)	1990s (%)	2000s (%)	Overall (%)
Norway	N/A[a]	66.7 (2/3)[b]	0 (0/1)	100 (3/3)	100 (1/1)	66.7 (2/3)	72.7 (8/11)
Portugal	–	–	50.0 (1/2)	50.0 (1/2)	N/A	100 (1/1)	60 (3/5)
France	0 (0/1)	0 (0/5)	0 (0/3)	100 (2/2)	100 (2/2)	0 (1/1)	35.7 (5/14)
Sweden	33.3 (1/3)	N/A	0 (0/2)	0 (0/1)	0 (0/1)	100 (1/1)	25 (2/8)
Ireland	0 (0/1)	N/A	100 (1/1)	0 (0/3)	0 (0/4)	0 (0/2)	9 (1/11)
Greece	–	–	N/A	0 (0/2)	N/A	N/A	0 (0/2)
Austria	0 (0/3)	0 (0/1)	N/A	0 (0/2)	0 (0/3)	0 (0/4)	0 (0/13)
Luxembourg	0 (0/3)	0 (0/2)	0 (0/2)	0 (0/2)	0 (0/2)	0 (0/2)	0 (0/13)
Denmark	0 (0/3)	0 (0/2)	0 (0/1)	0 (0/4)	0 (0/5)	0 (0/3)	0 (0/18)
Germany	0 (0/4)	0 (0/5)	0 (0/2)	0 (0/4)	0 (0/4)	0 (0/3)	0 (0/22)
The Netherlands	0 (0/5)	0 (0/4)	0 (0/4)	0 (0/5)	0 (0/2)	0 (0/3)	0 (0/23)
Belgium	0 (0/4)	0 (0/4)	0 (0/7)	0 (0/6)	0 (0/3)	0 (0/2)	0 (0/26)
Italy	0 (0/4)	0 (0/3)	0 (0/7)	0 (0/6)	0 (0/7)	0 (0/3)	0 (0/30)
Finland	0 (0/11)	0 (0/3)	0 (0/8)	0 (0/3)	0 (0/5)	0 (0/2)	0 (0/32)
Switzerland	0 (0/10)	0 (0/10)	0 (0/10)	0 (0/10)	0 (0/10)	0 (0/10)	0 (0/60)
Spain	–	–	N/A	N/A	N/A	N/A	N/A
United Kingdom	N/A	N/A	N/A	N/A	N/A	N/A	N/A
Overall	1.9 (1/52)	4.8 (2/42)	4.0 (2/50)	10.9 (6/55)	6.1 (3/49)	12.5 (5/40)	6.6 (19/288)

Sources: Allern and Aylott (2009); Alliance for Sweden Homepage (2010); The Department of the Taoiseach (2010); Golder (2006); Norwegian Centre Party Homepage (2010); Norwegian Venstre Party Homepage (2010); Ministère de L'intérieur (2010); Müller and Strøm (2000b); Portuguese Government Portal (2010).

Notes
a A decade receives the notation N/A when no coalition government has been formed in that particular decade.
b Figures in brackets illustrate the number of governments formed on the basis of pre-electoral coalition agreements as a proportion of all coalition governments in that decade.

do not occur. Established parties in Norway, Portugal and France should be able to dominate their party systems because of their high levels of construction of pre-electoral coalition agreements. By constructing pre-electoral agreements, these established parties are showing themselves to be open and responsive towards the electorate, but also seeking to direct the way that voters cast their votes. Established parties in Italy, Finland and Switzerland should achieve low levels of centrality within their national party systems due to their reluctance to engage in pre-electoral agreements, indicating a closed and unresponsive attitude towards the electorate.

2.5 Length of coalition agreements

Section 2.4 examined the prevalence of pre-electoral coalition agreements, but not the content of these agreements. In this section, the length of coalition agreements formed both before and after elections is analysed to determine the extent to which established parties construct coalition agreements in order to try to act in an open manner towards the electorate. Coalition agreements have already been defined in section 2.4 as 'the most binding written statements joined by all parties, that is, the most authoritative document which constrains party behaviour' (Müller and Strøm 2000a: 18). Some documents regulate coalition life in some detail and may contain specific conflict management mechanisms, impose discipline in parliamentary votes or apply rules to the selection of cabinet posts (Müller and Strøm 2000a: 18–19). Saalfeld (2000: 55) notes that post-electoral coalition agreements are usually well-publicised documents, summarise the results of coalition negotiations, attempt to insure each partner against changing preferences or opportunism of the other, and can lay down rules for conflict management. Saalfeld also highlights the importance of coalition agreements as strategic tools. He argues that parties are often faced with 'unresolvable conflicts' when constructing coalition agreements and parties are faced with a choice to either omit the issue entirely from the agreement, 'flag up' the issue and effectively postpone a settlement to a later stage, or deal with the issue comprehensively in the agreement (Saalfeld 2000: 57).

A consequence of a lengthy coalition agreement, outlining in detail the policies to be pursued during the course of the governmental term, is that the electorate is provided with access to a detailed agreement against which the performance of the government can be judged. This may make parties more accountable to the electorate and may demonstrate an open attitude towards the electorate, suggesting they should achieve high levels of centrality within their national party systems. Conversely, short coalition agreements may indicate a desire to engage in a closed relationship with the electorate, therefore established parties should expect to record lower levels of systemic centrality.

Table 2.8 shows that coalition agreements are publicly accessible in 12 of the 17 countries considered. The length of document ranges from an average of just 368 words in Italy, to 22,059 in Portugal. Some interesting trends are observable within the data. There has been a fairly consistent trend over time for longer coalition agreements to be constructed, perhaps indicating increasing levels of

Table 2.8 Average length of coalition agreements in western Europe, 1950–2009

	1950s	1960s	1970s	1980s	1990s	2000s	Overall
Portugal	–	–	19,388 (n=2/2)[a]	18,381 (n=2/2)	N/A[b]	34,756 (n=1/1)	22,059 (n=5/5)[c]
Norway	N/A	4,464 (n=3/3)	2,919 (n=1/1)	20,975 (n=3/3)	20,240 (n=1/1)	22,775 (n=3/3)	15,255 (n=11/11)
Austria	1,200 (n=3/3)	4,400 (n=1/1)	N/A	8,400 (n=2/2)	15,400 (n=3/3)	29,927 (n=4/4)	14,670 (n=13/13)
Belgium	0 (n=0/4)	2,325 (n=2/4)	12,757 (n=7/7)	19,200 (n=6/6)	25,233 (n=3/3)	24,888 (n=2/2)	13,049 (n=20/26)
The Netherlands	0 (n=0/5)	2,513 (n=3/4)	3,500 (n=2/4)	16,030 (n=4/5)	26,125 (n=2/2)	14,262 (n=4/4)	8,896 (n=14/24)
Germany	0 (n=0/4)	367 (n=1/5)	0 (n=0/2)	3,511 (n=4/4)	10,610 (n=3/4)	41,102 (n=3/3)	8,256 (n=11/22)
Ireland	0 (n=0/1)	N/A	1,248 (n=1/1)	7,797 (n=3/3)[d]	1,130 (n=3/4)	23,789 (n=2/2)	6,267 (n=9/11)
Denmark	0 (n=0/3)	455 (n=1/2)	0 (n=0/1)	0 (n=0/4)	2,693 (n=3/5)	18,363 (n=3/3)	3,859 (n=7/18)
Sweden	1,367 (n=3/3)	N/A	3,200 (n=2/2)	1,400 (n=1/1)	5,200 (n=1/1)	11,110 (n=1/1)	3,526 (n=8/8)
Finland	449 (n=11/11)	907 (n=3/3)	1,244 (n=8/8)	1,891 (n=3/3)	3,902 (n=5/5)	11,449 (n=3/3)	2,338 (n=33/33)
France	0 (n=0/1)	0 (n=0/5)	0 (n=0/3)	1,153 (n=2/2)	1,723 (n=2/2)	0 (n=0/1)	411 (n=4/14)
Italy	0 (n=0/4)	3,680 (n=1/3)	0 (n=0/7)	0 (n=0/6)	0 (n=0/7)	0 (n=0/3)	368 (n=1/30)
Greece	–	–	N/A	0 (n=0/2)	N/A	N/A	0 (n=0/2)
Switzerland	0 (n=0/10)	0 (n=0/10)	0 (n=0/10)	0 (n=0/10)	0 (n=0/10)	0 (n=0/10)	0 (n=0/60)
Luxembourg	Not published	Not published	Not published	Not published	Not published	Not published	Not published
Spain	–	–	N/A	N/A	N/A	N/A	N/A
United Kingdom	N/A	N/A	N/A	N/A	N/A	N/A	N/A
Overall	258 (n=17/49)	1,341 (n=15/40)	3,387 (n=23/48)	6,767 (n=30/53)	6,021 (n=26/47)	13,906 (n=26/40)	5,151 (n=137/277)

Sources: Alliance for Sweden Homepage (2010); Austrian Federal Chancellery (2010); Belgian Federal E-Portal (2010); German Christian Democratic Union Homepage (2010); The Department of the Taoiseach (2010); Dutch Government Homepage (2010); Finnish Government Homepage (2010); German Government Homepage (2010); German Green Party Homepage (2010); Müller and Strøm (2000b); Norwegian Centre Party Homepage (2010); Norwegian Venstre Party Homepage (2010); Portuguese Government Portal (2010); Prime Minister's Office Homepage (Denmark) (2010).

Notes

a Figures in brackets illustrate the number of coalition agreements made out of the total number of coalitions formed in that particular decade.

b A decade receives the notation N/A when no coalition is formed in that particular decade.

c Averages indicate the total number of words in all coalition agreements divided by the total number of coalitions formed. If a coalition is formed and is not based on a coalition agreement, then this is recorded as 0 for the purposes of length of words within the agreement. This ensures that an accurate overall picture is obtained. For example, coalition governments may dominate a system, but only one coalition is based on an agreement, containing 25,000 words. This would suggest that, according to these results, the established parties in this country are engaging in a responsive and open strategy towards the electorate. However, this distorts the real picture, as only one coalition was based on an agreement; all other coalitions did not form agreements and sought to keep the electorate ignorant of the policies, composition and organisation of the coalition. Awarding a coalition a value of 0 when no agreement is made should ensure that the results obtained are accurate.

d Three coalition agreements were formed in the 1980s in Ireland, but the data for the agreement made between Fianna Fáil and the Progressive Democrats in 1989 is unavailable, so the average length of the two recordable agreements is cited.

distrust between coalition partners (Saalfeld 2000: 55), or an increasing desire for established parties to communicate the operation and policies of coalition government to the electorate. The increase in length over time is a striking trend, with the average length of document increasing from a mere 258 words in the 1950s to 13,906 in the 2000s, reinforcing the trends observed in previous sections relating to an overall increase in the level of responsiveness.

The longest coalition agreements occur in Portugal, Norway and Austria, whereas established parties within Luxembourg have chosen to make their agreements unavailable to the public, and the established parties in Greece and Switzerland eschew agreements completely. Dumont and De Winter (2000: 413) argue that the 'secrecy of government agreements is surprising ... [c]onsidering the efforts made by the Luxembourg governments to politically inform its citizens'. Although they argue that, from the scarce information available, these are lengthy texts and increasing in length over time (2000: 415), the decision to keep the agreements private indicates a lack of willingness by the established parties to engage in an open and responsive strategy towards the electorate.

Established parties in Portugal, Norway and Austria should achieve a high level of centrality within their national party systems. Established parties in these three countries have constructed the longest coalition agreements in western Europe, informing the electorate about the 'inner workings' of the coalition and providing the electorate with a document against which the parties' performance can be judged at the end of the governmental term. High levels of engagement in this open strategy towards the electorate should positively influence the fate of the established parties in Portugal, Norway and Austria.

Conversely, established parties in Greece, Switzerland and Luxembourg should achieve low levels of centrality within their respective national party systems. In Luxembourg, agreements are not publicly available and established parties do not draw up agreements at all in Greece and Switzerland. The behaviour of established parties within these three countries indicates a desire to keep the electorate ignorant of the operation, membership and policies of the coalition. This closed and unresponsive strategy towards the electorate should negatively influence the fate of the established parties in Luxembourg, Greece and Switzerland.

2.6 Conclusion

This chapter has provided data concerning the levels of engagement by established political parties in western Europe in certain 'electorate-orientated strategies', measuring five dimensions: ideological change, electoral responsiveness, relations with anti-political establishment parties, pre-electoral coalition agreements and length of coalition agreements. The low use of electorate-orientated strategies should negatively influence the fate of established parties, whereas the high use of strategies should enable established parties to continue to dominate their party systems. However, the reverse causal relationship may also be in operation, suggesting that high levels of electorate-orientated strategies would negatively influence the fate of established parties, whereas the more beneficial strategy for established parties seeking to maintain their systemic dominance is to engage in low levels of electorate-orientated strategies. The cartel thesis of Katz and Mair (1995) further develops this argument.

The most beneficial strategy for established parties may be to create distance between themselves and the electorate, and to act in a closed and unresponsive manner. Katz and Mair (1995) argue that this creation of distance from the electorate can be achieved by established parties forming a closer relationship with the state and instead of relying on membership subscriptions for income and electoral results to determine government formation, a 'cartel' of political parties is created. This cartel has distanced itself from civil society and has become part of the state in which a small group of parties share the spoils of government and state subsidies; and by distancing themselves from the electorate, the established parties can create a certain amount of immunity from electoral trends. The creation of a cartel also implies a reduction in competition within the party system, as the cartel seeks to control entry to the system and keep challengers to the cartel outside. If the cartel hypothesis is accepted, parties engaging in cartel strategies may also engage in low levels of electorate-orientated strategies precisely because of their desire to reduce systemic competition. Therefore, low levels of engagement in electorate-orientated strategies may produce high levels of systemic centrality, due to the reduction of levels of competition within the party system. The analysis conducted in Chapter 5 should reveal if the data supports the hypotheses presented in this chapter.

Parties that engage in high levels of electorate-orientated strategies may be seeking to dominate the *electoral arena*, whereas parties that engage in low levels of electorate-orientated strategies are seeking to dominate the *governmental arena*. Parties that act in an open and responsive manner towards the electorate may engage in strategies such as an inclusive attitude towards antipolitical establishment parties and creating a close relationship between electoral results and governmental outcomes. These actions inevitably reduce the dominance that established parties could achieve within the governmental arena, as parties are welcomed into government by the established parties, responding to electoral trends. In contrast, parties that engage in low levels of electorateorientated strategies are eschewing responsiveness to the electorate in favour of the pursuit of governmental dominance. By adopting an exclusive strategy towards anti-political establishment parties and ensuring that there is a weak relationship between electoral trends and governmental outcomes, established parties can seek to retain their governmental status and ensure that nonestablished parties cannot challenge this dominance. These points reflect the work of Luther (1989), who assesses the Austrian party system by examining congruence between the party system operating in different arenas. Chapter 5 tests this interesting interpretation of the emphasis placed on dominance in different arenas by examining the impact on established parties' centrality of high and low levels of electorate-orientated strategies.

3 Institutional strategies

In addition to engagement in strategies relating to the electorate, parties can also engage in strategies relating to institutions, and this chapter investigates the extent to which the political institutions of western Europe favour established parties. Institutions play a major role in shaping the way that political parties operate and can facilitate or restrict certain activities, ultimately playing a role in determining the success of certain parties. Rules and regulations for the maintenance of the institutional structure are set out in most western European democracies' constitutions, yet governing parties are not always compelled to abide by rules concerning the operation of institutions. If the rules disadvantage certain parties, they can change the rules. This perspective is encapsulated by Müller's statement that 'political parties' motivation for playing the political game is not the Olympic principle; their rationale is not mere participation in the game, but winning it' (2002: 251).

Katz (2002: 90) argues that the major way that political parties can seek to change the rules of the game is by seeking refuge in the institutions of the state. This forms the basis of the cartel thesis (Katz and Mair 1995), which focuses on state subsidies and media access as ways in which parties can entrench themselves within state institutions. This chapter addresses these dimensions, alongside other dimensions relating to the institutional environment. The importance of political parties not only operating in, but also able to influence, the institutional framework is of vital importance for the purposes of this chapter. Parties have been the principal actors constructing the particular institutional arrangement in each country over time, so parties are constantly engaging in institutional strategies.

Established parties, acting as rational actors and in line with the cartel thesis, should seek to utilise the resources of the state and modify institutions to ensure that the institutional set-up in which they operate favours them. This chapter consider the extent to which the institutional arrangement in western Europe favours established parties by considering the following four dimensions: electoral laws, electoral systems, television campaigning airtime and state subsidies. Electoral laws and electoral systems are the first hurdles for parties when embarking on an election campaign and the pursuit of votes, policy and office (Müller and Strøm 1999b). Television campaigning airtime and state subsidies relate to the campaign process itself and the rewards that parties can expect to receive, often because of the share of the vote received at the election. These dimensions form an important part of the cartel thesis, enabling this chapter to provide an assessment of the levels of strategies engaged in by established parties and expected hypotheses, and provide an analysis of the applicability of the cartel thesis.

3.1 Electoral laws

Although not explicitly addressed in the cartel thesis of Katz and Mair (1995), electoral laws nonetheless provide an important opportunity for established parties to engage in institutional strategies. Electoral laws are those that specifically govern the conduct of elections *before* elections take place, that is, the electoral system translates vote shares into parliamentary seats and constitutes a separate dimension. The system of electoral laws in place within a country is a major determinant of whether non-established parties can challenge established parties and is the first hurdle that parties seeking to compete in elections must face. If the barriers put in place by a system of electoral laws are too high for some parties wishing to take part in elections, the possibility of challenging the established parties is reduced and cartel-like behaviours and institutional strategies are in operation.

One of the earliest seminal works to address the importance of electoral laws for party systems and the political systems as a whole was Douglas Rae's 1967 work *The Political Consequences of Electoral Laws.* Rae defines electoral laws as 'those which govern the processes by which electoral preferences are articulated as votes ... among the competing political parties' (1967: 14), reinforcing the earlier distinction made between electoral laws (governing the conversion of preferences to votes) and electoral systems (the process of converting votes to seats). Bernard Grofman and Arend Lijphart (1986: 2–3) supplement this view, arguing that there are 13 areas relevant for the purposes of the conversion of preferences to votes, the most important of which relate to the ease of party and candidate access to the political process and campaign financing rules.

Recent literature has begun to look in detail at the impact of electoral laws in place throughout western Europe. Two of the most important works are those of Shaun Bowler *et al.* (2003) and Elisabeth Carter (2005). Bowler *et al.* (2003: 86) emphasise that electoral laws contain not just counting rules relating to the electoral system, but also rules concerning ballot access and campaign finance. Carter (2005: 162) echoes this sentiment by arguing that the electoral system forms only part of the electoral laws of a country. An interesting point raised in the Bowler *et al.* study and important for the purposes of this study is that electoral laws may be easier to change than electoral systems. The constitution often does not protect electoral laws, which may be less visible and much more complex than the counting rules, and so less susceptible to public charges of 'rigging the rules' (Bowler *et al.* 2003: 87). Established parties may thus be more likely to alter the rules concerning campaign subsidies and ballot access than rules relating to electoral systems.

In order to assess the extent to which established parties create systems that are favourable to themselves, that is, the extent to which established parties engage in institutional strategies, the factors proposed by Bowler *et al.* (2003) can be assessed. Where laws for ballot access are restrictive and campaign finance weigh strongly in favour of the established parties, established parties should achieve high levels of centrality within their national party systems. Conversely, where laws governing ballot access are permissive and campaign finance is relatively equally distributed, competition may be more open within a given country and established parties may achieve low levels of systemic centrality.

This section focuses on ballot access and campaign finance as two areas of particular importance within the field of electoral laws. Each area of study must be broken down into sub-sections in order to produce comparable data. Within the area of ballot access, the deposit and signature requirements for political parties and candidates to stand at elections are significant, as are rules governing independent candidates. In relation to campaign finance, the system of campaign subsidies in place (if any) is relevant, in addition to limits to campaign expenditure. These five areas should provide thorough and comparable data to show in which countries the system of extant electoral laws is the most and least restrictive.

Deposit requirements

Where deposit requirements are high, established parties have engaged in high levels of institutional strategies in an attempt to maintain their systemic dominance. If parties pay a large deposit to run in elections, this should favour the established and generally richer parties. Smaller or newer competitors would be reticent about paying a high electoral deposit, especially if the party or candidate stands only a remote chance of attracting enough votes to be eligible for a reimbursement of the deposit (Carter 2005: 167). Where deposit requirements are low, established parties have engaged in low levels of institutional strategies and have created a permissive system where deposit requirements do not penalise non-established parties.[1]

Signature requirements

The second area, signature requirements, raises further problems concerning comparability of data. Many countries have signature requirements for a certain number of petitions in a district and this figure varies by district size. Conversely, other countries stipulate a national requirement, whereby a certain number of petitions are required throughout the whole country, making these requirements difficult to compare with countries that require a certain number of signatures per district.[2]

Where signature requirements are high, established parties are engaging in high levels of institutional strategies in an attempt to sustain their systemic dominance, but where signature requirements are low, engagement in institutional strategies is also low. Carter (2005) supports this view, arguing that:

> it is reasonable to assume that high ballot access requirements will be detrimental to small or new parties ... [as] such parties command little support and will thus find it harder to muster the necessary number of signatures to access the ballot than will a larger, more popular party.
>
> (Carter 2005: 167)

Independent candidates

The position of independent candidates within the political systems of western Europe is significant, as although independent candidates may not challenge the established parties' governmental positions, without the restraints imposed by political party affiliation, independent candidates are freer to criticise the government and undermine the authority of the established parties. With reference to the Irish example, some independent candidates (totalling 12.6 per cent of the membership of the Dáil following the 2011 election) 'wield disproportionate power and create a potentially serious underlying threat to the stability of government' (Sinnott 1999: 120). Restricting opportunities for independent candidates represents a further way in which established parties can engage in institutional strategies in an attempt to protect their own interests.[3]

Campaign subsidies

In certain countries, parties receive subsidies specifically to cover campaign costs, with the amount awarded usually reimbursed in proportion to the party's success at the election, but the impact of these subsidies has been a matter of dispute within the literature. Katz and Mair (1995: 15–16) argue that access to state subsidies is a key feature of the cartel party system and cartel parties can use subsidies to reinforce their positions and to freeze out challengers. Other studies such as Bowler *et al.* (2003) note that the introduction of subsidies has reinforced the status quo in most countries, but does also have benefits for smaller parties. Jon Pierre *et al.* (2000) and Susan Scarrow (2006) argue that the introduction of subsidies has had very little impact at all on the balance of power between the core parties and their smaller and newer competitors.

There is no consensus regarding the impact of campaign subsidies, although thresholds for eligibility play a vital role. A high threshold will clearly have the impact of reinforcing the cartel system outlined by Katz and Mair (1995), whereas a low or non-existent threshold may assist non-established parties. Where the threshold is low or non-existent, established parties are engaging in low levels of institutional strategies, but where the threshold is high, established parties engage in high levels of institutional strategies, restricting opportunities for non-established parties. High thresholds can reinforce the problems faced by minor parties, as outlined by Bowler *et al.* (2003). They argue that if the threshold for parties to receive state contributions towards their campaign expenses is 5 per cent, the offer of public money comes too late since the ability to gain 5 per cent of the vote depends on running expensive media campaigns (Bowler *et al.* 2003: 88).

Campaign expenditure limits

The costs of running electoral campaigns have increased dramatically over recent decades (see Katz and Mair 1992, Farrell 2002 and Plasser and Plasser 2002), with many established parties able to spend heavily in order to communicate their political message. Limiting campaign expenditure should ensure that all parties are competing relatively equally, as established parties generally still have more money to spend on election campaigns than non-established parties,[4] but a cap on expenditure may ensure that wealthy parties cannot spend excessively more than other parties and can prevent wealthy candidates or parties from buying votes (Nassmacher 2006: 446). Where there is no expenditure limit, established parties are engaging in high levels of institutional strategies, as the absence of a limit enables wealthy parties to dominate the campaign. In contrast, a cap on campaign expenditure may be an attempt to create a 'level playing field' for all parties and not favour the established parties. A cap on campaign expenditure may indicate the engagement of established parties in low levels of institutional strategies, not restricting opportunities for non-established parties.

Table 3.1 shows the criteria developed in order to determine if a system is restrictive, permissive or neutral, with a score of 1, 2 or 3 awarded for each factor, signifying a permissive (1), neutral (2) or restrictive (3) system for non-established parties for each aspect. Table 3.2 presents the results of the study, using the criteria developed in Table 3.1. The current system in place is the system that determines whether the area is restrictive, permissive or neutral for non-established parties, with changes over time also highlighted.

Table 3.2 shows that the countries in which the most restrictive systems of electoral laws are to be found are Austria and Denmark, whereas the least restrictive systems are to be found in Ireland, Spain and Belgium. In Austria and Denmark, the restrictive system of electoral laws in place should penalise non-established parties and assist the established parties to maintain their dominant positions within their national party systems. Established parties have engaged in high levels of institutional strategies by creating systems that are unfavourable towards non-established parties, with the Austrian example in particular indicating modifications to the system in favour of the established parties. The signature requirements increased from 200, to between 200 and 500 per district in 1970 and access to campaign subsidies, introduced in 1989, is reliant on parliamentary representation (Carter 2005: 164, 178), introducing an effective threshold for eligibility of 4 per cent. Established parties in Austria and Denmark should achieve high levels of dominance within their national party systems, as the strategies engaged in should restrict opportunities for non-established parties to achieve access to the ballot.

Table 3.1 Coding categories for electoral laws

Aspect considered	(1) Permissive	(2) Neutral	(3) Restrictive
Deposit requirements	No deposit required (or nomination by party)	Deposit of under £300 required	Deposit of more than £300 required, or deposit is non-refundable
Signature requirements	Under 200 signatures required (or nomination by party)	200–500 signatures required	More than 500 signatures required
Independent candidates	Independent candidates allowed	Independent candidates allowed but with signature/deposit requirement	Independent candidates not allowed
Campaign subsidies	Campaign subsidies awarded to parties with a maximum threshold of 2%	Campaign subsidies awarded to parties with a threshold of between 2% and 4%	Campaign subsidies awarded with a threshold of 4% or more in place
Expenditure limits	Campaign expenditure limit in place	Category not applicable	No campaign expenditure limit in place

Table 3.2 Electoral laws and non-established parties in western Europe, 1950–2009[a]

	Registration requirements for parties[b]		Independent candidates?	Campaign subsidies criteria	Limit on campaign expenditure?	Overall
	Deposit	Signatures				
Austria	(3) Since 1971, ATS6000 ($430, £290)[c] paid by each party in each constituency (non-refundable)	(2) Until 1970, 200 petitions. Now, 200–500 depending on district size or support of 3 outgoing MPs. Parties must formally register with the Ministry of the Interior	(3) No independent candidates	(3) Since 1989, €1.94 per vote received ($2.46, £1.34). Parliamentary representation needed (effective threshold of 4%)[d]	(3) No expenditure limits, although the larger parties sometimes agree informal limits	(2.8) Restrictive system
Denmark	(1) No deposit required	(3) Need a number of signatures equal to 1/175 of the previous votes cast (approximately 20,000)	(2) Independent candidates need 150–200 petitions from their district	No campaign subsidies[e]	(3) No expenditure limit	(2.25) Restrictive system
Italy	(1) No deposit required	(3) Candidates require support of at least 500 electors (previously 300) or backing by 1,500–4,000 signatures for party lists	(3) No independent candidates	Since 1999, no campaign subsidies. Previously, parties that contested seats in at least 2/3 of constituencies and won either at least 1 quotient and at least 300,000 votes, or at least 2% of the vote were eligible 20% of funds distributed in equal shares to all parties that contested seats in 2/3 of constituencies, the other 80% distributed in proportion to vote share	(1) Expenditure limits for candidates	(2) Restrictive system

	Deposit	Registration/signatures	Independent candidates	Campaign subsidies	Expenditure limits	System
The Netherlands	(3) Dfl25,000 ($10,400, £6,800) (previously Dfl1,000 ($1,600, £1,050) for one sub-district) required to present a list in one or more sub-districts, reimbursed if the party wins 3/4 of the electoral quotient (approximately 0.5%)	(1) Since 1989, 30 signatures required to present a list (previously 25)	(1) Independent candidates allowed	No campaign subsidies	(3) No expenditure limits	(2) Restrictive system
Sweden	(1) No deposit required	(1) No registration requirements		No campaign subsidies	(3) No expenditure limits	(2) Restrictive system
Norway	(1) No deposit required	A list of candidates can be submitted by a registered party, or (1) List of candidates can be approved by 500 registered voters. 5,000 signatures required to register a party (previously 3,000)	(3) No independent candidates	No campaign subsidies	(3) No expenditure limits	(2) Restrictive system
France	(3) 1,000 FF ($200 in 1965, worth $1,100, £700 today) per candidate, returned if the candidate receives 5%+ of the vote	(1) Candidates must draw up a signed declaration giving their personal details and those of their substitutes. These are lodged with the prefect	(1) Independent candidates allowed	(3) Since 1988, candidates winning more than 5% of the vote are reimbursed FF50,000 ($9,200, £5,100 today)	(1) Since 1993, FF250,000 ($48,478, £25,500) per candidate plus FF1 ($0.19, £0.10) per inhabitant (previously FF500,000 ($96,957, £51,000) per candidate)	(1.8) Neutral system

continued overleaf

Table 3.2 continued

	Registration requirements for parties[b]		Independent candidates?	Campaign subsidies criteria	Limit on campaign expenditure?	Overall
	Deposit	Signatures				
Luxembourg	(1) No deposit required	(1) Since 2003, lists are formally accepted on the ballot when supported by 100 registered voters in their respective district (previously 25)	(3) No independent candidates	(3) Political parties that receive more than 5% of the vote in national elections benefit from some reimbursement for expenditures in relation to electoral campaigns	(1) Expenditure limits apply	(1.8) Neutral system
Germany	(1) No deposit required	(2) 200 signatures in each single-member constituency and 0.1% of eligible voters within the state to submit a candidate list at state level (up to a maximum of 2,000 voters)	(1) Independent candidates allowed in single-member constituencies	From 1989 until 1993, parties winning 2%+ of the vote were eligible for a modest reimbursement. Declared unconstitutional in 1994	(3) No expenditure limits	(1.75) Neutral system
Switzerland	(1) No deposit required	(2) Since 1994, between 100 and 400 signatures required depending on size of canton. Previously 50 signatures in cantons with two or more seats	(1) Independent candidates allowed	No campaign subsidies	(3) No expenditure limits	(1.75) Neutral system

	Nomination / Deposit	Registration requirements	Independent candidates	Campaign subsidies	Expenditure limits	Media system
Portugal	Candidate are nominated by political parties and (1) No deposit required	(1) Signatures of 5,000 electors required to register a party	(3) No independent candidates	(2) Since 1993, parties awarded campaign reimbursement, of which 80% is distributed proportionally according to electoral result, if a party obtains 2%+ of the vote (and fields candidates in 51%+ of seats). Parties receive 2,500 times the national monthly salary	(1) Expenditure limits for parties (€3 million, $3.8 million, £2.0 million) and candidates	(1.6) Neutral system
Greece	(3) Deposit of $180, £120 per candidate to be paid. Non-refundable. Previously, until 1990, Dr.8,000 (worth $70, £40 today)	(1) 12 signatures required, but must formally register with the Supreme Court	(1) Independent candidates allowed	(2) Since 1984, parties receive funding in proportion to their share of the vote if they receive 3% of the vote (5–6% in coalition) and presented a list in 2/3 of electoral districts	(1) Expenditure limits for candidates	(1.6) Neutral system
Finland	Candidates may be nominated by a registered political party or (1) No deposit required	(1) Candidates require the backing of an electoral association in their constituency (100 voters). Since 1969, parties need 5,000 adherents eligible to vote to become a registered party	(1) Independent candidates allowed	No campaign subsidies	(3) No expenditure limits	(1.5) Neutral system

continued overleaf

Table 3.2 continued

	Registration requirements for parties[b]		Independent candidates?	Campaign subsidies criteria	Limit on campaign expenditure?	Overall
	Deposit	Signatures				
United Kingdom	(3) Since 1985, £500 deposit per candidate ($735). Refunded with 5%+ of the vote. Previously, deposit of £150 per candidate (worth $2,930, £2,000, today), refunded with 12.5%+ of the vote	(1) 10 signatures required	(1) Independent candidates allowed	(1) No campaign subsidies	(1) Expenditure limits for candidates: £30,000 ($57,034) per contested constituency	(1.4) Permissive system
Belgium	(1) No deposit required	(2) 200–500 voters per district, or, since 1976, 3 outgoing MPs' support	(1) Independent candidates allowed	No campaign subsidies	(1) Expenditure limits for individual candidates and parties (€1 million per election cycle, $1.3 million, £669,071)	(1.25) Permissive system
Spain	Candidates are nominated by registered political associations, federations and coalitions, or (1) No deposit required	(1) Candidates must receive the support of at least 0.1% (and no fewer than 500) of the constituency's electorate	(1) Independent candidates allowed	(2) Since the late 1970s, parties receive 101 pesetas ($0.74, £0.40 today) for each vote won in a district where the party wins a seat (effective threshold of 3%). Parties also receive 2,692,000 pesetas ($20,400, £11,200) for each seat obtained in the two houses	(1) Expenditure limits for candidates (established for each electoral cycle by the General Accounting Court)	(1.2) Permissive system

	Candidates may nominate themselves or are nominated by a registered elector of the constituency, or	(1) Independent candidates allowed	(2) Campaign subsidies	(1) Expenditure limits for individual candidates	(1.2) Permissive system
Ireland		(1) No signature requirements	Campaign subsidies introduced in late 1990s. Parties must win 2%+ of the vote to be eligible. Partial reimbursement of election expenses up to a maximum of £5000 for every candidate who contested the election without losing his or her deposit		
	(1) Deposit of IR£300 ($350, £240), refundable if candidate receives more than a quarter of the quota			(IR£14,000 ($22,717, £12,044) in a three-seat constituency, IR£17,000 ($27,586, £14,625 in a four-seat constituency, £IR20,000 ($32,463, £17,208 in a five seat constituency)	

Sources: Administration and Cost of Elections (2010); Austin and Tjernström (2003); Bowler and Farrell (1992); Bowler *et al.* (2003); Carter (2005); Casas-Zamora (2005); Centre for European Constitutional Law – Themistokles and Dimitris Tsatsos Foundation (2010); Clift and Fisher (2004); Inter-Parliamentary Union Parline Database (2010); Laver and Marsh (1999); Müller and Sieberer (2006); Norris (2005); Papathanassopolous (2000); Plasser and Plasser (2002); Van Biezen (2004)

Notes

a Each aspect for each country is examined in turn and a score is given according to whether the aspect is permissive, restrictive or neutral for non-established parties. These figures are shown in brackets at the start of the data for each aspect for each country. Scores are added together and an average taken, with all aspects carrying equal weight. The countries are then ranked according to their average scores, reflecting the overall nature of the electoral laws regime, with a low score reflecting a permissive system, and a high score indicating a restrictive system. The classification for the final column is as follows: if a country's average score is between 1 and 1.4, the regime is classified as permissive. A score of between 1.5 and 1.9 indicates a system of electoral laws that is neutral and a score of between 2 and 3 indicates a restrictive system of electoral laws.

b In many of the countries presented in Table 3.2, parties already represented in parliament are exempt from having to pay deposits and obtain signatures.

c All monetary data is converted to US$ and GB£ to assist with comparability.

d Parliamentary representation is required to be eligible for campaign subsidies in Austria so the 4% legal threshold for entry into parliament is the effective threshold for access to campaign subsidies.

e Where a country does not have a system of campaign subsidies in place, this area for this country does not receive a score.

Conversely, in Ireland, Spain and Belgium, the system of electoral laws should not restrict opportunities for non-established parties and, instead, should create relatively equal ballot access for all parties. A permissive system of electoral laws for non-established parties should not penalise these parties to the same extent as those laws found in Austria and Denmark. Established parties in Ireland, Spain and Belgium have engaged in low levels of institutional strategies and have created systems that favour their own interests less than in Austria and Denmark. In Ireland, Spain and Belgium, established parties should achieve low levels of centrality within their national party systems, as the strategies engaged in do not restrict ballot access for non-established parties.

Established parties in Austria and Denmark are engaging in 'cartel' strategies, as these strategies should 'help to ensure the maintenance of existing parties while at the same time posing barriers to the emergence of new groups' (Katz and Mair 1995: 15). Conversely, established parties in Ireland, Spain and Belgium have not engaged in cartel strategies, hence levels of established party dominance should differ. In Austria and Denmark, a cartel party system might emerge, where several parties achieve high levels of centrality, particularly in the governmental arena. However, the high levels of engagement in cartel strategies may produce an electoral backlash, as the 'success of the cartel inevitably generates its own opposition' (Katz and Mair 1995: 24). A perverse hypothesis would suggest that the established parties in Ireland, Spain and Belgium might achieve high levels of centrality, particularly in the electoral arena, precisely due to their lack of engagement in cartel strategies. By adopting permissive systems of electoral laws, established parties are not seeking to restrict opportunities for non-established parties and the electorate may respond favourably to the established parties because of the open and 'non-cartel' nature of competition. Chapter 6 studies the impact of institutional strategies on the fate of established parties and will assess these competing hypotheses in greater depth.

3.2 Electoral systems

An electoral system, part of the regime of electoral laws, is a set of rules that structures how votes are cast at elections for a representative assembly and how these votes are then converted into seats in that assembly (Gallagher and Mitchell 2005a: 3). Of interest for the purposes of this dimension is the process by which votes are converted into seats and how permissive or restrictive the electoral system is for non-established parties. Maurice Duverger (1954) was one of the first political scientists to emphasise the importance of the impact of electoral systems on party systems, stating that 'the simple-majority single-ballot system favours the two-party system' (1954: 217), whereas proportional representation 'put(s) to an end any tendency towards a two-party system' (1954: 248). The type of electoral system can strongly influence the shape of the party system and competitive relations found within party systems. Established parties may put a restrictive electoral system in place in order to restrict opportunities for non-established parties, in line with the cartel thesis.[5] A permissive electoral system, which does not favour the established parties to the same extent as a restrictive electoral system, can be seen as an indication of the engagement by established parties in low levels of institutional strategies. In order to describe western European electoral systems, note any changes made and assess the restrictive or permissive nature of electoral systems for non-established parties, the key features of an electoral system need to be highlighted.

Electoral formula

Deriving from Duverger's (1954) work, the first important feature of an electoral system is the electoral formula employed. Whether an electoral system contains a majoritarian or proportional formula influences the shape of the party system and the role non-established and established parties can play within the system. A majoritarian formula should favour the established parties, whereas a proportional formula should favour the non-established parties, precisely because of the closer relationship between votes cast and seats received achieved under a proportional formula.

Ballot structure

In addition to the formula adopted, Rae (1967: 17–20) highlights ballot structure as an additional area that can influence the proportionality of a particular electoral system and influence party competition. Whether a ballot structure is ordinal (allowing voters to express preferences for multiple candidates or parties) or categorical (allowing voters to choose only one party or candidate) can influence party systems, as the categorical ballot structure favours the status quo and the established parties, whereas ordinal structures favour the dispersion of power amongst multiple parties (Rae 1967: 17–18).

District magnitude

A third important area is district magnitude, referring to the number of representatives elected in a given district, with distinctions made between multi-member and single-member districts, as 'the larger the number of seats in the constituency, the more exact is the proportionality that can be achieved' (MacKenzie 1958: 61). Rae supplements this view arguing that small district magnitudes will tend to concentrate seats in the already strong parties and large district magnitudes will leave the seats relatively dispersed among the smaller parties (1967: 21).

Where systems have one tier of representation, district magnitude is simple to calculate: the size of the assembly is divided by the number of districts to produce the average district magnitude. However, with multi-tier systems, calculating the average district magnitude becomes more complex and it is important to establish the tier that is the most important for determining the overall proportionality of the system. Carter (2005: 152) has summarised the problems associated with district magnitude measurement and, based on the work of Lijphart (1994), has established which is the most important tier for determining overall proportionality within multi-tier systems. The data of Carter (2005) helps to establish the average district magnitude of the countries under consideration.[6]

Number of tiers

The number of tiers of districting in operation also influences the restrictive or permissive nature of the system, as each tier has a different district magnitude. The addition of an extra tier of districting generally reduces the distortions resulting from the allocation of seats in the first tier and so should favour the smaller parties as the introduction of an extra tier should make the overall elect-oral result more proportional (Blais and Massicotte 2002: 49).

Legal thresholds

The presence of a legal threshold mitigates the potentially favourable impact of multi-level districting and large district magnitudes for small parties. Many western European electoral systems have legal thresholds in place that require parties or independent candidates to achieve a certain percentage of the vote (or win a certain number of seats), nationally or regionally, in order to obtain a pro-portional share of the seats. A threshold is an important barrier in the electoral system, with the effect of penalising smaller, generally non-established parties and keeping them out of the system. Electoral systems that have a threshold in place should benefit the established parties, especially if the threshold is set at a high level. A:

> threshold flatly states that political parties that fail to secure a given percent-age of the vote, either in districts or nationally, are deprived of parliament-ary representation or at least of some of the seats they would otherwise be entitled to.
>
> (Blais and Massicotte 2002: 51)

Where countries do not have legal thresholds in place, an 'effective' threshold gives an indication of the share of the vote needed by a party in order to enter parliament. The concept of the effective threshold originates in the work of Lijphart (1994: 26–30) and is based upon the district magnitude of a given elect-oral system.

Assessing disproportionality data can determine how restrictive or permissive an electoral system is for non-established parties, and can empirically compare electoral systems by capturing the differences between the votes cast for a party and the number of seats received. The most widely used and commonly accepted measure for calculating the disproportionality of electoral systems is Michael Gallagher's least squares method (1991). One of the main advantages of this method is that it takes into account the total amount of vote-seat disparity and the way that this difference came about, regarding one large disparity as more significant than several small differences (Gallagher and Mitchell 2005c: 602). The measure provides a snapshot of the proportionality of a particular electoral system at a certain election and does not provide continuous data, but can produce average figures relating to disproportionality. The formula for calculating the measure is as follows:

$$LS_q = \sqrt{\tfrac{1}{2}\Sigma(V-S)^2}$$

Where V is the share of votes obtained by a party and S is the share of seats obtained by a party.[7]

Table 3.3 shows average disproportionality values for all electoral systems since 1950 in all 17 countries based on all elections that have taken place under a particular electoral system, taking into account changes in electoral systems. These values provide an indication of the disproportionality of each electoral system, and whether the system is permissive or restrictive for non-established parties. If the disproportionality of an electoral system has increased, non-established parties should be restricted in their potential to access parliament. However, if the disproportionality figure has fallen, these parties could benefit from the change.

Table 3.3 shows that the most restrictive electoral systems for non-established parties occur in France, the United Kingdom and Greece, whereas the least restrictive are found in the Netherlands, Denmark and Sweden. In France, the United Kingdom and Greece, established parties have engaged in high levels of institutional strategies in an attempt to restrict opportunities for challenges to their established status. It is also interesting to note that Greece and France have experienced frequent changes in their electoral system, with the French system undergoing five changes since 1958 and the Greek system changing on four occasions since 1975. These frequent changes reinforce the argument that French and Greek established parties have engaged in high levels of institutional strategies, as not only is the present system restrictive for non-established parties, the electoral system is regarded as a 'political football' by the established parties, with proportional representation in Greece regarded as 'a useful tool for ... short-term tactics' (Dimitras 1994: 155).

In contrast, the most permissive electoral systems for non-established parties occur in the Netherlands, Denmark and Sweden, where established parties have engaged in low levels of institutional strategies and do not use the electoral system as a tool through which access to parliament for non-established parties can be restricted. The Danish and Swedish electoral systems have changed, yet in Sweden, these changes significantly reduced disproportionality within the electoral system and the changes made in Denmark did not have a significant impact on levels of proportionality. In the Netherlands, Denmark and Sweden, established parties have created permissive electoral systems for non-established parties suggesting low levels of engagement in institutional strategies.

Table 3.3 Electoral systems and non-established parties in western Europe, 1950–2009

	Electoral system[a]	Changes to the electoral system[b]	Average disproportionality of elections held under each electoral system	Overall[c]
France				
Formula[d]	Majority-plurality	*1958: introduction of two-ballot majority-plurality system replacing a system that varied between Paris and the rest of the country. Vote share equating to 5% of the electorate required to progress to next round	1956–58: 3.75 (n=1)	Restrictive system
Ballot structure	Non-preferential		*1958–66: 17.91 (n=2)	
Average district magnitude[e]	1		*1967–76: 14.89 (n=3)	
		*1967: threshold to progress to next round increased to 10% of the electorate	*1978–85: 10.88 (n=2)	
Number of tiers	1		*1986: 6.71 (n=1)	
Legal threshold (%)[f]	(37.5)	*1978: threshold to progress to next round increased to 12.5% of the electorate	*1988–present: 18.92 (n=5)	
		*1986: introduction of a department-based list proportional representation system, replacing the two-ballot system		
		*1988: re-introduction of two-ballot majority-plurality system		
United Kingdom				
Formula	Plurality	No major changes	1950–present: 11.87 (n=16)	Restrictive system
Ballot structure	Non-preferential			
Average district magnitude	1			
Number of tiers	1			
Legal threshold (%)	(37.5)			

Greece			Restrictive system
Formula	Proportional (highest-average d'Hondt)[g]	*1977: change in formula to Hagenbach-Bischoff from Hare. Change in distribution of seats between tiers biased in favour of first round seats	*1975–77: 15.76 (n=1) *1977–85: 10.95 (n=2) *1985–89: 7.12 (n=1) *1989–90: 4.07 (n=3)
Ballot structure	Preferential	*1985: barriers for inclusion in post-first round seat allocations (17% threshold) abandoned. Change in formula to d'Hondt	*1993–present: 7.82 (n=6)
Average district magnitude	12	*1989: abolition of the third tier and introduction of proportional representation system instead of reinforced proportional representation. Change to the Droop quota for the decisive tier	
Number of tiers	4	*1993: reversion to reinforced proportional representation with a 3% legal threshold and a 4 tier system, using d'Hondt for most tiers	
Legal threshold (%)	3		
Spain			Restrictive system
Formula	Proportional (highest-average d'Hondt)	No major changes	1977–present: 7.18 (n=10)
Ballot structure	Non-preferential		
Average district magnitude	6.73		
Number of tiers	1		
Legal threshold (%)	3		
Belgium			Neutral system
Formula	Proportional (highest-average d'Hondt)	*1995: reduction in number of constituencies from 30 to 20	1950–95: 3.00 (n=14) *1995–2003: 2.80 (n=2) *2003–present: 5.70 (n=2)
Ballot structure	Preferential	*2003: simplified the allocation of seats by applying the d'Hondt system in every constituency and enlargement of these constituencies. Abolition of the second tier of allocation. Introduction of 5% threshold	
Average district magnitude	13.64		
Number of tiers	1		
Legal threshold (%)	5		

continued overleaf

Table 3.3 continued

	Electoral system[a]	Changes to the electoral system[b]	Average disproportionality of elections held under each electoral system	Overall[c]
Portugal				
Formula	Proportional (highest-average d'Hondt)	No major changes. The number of MPs was reduced from 250 to 230 for the 1991 election, resulting in a minor reduction in the average district magnitude (from 12.5 to 11.5)	*1975–present: 5.64 (n=13)	Neutral system
Ballot structure	Non-preferential			
Average district magnitude	11.5			
Number of tiers	1			
Legal threshold (%)	(6.0)			
Luxembourg				
Formula	Proportional (Hagenbach-Bischoff)	No major changes	*1950–present: 4.85 (n=13)	Neutral system
Ballot structure	Preferential			
Average district magnitude	15			
Number of tiers	1			
Legal threshold (%)	(14)			
Italy				
Formula	Proportional (largest-remainder)	*1958: change in the formula for lower tier votes to Imperiali *1979: change in the formula for lower tier votes to Hare *1994: adoption of mixed member proportional system where 75% of candidates are elected by the plurality rule in single member districts and 25% from higher tier party lists *2006: change of system to list proportional representation, with a 4% legal threshold and a single tier of districting	1950–58: 3.65 (n=1) *1958–79: 2.70 (n=5) *1979–94: 2.46 (n=4) *1994–2005: 7.35 (n=3) *2006–present: 4.16 (n=2)	Neutral system
Ballot structure	Non-preferential			
Average district magnitude	24.23			
Number of tiers	1			
Legal threshold (%)	4			

Ireland

Formula	Proportional (Single Transferable Vote)	No changes made to the electoral system, despite two referendums regarding a change taking place in 1959 and 1968	1950–present: 3.95 (n=17)	Neutral system
Ballot structure	Preferential	
Average district magnitude	4.05	
Number of tiers	1	
Legal threshold (%)	(14.9)	

Norway

Formula	Proportional (highest-average Modified Sainte Laguë)	*1989: adoption of two tiers of districting and introduction of formal 4% legal threshold	1953–89: 4.48 (n=9) *1989–present: 3.38 (n=6)	Neutral system
Ballot structure	Non-preferential	
Average district magnitude	165	
Number of tiers	2	
Legal threshold (%)	4	

Finland

Formula	Proportional (highest-average d'Hondt)	No major electoral reforms. Minor reforms include alphabetically-ordered candidates on party lists instead of a party-chosen order in 1955 and changes concerning the number of constituencies in 1952 and 1962	1950–present: 3.03 (n=16)	Neutral system
Ballot structure	Preferential	
Average district magnitude	13.33	
Number of tiers	1	
Legal threshold (%)	(5.2)	

continued overleaf

Table 3.3 continued

	Electoral system[a]	Changes to the electoral system[b]	Average disproportionality of elections held under each electoral system	Overall[c]
Germany				
Formula	Mixed Member Proportional (corrective) (largest-remainder Hare)	*1953: equalisation of candidates elected from single member districts and party lists (instead of 60:40), each voter given two votes instead of one, threshold changed: 5% of the national vote or one direct district mandate required to qualify for list seats instead of 5% requirement in any Land	1949–53: 4.09 (n=1)	Neutral system
			*1953–56: 4.06 (n=1)	
			*1957–87: 2.29 (n=8)	
Ballot structure	Non-preferential		*1987–90: 0.74 (n=1)	
Average district magnitude	598	*1957: threshold changed to 5% of the national vote or three direct district mandates	*1990–94: 4.83 (n=1)	
			*1994–98: 2.66 (n=2)	
Number of tiers	2	*1987: change in formula from d'Hondt to Hare	*2002–present: 2.92 (n=3)	
Legal threshold (%)	5	*1990: change for the first all-German elections to 5% requirement in either the former West or East Germany.		
		*1994: reversion to 5% of the national vote or three direct district mandates as a threshold		
		*2002: number of constituencies reduced from 328 to 299		
Switzerland				
Formula	Proportional (Hagenbach-Bischoff)	No major changes in the period covered. The extension of suffrage to women in 1971 increased the numbers of voters, but did not alter the system per se	1950–present: 2.88 (n=15)	Neutral system
Ballot structure	Preferential			
Average district magnitude	7.69			
Number of tiers	1			
Legal threshold (%)	(8.6)			

Austria

Formula	Proportional (largest-remainder Hare)	*1971: increase in the size of electoral districts from relatively small to large (sometimes encompassing 1.1 million voters). Change in allocation of remainders from four districts to two regional super-districts *1994: increased the number of electoral districts from 9 to 43 (adding a third tier of representation). Introduction of the 4% legal threshold	1950–70: 3.74 (n=6) *1971–92: 1.88 (n=6) *1994–present: 1.88 (n=6)	Permissive system
Ballot structure	Preferential		
Average district magnitude	4.26		
Number of tiers	3		
Legal threshold (%)	4		

Sweden

Formula	Proportional (highest-average Modified Sainte Laguë)	*1952: change in electoral formula from d'Hondt to Modified Sainte Laguë *1970: introduction of two tier system with a 4% legal threshold	1948–52: 3.48 (n=1) *1952–70: 2.33 (n=7) *1970–present: 1.77 (n=12)	Permissive system
Ballot structure	Preferential		
Average district magnitude	349		
Number of tiers	2		
Legal threshold (%)	4		

continued overleaf

Table 3.3 continued

	Electoral system[a]	Changes to the electoral system[b]	Average disproportionality of elections held under each electoral system	Overall[c]
Denmark				
Formula	Proportional (largest-remainder Hare)	*1953: reduction in the percentage of compensatory seats awarded, change in the formula for the allocation of lower tier seats from d'Hondt to Modified Sainte Laguëw *1964: 2% formal legal threshold introduced *1971: number of multi-member constituencies reduced from 23 to 17	1950–53: 0.28 (n=1) *1953–61: 1.08 (n=4) *1964–70: 1.56 (n=3) *1971–present: 1.55 (n=15)	Permissive system
Ballot structure	Preferential			
Average district magnitude	179			
Number of tiers	2			
Legal threshold (%)	2			
The Netherlands				
Formula	Proportional (highest-average d'Hondt)	No significant changes but an enlargement of parliament from 100 to 150 seats means a reduction in the effective threshold from 1% to 0.67%	1950–present: 1.26 (n=17)	Permissive system
Ballot structure	Preferential			
Average district magnitude	150			
Number of tiers	1			
Legal threshold (%)	(0.67)			

Sources: Administration and Cost of Elections (2010), Baum and Freire (2002), Blais and Massicotte (2002), Bowler *et al.* (2003), Carter (2005), Dimitras (1994), Gallagher and Mitchell (2005b), Inter-Parliamentary Union Parline Database (2010), Katz (2003), Leonard (1983), Lijphart (1994), Mackie and Rose (1991), Scarrow (2006), Shugart (1992), Taagepera (1984)

Notes

a Figures in brackets denote effective threshold values where no legal threshold is present.

b Years denote the first election held under the reformed electoral system.

c The permissive or restrictive nature of the system is based on the average disproportionality figures for elections held under the present electoral system. Where the average value of disproportionality is under 2, the system is classified as permissive for non-established parties. Where the value is between 2 and 7, the system is neutral and where the value is over 7, the system is noted as restrictive for non-established parties.

d The formula relates to the formula used for the decisive tier of districting for the purposes of the overall proportionality of the electoral system in a multi-tier system.

e The average district magnitude figure relates to the average district magnitude for the decisive tier of districting for the purposes of the overall proportionality of the electoral system.

f The data for the effective thresholds is taken from Carter (2005) and Scarrow (2006) and is a useful tool for determining to what extent electoral systems are permissive or restrictive for small parties.

g Proportional formulae can be sub-divided into highest-average formulae (such as D'Hondt, Sainte-Laguë and Modified Sainte-Laguë) and largest-remainder formulae (that rely on quotas such as the Droop, Hare and Imperiali). A combination of a highest-average formula with a quota is the Hagenbach–Bishoff formula (Carter 2005: 157–8).

Established parties in France, Greece and the United Kingdom should achieve high levels of centrality within their party systems, as opportunities for non-established parties to enter parliament are restricted by the electoral system. However, it will be interesting to examine in Chapter 6, which provides an ana-lysis of the impact of the high and low engagement in institutional strategies, whether established parties achieve high levels of centrality in the parliamentary, electoral and governmental arenas (Luther 1989). Parliamentary and govern-mental centrality should be high, but perhaps electoral centrality may be lower, as the parliamentary arena data may hide some more interesting trends in the electoral arena. Established parties in the Netherlands, Denmark and Sweden should achieve low levels of centrality within their national party systems, as non-established parties are not penalised by a highly disproportional electoral system. Levels of centrality may be low in all three arenas, as the party system is likely to contain a large number of parties, as parliamentary access is not restricted. It may be more problematic for established parties to continue to achieve high levels of centrality in a system that should contain many more par-ties than within a more limited party system format, as expected in Greece, the United Kingdom and France due to the threshold in place for parliamentary access.

3.3 Television campaigning airtime

Political television advertising can be defined as encompassing all moving image programming that is designed to promote the interests of a given party or candi-date (Kaid and Holtz-Bacha 1995: 2). This includes all television advertising, whether given or bought by political parties or candidates. This dimension inves-tigates to what extent the system regulating access to television campaigning airtime is restrictive for non-established parties. Although other media outlets such as radio campaigning, written press advertising or any form of internet communication are also important avenues through which parties can com-municate with voters, television advertising is the principal political communica-tion medium. Television penetration in western Europe (based on the number of households with at least one television) is close to 100 per cent (Plasser and Plasser 2002: 182), so parties that wish to compete successfully in elections must make use of this vital media tool.

Literature concerning the prominence of television advertising as a political tool began to emerge at the end of the 1950s, as a study carried out during the 1959 British general election found that television played a major role and that it had replaced radio 'as an instrument of political communication' (Mughan and Gunther 2000: 21). Lynda Lee Kaid and Christina Holtz-Bacha (1995) argue that television spots have been a dominant part of American elections for several decades, but it has only been in recent decades that 'American style' television advertising has gained significance in the political processes of western European democracies. The 'American style' of election campaigning comprises the prevail-ing role of television among the different campaign channels, the predominance of

images instead of issues, a personalisation of the political process and a profes-
sionalisation of political actors in the development of their media strategies (Kaid
and Holtz-Bacha 1995: 9). Western European campaigns have become more similar to those found in the United States, but some differences remain, such as the
impact of media privatisation.

The increasing importance of television as an advertising tool for political
parties is clear, but the impact of television advertising on voters is less obvious.
Indeed, by addressing television advertising as an important dimension, the
assumption is that television advertising influences voters and that the more television coverage a party receives, the higher the share of the vote the party can
expect to receive. There has been only inconsistent evidence presented in the
literature to support this assumption. Anthony Mughan and Richard Gunther
(2000: 16) summarise the literature concerning micro-level media effects and
highlight the contradictory evidence found. Early studies concerning the impact
of the broadcast media on political attitudes and behaviours (for example,
Klapper 1960) found only minimal or negligible effects. However, recent studies
have highlighted the role that television can play in persuasion and learning. Television advertising encourages voters to be more aware and informed and to
reconsider 'their preferences for a candidate, policy, or some other object or idea
in response to a particular message' (Ansolabehere *et al.* 1993: 146). Television
advertising can have an impact on the electorate and shape the way that voters
perceive issues and candidates, although the role that television plays is often to
reinforce previously held beliefs rather than encouraging voters to form new
opinions. The restrictive or permissive nature of television advertising systems
for non-established parties focuses on the following four areas, derived from the
literature on media and campaigning.

Paid television spots

The difference between the American private media system and the western
European model of public television services highlights the first important issue:
whether parties can buy airtime. The potential for parties to purchase airtime is
generally an advantage for the established parties, as non-established parties
generally have less financial resources available to them, although Forza Italia
emerges here again as an exception due to Berlusconi's influence within the
Italian media sector. Kaid and Holtz-Bacha (1995: 4) have argued that 'the
expansion of private media systems has generally led the way for an opening up
of potential distribution of party/candidate messages to voters', thus where parties are allowed to buy private media airtime, the system should be favourable
for established parties.

Free airtime[8]

The second important area also relates to the western European model of the
dominance of the public broadcasting sector. Whether parties are allocated free

television airtime has an impact on the overall potential for non-established parties to challenge the established parties. Parties may receive some free airtime to convey their political message, and where parties receive free airtime, non-established parties should benefit and be in a stronger position to compete with the established parties. However, many other issues can influence free television airtime; the method of allocation of this free airtime can severely restrict opportunities for non-established parties.

Criteria for eligibility

Criteria for eligibility to free airtime is generally based on parliamentary representation or presenting candidates in a certain number of constituencies. A high threshold for eligibility should make it more difficult for non-established parties to compete in the election. However, although winning a seat in parliament or presenting a certain number of candidates may allow a party to access free political television advertising airtime, the method of allocation can severely restrict the distribution of free airtime.

Method of allocation

Political parties receive free airtime according to the principles of equality or proportionality. Where political parties receive free airtime equally, all parties that have crossed the threshold of eligibility for free airtime receive the same amount of airtime. Where a principle of proportionality is in place, each party receives airtime in proportion to either their seat or vote share at the previous election. Equal free airtime is clearly favourable for non-established parties, as these parties receive a chance to compete with the established parties on a relatively level playing field, as all parties regardless of size receive the same amount of free airtime.

Table 3.4 presents the coding categories for political television advertising, and Table 3.5 presents the results of the data collection. Table 3.5 shows the most restrictive television advertising regimes are in Austria, Greece and Germany, whereas the least restrictive are in Italy, Denmark and Norway. Established parties in Austria, Greece and Germany have engaged in high levels of institutional strategies and have created systems whereby non-established parties have restricted access to television campaigning. The behaviours of the established parties in Austria, Greece and Germany are in line with the cartel thesis, as: 'the rules regarding the electronic media … offer a means by which those in power can acquire privileged access, whereas those on the margins may be neglected' (Katz and Mair 1995: 15). Established parties in Austria, Greece and Germany should achieve high levels of centrality within their national party systems, as the political television advertising regime in place in the three countries strongly favours the established parties and restricts opportunities for non-established parties.

Conversely, established parties in Italy, Denmark and Norway have engaged in low levels of institutional strategies and have created systems of television

Table 3.4 Coding categories for political television advertising

Aspect considered	(1) Permissive	(2) Neutral	(3) Restrictive
Paid political television spots allowed	Paid political television spots not allowed	Not applicable	Paid political television spots allowed on private television channels
Availability of free airtime	Free airtime available for parties	Not applicable	Free airtime not available for parties
Criteria for eligibility to free airtime	No criteria for eligibility to free airtime	Non-parliamentary parties have access to only a minimal amount of free airtime, or parties must present candidates in a certain number of districts or must have received a certain percentage of the vote at previous elections	Parties must already be represented in parliament. No free airtime to parties not represented in parliament
Method of allocation of free airtime	Equal allocation for all parties	Proportional allocation of airtime based on vote share at previous election	Proportional allocation of airtime based on seat share at previous election

Table 3.5 Television advertising regimes and non-established parties in western Europe, 1950–2009

	Paid political television spots	Free airtime available	Criteria for eligibility for free airtime	Method of allocation of free airtime	Overall
Austria	(3) Yes, on private television channels. The government can buy airtime to inform the public about policy issues	(1) Yes, but mainly leader debates	(3) Parties must hold seats in parliament to be eligible	(3) Proportional to party strength in parliament	(10) Restrictive system
Greece	(3) Yes. Greek parties have unlimited access to private spots	(1) Yes	(2) Eligibility based on parliamentary representation, although parties with no representation in parliament but with a list of candidates in 75% of electoral districts are entitled to 5 minutes of free airtime per week	(3) Proportional to seats obtained at previous election	(9) Restrictive system
Germany	(3) Yes, but only on private television stations (since the early 1980s)	(1) Yes	(2) New and previously unsuccessful parties allocated a minimum amount of airtime	(2) Proportional to parties' percentage of the vote at the previous election	(8) Restrictive system
Spain	(3) Yes, although total expenditures on paid television advertising must not exceed 25% of the parties' overall expenditure on political advertising	(1) Yes	(1) No criteria for eligibility. Since 1985, all parties receive free airtime	(2) Proportional to parties' vote share in previous elections. Parties fielding candidates in 75%+ of electoral districts receive additional broadcasting time	(7) Neutral system
The Netherlands	(3) Yes. Since 1994, a minor amount of advertising takes place on private channels	(1) Yes	(2) If parties present candidates in all 19 electoral sub-districts (since 1982). Previously, parties needed to present a list in only one sub-district	(1) Equal, but with some concessions made to the larger parties	(7) Neutral system

Country			
Luxembourg	(1) No	(2) Parties must be represented in parliament, although a minimal amount of time is available for parties not represented in parliament	(3) Proportional to share of seats at the previous election	(7) Neutral system
France	(1) No (since 1994)	(2) Parties must hold parliamentary seats, although parties not represented in parliament can receive a minimal amount of airtime if they nominate at least 75 candidates for the first ballot	(3) Since 1986, proportional to seat share at the previous election. Previously, airtime was distributed equally between all parties represented in parliament	(7) Neutral system
Finland	(3) Yes, but only on private television stations (introduced in 1990)	(1) Yes, but mainly leader debates	(2) Parties must be represented in parliament. Non-parliamentary parties rarely take part in television debates and are pooled together to receive their free airtime	(1) Equal	(7) Neutral system
Sweden	(3) Yes – but only on direct satellite television since the early 1980s	(1) Yes, but mainly leader debates	(2) Free airtime has mainly been restricted to parties represented in parliament, although on a few occasions, parties not represented in parliament have been included	(1) Equal	(7) Neutral system
United Kingdom	(1) No	(1) Yes	(2) Eligibility is based on a 'balance' between the major three parties based on vote share at the previous election. Other parties may also qualify if they have presented candidates in 50 or more constituencies	(2) Proportional to share of the vote at the previous election	(6) Neutral system

continued overleaf

Table 3.5 continued

	Paid political television spots	Free airtime available	Criteria for eligibility for free airtime	Method of allocation of free airtime	Overall
Portugal	(3) Yes, on private television channels	(1) Yes	(1) No criteria for eligibility. All competing parties, including those not represented in parliament, receive free airtime	(1) Equal	(6) Neutral system
Ireland	(1) No	(1) Yes (since 1968)	(2) Election broadcasts are available to any group or party fielding at least 7 candidates	(2) Proportional to share of the vote at the previous election	(6) Neutral system
Switzerland	(1) No	(1) Yes	(2) Parliamentary representation. Small parties without parliamentary representation are entitled to free airtime if they have had success in the previous cantonal elections	(2) Proportional to vote share at the previous election. Equal coverage is given to the four main parties and smaller parties are accorded less free airtime	(6) Neutral system
Belgium	(1) No	(1) Yes	(2) French-speaking: only groups with more than 2% of the seats are eligible for free airtime. Dutch-speaking: groups with a minimum of two members in the Culturrad can create a broadcasting organisation. Since 1982, every group with more than three members in the Vlaamse Raad can create a broadcasting organisation	(2) French-speaking: proportionate to number of seats in the Conseil Culturel. Dutch-speaking: half the time is allocated equally and half allocated proportionally	(6) Neutral system

Norway	(1) No	(1) Yes (since 1968), but mainly leader debates	(2) Parties must have been represented in parliament in at least one of the last two parliamentary periods, to nominate candidates in a majority of constituencies and to have a national organisation. Parties that do not meet these criteria can be accorded a minimal amount of free airtime	(1) Equal	(5) Permissive system
Denmark	(1) No	(1) Yes, mainly leader debates	(1) No criteria for eligibility. All parties participating in the ballot are eligible for free airtime	(1) Equal	(4) Permissive system
Italy	(1) No, since 2000	(1) Yes	(1) No criteria for eligibility. All parties, coalitions and candidates receive free airtime	(1) Since 2000, equal access for all parties, candidates and coalitions (previously proportional)	(4) Permissive system

Sources: Administration and Cost of Elections (2010); Austin and Tjernström (2003); Bergman *et al.* (2003); Bowler *et al.* (2003); Carter (2005); Casas-Zamora (2005); Farrell (2002); Farrell and Webb (2000); Gunther and Mughan (2000); Kaid and Holtz-Bacha (1995); Müller and Sieberer (2006); Nassmacher (2001c); Norris (2000); Plasser and Plasser (2002); personal communication with Professor Kurt Richard Luther.

Note

If a country scores 4 or 5, the regime is permissive. A score of 6 or 7 indicates television advertising rules are neutral and a score of 8 or more indicates a restrictive system of television advertising for non-established parties. Cumulative scores are presented as all countries score on all dimensions. The lower the score, the more permissive a system and the higher the score, the more restrictive a system, with all columns carrying equal weight. The countries are ranked from high to low, from most restrictive to most permissive.

advertising that are not biased towards the established parties and do not restrict opportunities for non-established parties. Established parties in Italy, Denmark and Norway do not engage in cartel strategies and have instead created equal systems of access for all parties and candidates. This strategy should negatively influence the positions of established parties in these countries. In these countries, established parties should achieve only low levels of centrality within their national party systems, as non-established parties are not restricted in their access to television advertising opportunities.

Access to media resources is one of the major features of the cartel party system, so the party systems of Austria, Greece and Germany should resemble cartel party systems, where competition is restricted and outsiders excluded. This should produce high levels of systemic centrality for the established parties, yet, as argued in Chapter 2, 'the cartel inevitably generates its own opposition' (Katz and Mair 1995: 24). The cartel strategies engaged in by the established parties in Austria, Greece and Germany might legitimate the protest of some non-established parties against the cartel, as the actions of the cartel parties themselves fuel the challenge (Katz and Mair 1995: 24). Chapter 6 tests these claims, by assessing the impact of high and low levels of institutional strategies.

3.4 State subsidies

State subsidies are funds provided by the state to political parties for any purpose, although campaign expenses do not feature here as section 3.1 assessed these expenses. Recent literature concerning the role of established parties in the construction of systems of state subsidies takes its lead from the cartel thesis of Katz and Mair (1995). Following on from their studies on party organisations (1992, 1994) that addressed the issue of party funding, Katz and Mair drew the conclusion that parties were increasingly reliant on state subsidies as a form of party income to compensate for declining party membership. The cartel thesis emerged following this finding. According to Katz and Mair, cartel parties create systems of state subsidies to reinforce the cartel, that is, to support those within and to penalise those outside. Katz and Mair note that:

> Because these subventions are often tied to prior party performance or position, whether defined in terms of electoral success or parliamentary representation, they help to ensure the maintenance of existing parties while at the same time posing barriers to the emergence of new groups
>
> (Katz and Mair 1995: 15)

State subsidies have changed the way in which parties operate and have had important implications for competition within party systems. However, other studies that have sought to test empirically the effect of state subsidies on party systems have found little evidence to support Katz and Mair. Pierre *et al.* (2000)

find no support for the hypothesis that party subsidies lead to the petrification of the party system, nor have subsidies meant that other income sources have lost their significance for political parties. Likewise, Scarrow (2006) concludes that 'changes in the vote share of parties and in the number of competitors have not coincided in any systematic way with the introduction of party subsidies' (Scarrow 2006: 635).

'State subsidies' include money awarded to parliamentary groups, central party organisations and youth groups, as well as funds that may have been awarded for general party organisation or as 'non-earmarked' (Austin and Tjernström 2003). Furthermore, only direct subsidies are included as part of this dimension; indirect subsidies that the state may provide such as funding to auxiliary organisations are not included. The restrictive or permissive nature of state subsidies for non-established parties focuses on the following four areas.

Funded institutions

All countries in western Europe provide some form of state funding to political parties, so this first dimension allows the comparison of systems that have a comprehensive system of state subsidies with countries that have minimal systems. Within comprehensive systems of state subsidies, party central organ-isations and parliamentary groups receive state subsidies, with other areas of the party included for highly comprehensive systems. Patterns of change are also significant, as Pierre *et al.* (2000: 9) argue that there is a clear tendency in many countries to increase the number of recipients as a means of diversifying the sub-sidies. Party research institutes, educational institutions, and local and regional branches of the party organisations also receive subsidies in many jurisdictions. Whether comprehensive systems are restrictive or permissive for non-established parties depends largely on the method of allocation of funds and any thresholds for eligibility in place.

Level of state subsidies

This area focuses on state funding to party central organisations, as this data is most readily available, thanks to the Katz and Mair project (1992, 1994). Through the assessment of levels of subsidies awarded to central party organisa-tions and the percentage of this funding that comes from the state, trends in the amounts of subsidies received can be highlighted to observe whether parties are becoming more or less reliant on party subsidies. Recent data suggests that there is no trend to suggest the party dependency on state subsidies is increasing, although levels of state-dependency are high (Katz 2002: 114). Although state subsidies may be generous or meagre, the amount of funding received by non-established parties is contingent upon the method of allocation and the thresholds in place, which can severely restrict access to state subsidies for non-established parties.

Method of allocation

The method of allocation is one of the two most important areas for determining the permissive or restrictive nature of the system of state subsidies for non-established parties. There are two main methods of allocating state subsidies in operation in western Europe: parties receive funds in proportion to votes or seats, or with a base amount for all parties and a subsequent amount in proportion to seats and votes. A further, less used method is the 'matching funds' model, where subsidies are tied to electoral support and the ability of candidates and parties to raise funds themselves (Pierre *et al.* 2000: 9). Non-established parties should be favoured the most by methods of allocation that distribute a base amount of funding and an additional amount in proportion to the share of the vote received, as this guarantees all parties (that meet the threshold of eligibility) a certain amount of funding, so introduces an element of equality into an otherwise proportional distribution of resources.

Payout threshold

The presence of a threshold can strongly influence the method of allocation, the fourth and most important area of state subsidies to consider. Some countries state that eligibility for funding is dependent upon a minimum number of votes or seats, whereas others require only parliamentary representation. To compare these two thresholds, Scarrow's (2006) concept of a 'payout threshold' is particularly useful. The 'payout threshold' is a figure that corresponds to the minimum percentage of the vote that parties need to be eligible for state funds. Where parliamentary representation is not required, the payout threshold corresponds with the eligibility threshold stated within the state subsidy laws. However, where parliamentary representation is required, the payout threshold for state subsidies is the same as the 'effective' threshold calculated in section 3.2, or the legal threshold if present. The 'effective' threshold seeks to estimate the percentage of the vote needed for a party to obtain a parliamentary seat and is the payout threshold within systems where parliamentary representation is the criteria for eligibility for funding and where no legal electoral threshold is in place. Scarrow (2006: 624) notes that the 'payment threshold is the aspect of subsidy regime that seems most likely to influence the possible effect of public funds on political competition'.

Table 3.6 presents the coding categories for state subsidies, with two areas determining the permissive or restrictive nature of the system. The method of allocation and the payout threshold are the two most important areas of state subsidies for the restrictive or permissive nature of the system, as both areas have an important impact on the other areas considered. The importance of the payout threshold is particularly considerable, therefore the score received for this area is weighted double.

Table 3.7 shows that the countries with the most restrictive systems of state subsidies for non-established parties are the United Kingdom and Finland. Established parties within these countries have created systems of state subsidies that

Table 3.6 Coding categories for state subsidies

Aspect considered	Permissive (1)	Neutral (2)	Restrictive (3)
Method of allocation	Base amount plus an amount per vote	Base amount plus an amount per seat, or proportional to number of votes won at the previous election	Proportional to number of seats won at the previous election
Payout threshold (weighted double)	Less than 1%	Between 1% and 4%	4% or more

reward the established parties and restrict the potential for non-established parties to achieve success within the party system. Established parties in Finland and the United Kingdom have engaged in cartel strategies using the tool of state subsidies to restrict challenges. In the United Kingdom, the state subsidy system in place is minimal and the system that is in place restricts funding to parties represented in parliament (Katz and Mair 1992: 869). The Finnish example is very different, as a system of subsidies is in place and parties are heavily reliant on these subsidies (Katz and Mair 1992: 309–16), but as in the United Kingdom, only parties with parliamentary representation receive subsidies. This behaviour is in line with the cartel thesis, with subventions tied to prior performance (Katz and Mair 1995: 15), and the 'prior performance' required in the cases of the United Kingdom and Finland is highly restrictive for non-established parties, further reinforcing the cartel. In the United Kingdom and Finland, established parties should achieve high levels of systemic centrality, as barriers restrict entry into the system for non-established parties.

Conversely, the most permissive systems of state subsidies for non-established parties occur in Denmark, Germany, the Netherlands, Norway, Portugal and Austria, indicating that engagement in cartel strategies does not appear to be widespread. In these six countries, established parties have not engaged in cartel strategies, and have not created systems of state subsidies that reinforce the status quo and restrict opportunities for non-established parties. Instead, access to state subsidies is available for non-established parties, demonstrating a lack of willingness to engage in cartel strategies. This behaviour is somewhat counter-intuitive, as according to the cartel thesis, 'the growth in state subventions ... has come to represent one of the most significant changes to the environment in which parties act' (Katz and Mair 1995: 15). If all parties were self-interested, rational actors, established parties would engage in cartel strategies to preserve their systemic dominance. However, the evidence found in Table 3.7 appears to suggest that parties in more than a third of countries considered have eschewed posing barriers to non-established parties in terms of restricting access to state subsidies. Therefore, in Denmark, Germany, the Netherlands, Norway, Portugal and Austria, established parties should experience low levels of systemic centrality, as access to state subsidies for non-established parties is less restricted than elsewhere.

Table 3.7 State subsidies and non-established parties in western Europe, 1950–2009

	State subsidies system in place	Total amount of subsidies awarded to party central organisations (average per year)	Percentage of party central organisation income comprised of state subsidies (averages)	Method of state subsidies allocation[a]	Payout threshold (weighted double)[b]	Overall[c]
United Kingdom	Since 1975, to parliamentary opposition parties	No funding for party central organisations		(3) Awarded according to seat and vote share at last election. Minimum of two seats to be eligible, or one seat and 150,000 votes. In 2001–02, opposition parties received £11,012 ($16,180) per year per seat plus £21.99 ($32) per 200 votes won[d]	(3) (37.5%)	(9) Restrictive system
Finland	Since 1967, to parliamentary groups and to central party	1965–69: FIM1.8 million ($0.4 million, £0.2 million) 1970–4: FIM2.1 million ($0.4 million, £0.2 million) 1975–79: FIM8.4 million ($1.8 million, £1.0 million) 1980–84: FIM14.6 million ($3.1 million, £1.7 million) 1985–89: FIM17.2 million ($3.6 million, £2.0 million)	1967–69: 98.2% 1970–74: 90.1% 1975–79: 75.0% 1980–84: 82.7% 1985–89: 74.3%	(3) Awarded in proportion to number of MPs (1 MP required to form a group)	(3) (5.2%)	(9) Restrictive system
Switzerland	Since 1972, to parliamentary groups (minimum 5 MPs, but do not have to come from the same party)	No funding for party central organisations		(2) An annual sum and a sum per member for parliamentary groups. In 2000, the amounts received were CHF90,000 ($56,750, £38,620) as an annual sum and CHF16,500 ($10,400, £7,080) per member	(3) (8.6%)	(8) Restrictive system

Country						
Belgium	Since 1971, to parliamentary groups (minimum 3 MPs) Since 1989, to central party organisation (minimum 1 MP)	1989: BEF141.9 million ($4.4 million, £2.4 million)e		(2) A sum per group and a sum per MP are awarded to the parliamentary group Central party organisations receive a fixed amount and an amount per valid vote cast at the last election on its list. In 1995, the fixed amount was BEF5 million ($113.700, £77,350) and the amount per vote BEF50 ($1.14, £0.77)	(3) 5%	(8) Restrictive system
Sweden	Since 1965, to party central organisations Since 1979, press subsidies. Also subsidies to parliamentary group awarded and for youth and women's organisations	1965–69: SEK3.5 million ($0.5 million, £0.3 million) 1970–74: SEK6.3 million ($0.9 million, £0.5 million) 1975–79: SEK12.4 million ($1.7 million, £0.9 million) 1980–84: SEK16.2 million ($2.2 million, £1.2 million) 1985–89: SEK22.8 million ($3.1 million, £1.7 million) 1999: SEK140.0 million ($19.1 million, 10.3 million)f	1965–69: 52.7% 1970–74: 59.2% 1975–79: 62.9% 1980–84: 58.0% 1985–89: 52.0% 1999: 63.3%	(2) Per-seat subsidy paid to the central organisations with 4% of the vote or more. For parties with no seats and with less than 4% of the vote, one per seat subsidy is paid for every 0.1% gained above 2.5% of the vote. For parties with seats but with less than 4% of the vote, one per seat subsidy is paid per seat and one per seat subsidy for every 0.1% gained above 2.5% of the vote. Basic subsidies for parties who have previously received 4%+ of the vote but have no current parliamentary representation Per-seat subsidies, with bonus for opposition parties to parliamentary groups. In 1966, governing parties received SEK3,000 per seat, ($3,150 today), non-governing parties SEK4,500 per seat, ($4,700 today). Since 1972, parties receive a basic grant and per-seat subsidy from parliament. Subsidies for parties who have previously received 4%+ of the vote but have no current parliamentary representation	(2) 2.5%	(6) Neutral system

continued overleaf

Table 3.7 continued

	State subsidies system in place	Total amount of subsidies awarded to party central organisations (average per year)	Percentage of party central organisation income comprised of state subsidies (averages)	Method of state subsidies allocation[a]	Payout threshold (weighted double)[b]	Overall[c]
Spain	Since 1978, to national party organisations and to parliamentary party groups (minimum of 5 MPs)	1978: ESP1.7 billion (£12.6 million, £6.8 million) 1994: ESP12.0 billion ($91.3 million, £49.3 million)	1987: 77.3% 1988: 79.3% 1989: 64.5% 1990: 76.3% 1991: 71.2% 1992: 66.2%	(2) Since 1978, a fixed amount paid to parliamentary party central organisations for each seat, with additional funds for each vote. 1987 change: central organisation is awarded one third of the funding according to seats in parliament and the other two-thirds according to previous election vote share Since 1978, all parliamentary groups receive a base amount of funding, with additional funds according to number of seats	(2) 3%	(6) Neutral system
Italy	From 1974–93, state subventions to parliamentary groups Since 1999, state subventions have taken the form of electoral reimbursement	1974–79: ITL40.6 billion ($26.6 million, £14.4 million) 1980–84: ITL84.1 billion ($55.2 million, £29.9 million) 1985–89: ITL85.1 billion ($55.8 million, £30.2 million)	1974–79: 27.4% 1980–84: 21.1% 1985–89: 27.1%	(2) From 1974–93, subsidies distributed in proportion to membership of parliament Since 1999, the state subsidy system has been based on campaign reimbursement for parties with more than 4% of the vote, or with one elected candidate and 1% of the vote receive ITL4,000 per vote received ($2.61, £1.43 today)	(2) 4%	(6) Neutral system

France	Public funding to parties has existed since 1988	1989–90: FF182.9 million ($35.2 million, £19.0 million) 1991–93: FF373.0 million ($71.8 million, £38.8 million) 1994–96: FF526.3 million, ($101.4 million, £54.7 million)	1993: 46.1% 1997: 51.7% 1998: 54.1%	(2) Distributed in two equal parts. Since 2003, funds are allocated to parties that have received at least 1% of the vote in at least 50 districts (previously 75), distributed in proportion to vote won by candidates on the first ballot (previously with a 5% threshold in place). Funds also allocated to parties on basis of their parliamentary representation Some extra help for smaller parties that do not meet threshold criteria (2) 1%	(6) Neutral system
Ireland	Since the 1960s, to the leaders of both government and opposition parties Since the late 1990s, to party organisations	Funds, until the late 1990s, were payable only to party leaders and were not part of central party income.		(2) Party leaders with over 7 MPs in their parties eligible for funds. Parties continue to receive the 'Oireachtas' grant, which is weighted in favour of the opposition parties, but since 1996 has also taken into account the number of MPs belonging to each party 2% of the vote at the previous election to be eligible for party organisation subsidies. Qualified parties are entitled to share approximately IR£1 million annually, distributed in proportion to first preference votes received (2) 2%	(6) Neutral system

continued overleaf

Table 3.7 continued

	State subsidies system in place	Total amount of subsidies awarded to party central organisations (average per year)	Percentage of party central organisation income comprised of state subsidies (averages)	Method of state subsidies allocation[a]	Payout threshold (weighed double)[b]	Overall[c]
Greece	Since 1984, operational costs of parties subsidised	Funding data for party central organisations not available		(1) More than 3% of the vote needed to receive a flat grant with additional funds according to votes received at the previous election. Parties must have presented candidates in two-thirds of constituencies	(2) 3%	(5) Neutral system
Austria	Since 1963, to parliamentary group (minimum 5 MPs). Since 1972, to party academies/educational institutions. Since 1975, to party central organisations	1975–79: ATS54 million ($5.0 million, £2.7 million) 1980–85: ATS83 million ($7.6 million, £4.1 million) 1986–90: ATS127 million ($11.7 million, £6.3 million)	1975–79: 30.6% 1980–85: 28.1% 1986–90: 29.8%	(2) Base amount and supplementary amount awarded to the parliamentary group according to number of seats Base amount plus an amount per seat for parties with 5+ MPs to party academies/educational institutions Fixed sum to central party organisations with at least 5 MPs, with a fixed base amount and supplementary amount according to vote share at the previous election. Parties receiving more than 1% of the vote receive money in election years	(1) 1%	(4) Permissive system

					(2)	(1)	(4)
Portugal	Since 1977, to parliamentary groups Since 1988, to central organisations	1978: PTE120.1 million ($0.8 million, £0.4 million) 1995: PTE1.3 billion ($8.0 million, £4.3 million)	Reliance on party funding is similar to levels in Spain		To central organisations based on vote share at the previous election. The threshold for funding is representation in the legislature. Since 1993, parties with at least 50,000 votes (c.0.6% of the electorate) are also eligible for funding All parliamentary groups (no minimum number of MPs) receive a base amount of funding, with additional funds according to number of seats Parties receive 1/225 of national minimum salary for each vote received	0.6%	Permissive system
Norway	Since 1960, to parliamentary groups (minimum 1 MP) Since 1970, to central party organisations Since 1978, to youth and educational organisations	1970–74: NoK11.0 million ($1.7 million, £0.9 million) 1975–79: NoK18.8 million ($2.9 million, £1.6 million) 1980–84: NoK29.8 million ($4.6 million, £2.6 million) 1985–89: NoK44.1 million ($6.8 million, £3.8 million)	1970–74: 48.9% 1975–79: 50.4% 1980–84: 51.5% 1985–89: 51.5%		An amount per vote for central party organisations. Since 2005, all registered parties are eligible for funds (previously 2.5% or more of the vote was needed to be eligible and the party had to present candidates in at least half of the constituencies) Parliamentary parties receive a basic sum and an additional sum per MP. Since 1983, the three smallest parties in parliament receive increased support, in 1991 worth NoK432,136 (US$66,585), plus an extra amount per vote. Extra support for MPs from small parties since 1991	None. Since 2005, all registered parties are eligible for funds (parties need 5,000 signatures to register, see Table 3.2)	Permissive system

continued overleaf

Table 3.7 continued

	State subsidies system in place	Total amount of subsidies awarded to party central organisations (average per year)	Percentage of party central organisation income comprised of state subsidies (averages)	Method of state subsidies allocation[a]	Payout threshold (weighted double)[b]	Overall[c]
Germany	Since 1969, to parliamentary groups (26 MPs) Funding to party central organisation Since 1962, to party foundations Since 1959, for educational activities	1960–64: DM17.3 million ($11.2 million, £6.0 million) 1965–69: DM29.0 million ($18.7 million, £10.1 million) 1970–74: DM29.7 million ($19.2 million, £10.3 million) 1975–79: DM71.5 million ($46.2 million, £24.9 million) 1980–84: DM109.0 million ($70.4 million, £38.0 million) 1985–89: DM117.9 million ($76.2 million, £41.1 million)[g]	1960–64: 65.1% 1965–69: 67.1% 1970–74: 46.7% 1975–79: 64.2% 1980–84: 68.7% 1985–89: 68.0%	(2) Since 1994, each party annually receives €0.70 (US$0.89, £0.47) for each valid vote cast on its list, or €0.70 or each valid vote cast for it in a constituency or polling district in a Land where its list was not approved and €0.38 (US$0.49, £0.26) for each euro obtained through membership fees, deputy fees or rightfully obtained donations. Parties annually receive €0.85 (US$1.08, £0.58) (rather than €0.70) for the first 4 million valid votes it wins. Parties are eligible for this money if they win 0.5% of the valid votes cast for lists at the last election, or if have obtained 10% of the valid votes cast in a constituency or polling district Previously, a set sum per eligible voter was shared out proportionally among the parties according to their vote percentage. Parties had to win 0.5% of the second list votes to be eligible for these funds	(1) 0.5%	(4) Permissive system

Denmark	Since 1965 to parliamentary groups (minimum 1 MP) for administrative assistance and since 1969 for 'expert' assistance Since 1987, to central party	1987–89: DKK9.7 million ($1.6 million, £0.8 million)[h]	1987–89: 19.3%	(2) To parliamentary groups based on the numbers of seats held and since 1969 the grant for expert assistance is based on a sum per month per seat plus a sum for opposition parties in parliament. Change in 1986: each group receives DKK15,000 (US$1,840, £1,250) per month per seat plus DKK60,000 (US$7,360, £5,010) Central party organisations receive DKK5 (US$0.61, £0.42) per vote if minimum of 1,000 votes received. From 1995, the amount was raised to DKK19.50 (US$2.39, £1.63) per vote	(1) 1,000 votes	(4) Permissive system
The Netherlands	Since 1964, to parliamentary groups (minimum 1 MP) Since 1972, to research institutes Since 1975, to educational institutes Since 1976, to youth organisations	1989: Dfl4.2 million ($2.4 million, £1.3 million) 1995: Dfl8.2 million ($4.7 million, £2.5 million) 1999: Dfl10.0 million (£5.7 million, £3.1 million)[j]	1989: 18.0% 1995: 25.3%	(2) To parliamentary groups awarded as a fixed amount that increases with the number of seats obtained To research institutes as a fixed amount and an amount per seat To educational institutes as a fixed amount and an amount per seat To parties' youth organisations dependent on size of parliamentary group	(1) (0.67)	(4) Permissive system

continued overleaf

Table 3.7 continued

State subsidies system in place	Total amount of subsidies awarded to party central organisations (average per year)	Percentage of party central organisation income comprised of state subsidies (averages)	Method of state subsidies allocation[a]	Payout threshold (weighted double)[b]	Overall[c]
Luxembourg Since 1965 to parliamentary group (minimum 5 MPs)	No funding for party central organisations		Data not available	(3) (14%)	Not enough data available to reach a conclusion

Sources: Austin and Tjernström (2003); Bowler *et al.* (2003); Carter (2005); Casas-Zamora (2005); Clift and Fisher (2004); Katz and Mair (1992, 1994); Koss (2010); Ladner (2001); Nassmacher (2001c, 2003, 2006); Pierre *et al.* (2000); Scarrow (2006); Van Biezen (2000, 2004); Webb *et al.* (2002).

Notes

a Where different methods of allocation to different parts of the party exist, an average score is taken. If a country allocates funding as a base amount plus an amount per vote (1) to central party organisations, but in proportion to seats won at the previous election (3) to parliamentary groups, then an average score of 2 is allocated.

b Where different payout thresholds exist, the lowest threshold is cited, as this value represents the minimum percentage of the vote that parties need to be eligible for any funding. Figures in brackets denote the 'effective' threshold cited in the absence of a legal threshold, or a threshold in place as part of the eligibility criteria for state funding

c A score of between 7 and 9 indicates a restrictive system for non-established parties, 5 or 6 a neutral system and a score of 4 or less indicates a permissive system. Cumulative scores are presented as all countries (with the exception of Luxembourg) score on each dimension.

d All currencies are converted into US$ and GB£ using www.xe.com in order to ascertain a basic level of comparability.

e Information for Belgium is relatively limited, as Deschouwer notes that 'nothing, or almost nothing, is known about income and expenditure of the Belgian parties' (Deschouwer 1994: 104).

f All figures include subsidies to parliamentary groups.

g Figures relate to the total amount of subsidy received.

h Excludes V (Left) and KF (Conservative People's Party), as these parties do not publish their accounts.

i Data for the central party income of Dutch parties is generally limited, as government-released figures only refer to state subventions given for the use of broadcasting on radio and television and not to the many other forms of state subsidies awarded to Dutch parties.

3.5 Conclusion

This chapter has suggested that the low use of institutional strategies should negatively influence the fate of established parties, whereas the high use of institutional strategies should enable established parties to continue to dominate their party systems, strongly influenced by the cartel thesis of Katz and Mair (1995). The assumptions of this chapter are that parties are self-interested actors, engaging in strategies in order to preserve their systemic dominance. Applying the Katz and Mair logic to this chapter, some established parties should engage in high levels of institutional strategies, by creating systems of electoral laws, electoral systems, television campaigning airtime and state subsidies that operate in ways that are favourable to the established parties. However, the evidence presented in this chapter has shown that this behaviour is far from widespread.

In many countries, established parties have not acted as self-interested actors and do not restrict potential challenges to their systemic dominance. One possible reason for this interesting finding may be that self-interest does not motivate established parties, but they instead seek to shape institutions to favour *democracy* as a whole, by not posing barriers to challengers. Although this perspective may have some relevance, a more convincing argument is in line with rational choice assumptions. In Chapter 1, it was argued that 'situations in which actors do *not* choose the apparently optimal alternative ... [are] because they are involved in nested games, that is, contextual or institutional factors have an overriding importance' (Tsebelis 1990: 11), thus the behaviour of some established parties is perfectly rational from a wider context. For example, for established parties that operate in coalition systems, where one party rarely achieves a parliamentary majority, engagement in low levels of institutional strategies is the rational option to choose. These parties do not operate in a void and are often reliant on non-established parties' support to achieve a governing majority. Rational behaviour may be to eschew restrictions for non-established parties so that the established parties' coalition partners can continue to achieve electoral success and remain viable coalition partners.

Although, in many countries, permissive systems are in place for non-established parties, the data has shown that there are many countries in which the cartel thesis appears to be realised and where restrictive institutional arrangements are in place. Thus, the theory of the 'cartelisation' of western European political systems receives only mixed support, as established parties in many countries have not made full use of the resources of the state and their positions as legislators. Yet, this mixed picture is not surprising, as the cartel model is merely that; a model suggesting that political parties in modern democracies have been moving in a certain direction over recent decades. This movement from civil society to the state takes place in different countries, to different extents and at different times. Although the cartel thesis may not be applicable in all the countries in the study, it does not undermine the relevance of the thesis as a statement of the hypothesised direction of party development. Chapter 6 studies the relevance of the cartel thesis further, examining the impact of institutional strategies on the fate of established parties in detail. From the analysis conducted in Chapter 6, conclusions can be drawn regarding the success of cartel strategies.

4 Selection of cases and measurements

In order to assess the extent to which engagement in strategies impacts upon the fates of established parties in western Europe, this chapter selects cases and proposes measures to assess this impact. The task of the first part of this chapter is to select the countries that have experienced high and low levels of use of electorate-orientated and institutional strategies. Subsequent chapters analyse these countries as case studies to learn more about the effect of these strategies. The second part of this chapter discusses how the impact of party strategies on established parties and party systems can be assessed, focusing on developing the ideas of Peter Mair, and also putting forward the concept of 'systemic centrality' to assess the fate of established parties.

4.1 Electorate-orientated strategies

Table 4.1 presents data based on the results presented in Chapter 2. Each country receives a ranking on each dimension, based on the country's position in the tables constructed in Chapter 2. Each of the 17 countries in this study receives a score of between 1 and 17. A score of 1 indicates that the country ranked first in the previous tables constructed, suggesting that parties within this country have engaged in high levels of the strategy discussed. A score of 17 indicates that parties in that particular country have engaged in only low levels of these strategies.

There are problems when summarising findings in a table using rankings, and one of the major practical problems faced when constructing Table 4.1 was that not all countries scored on each dimension. For example, countries that have never experienced a coalition government (Spain and the United Kingdom) do not record scores on the pre-electoral coalition agreements or content of coalition agreements dimensions. When not all countries score on a particular dimension, the analysis excludes lower and upper values in order not to distort the results. For example, only 15 countries score on the pre-electoral coalition agreements dimension, so data excludes the middle two values of 9 and 10,[1] and countries receive scores from 1–8 and 11–17, allowing the countries that rank first and last in the tables to receive scores of 1 and 17. Disregarding the top two or bottom two values would bias the results, but by removing the middle two values, minimal distortion will occur. Another problem occurs when countries receive the same scores on the individual dimensions. For example, eight countries engage in a strategy of exclusion regarding anti-political-establishment parties. Where this occurs, all the countries within that group receive an average mark, with eight countries receive marks ranging from 10–17. An average score is calculated and all countries that score the same within the group receive this average score. In this example, the average score is 13.5, so all countries receive the rounded score of 14 for this dimension.

Table 4.1 presents the cumulative and average scores of countries based on the data collected in Chapter 2, with the average score used to place the countries in rank order from low to high scores.[2] The lower the overall value obtained, the more established parties within a certain country have engaged in electorate-orientated strategies. The higher the mark, the less the established parties have engaged in these strategies.

Table 4.1 shows that the two countries with the lowest average values are Portugal and Germany, suggesting that in these countries established parties have engaged in the highest levels of electorate-orientated strategies. The lowest levels of electorate-orientated strategies occur in Switzerland and Luxembourg. Chapter 5 assesses the countries where parties engage in the highest, second highest, lowest and second lowest levels of use of electorate-orientated strategies, allowing comparison and differences in terms of party system change and established parties' success to be drawn and enables a fuller analysis of the effect of electorate-orientated strategies.

Portugal is the country that has experienced the highest levels of electorate-orientated strategies, scoring 24 points where the lowest possible value obtained could have been 5 and the maximum potential value is 85. Portuguese established parties engage in high levels of ideological change, and have proved to be highly responsive. Portuguese established parties are the most eager in western Europe to respond to the electorate and in 75 per cent of governments formed between 1976 and 2009, all governing parties had improved their share of the vote at the previous election (see Table 2.5). These figures appear to suggest that Portuguese established parties are keen to follow trends within the electorate, as ideologies have changed often and sometimes radically and governments are predominantly comprised of parties that have increased their share of the vote at the previous election.

Portuguese established parties reject anti-political establishment parties, as the CDU (United Democratic Coalition), a union between the PCP (Portuguese Communists) and the Greens, has, since its inception in the late 1980s, received around 10 per cent of the vote, yet has never been in government. Similarly, the vote share of the previous incarnation of the CDU, a union between the PCP and the APU (United People's Union), never fell below 12.5 per cent between 1976 and the late 1980s, yet the party never featured in government. Yet, this is the only dimension where Portugal does not demonstrate a high use of electorate-orientated strategies. With regard to coalition agreements, established parties in Portugal have formed these agreements on a regular basis compared to the rest of western Europe. Parties have made formal agreements on every occasion in

Table 4.1 The use of electorate-orientated strategies by country, 1950–2009

	Ideological change	Electoral responsiveness	Relations with anti-political-establishment parties	Pre-electoral coalition agreements	Coalition agreements	Overall (mean averages)
Portugal	6	1	14	2	1	**24 (4.8)**
Germany	2	9	7	12	6	**36 (7.2)**
Ireland	3	8	14	5	7	37 (7.4)
Finland	1	12	1	12	12	38 (7.6)
France	12	2	8	3	13	38 (7.6)
The Netherlands	13	7	3	12	5	40 (8.0)
Austria	4	17	6	12	3	42 (8.4)
Norway	16	13	14	1	2	46 (9.2)
Greece	9	6	5	12	16	48 (9.6)
Italy	14	4	4	12	14	48 (9.6)
Belgium	15	15	3	12	4	49 (9.8)
Sweden	5	15	14	4	11	49 (9.8)
Denmark	7	11	14	12	8	52 (10.4)
United Kingdom	11	10	N/A	N/A	N/A	21 (10.5)
Spain	17	3	14	N/A	N/A	34 (11.3)
Luxembourg	10	5	14	12	16	**57 (11.4)**
Switzerland	8	16	14	12	16	**66 (13.2)**

which Portugal has experienced coalition governments. Allied to this figure, Portuguese established parties have constructed the longest written coalition agreements in western Europe, averaging 22,059 words per written coalition agreement (see Table 2.8). Overall, Portuguese established parties have engaged in high levels of electorate-orientated strategies, and Chapter 5 examines the effect of the use of these strategies on the fate of the established parties and the party system as a whole.

Germany ranks second in terms of the level of electorate-orientated strategies used. Established parties in Germany have engaged in high levels of ideological change, ranking second on this dimension behind Finland. Responsiveness in Germany is only moderate, yet the figures obtained suggest that overall, German established parties are more responsive than not, in terms of reacting to the voters' preferences at election time. An average level of responsiveness of 1.1 indicates that German parties are responsive, but only at a moderate level.[3] Established parties treat anti-political establishment parties in a relatively inclusive way in Germany, as demonstrated by the inclusion of the Green Party in government; a party that started life within the Bundestag in 1983 as a somewhat radical party.

German established parties have never formed a formal pre-electoral coalition agreement, although on 57.1 per cent of occasions where a coalition government occurred between 1950 and 1999, the coalition parties made an informal agreement (Saalfeld 2000: 54). This may demonstrate that the established parties in Germany wish to communicate their preferences to the voters before the election has taken place and not engage in drawn-out coalition negotiations behind closed doors, away from the eyes of the voters after the votes have been cast. Coalition agreements are relatively long, averaging 8,256 words (see Table 2.8). The length of these agreements may indicate that German established parties believe it important to define the policies the coalition will be pursuing in the forthcoming governmental term in detail, thereby informing the voters about their intentions. Overall, German established parties have engaged in high levels of electorate-orientated strategies, and Chapter 5 assesses the impact of these strategies on the party system, to compare the effects of the adoption of similar strategies in Germany and Portugal.

The countries that demonstrate the lowest levels of electorate-orientated strategies are Luxembourg and Switzerland. Swiss parties have engaged in only moderate levels of ideological change, suggesting that Swiss parties are reluctant to move their policies in line with the changing views of the voters. Electoral responsiveness in Switzerland is very low, as on only one occasion have all parties entering government increased their share of the vote since the previous election. An overall level of responsiveness of 0.1 indicates that on average, the parties of government had gained a combined 0.1 per cent of the vote compared to their electoral share at the previous election, indicating that the parties had not significantly gained voter confidence since the previous election.

Established parties in Switzerland reject anti-political establishment parties, although there is certainly a case to argue that the SVP (Swiss People's Party) has become an anti-political establishment party over recent decades and Chapter 5 assesses this argument in more detail. Government access is restricted to the major four parties, despite the challenge of numerous anti-political establishment parties over the period covered. The Labour Party (PdA), the Swiss Democrats (SD) and the Freedom Party (FPS) have all received significant shares of votes and seats, yet have remained excluded from government. Swiss parties do not produce pre-electoral coalition agreements, although an overarching agreement exists between the major parties: the 'magic formula' whereby all four parties receive a set number of seats within government.[4] Nonetheless, Swiss parties do not inform the electorate before or after the election about their plans for ministerial positions or policy.

Swiss established parties engage in only low levels of electorate-orientated strategies. They have proven to be relatively unresponsive to the electorate and reluctant to change ideologically. Established parties exclude anti-political establishment parties from government (until the SVP changed ideologically) and established parties do not make pre-electoral or post-electoral coalition agreements. Swiss political parties do not engage in strategies to influence the electorate and maintain their own positions; in fact, they appear to engage in the opposite strategy of detachment from the electorate. This may suggest that Swiss parties engage in 'cartel strategies' rather than the electorate-orientated strategies discussed in Chapter 2. Swiss parties distance themselves from the electorate, fitting into the cartel thesis' concept of the cartel party moving away from civil society and becoming part of the state. Chapter 5 discusses the impact of this cartel-like behaviour on the fate of established parties within Switzerland.

The country with the second lowest levels of use of electorate-orientated strategies is Luxembourg. Established parties in Luxembourg engage in moderate levels of ideological change and are relatively responsive. 23.1 per cent of governments formed in Luxembourg between 1950 and 2009 contained parties that all increased their share of the vote at the previous election (see Table 2.5). Established parties reject anti-political establishment parties in Luxembourg, as only three parties have been in government since 1950. The KPL (the Communist Party) took part in a coalition in 1945, but since then has not entered government, despite receiving a post-war high of 16.9 per cent of the vote in 1951. More recently, the fortunes of the KPL have faded and the Green Party has gained prominence. Entering parliament in 1984, the Greens have not entered government, despite receiving 11.6 per cent and 11.7 per cent of the vote at the 2004 and 2009 elections respectively.

Parties in Luxembourg do not create pre-electoral coalition agreements, suggesting a lack of engagement with the electorate. Coalition agreements are sometimes agreed upon, but these are not made public (Dumont and De Winter 2000: 412–15), again, demonstrating a distance from the electorate. Established parties in Luxembourg engage in only low levels of electorate-orientated strategies, in common with the Swiss example. Instead, the behaviour of the established parties in Luxembourg is 'cartel-like', as established parties distance themselves from the electorate and do not try to influence the voters. Chapter 5 assesses the impact of this behaviour on the fate of established parties within Luxembourg and the party system as a whole, comparing the systemic impact of the similar strategies employed by established parties within Switzerland and Luxembourg, and the results obtained for Portugal and Germany. This analysis will determine which electorate-orientated strategy is the more beneficial for the maintenance of established parties' dominance within western European party systems.

The impact of these electorate-orientated strategies may occur in two different ways. From a Downsian, rational choice perspective, established parties within Portugal and Germany should have the most success in maintaining their systemic dominance. Established parties within these countries have engaged in strategies to be responsive to the electorate and to inform the electorate of coalition choices and the content of agreements. In contrast, taking a perspective more akin to the cartel thesis, established parties within Portugal and Germany should have the *least* success and established parties in Luxembourg and Switzerland should enjoy continuing success precisely because of their lack of responsiveness to the electorate. Established parties within Luxembourg and Switzerland have engaged in cartel strategies to restrict competition and to keep non-established parties outside the system, so established parties within these countries should have the most success maintaining their dominant systemic positions. Chapter 5 tests these two competing hypotheses.

4.2 Institutional strategies

Table 4.2 presents data based on the results presented in Chapter 3, with similar methodological considerations applying in relation to calculating scores where not all countries score on a particular dimension, or where countries receive the same score.

Table 4.2 suggests that established parties in France have engaged in the highest levels of institutional strategies. The system of electoral laws in France is somewhat restrictive, as candidates must pay approximately £700 in order to stand and this deposit is only refundable if a candidate wins 5 per cent of the vote (Inter-Parliamentary Union Parline Database 2010). Likewise, parties are only able to receive campaign subsidies if they win 5 per cent of the vote in a district (Carter 2005: 180). The French electoral system is the most disproportional in western Europe and hence the most restrictive for non-established parties, recording a disproportionality value of 18.92 and has changed on several occasions, arguably with partisan motives in mind. Robert Elgie (2005) discusses the electoral system change for the 1986 election and suggests that the change in electoral formula from majority-plurality to proportional may have been partisan. He argues that 'the size of the defeat [for the Socialist government] was greatly reduced' and the subsequent return to the previous system was controversial, as 'the right seemed to stand to gain the most from a return to the previous system' (Elgie 2005: 120).

The French system of television advertising is neutral for non-established parties, although the allocation criteria for free airtime are particularly strict. Seat share at the previous election determines the proportion of free airtime (Plasser and Plasser 2002: 226), so given the disproportionality of the French electoral system, the system of television advertising in France is somewhat restrictive for non-established parties.[5] The system of state subsidies is not restrictive for non-established parties, although it should be noted that France introduced a system of state subsidies relatively recently in 1988 (Knapp 2002: 125), so for much of the period considered, there was no system of state subsidies in place.

The French institutional arrangement is restrictive for non-established parties because of somewhat restrictive electoral laws, a highly disproportional electoral system and a system of television advertising that favours parliamentary parties, suggesting that established parties in France have created systems that disadvantage competitors and favour their own interests. The electoral system changes made in the Fifth Republic reinforce this view, suggesting that established parties in France are willing and able to change political institutions for their own benefit. Engagement in these strategies is an indicator of cartel-like strategies in action, as the French institutional system clearly favours the established parties' interests. Chapter 6 examines the impact of these strategies on the fate of the established parties (the creators of much of the institutional set-up) and the impact on the party system as a whole.

The Greek established parties have engaged in the second highest levels of institutional strategies in this study. Greek electoral laws are relatively restrictive for non-established parties, as a non-refundable deposit is required (Inter-Parliamentary Union Parline Database 2010) and a threshold of 3 per cent is in place for eligibility for campaign subsidies (Carter 2005: 184). The electoral

Table 4.2 The use of institutional strategies by country, 1950–2009

	Electoral laws	Electoral system	TV advertising	State subsidies	Overall
France	8	1	7	7	**23 (5.8)**
Greece	12	3	2	10	**27 (6.8)**
Luxembourg	8	7	7	N/A	22 (7.3)
United Kingdom	14	2	12	2	30 (7.5)
Austria	1	14	1	14	30 (7.5)
Finland	13	11	7	2	33 (8.3)
Sweden	5	15	7	7	34 (8.5)
Spain	17	4	7	7	35 (8.8)
Belgium	15	5	12	4	36 (9.0)
Italy	5	8	17	7	37 (9.3)
Switzerland	10	13	12	4	39 (9.8)
Germany	10	12	3	14	39 (9.8)
The Netherlands	5	17	7	14	43 (10.8)
Norway	5	10	15	14	44 (11.0)
Portugal	12	6	12	14	44 (11.0)
Ireland	17	9	12	7	**45 (11.3)**
Denmark	2	16	17	14	**50 (12.5)**

system is one of the most disproportional in western Europe and as with the French example, has changed several times, potentially with partisan motives in mind. The electoral system changed in 1989, and saw Greece adopt a proportional representation system compared to the 'reinforced' proportional representation system used since 1958, although this change reversed for the next election. Panayote Dimitras suggests that the elites of Greek established parties viewed proportional representation as 'a useful tool for ... short-term tactics'. He goes on to propose that the electoral system change was enforced because 'the outgoing ... government knew it stood no chance of coming out ahead of the opposition' (1994: 155). Greek established parties are willing to engage in institutional engineering if they believe a change in the electoral system will enhance their short-term interests.

The Greek system of television advertising is highly restrictive for non-established parties as parties can buy unlimited airtime on private television channels. In 1996, these paid spots comprised 83 per cent of parties' total campaign expenditure (Papathanassopoulos 2000: 56). The method of allocation of free airtime is proportional to seats obtained (Carter 2005: 171), so the disproportionality of the electoral system influences the television advertising regime. The allocation of state subsidies is relatively restrictive for non-established parties as a 3 per cent threshold is in place (Carter 2005: 184). Greek institutions are restrictive for non-established parties and, as in France, Greek established parties are willing to engage in institutional manipulation for short-term gain. Thus, if the cartel thesis holds, established parties in Greece and France should be the most successful in western Europe at maintaining their dominant positions within their national party systems because of the strategies in which they engage. The analysis presented in Chapter 6 will assess this hypothesis in greater depth.

Denmark records the highest score in the sample, suggesting that established parties are reluctant to mould Danish institutions to support their own needs and to restrict opportunities for non-established parties. Electoral laws are highly restrictive in Denmark, as parties need approximately 20,000 signatures to stand in an election (Inter-Parliamentary Union Parline Database 2010) and there are no limits to campaign expenditure (Plasser and Plasser 2002: 177). However, this is the only aspect where the Danish institutional arrangement is not permissive for non-established parties. The Danish electoral system in one of the most proportional in western Europe, recording an average disproportionality score of 1.55 for elections held under the present system. The highly proportional electoral system should favour new and small parties, suggesting that Danish established parties do not restrict opportunities for non-established parties to gain parliamentary representation.

Access to television advertising is also easily available to non-established parties. All parties participating in the ballot are eligible for free airtime (Sundberg 2002: 218), which is allocated on an equal basis (Plasser and Plasser 2002: 219). Sundberg (2002) notes that opportunities are available for the major parties to discriminate against political rivals, especially as equal and free access for all parties in Denmark is only provided for by unofficial convention (2002: 208). Despite the opportunities available, established parties in Denmark have abided by the convention of equality and have not sought to take advantage of their dominant systemic positions. The system of television advertising does not favour the interests of the established parties and is highly permissive for the non-established parties. The system of state subsidies in place is also highly permissive for non-established parties, as parties need to receive only 1,000 votes to be eligible for a share of state subsidies (Carter 2005: 179).

The institutional arrangements in Denmark are highly permissive for non-established parties, as new and small parties have benefited from a highly proportional electoral system, a permissive system of television advertising and a generous system of state subsidies with a low threshold for eligibility. Chapter 6 examines the effect that the choices made by the established Danish parties have had on the party system, with Danish established parties expected to struggle to maintain their systemic centrality, as the institutional system is permissive for non-established parties. In line with the cartel thesis, the reluctance to engage in cartel strategies demonstrated by Danish established parties may have a negative impact on their dominance within the party system.

The country that demonstrates the second lowest levels of institutional strategies is Ireland, which has the most permissive system of electoral laws in western Europe for non-established parties. A small deposit is required (Inter-Parliamentary Union Parline Database 2010), independent candidates can stand (ibid.) and campaign subsidies have recently been introduced with a low threshold for eligibility (Murphy and Farrell 2002: 229). The electoral system in Ireland is neither restrictive nor permissive for non-established parties, registering a disproportionality score of 3.95. The results obtained from these two dimensions suggest that established parties in Ireland have not attempted to manipulate institutional arrangements, or to create systems that favour their own interests.

Access to television advertising is permissive for non-established parties as free election broadcasts are available to any group or party fielding at least seven candidates (Bowler *et al.* 2003: 103) and this free airtime is distributed in proportion to the share of the vote obtained at the previous election (Murphy and Farrell 2002: 235–6). Ireland introduced state subsidies only at the end of the 1990s, so their full impact is still uncertain. However, the new system in place is relatively permissive for non-established parties as the system has a small threshold of 2 per cent and the proportion of votes received at the previous election determines funds (Murphy and Farrell 2002: 229).

Irish institutions are highly permissive for non-established parties and established parties appear reluctant to engage in institutional strategies that should enable them to maintain their dominant systemic positions. Irish established parties should therefore struggle to maintain their systemic dominance due to the permissive institutional arrangement in Ireland. Chapter 6 compares the impact of the choices made by the established parties in Ireland to the effect of similar choices made by Danish established parties.

Established parties that engage in high levels of institutional strategies should be able to maintain their systemic dominance more effectively than those that choose not to engage in these strategies. However, the evidence may not support this hypothesis. The cartel thesis addresses the potential for challenges to the cartel to emerge as a result of parties engaging in cartel-like behaviour 'ceas(ing) to be effective channels of communication from civil society to the state' (Katz and Mair 1995: 23). Katz and Mair argue that although established parties can create institutions that favour their own interests, as in France and Greece, 'attempts at exclusion may prove counter-productive, offering to the excluded neophytes a weapon with which to mobilise the support of the disaffected' (Katz and Mair 1995: 24). This was a point raised in section 2.6 and is discussed further in Chapter 6. Although established parties that engage in high levels of institutional strategies should prove to be the more successful in terms of maintaining systemic dominance, the restrictive systems put in place may ultimately prove to be counter-productive. Chapter 6 tests these hypotheses and examines the systemic effect of the different strategies engaged in by established parties.

In order to test the impact of these strategies on the systemic positions of western European established political parties, a measure of exactly *how* this impact can be measured needs to be developed, to determine how the success or failure of established parties should be measured and how party system change can be assessed. For answers to many of these questions, the work of Peter Mair provides a vital starting point.

4.3 The Mair typology and party system change

Mair has presented his own unique measure of party system change (2002), which argues that the structure of competition is the most important factor to consider when examining party systems and processes of change. The way parties compete with each other has an importance beyond merely counting parties (Duverger 1954; Rae 1967; Laakso and Taagepera 1979), or measuring systemic volatility (Pedersen 1979). Competition for government is the vital aspect of the structure of competition and identifying the structure of competition for government allows the comparison of party systems over time and across countries. The Mair typology appears to be the most intuitively useful measure for analysing the success of parties in maintaining their positions at the heart of party systems. As the structure of competition for government is deemed to be the crucial factor, the measure fits in well with the study of established parties, as it is these parties that form the majority of governments and to a certain extent, can control entry into the party system and the roles played by new parties when they gain parliamentary representation.

A major advantage that the Mair typology has over other party system typologies is that it argues against the widely accepted notion that 'party system change is largely, if not exclusively, a function of, or even a synonym for, electoral change' (Mair 2002: 101). Instead, Mair conceives of the possibility that party system change may find its origins *within* the party system itself and that forces for change may not necessarily originate from *outside* the party system. This theory underpins this study – the idea that parties may be able to influence their own fate and, through the adoption of certain strategies, may be able to maintain or improve their position within the party system. The Mair typology is summarised in Table 4.3.

The three components of Mair's typology depict elements over which established parties have a certain element of control: alternation in government, innovation and familiarity and which parties govern. Mair argues that determining whether a party system is closed or open can be achieved by assessing these three factors, which also allow an assessment of differences between party systems and a measurement of party system change over time.

Alternation in government

Mair sees three conceivable patterns of alternation in government – wholesale alternation, partial alternation and non-alternation – and this factor is relatively easy to measure as each category is distinct. If all of the parties in government at time *t* are removed from office and are replaced at time $t+1$ by a new government made up of a party or parties who were previously in opposition, then wholesale alternation has taken place. One possible problem that may emerge is the issue of party splits, fusions and name changes. France provides the most complex issues regarding alternation in government. The centre-right groups in France have had various names throughout the history of the Fifth Republic (see Thiébault 2000: 500), so it is arguable whether a party name change constitutes alternation in government. On a similar note, the French party system exhibits wholesale alternation between two coalitions, which raises the question whether alternation in government depends on *individual* parties or *coalitions* of parties. For the purposes of this study, alternation in government is an action that individual parties engage in, rather than coalitions. Party name changes, splits (such as the disintegration of the Belgian party system in the 1970s) and fusions (such as the fusion of the Christian parties into the CDA, Christian Democratic Appeal, in the Netherlands in the 1970s) are also evidence of non-alternation.

Table 4.3 The Mair typology

Closed structure of competition	Open structure of competition
Wholesale alternation in office, or non-alternation in office	Partial alternation, or mix of both partial and wholesale alternation
Familiar governing formulae	Innovative governing formulae
Access to government restricted to a limited number of parties	Access to government open to (almost) all parties

Source: Mair (2002).

Innovation or familiarity in government formation patterns

The second component of the Mair typology is the presence of innovative or familiar governing formulae. This particular component is concerned with assessing whether or not the party or combination of parties has governed before in that particular format (Mair 2002: 96). Innovation reflects an open party system, whereas familiarity is a component of a closed party system. Classifying whether there has been innovation or familiarity should be relatively straightforward.[6] If a government has previously governed in that form (that is, the same combination of parties has governed before), then familiarity can be seen. If a party enters government for the first time, no matter how small that party, this signifies innovation in terms of government formation patterns. Similarly, if parties form a coalition where parties may have all governed previously, but not in that particular alliance, then innovation occurs. Over time, levels of familiarity should increase, simply because the numerical possibilities of coalitions decline over time and innovation may only be possible when new parties enter the system. Likewise, in a party system with a limited format, low levels of innovation should be present, with most governing combinations exhausted relatively quickly.

Access to government

The final component of the Mair typology is concerned with examining which parties govern and which do not. This component is the most difficult to measure and involves a qualitative judgment. The distinction Mair makes involves deciding whether *almost* all parties eventually cross the governing threshold (Mair 2002: 97). Mair compares this factor to Sartori's (1976) concept of polarised pluralism, where established parties consider some parties as unacceptable partners for office and permanently exclude them from office. This raises a problem with this component, as the exclusion of a moderate, centrist party from governing patterns may still constitute either an open or a closed pattern of government access. According to Mair's first definition, if the party does not cross the governing threshold, then the pattern of government access is restricted. Yet according to the Sartori definition, the party would have coalition potential and may eventually cross the governing threshold, and thus government remains open.

The analysis adopts the first definition of Mair, viewing access to government as dependent on whether almost all parties eventually cross the governing threshold, as this provides data that are more comparable by using a quantitative assessment of systemic relevance. If a party that has never governed before receives over 5 per cent of the vote and does not enter government, then patterns of government formation are restricted. A party is relevant if it passes the threshold of 5 per cent, as section 2.3 adopted this threshold in relation to anti-political establishment parties. However, if the party obtains between 0 per cent and 4.9 per cent, then access is open. A further problem with the Mair typology emerges when considering parties that have undergone ideological changes. Parties such as the FPÖ (Austrian Freedom Party) had crossed the governing threshold, but then made a radical swing to the right in the mid-1980s, following which the party was a pariah within the Austrian party system for 14 years. Although the Mair definition sees the party system as remaining open, the established parties' response to the ideological change that the FPÖ underwent in the 1980s sees the Austria party system as closed until 2000.

The overall typology

One problem with the typology as a whole is that the categories are not exclusive, as wholesale alternation is a characteristic of both an open and closed structure of competition. Lijphart (1968: 7) argues that an effective typology should be exhaustive and mutually exclusive, that is, it should be capable of sorting all relevant cases into one and only one category, but should also be parsimonious (Wolinetz 2004: 11). It is questionable whether the Mair typology meets these criteria, as not every country clearly falls within one category. For example, a country that has a mix of innovative and familiar governing formulae does not clearly fall into either category. These problems do not hinder the use of the Mair typology for this study; however, as for each aspect of the typology, the two categories are different ends of a scale rather than as independent, distinct categories. This allows for comparison between countries, as some have a more familiar pattern of government formation than others do, and some countries less open system of access to government than others.

The presence of 'wholesale patterns of alternation' in two categories is problematic but justified. Regarding the alternation in office factor, Mair seeks to differentiate between systems where wholesale change in government is the norm and where no partial alternation occurs, and those systems where partial alternation is the norm and where wholesale alternation occurs far less frequently. The most obvious example of wholesale alternation in government is the United Kingdom, where Labour and the Conservatives alternate in government. Wholesale alternation is the dominant pattern (a Labour government replaced by a Conservative government or vice versa), with non-alternation taking place when a government enjoys successive terms in office. The key factor within these systems is the *absence of partial alternation*. Partial alternation necessarily needs coalition government as a basic principle, which did not occur in the United Kingdom at the national level in the period covered.

Partial alternation is instead a major part of an open structure of competition. Coalition systems are more likely to produce patterns of partial alternation, as some parties move into government, some out, while others remain. Wholesale alternation and non-alternation are much less likely to occur within open party systems as partial alternation dominates. Systems where governments regularly contain many parties, such as Finland, are likely to demonstrate high incidences of partial alternation in government. It is for these reasons that Mair is justified in using wholesale alternation within both categories. Perhaps a minor modification would see the reframing of the categories as 'wholesale alternation and non-alternation, with no/limited partial alternation' as an aspect of a closed party system. 'Dominance of partial alternation' could then be seen as an aspect of an open party system, as it is within the category of partial alternation that the distinction between the forms is most useful.

Thus, a party system has changed if patterns of competition change from open to closed or vice versa. However, a further problem occurs as there are three component elements of the closed and open systems of competition and so it may often be difficult to determine if a system is completely open or closed. It is beneficial to view party systems as closed, semi-closed, semi-open or open. A closed party system would be characterised by wholesale alternation in office (or non-alternation), familiar governing formulae and restricted access to government. A semi-closed system would contain two of the three characteristics, a semi-open system one of the three and an open system, none. An open system would demonstrate partial alternation (or a mix of partial and wholesale), innovative governing formulae and open access to government. The use of four categories rather than two means allows the more accurate classification of party systems. This revision of the typology overcomes another problem: the increasingly open nature of most party systems within western Europe. The simple dichotomy between open and closed would force, for example, the Luxembourg party system to be categorised as closed, despite several instances of partial alternation. These changes improve the discriminatory value of the typology and allow the categorisation of Luxembourg party system as semi-closed. Table 4.4 shows the revised Mair typology, taking into account the new distinctions between the categories.

Despite the earlier assumption that the Mair typology is useful because it steps away from traditional interpretations of party system change, one crucial element, acknowledged by Mair, is missing from his typology. The number of parties within a party system is vital for determining how competition operates and although it should not be the only measure used for classifying party systems, it adds further discriminatory value to the Mair typology. Sartori (1976) most clearly expresses the importance of numbers for the interpretation, classification and comparison of party systems.

Sartori's distinction between format and mechanics is one of the key ideas within the study of party system typologies. The format relates to how many parties a party system contains and their relative size at either the electoral or the parliamentary level. Formats contain mechanical dispositions (Sartori 1976: 128), so despite Mair's downplaying of the importance of numbers, numbers clearly have a vital role to play in the assessment of party systems. The number of parties within a system is an indicator of fragmentation and indicates the number of 'streams of interaction' (Sjöblom 1968: 174); that is, the more parties there are, the more relationships with other actors parties have to consider and the more complex these relationships become. The relative size of parties is the best indicator of the coalition potential a party has and can provide an indication of likely governing coalitions, based on concepts such as the minimum-winning coalition. The

Table 4.4 The revised Mair typology

Closed structure of competition (demonstrating all of the following characteristics)	Semi-closed structure of competition (demonstrating two of the following characteristics)	Semi-open structure of competition (demonstrating two of the following characteristics)	Open structure of competition (demonstrating all of the following characteristics)
Wholesale alternation and non-alternation, with no/limited partial alternation	Wholesale alternation and non-alternation, with no/limited partial alternation	Dominance of partial alternation	Dominance of partial alternation
Familiar governing formulae	Familiar governing formulae	Innovative governing formulae	Innovative governing formulae
Access to government restricted to a limited number of parties	Access to government restricted to a limited number of parties	Access to government open to (almost) all parties	Access to government open to (almost) all parties

mechanics of a party system is the focus of the Mair typology but, equally, the format of a party system has a major impact on the mechanics.

By introducing a numerical aspect into the Mair typology, party systems such as the British and the Norwegian (at least until very recently) show differences. The classification of both systems is 'closed' due to the lack of partial alternation, the familiarity of government formation patterns and the restricted nature of access to government. However, these party systems operate under very different circumstances, the principal being that the Norwegian party system contains many more parties than the British system and governments in Norway are sometimes coalitions, rather than the single-party government format that dominates in the United Kingdom.

Comparisons between the party system of modern-day Austria and those of the Netherlands and Finland are also useful. All three systems are open, yet the Austrian party system contains far fewer parties than Finland or the Netherlands. This influences the operating principles of the party system and simply means that parties in Austria have fewer options available to them than in the Netherlands and Finland, so the open party systems operate under different conditions. The introduction of the effective number of parties (Laakso and Taagepera 1979) measure into the Mair typology could be an interesting way of increasing the discriminatory value of the measure. The proposed typology may resemble something akin to that presented in Table 4.5.

It should be possible to classify each party system within one of the categories in Table 4.5 and a change from one category to another would indicate a party system change. The extent of this change would be dependent on the number of 'boxes' covered by the change. For example, a minor party system change could see a move from a closed party system with fewer than four

Table 4.5 Introducing the numerical factor into the Mair typology

	Effective number of parties	
Structure of competition	<4	≥4
Closed	a↓ y↘	
Semi-closed	b	
Semi-open		
Open		z

Note
The distinction between the number of parties for classification purposes has been set at 4 for this example; however, the number used in the case studies will depend on the individual party system. The addition of the numerical criterion does not imply that certain numbers have mechanical properties, in the same way that Sartori identifies. It does, however, provide a useful heuristic tool to enable the identification of a change in the numbers of parties present within the party system. Where change in numbers occurs, an electoral change has taken place, which may affect the mechanics of the party system, but this relationship is not deterministic.

effective parties to a semi-closed system with fewer than four effective parties (see the movement of 'a' to 'b' in Table 4.5). However, a more significant change would see a move from a closed party system with fewer than four parties to an open system of competition with more than four effective parties (see the movement of 'y' to 'z' in Table 4.5). Clearly, this is an exaggerated example, but the typology can determine when a party system has changed, and also the extent or significance of the change.

A further benefit of the revised typology is that it can highlight processes of change that the original typology ignored. One of the strengths of Mair's typology is that it dissociates the processes of party system change and electoral change. However, this is also one of its biggest drawbacks. The revised typology proposed can capture electoral changes (a change in the effective number of parties) and party system change (a change in the structure of competition), allowing the relationship between the two processes to be examined.

A crucial feature of the revised Mair typology is the addition of the effective number of parties index. The index developed by Laakso and Taagepera (1979) is an intuitive measure that captures the effective number of parties within a party system based on vote shares obtained by various parties. It develops the fractionalisation index developed by Rae (1967) and both measures originate from the same mathematical basis, which has also spawned a number of more complex measurements intended to improve upon numerical output (see Dunleavy and Boucek 2003, Molinar 1991, and Dumont and Caulier 2005). Both measures adopt the sum of squared shares of the vote method, and produce figures that are sensitive to both the number and relative size of parties. Rae's scores range from 0, which represents a perfect one-party regime, to 1 where no two voters choose the same party, whereas the values produced by Laakso and Taagepera range from 1 to infinity. The Rae index provides an indicator of the frequency with which pairs of voters would disagree in any given election (Rae 1967: 55) based on simple probability statistics, and Laakso and Taagepera calculate the inverse of the Rae values.

The formula for calculating the effective number of parties is as follows. The calculation squares and adds together the fractions of the vote received by each party. The inverse of this figure produces a value denoting the effective number of parties:

$$N_v = \frac{1}{\sum_{1}^{x} v_i^2}$$

Where N_v is the effective number of electoral parties and v_i is the vote shares of the parties.

The principal strength of the Rae and Laakso and Taagepera measures are that they capture two vital elements of party systems: both the number and relative size of parties. The format of the party system contains important mechanical properties (Sartori 1976) and the figures produced by the measure provide a gauge of the fragmentation of political power, the number of possible interaction streams, likely tactics of party competition, the opportunity for clear decisions and electoral accountability and government formation possibilities (Bennett 1997: 187). The figures are easy to calculate and the values produced by Laakso and Taagepera in particular match intuitive thinking about the number of parties contained in a system. The figures produced represent an accurate estimate of the number of 'relevant' parties in a system, coming as close as any operational index based on seat or vote shares alone can come, without detailed knowledge about the given country (Taagepera 1999: 498). For example, a two-party system where both parties receive 50 per cent of the vote would record a value of 2 utilising the Laakso and Taagepera measure. The effective number of parties index has become the most widely used measure in the field of political science for interpreting the number of 'relevant' parties within a system. Despite its widespread use, however, there are problems with both the theoretical basis and empirical values produced by the measure.

The Laakso and Taagepera measure and previously the Rae measure give too much weight to the larger parties within the system, due to the reliance of the measure on the sum of squared shares method. For example, a party obtaining 40 per cent of the vote contributes a value of 0.16 to the measure, whereas a party with 10 per cent of the vote only contributes 0.01, a disproportionately low value (Sartori 1976: 307). Although some weight is given to all parties, small parties receiving under 10 per cent of the vote count for very little and tiny parties under 1 per cent hardly count at all (Dunleavy and Boucek 2003: 292). The claim that these indices are sensitive to the number and relative size of parties is questionable, as the index is not sensitive to the numbers of parties as such, as very small parties do not even register on the fractionalisation index (Mayer 1980: 518). Additionally, the figures produced by the application of the measure are artificial and correspond to 'the number of hypothetical *equal*-size parties that would have the same *total* effect on fractionalisation of the system as have the actual parties of *unequal* size' (Laakso and Taagepera 1979: 4). The measure fails to distinguish between the number and relative size of parties, to a certain extent inhibiting the utility of the measure. These problems aside, the effective number of parties index is the most widely used and efficient method for providing a tool allowing the quantitative comparison of party systems over time within a country and between countries,[7] and is applied to the Mair typology in order to produce results that are more discriminating.

The revised Mair typology thus provides a proposed solution for the problem of how to study party systems and whether they have changed, but still leaves many questions open regarding the assessment whether established parties remain the key actors within their national party systems.

4.4 Assessing the fate of established parties

Established parties have been defined in section 1.3 as parties that have over a substantial period, been in leading positions and have been especially influential for the functioning of the system (Smith 1989b). Following this definition, it is necessary to determine how the impact of the strategies that established parties have engaged in can be measured, utilising the concept of 'systemic centrality'[8] which relates to how important or dominant established parties are within their national party systems. The problem of circularity first raised in Chapter 1 is significant, as established parties are those parties that have been particularly significant within their party systems between 1950 and the early 1970s and how successful they are within their national party systems determines the enduring success of these parties. Clearly, established parties achieved relatively high levels of centrality until the early 1970s, as this is why they are established parties. However, by extending the study to 2009, the study can determine if established parties have continued to achieve high levels of centrality throughout the period covered and not just in the period between 1950 and the early 1970s.

Chapter 1 highlighted the importance of the work of Luther (1989) in terms of assessing party system change through different arenas, and this approach applies to the study of systemic centrality. Françoise Boucek adopts a similar approach and argues that parties can dominate their party systems in the electoral, parliamentary and executive arenas (1998: 105–7). Parties must maximise their electoral appeal and parliamentary representation (relating to dominance in terms of size) and be able to transform parliamentary outcomes into office benefits. This relates to the concept of influence on government formation, as coalition potential allows the largest party to dominate the government formation process. From the work of Smith (1989a, 1989b), Boucek (1998) and Luther (1989), a number of measures can be constructed to determine the 'centrality' of established parties within party systems.

Share of the vote

If the share of the vote that established parties receive has fallen, parties have failed to maintain their dominant positions within their party systems. However, this measure is not a reliable measure of established parties' centrality. The share of the vote received by established parties has declined relatively consistently across western Europe over recent decades, so a fall of support from, for example, 50 per cent of the vote to 45 per cent of the vote may not indicate a dramatic decline in an established party's fortunes. Mair has argued that in the early 1960s, 'old' parties gained an average of 95 per cent of the vote in western Europe and in the late 1980s and early 1990s, these same parties averaged 84 per cent of the vote (Mair 1993a: 126–8). Established parties' support has declined somewhat since the 1960s, and this is not surprising, as the decline in party identification (see Dalton and Wattenberg 2000b), decline in party membership (see Mair and Van Biezen 2001) and the rise of new issues and new political parties (see Poguntke 1993; Ignazi 1992) have challenged established parties' systemic stranglehold. The number of new party actors within party systems since the 1960s has increased the fragmentation of many western European party systems, so established parties should suffer a decline in their share of the vote. Yet, this decline, as has already been stated, should not be read as a 'terminal' indication of party decline and loss of centrality for established parties, especially as established parties often do not respond to a loss of votes, as was shown in section 2.2.

Indeed, Mair argues that because of the expansion on the electorate in western Europe since the 1960s, the 'old' parties have actually increased their vote in absolute terms (Mair 1993a: 127). A decline in vote percentage does not necessarily indicate a decline in centrality and although the share of the vote a party receives is important, it can only form part of the measure of a party's systemic centrality. A significant loss, of perhaps 20–25 per cent of the party's vote, may signify a loss of centrality within the party system, yet the context of the losses or gains is significant.

Share of parliamentary seats

The share of parliamentary seats determines established party centrality within the *parliamentary* arena. Due to the proportional nature of many of the electoral systems within western Europe, trends in the electoral and parliamentary arenas should reflect each other relatively closely. However, in some countries with disproportional electoral systems, the results obtained from comparing vote and seat shares, that is, comparing levels of centrality within the electoral and parliamentary arenas, may produce some interesting findings.

Although the share of the vote and the share of parliamentary seats received are important measures for assessing the centrality of established parties, of greater importance for the purposes of measuring the fate of established parties and in keeping with the assumptions behind much of this study, is participation in government. If an established party has lost importance in terms of the potential to influence the party system and, in particular, the composition in government, then a party can be seen to have lost its central position within a party system. Various measures related to government participation indicate the extent to which established parties dominate the governmental arena.

Largest party in parliament (seats)

The first measure for capturing the *governmental centrality* of established parties is the number of times the party has been the largest party within parliament in terms of seat share. Clearly, size is not the only factor that determines whether parties maintain centrality within party systems, but size can influence the options available to parties. The largest party within a system generally has the first opportunity to form a government and is a key actor within the system.[9] The fate of other parties, especially in terms of access to government, is often reliant upon decisions made by the largest party within the system. The largest party does not always succeed in forming a government and may sometimes not enter government, but by winning more seats than any other party wins, the largest party is in a position to direct coalition negotiations.

Time spent in government

The second governmental arena measure relates to the number of years parties have spent inside and outside government. Some established parties in western Europe have spent the majority of the post-war period in government and this is a strong indicator of systemic dominance. Parties such as the CVP (Christian People's Party) in Belgium and the DC (Christian Democrats) in Italy have been their country's 'natural' party of government and an inherent part of the political system, dominating their respective party systems, and were successful in maintaining their leading role until the 1990s. Other parties such as the FDP (Free Democrats), crucial coalition allies for the SPD (Social Democrats) and CDU/CSU (Christian Democrats) in Germany, were also rarely out of government. Although not as dominant as the CVP and DC, the FDP has managed to consolidate its central role within the German party system throughout much of the post-war period, although the rise of the Greens as an alternative coalition ally for the SPD has seen the considerable influence of the FDP challenged over recent years.

Median legislator

A third measure relates to whether a party is in a 'king-maker' or the median legislator position within a party system. This concept relates to whether a party occupies the crucial central seats in parliament when parties are placed on a left-right scale according to ideology. If a party occupies the central seats then, theoretically, the party can decide if it should ally with the left or the right and has a crucial role to play within the party system. Parties that occupy this king-maker position have a crucial role to play in any coalition negotiations and although they may not automatically win a place in government, these parties often have enormous bargaining power at their disposal. A party that occupies the ideological centre in a party system has in its possession the crucial seats that could determine which coalition obtains a majority and is able to govern. This concept takes its lead from the work of Abram De Swaan and his theory regarding the 'median legislator'. This model assumes that the party that controls the median legislator in any potential coalition is decisive because it blocks the axis along which any connected winning coalition must form (De Swaan 1973; see also Laver and Budge 1992 and Klingemann *et al.* 1994).

Percentage share of government positions

The final three measures relate to the share of positions obtained within government by established parties. If the number of government positions that these parties obtain stays constant or increases (as a percentage of total positions within government), then the established party in question has maintained its position at the heart of the party system. Using the number of government positions as a measure has various associated problems; primarily, it does not take into account the nature of the positions. Clearly, some positions within government allow greater influence and are more important in terms of directing future policy direction and a simple measure of the number of positions equates the holding of a core position with a relatively minor position. However, the percentage of government positions held is important, as it influences the power that a party can exert within government, both in terms of dominating other parties and playing a major policy-making role.

Prime minister's party

This problem is addressed by stating the party to which the prime minister belongs, as the prime minister's party should wield the most weight within the coalition and is a suitable indicator for measuring the governmental centrality of established parties.

Ratio of portfolios obtained to share of seats

A final, similar measure relates to the share of portfolios obtained within government compared to the share of parliamentary seats. The relationship between these two figures should reveal that larger parties are penalised to a certain extent, as smaller parties usually receive more government positions than a proportionate distribution of government positions should entail, given the share of seats received, as smaller parties regularly achieve 'bonus portfolios' due to the pivotal position they often occupy (De Winter 2002: 190). Lieven De Winter expresses this point well, arguing that the small size of minor parties is compensated by their larger bargaining or 'walk-away' power (ibid.), that is, the threat that smaller parties can leave the government, potentially removing the governing majority.

These eight measures, summarised in Table 4.6, determine the centrality of established parties within western European party systems over time in order to determine whether centrality is declining or increasing.

Table 4.6 Measuring the centrality of established parties in western Europe

Arena in which centrality is to be measured	*Measure to be applied*
Electoral centrality	1. Percentage share of the vote
Parliamentary centrality	2. Percentage share of parliamentary seats
Governmental centrality	3. Largest party in parliament (seats)
	4. Time spent in government
	5. Median legislator
	6. Percentage share of government positions
	7. Prime minister's party
	8. Ratio of portfolios obtained to share of seats

4.5 Conclusion

This chapter has played a facilitating role in the study, with the first part of the chapter selecting the case studies to show the impact of strategies on the fate of established parties. Chapters 5 and 6 will assess the competing hypotheses of the rational choice model of party action in line with the work of Downs, and Katz and Mair's cartel thesis, applied to the eight case study countries selected in this chapter. The application of the revised Mair typology and the eight measures relating to systemic centrality, provide data to show the impact of strategies on the fates of established western European political parties. These measures enable the next two chapters to compare and contrast systems in a meaningful way and to assess change over time. Descriptive case studies will draw out some of the key areas of importance within national party systems and the use of measures and a typology will determine change and enable comparison in a more meaningful way. The study of the impact of strategies begins with the impact of electorate-orientated strategies in Portugal, Germany, Luxembourg and Switzerland.

5 The use of electorate-orientated strategies

Chapter 2 examined the use of five electorate-orientated strategies by established parties: ideological change; electoral responsiveness; relations with anti-political establishment parties; pre-electoral coalition agreements and length of coalition agreements. Chapter 4 identified the countries in which established parties engaged in the highest and lowest levels of these strategies, with Portugal and Germany demonstrating the highest use of electorate-orientated strategies and Switzerland and Luxembourg the lowest. Established parties in Portugal and Germany engage in responsive, 'Downsian' strategies (Downs 1957), attempting to satisfy the needs of the median voter. In contrast, established parties in Luxembourg and Switzerland have engaged in 'cartel' strategies (Katz and Mair 1995), by creating distance between themselves and the voters. The aim of this chapter is to examine the effectiveness of these two strategies upon established parties' centrality in their respective national party systems.

This chapter analyses each of the four countries in the same way. Each section begins with a brief overview placing the operation of the party system into context. This is achieved with reference to the work of Smith (1976, 1982, 1989a, 1989b; Padgett and Poguntke 2002) in order to place each country's party system into its institutional and historical context in order to understand the operation of the party system. Understanding the context of the operation of the party system will then enable the study to determine whether parties are established or non-established.[1]

This analysis explores the data regarding the centrality of the established parties, followed by a brief section highlighting the key trends in terms of the centrality of the established parties in the electoral, parliamentary and governmental arenas, and patterns of party system change. Following each pair of country studies, the chapter assesses the impact of the use of strategies on the fate of established parties, focusing on the relationship between established party system centrality within different arenas (Luther 1989), explaining levels of systemic change and established party centrality in the two countries.

5.1 Portugal

Analyses concerning the party system of Portugal must address the rupture in democracy that has so strongly influenced Portugal's present day democratic system. The adoption of a new constitution on 2 June 1976 marked the start of Portugal's post-war democratic era, following the rule of authoritarian dictator António de Oliveira Salazar between 1926 and 1968 and the subsequent period of revolution and democratic transition. The PS (Socialist Party) was one of the main parties of the resistance against the authoritarian regime and as such was able to call upon a certain amount of democratic legitimacy in the post-1976 era. The PSD (Social Democrats) and CDS (Christian Democrats) emerged only during the revolutionary period (Magone 2000: 530) and so were untainted by the experiences of the Salazar era. These three parties comprise the group of established parties within the Portuguese party system.

Despite its role as another of the most important forces against the authoritarian regime, since 1976 the PCP (Communist Party) has been 'isolated within the party system' and 'ostracized from the national decision-making structures' (Magone 2000: 533). This is because of the PCP's association with the armed forces and the role the party played in the transition to democracy, leaving the party suspect in the eyes of many moderate voters (Macridis and Lancaster 1987: 321). The rupture in democracy has played a vital role in shaping the post-1976 Portuguese party system and has strongly influenced which parties constitute the group of established parties.

The classification of the parties as either established or non-established is important to identify levels of centrality within the Portuguese party system, with the established and non-established parties and the first and most recent election in which they participated since 1976[2] summarised in Table 5.1. The parties considered as established parties are the PS, PSD, PP-CDS and the AD, with these parties assessed in terms of their centrality within the party system, and how party system change has affected their position. Table 5.2 presents the results of the study into the centrality of established parties within the Portuguese party system. The table features the measures of centrality proposed in the previous chapter and shows trends in the centrality of the established parties within different arenas over time.

Table 5.1 Established and non-established parties in Portugal, 1976–2009

Established parties	*Non-established parties*
PS (Socialist Party) (1976–present)	CDU (Democratic Unity Coalition) (1987–present, previously PCP, Communist Party and APU, United People's Union 1975–85)
PSD (Social Democrat Party) (1976–present, part of AD 1979–80)	BE (Left Bloc) (1999–present, previously UDP, Democratic People's Union 1976–95)
PP-CDS (People's Party) (1993–present, previously CDS, Christian Democrats 1976–93, part of AD 1979–80)	PRD (Democratic Renewal Party) (1985–91)
AD (Democratic Alliance) (1979–80, including PSD, CDS and PPM (Monarchic People's Party))	PEV (Ecological Party The Greens) (1982–present)

Table 5.2 Centrality of established parties in the Portuguese party system, 1976–2009

	1976	1978a	1978b	1979	1980	1981	1983	1985
Percentage share of the vote	PS: 34.9 PSD: 24.4 CDS: 16.0 Total: 75.3%			PS: 27.8 AD: 45.3 Total: 72.6%	PS: 27.8 AD: 47.6 Total: 75.4%		PS: 36.1 PSD: 27.2 CDS: 12.4 Total: 75.7%	PS: 20.8 PSD: 29.8 CDS: 10.0 Total: 60.6%
Percentage share of seats	PS: 40.7 PSD: 27.8 CDS: 16.0 Total: 84.5%			PS: 29.6 AD (PSD, CDS and PPM): 51.2 Total: 80.8%	PS: 29.6 AD (PSD, CDS and PPM): 53.6 Total: 83.2%		PS: 40.4 PSD: 30.0 CDS: 12.0 Total: 82.4%	PS: 22.8 PSD: 35.2 CDS: 8.8 Total: 66.8%
Largest party within parliament (seats)	PS	PS	PS	AD	AD	AD	PS	PSD
Time spent inside government								
PS								
PSD								
PP–CDS								
PPM								
Median legislator[b]	PS	PS	PS	AD	AD	AD	PS	PRD
Percentage share of government positions[c]	PS: 64.3 Inds: 35.7[d]	PS: 64.7 CDS: 17.6 Inds: 18.8	Inds: 100	AD: 100 (PSD: 62.5 CDS: 31.2 PPM: 6.3)	AD: 100 (PSD: 62.5 CDS: 31.2 PPM: 6.3)	AD: 94.1 (PSD: 58.8 CDS: 29.4 PPM: 5.9 Inds: 5.9	PS: 44.4 PSD: 50.0 Inds: 5.6	PSD: 85.7 Inds: 14.3
Prime minister's party[e]	PS	PS	Ind	AD (PSD)	AD (PSD)	AD (PSD)	PS	PSD
Ratio of portfolios obtained to share of seats	PS: 1.6:1	PS: 1.6:1 CDS: 1.1:1	N/A	AD: 2.0:1	AD: 1.9:1	AD: 1.8:1	PS: 1.1:1 PSD: 1.7:1	PSD: 2.43:1

	1987	1991	1995	1999	2002	2004	2005	2009
Percentage share of the vote	PS: 22.2 PSD: 50.3 CDS: 4.4 Total: 76.9%	PS: 29.1 PSD: 50.6 CDS: 4.4 Total: 84.1%	PS: 43.8 PSD: 34.1 PP-CDS: 9.1 Total: 87.0%	PS: 44.1 PSD: 32.3 PP-CDS: 8.3 Total: 84.7%	PS: 37.9 PSD: 40.1 PP-CDS: 8.3 Total: 86.3%		PS: 45.1 PSD: 28.7 PP-CDS: 7.3 Total: 81.1%	PS: 36.6 PSD: 29.1 PP-CDS: 10.4 Total: 76.1%
Percentage share of seats	PS: 24.0 PSD: 59.2 CDS: 1.6 Total: 84.8%	PS: 31.3 PSD: 58.7 CDS: 2.2 Total: 92.2%	PS: 48.7 PSD: 38.2 PP-CDS: 6.5 Total: 93.4%	PS: 50.0 PSD: 35.2 PP-CDS: 6.5 Total: 91.7%	PS: 41.7 PSD: 45.7 PP-CDS: 6.1 Total: 93.5%		PS: 52.6 PSD: 32.6 PP-CDS: 5.2 Total: 90.4%	PS: 42.2 PSD: 35.2 PP-CDS: 9.1 Total: 86.5%
Largest party within parliament (seats)	PSD	PSD	PS	PS	PSD	PSD	PS	PS
Time spent inside government								
PS								
PSD								
PP-CDS								
Median legislator	PSD	PSD	PS	PS	PSD	PSD	PS	PS
Percentage share of government positions	PSD: 93.3	PSD: 100	PS: 100	PS: 73.7 Inds: 26.3	PSD: 77.8 PP-CDS: 16.7 Inds: 5.6	PSD: 80.0 PP-CDS: 15.0 Inds: 5.0	PS: 52.9 Inds: 47.1	PS: 58.8 Inds: 41.2
Prime minister's party	PSD	PSD	PS	PS	PSD	PSD	PS	PS
Ratio of portfolios obtained to share of seats	PSD: 1.6:1	PSD: 1.7:1	PS: 2.1:1	PS: 1.5:1	PSD: 1.7:1 PP-CDS: 2.7:1	PSD: 1.8:1 PP-CDS: 2.5:1	PS: 1:1	PS: 1.4:1

Sources: Comissão Nacional de Eleições (2010); Magone (1998; 1999; 2000; 2002; 2003; 2004; 2005; 2006; 2010); Woldendorp *et al.* (2000).

Notes

a Where the percentage of the vote and seats received is not cited for a particular year, the composition of government changed but no election took place.

b Median legislator details taken from individual country chapters, based on the ordering of parties from left to right according to Laver and Hunt's (1992) policy scales.

c Governments are the units of analysis for the purposes of this table rather than cabinets (see note 7); government composition referred to represents the composition at the start of the governmental term and does not take into account any changes made to control of ministries.

d Independent candidates.

e Although the title of this dimension is 'prime minister's party', in some countries, this title may refer to the first minister or chancellor.

Centrality of established parties

Within the electoral arena, the PS, PSD and PP-CDS have increased their centrality over the period covered, although the parties receive a relatively low combined share of the vote. 1985 marks a turning point in the centrality of the established parties. Before 1985, the three parties together received around 75 per cent of the vote. In 1985, this value fell to 60.6 per cent as the PRD received 17.9 per cent of the vote. However, this electoral shock was to be short-lived and since 1987, the three parties have increased their electoral centrality to a high in 1995 of 87 per cent. There has been a trend for the centrality of the established parties within the electoral arena to increase over the period covered. Ironically, it appears that the collapse of electoral centrality in 1985 acted as a catalyst for the established parties to increase their centrality to the present high levels.

The parliamentary arena reflects the electoral arena relatively closely due to Portugal's proportional electoral formula. The data shows that 1985 again is the low point of established party centrality within the parliamentary arena, with the three established parties receiving a combined share of only 66.8 per cent of seats. Previously, the parties had received around 83 per cent, but after 1985, their parliamentary centrality increased dramatically. The major trend in the parliamentary arena is similar to that found in the electoral arena. Before 1985, Portuguese established parties demonstrated low levels of systemic centrality and the shock of 1985 actually served to increase their centrality, as over the past two decades, Portuguese established parties have maintained high levels of parliamentary centrality.

Levels of governmental centrality are similarly high. One of the most interesting features of the Portuguese data is the monopoly of government by the PS, PSD and PP/CDS. This demonstrates high levels of centrality, as the established parties have been able to maintain their monopoly on governing positions and have not allowed new parties to enter government. However, independent ministers have an important role to play in government formation in Portugal, so although only the three established parties have participated in government, independent ministers have often proved to be important governmental actors. Indeed, the second government of 1978 was made up entirely of independent ministers under the control of the president (Magone 2000: 238), but more recently, 47.1 per cent and 41.2 per cent of ministers in the governments formed in 2005 and 2009 respectively have no party affiliation. Within the governmental arena, a clear trend is for the monopoly of *party* governing positions by the three established parties, but not a monopoly on government *as a whole*.

Having considered the centrality of the established parties within the Portuguese party system, it is also important to consider whether any changes have occurred in the party system as a whole. The study has found increasing levels of centrality of established parties within the party system, with levels of centrality in all three arenas relatively high, and wider party system trends should similarly reflect established party dominance.

Party system change

The Portuguese party system, as has already been stated, has a four party format and this has been relatively consistent over the period covered. The presence of the PRD in the mid-1980s briefly changed the format to that of a five-party system, but this change was not enduring. Indeed, as Table 5.3 shows, the effective number of electoral parties declined after 1985 from an average of 4.01 between 1976 and 1985, to 3.26 between 1987 and the present. The 1985 election again proves to be an important turning point in the history of Portuguese party system, as was shown with the data concerning centrality.

The modified typology used proposes that if the format of a party system changes from an effective number of parties value of fewer than four to greater than four, then electoral change has taken place. The change in the average effective number of parties from 4.01 to 3.26 constitutes an electoral change and the decline in number of parties influences governing options available to the parties and the 'streams of interaction' (Sjöblom 1968) in which parties engage. The effective number of parties figures suggest that the Portuguese party system has consolidated since 1987; a conclusion that was also found in the study concerning the centrality of established parties. The format of the party system may have changed, but has this affected the mechanics of the party system? According to Sartori (1976), the format of a party system contains mechanical dispositions, so the mechanics of the party system should have changed too.

Table 5.3 Party system change in Portugal, 1976–2009

	Effective number of parties	
Structure of competition[b]	<4[a]	≥4
Closed	1987–present, N_v^c: 3.26, N_s^d: 2.57 (n=7)	
Semi-closed		
Semi-open		1976–85, N_v: 4.01, N_s: 3.29 (n=5)
Open		

Notes
a Although the boundary for the effective number of parties data will vary from four, for the Portuguese case, the most heuristically useful number to use to determine where electoral change has occurred is four.
b The structure of competition at each point at which a new government gains power is determined according to the amended Mair typology outlined in the previous chapter. A judgment is then made concerning when the structure of competition has changed. The judgment is based on a perception of the 'dominant' structure of competition over a period of several years. If this 'dominant' structure is replaced by another dominant structure of competition, then a change can be said to have occurred.
c Effective number of electoral parties.
d Effective number of parliamentary parties.

Table 5.3 shows whether party system change has taken place according to the modified typology developed. The table shows that the Portuguese structure of competition, as well as the format, changed after 1985 from a semi-open to a closed structure. Between 1976 and 1985, the structure of competition was characterised by partial alternation and innovation in government formation patterns but restricted access to government. The system was restricted as the PCP did not enter government in the period between 1976 and 1985, and similarly the PRD did not govern, despite receiving 17.9 per cent of the vote in the 1985 election.

Innovation was prevalent as government formation patterns were unsettled and unstructured in the early years of the post-1976 era, and parties were flexible in their choices of coalition partners (Bruneau 1984: 75). Partial alternation also dominated, as a majority of governments formed were coalitions, which naturally lend themselves to partial alternation in governing patterns.

After 1985, a major change occurred in the structure of competition within the Portuguese party system. Patterns of government formation changed considerably as familiarity, along with wholesale or no alternation in governing patterns began to dominate. Instead of coalition politics being the norm, single-party governments dominated, as the PSD and then the PS each had periods governing alone, demonstrating patterns of wholesale or non-alternation. Governing formations have become more familiar as only four parties have ever governed in Portugal and, with only around three effective parties active within the party system, parties had exhausted most possible governing options by 1987. Additionally, established parties continued to exclude the PCP from all governments, along with several other non-established parties such as the PRD and BE, further reinforcing the closed and familiar nature of governing options. Although party system change has occurred, the change served to consolidate and solidify the party system. José Magone (1999) views the destabilisation of the Portuguese party system in the mid-1980s as an important moment in the development of the party system. He argues that '[p]aradoxically, the new party system consolidated itself in the 1980s partly via the destabilisation of 1985–7' and concludes that the Portuguese party system is 'fluid, [but] ultra-stable' (1999: 254).

In conclusion, the Portuguese party system changed after 1985, yet this change served to stabilise the party system. The format of the party system changed as the number of parties within the system reduced and the structure of competition changed from semi-open to closed. Both aspects of the change should have improved the centrality of the established parties within the Portuguese party system and the data concerning centrality appears to support this hypothesis.

This section has shown that Portuguese established parties have achieved relatively high levels of centrality within the electoral, parliamentary and governmental arenas. Additionally, recent trends point towards a steady increase of centrality within the electoral and parliamentary arenas. The party system has changed only once, in the mid-1980s, and although the impact of this change was temporarily to destabilise the system, the long-term effect was to reinforce and increase the established parties' centrality and to change the structure of competition within the party system from semi-open to closed.

5.2 Germany[3]

As with the Portuguese case study, it is necessary to examine the evolution of the German party system by paying due regard to the historical context from which it emerged. Smith (1982: 60) strongly argues that it was the rupture in democracy, producing a changed political culture and new political institutions that enabled Germany to develop into a stable democracy in the post-war era. Competitive party politics in occupied Germany commenced in the late 1940s, but was short-lived in the German Democratic Republic (GDR). However, in the Federal Republic of Germany (FRG), a competitive party system began to take shape after elections to the Bundestag in 1949. The shape of the party system and the key actors soon began to develop. The CDU/CSU (Christian Democrats/ Christian Socialists) had particular success during this early period, perhaps due to the party's emergence as a new party with no links to the Weimar period. The FDP (Free Democrats) also emerged as a new nationwide party untainted by the Weimar experience. Although a much smaller party than the CDU/CSU in elect-oral terms, the FDP played a vital role in the development of the German 'two-and-a-half' party system as an important coalition ally for both centre-left and centre-right.

The SPD (Social Democrats) was the most successful party electorally in the Weimar system until 1932 when the National Socialist Party became the largest party in parliament. The early post-war years saw the SPD continue to pursue its democratic Marxist ideology (Jeffery 1999: 103) and it took several years until it embarked on an ideological change that would see the party become electable again. These three parties constitute the established parties within the West German party system. The SPD, CDU/CSU and FDP have formed the core of the German party system for most of the period considered since 1950, so must be noted as established parties. Other parties such as the Die Linke (Left Party) and especially the Greens may become significant actors over subsequent decades, but they are not established parties as they had not been major actors before the early 1970s.

Table 5.4 shows that there are three main parties under consideration as estab-lished parties: the SPD, CDU/CSU and FDP. These three parties form the basis of the analysis concerning the centrality of established parties, which is the next task for this chapter. Table 5.5 outlines the levels of centrality experienced by these parties since 1950.

Centrality of established parties

Table 5.5 shows that established parties in Germany over the entire period covered have proved themselves more dominant than their Portuguese counterparts in the electoral arena. The peak of German established parties'

Table 5.4 Established and non-established parties in Germany, 1953–2009

Established parties	Non-established parties
SPD (Social Democratic Party) (1953–present)	GB/BHE (Refugee Party) (1953–69, part of an alliance with DP in 1961)
CDU/CSU (Christian Democratic Union/Christian Social Union) (1953–present)	Die Linke (The Left) (2005–present, previously PDS, Party of Democratic Socialism 1987–2002; DKP, German Communist Party 1961–83; KPD, Communist Party of Germany 1953)
FDP (Free Democratic Party) (1953–present)	DP (German Party) (1953–61, part of an alliance with GB/BHE in 1961) The Greens (1983–present) REP (Republican Party) (1990–present) BP (Bavaria Party) (1953–present) NPD (National Democratic Party) (1961–present, previously DRP, German Reich Party 1953–61)

dominance occurred in the early 1970s, as the three parties received 99.1 per cent of the vote between them in 1972 and 1976. However, this centrality has reduced over recent decades. At the most recent election in 2009, the three parties received a combined vote share of only 71.4 per cent, the lowest value recorded. Although levels of centrality have fallen recently, over the entire period covered, levels of established party centrality within the electoral arena have been very high.

Within the parliamentary arena, the centrality of the German established parties reaches even higher levels. Between 1957 and 1983, the three established parties received 100 per cent of the seats in parliament between them. This exceptional level of centrality meant that the established parties enjoyed a complete monopoly within the parliamentary arena over a 26-year period. Since 1983, this level of centrality has fallen slightly, but remains relatively high. The governmental arena reinforces the dominance of the German established parties demonstrated in the electoral and parliamentary arenas. Between 1960 and 1998, only three parties governed in Germany, reflecting the same governing patterns found in Portugal. However, in Portugal, only three parties have governed since 1983, suggesting increasing governmental arena centrality. In Germany, the Green/SPD coalition of 1998 marked the entrance of a new actor into the governing arena. The entrance of the Greens into the governing fold suggests a potential decline in governmental centrality for the historic three established parties within the German system, the CDU/CSU, SPD and FDP.

In Germany, the established parties have enjoyed exceptionally high levels of party system centrality particularly in the 1960s and 1970s, although these levels have declined recently. A study of the German party system will show if any change has occurred and the impact that any changes have had on the established parties.

Table 5.5 Centrality of established parties in the German party system, 1953–2009

	1953	1955	1957	1960	1961	1962a	1962b
Percentage share of the vote	SPD: 28.8 CDU/CSU: 45.2 FDP: 9.5 Total: 83.7%		SPD: 31.8 CDU/CSU: 50.2 FDP: 7.7 Total: 82.0%		SPD: 36.2 CDU/CSU: 45.3 FDP: 12.8 Total: 94.3%		
Percentage share of seats	SPD: 31.8 CDU/CSU: 48.9 FDP: 10.4 Total: 91.1%		SPD: 34.9 CDU/CSU: 53.6 FDP: 8.3 Total: 96.7%		SPD: 39.0 CDU/CSU: 48.4 FDP: 12.9 Total: 100.0%		
Largest party within parliament (seats)	CDU/CSU	CDU/CSU	CDU/CSU	CDU/CSU	CDU/CSU	CDU/CSU	CDU/CSU
Time spent in government							
CDU/CSU							
FDP							
DP							
GB/BHE							
Median legislator	CDU/CSU	CDU/CSU	CDU/CSU	CDU/CSU	FDP	FDP	FDP
Percentage share of government positions	CDU/CSU: 60.9 FDP: 21.7 DP: 8.7 GB/BHE: 8.7	CDU/CSU: 68.4 FDP: 21.1 DP: 10.5	CDU/CSU: 88.9 DP: 11.1	CDU/CSU: 89.5 FDP: 10.5	CDU/CSU: 77.3 FDP: 22.7	CDU/CSU: 100.0	CDU/CSU: 77.3 FDP: 22.7
Prime minister's party	CDU/CSU	CDU/CSU	CDU/CSU	CDU/CSU	CDU/CSU	CDU/CSU	CDU/CSU
Ratio of portfolios obtained to share of seats	CDU/CSU: 1.2:1 FDP: 2.1:1 GB/BHE: 1.6:1 DP: 3.0:1	CDU/CSU: 1.2:1 FDP: 2.0:1 DP: 3.6:1	CDU/CSU: 1.4:1 DP: 3.4:1	CDU/CSU: 1.7:1 FDP: 0.8:1	CDU/CSU: 1.8:1 FDP: 1.8:1	CDU/CSU: 2.1:1 FDP: 1.8:1	CDU/CSU: 1.6:1 FDP: 1.8:1

continued overleaf

Table 5.5 continued

	1965	1966a	1966b	1969	1972	1976	1980	1982a	1982b
Percentage share of the vote	SPD: 39.3 CDU/CSU: 47.6 FDP: 9.5 Total: 96.4%			SPD: 42.7 CDU/CSU: 46.1 FDP: 5.8 Total: 94.6%	SPD: 45.8 CDU/CSU: 44.9 FDP: 8.4 Total: 99.1%	SPD: 42.6 CDU/CSU: 48.6 FDP: 7.9 Total: 99.1%	SPD: 42.9 CDU/CSU: 44.5 FDP: 10.6 Total: 98.0%		
Percentage share of seats	SPD: 41.9 CDU/CSU: 48.5 FDP: 9.7 Total: 100.0%			SPD: 45.8 CDU/CSU: 48.3 FDP: 6.0 Total: 100.0%	SPD: 46.7 CDU/CSU: 45.2 FDP: 8.1 Total: 100.0%	SPD: 43.2 CDU/CSU: 49.0 FDP: 7.7 Total: 100.0%	SPD: 43.9 CDU/CSU: 45.7 FDP: 10.4 Total: 100.0%		
Largest party within parliament (seats)	CDU/CSU	CDU/CSU	CDU/CSU	CDU/CSU	SPD	CDU/CSU	CDU/CSU	CDU/CSU	CDU/CSU
Time spent in government									
SPD									
CDU/CSU									
FDP									
Median legislator	FDP	FDP	FDP	CDU/CSU	CDU/CSU	CDU/CSU	CDU/CSU	CDU/CSU	CDU/CSU
Percentage share of government positions	CDU/CSU: 78.3 FDP: 21.7	CDU/ CSU:100	CDU/CSU: 52.3 SPD: 47.6	SPD: 70.6 FDP: 23.5 Ind: 5.9	SPD: 68.4 FDP: 31.6	SPD: 70.6 FDP: 29.4	SPD: 72.2 FDP: 27.8	SPD: 100	CDU/CSU: 72.2 FDP: 27.8
Prime minister's party	CDU/CSU	CDU/CSU	CDU/CSU	SPD	SPD	SPD	SPD	SPD	CDU/CSU
Ratio of portfolios obtained to share of seats	CDU/CSU: 1.6:1 FDP: 2.2:1	CDU/CSU: 2.1:1	CDU/CSU: 1.1:1 SDP: 1.1:1	SPD: 1.5:1 FDP: 3.9:1 Ind: N/A	SPD: 1.5:1 FDP: 3.9:1	SPD: 1.6:1 FDP: 3.8:1	SPD: 1.6:1 FDP: 2.7:1	SPD: 2.3:1	CDU/CSU: 1.6:1 FDP: 2.7:1

	1983	1987	1990	1991	1994	1998	2002	2005	2009
Percentage share of the vote	SPD: 38.2 CDU/CSU: 48.8 FDP: 7.0 Total: 94.0%	SPD: 37.0 CDU/CSU: 44.3 FDP: 9.1 Total: 90.4%	SPD: 33.5 CDU/CSU: 43.8 FDP: 11.0 Total: 88.3%		SPD: 36.4 CDU/CSU: 41.5 FDP: 6.9 Total: 84.8%	SPD: 40.9 CDU/CSU: 35.1 FDP: 6.2 Total: 82.4%	SPD: 38.5 CDU/CSU: 38.5 FDP: 7.4 Total: 84.4%	SPD: 34.2 CDU/CSU: 35.2 FDP: 9.8 Total: 79.2%	SPD: 23.0 CDU/CSU: 33.8 FDP: 14.6 Total: 71.4%
Percentage share of seats	SPD: 38.8 CDU/CSU: 49.0 FDP: 6.7 Total: 94.5%	SPD: 37.2 CDU/CSU: 45.1 FDP: 9.2 Total: 91.5%	SPD: 36.1 CDU/CSU: 48.2 FDP: 11.9 Total: 96.2%		SPD: 37.5 CDU/CSU: 43.8 FDP: 7.0 Total: 88.3%	SPD: 44.5 CDU/CSU: 36.6 FDP: 6.4 Total: 87.5%	SPD: 41.6 CDU/CSU: 41.1 FDP: 7.8 Total: 90.5%	SPD: 36.2 CDU/CSU: 36.8 FDP: 9.9 Total: 82.9%	SPD: 23.5 CDU/CSU: 38.4 FDP: 15.0 Total: 76.9%
Largest party within parliament (seats)	CDU/CSU	CDU/CSU	CDU/CSU	CDU/CSU	CDU/CSU	SPD	SPD	CDU/CSU	CDU/CSU
Time spent inside government SPD									
CDU/CSU									
FDP									
Greens									
Median legislator	CDU/CSU	CDU/CSU	CDU/CSU	CDU/CSU	CDU/CSU	SPD	SPD	SPD	CDU/CSU
Percentage share of government positions	CDU/CSU: 80.0 FDP: 20.0	CDU/CSU: 81.0 FDP: 19.0	CDU/CSU: 73.1 FDP: 23.1 DSU: 3.8	CDU/CSU: 71.4 FDP: 28.6	CDU/CSU: 78.9 FDP: 21.1	SPD: 70.6 Greens: 23.5 Inds: 5.9	SPD: 78.6 Greens: 21.4	CDU/CSU: 50.0 SPD: 50.0	CDU/CSU: 68.8 FDP: 31.2
Prime minister's party	CDU/CSU	CDU/CSU	CDU/CSU	CDU/CSU	CDU/CSU	SPD	SPD	CDU/CSU	CDU/CSU
Ratio of portfolios obtained to share of seats	CDU/CSU: 1.6:1 FDP: 3.0:1	CDU/CSU: 1.8:1 FDP: 2.1:1	CDU/CSU: 1.5:1 FDP: 1.9:1 DSU: N/A	CDU/CSU: 1.5:1 FDP: 2.4:1	CDU/CSU: 1.8:1 FDP: 3.0:1	SPD: 1.6:1 Greens: 3.4:1 Inds: N/A	SPD: 1.9:1 Greens: 2.4	CDU/CSU: 1.4:1 SPD: 1.4:1	CDU/CSU: 1.8:1 FDP: 2.1:1

Sources: German Government homepage (2010); Poguntke (2003); Saalfeld (2000); Woldendorp *et al.* (2000).

Note

The East German DSU was included in the first government following unification in 1990.

Party system change

Table 5.6 presents an amended version of the table used for the Portuguese case. The effective number of parties figure in Germany was consistently less than four throughout the period covered, so the effective number of parties boundary reduces from four to three, which should more adequately show where the format of the party system has changed. The revised table highlights three distinct periods regarding the format of the party system. At the beginning of the period covered – the 'formative' period (Roberts 1989: 101) from 1950 to 1961, when the party system of the FRG was consolidating – the average effective number of parties was 2.97. Between 1965 and 1983 the German party system was extremely stable and the average effective number of parties fell to 2.48, revealing the intuitive nature of the Laakso and Taagepera index in reflecting the 'two-and-a-half' party system. After the entrance of the Greens into parliament, the effective number of parties increased again, with the six elections held since 1987 averaging 3.44 (noted as the 'unpredictable' period by Jeffery 1999: 116). The figures clearly reflect the period of consolidation within the German party system, the stability that followed and the changes that have occurred within the system since the mid-1980s.

In terms of format, the two-party systems in Germany and Portugal bear striking similarities. The description of the German system as a 'two-and-a half' party system could equally be applied to the Portuguese case, as both systems (until the mid-1980s in Germany) are characterised by the presence of a large centre-left and centre-right party and a smaller third party. However, the changes in the format of the German party system in the 1980s were more permanent and enduring than the changes in Portugal. The entrance of the Greens in Germany marked the start of the expansion of the party system format that has continued to the present day. The effective number of parties within Germany appears to be still increasing, whereas in Portugal, the party system format appears to be becoming more restricted. However, these changes only indicate changes in format; changes in the structure of competition can show whether party system change has occurred.

Table 5.6 Party system change in Germany, 1953–2009

	Effective number of parties	
Structure of competition	<3	≥3
Closed		
Semi-closed	1965–83, N_v: 2.48, N_s: 2.37 (n=6)	1987–present, N_v: 3.44, N_s: 3.07 (n=7)
Semi-open	1953–61, N_v: 2.97, N_s: 2.57 (n=3)	
Open		

In the early 1960s, the German system changed from semi-open to semi-closed as familiar governing patterns came to dominate, alongside a reduction in partial alternation. The German party system had consolidated and the established parties dominated the party system. Their centrality gradually declined since the entrance of the Greens into parliament in the mid-1980s, with some commentators noting that the parties had become too similar (Jeffery 1999: 110) and the German electorate was seeking a change. The German party system is a 'two-bloc' party system (Jeffery 1999: 109), with the coalitions of the CDU/CSU and FDP and the SPD and Greens battling for government, although the formation of a grand coalition following the 2005 election appears to challenge this assumption. Despite the Greens' entrance into the governing fold in 1998, this did not constitute a party system change using this typology as it represented a one-off example of a semi-open system during a period where the system remained semi-closed, as Die Linke continue to be excluded from government and governing patterns remain familiar.

The levels of party system change found in Germany are lower than the change found in Portugal. In the German example, the changes that have occurred have been minor, but have pushed the party system in an interesting and challenging direction from the perspective of the established parties. The period between 1962 and 1986 was a period of almost complete dominance for the FDP, SPD and CDU/CSU, but since the change in format in the mid-1980s, the centrality of the established parties has been declining.

This section has shown that German established parties have achieved high levels of parliamentary, electoral and governmental centrality throughout the period covered, and although these levels have fallen since the early 1980s, overall levels of centrality remain high. Limited party system change has taken place, but recent changes have threatened the centrality of the established parties. Having drawn these conclusions from the study carried out into the fate of German established parties, this chapter now moves on to examine the overall impact of the high use of electorate-orientated strategies on the fate of established parties in Portugal and Germany.

5.3 The frequent use of electorate-orientated strategies and established parties' centrality

Chapter 2 showed that established Portuguese and German parties engaged in particularly high levels of electorate-orientated strategies, partaking in high levels of ideological change and electoral responsiveness, and that pre-electoral agreements are a feature of a large percentage of coalition governments[4] with the agreements proving to be amongst the longest in western Europe. German established parties have also demonstrated a relatively inclusive attitude towards non-established parties.

However, the study of centrality and party system change has revealed that the established parties within Portugal and Germany have experienced somewhat different fates. In Portugal, the established parties had achieved moderate levels of centrality, but these levels have been increasing since the early 1980s. In contrast, in Germany, the established parties enjoyed exceptionally high levels of centrality throughout the 1960s and 1970s, yet their centrality began to decline in the early 1980s. Party system change has occurred in Portugal in the mid-1980s, yet this change only reinforced the centrality of the Portuguese established parties. The German party system has remained relatively stable, with only minor system changes occurring, but the most recent change in format in the mid-1980s instigated a steady decline in the centrality of the established parties. How can these contrasting findings be explained? According to a Downsian interpretation of party competition, parties should be more successful if they engage in high levels of electorate-orientated strategies and respond to the needs of the voters. If established parties engage in high levels of the electorate-orientated strategies addressed previously, then parties should experience high and consistent levels of centrality within their party systems.

In Portugal, established parties initially achieved relatively low levels of centrality despite scoring exceptionally highly in terms of the use of electorate-orientated strategies. Portugal's short democratic history in the post-war era can explain this apparent paradox. Given the historical context in which the party system operates, in the early years of democracy, a multitude of parties would be present and no clear, stable pattern of competition would emerge. Pridham and Lewis (1996: 1) note that 'new democracies ... [are] vulnerable to collapse, or at least involve a lengthy and complicated period of transition with uncertain prospects for their consolidation'. It is perhaps understandable that it has only been in recent years that Portugal's party system has exhibited an increasing trend towards high levels of centrality. The parties comprising the new party system were very new themselves; only the PS and PCP existed during the Salazar era. The new parties lacked any strong social roots, strong party organisations and mass membership (Magone 1999: 252) and were more vulnerable to an electorate that was essentially unstable (Mair 1993b).

The high levels of centrality demonstrated in the governmental arena, coupled with the increasing levels of centrality within the electoral and parliamentary arenas, are evidence of party system consolidation, centring on the three established parties. Although levels of centrality within Portugal have only been moderate for much of the period considered (especially when compared to the German example), the stable and consolidated nature of the party system is a testament to the three established parties. The increasing systemic centrality of the established parties runs concurrently with the stabilisation and consolidation of the Portuguese party system and the strategies pursued by the established parties strongly influenced this process. Thomas Bruneau (1997: 1) argues that 'in no other country ... have political parties played anywhere near as important a role in the democratization [process] as in Portugal', highlighting the crucial role that the parties have played in the reinvigoration and consolidation of democracy within Portugal.

The electorate-orientated strategies that these parties engaged in appear to have influenced the rapid consolidation of the party system. An open, engaged and responsive attitude towards the electorate appears to have secured the position of the three established parties at the centre of the party system as shown by the continuing rise in levels of centrality. The rupture in Portugal's democratic history may be an important factor explaining the low levels of centrality found within the early years of the post-Salazar regime, but the actions of the political parties themselves constitute a vital explanatory factor when considering the steady rise of centrality of the established parties within the party system. Causality is an important issue when considering the impact of established parties on systemic centrality. The strategies employed by established parties influence their centrality within the party system, but it may equally be true that the centrality of the established parties provides a greater or lesser degree of 'manoeuvrability' within the party system. This allows for the engagement in certain strategies, and section 5.7 examines this alternative direction of causality in more detail.

Although the established parties in Germany and Portugal have engaged in very similar strategies, the impact on the fate of these parties has been somewhat different. The exceptionally high levels of centrality experienced by the established parties within Germany appears to support the hypothesis that a relationship exists between high levels of electorate-orientated strategies and high levels of centrality. The established parties within Germany are responsive and open towards the electorate and have obtained high levels of systemic centrality. Indeed, Germany is a model of a 'catch-all' party system, with Smith concluding that the SPD and CDU/CSU are 'Volksparteien' (Smith 1976). The CDU/CSU achieved a broad electoral base and embarked on a 'de-ideologisation' of party ideology in the early years of the FRG's existence. In keeping with the catch-all thesis, the SPD reacted to these changes within the CDU/CSU and following the Godesberg programme in 1959, pushing the party in a catch-all direction.

Germany is very much a 'party state' where the state awards a sizeable role to the parties in the functioning of democracy. The high levels of centrality achieved within the German party system may be a result of the important position in which political parties find themselves within the German party system, as all parties, not just established parties are important actors within the German 'party state'.

Thus, a link appears to exist between strategies employed by the established parties within Germany and their exceptional levels of centrality until the 1980s. It appears plausible to conclude that the strategies employed by the German established parties have enabled them to monopolise the electoral, parliamentary and governmental arenas until the 1980s. Perhaps assisted by their open and responsive relationship with the electorate, they increased their levels of systemic centrality and came to dominate the German party system.

However, assuming the established parties continued to engage in the same strategies (as the data presented in Chapter 2 suggests), how can the declining centrality of the established German parties over recent decades be explained? Various factors such as the problems caused by unification (Jeffery 1999: 97), popular disillusion with the party system as a whole (Jeffery 1999: 109), declining party membership (Scarrow 2002: 77) and the emergence of a 'new politics' dimension (Chandler 1988: 66) have been proposed to explain this decline.

The decline in centrality of the German established parties may ironically have been a product of the exceptionally high levels of centrality achieved throughout the 1960s and 1970s. Scarrow (2004) argues that the CDU/CSU and SPD held considerable information about voters' preferences and were able to steer their parties in classic Downsian strategies. Yet, having captured the ideological centre ground, both parties moved to mobilise the weakly aligned and have instead alienated their existing voters (Scarrow 2004: 104–6), suggesting that the use of electorate-orientated strategies has backfired for the established parties in Germany. This view put forward by Scarrow raises the possibility of perverse effects. Much of the literature concerning German politics highlights the concept of *Parteieinverdrossenheit*, 'tiredness' of the dominance of parties. This concept may help to explain why the centrality of established parties appears to be declining. Scarrow argues that there is now a growing gap between popular regard for parties and parties' ability to dominate public resources and political agendas (2002: 101).

Yet, the decline in centrality should not be exaggerated, as the established parties still receive around 80 per cent of votes and seats within the German parliament and have maintained relatively high levels of centrality despite a recent fall in support. Saalfeld (2002) argues that despite considerable political and socio-economic change, the established parties have proved adaptable and have maintained their positions. Although there has been significant change regarding the parameters of electoral competition and party organisation, change at the governmental level has been modest and the established parties have continued to produce stable and ideologically moderate governments (Saalfeld 2002: 125). Smith (1993) echoes these sentiments and argues that unification was a telling testament to the integrative capacities of the core parties and, by implication, to the enduring stability of a party system robust enough to accommodate even the upheavals of unification.

The strategies employed by the established parties within Germany and in Portugal may have had a significant impact on their centrality within the party system. Although neither country completely supports the hypothesis that there is a link between the high level of the use of electorate-orientated strategies and high levels of systemic centrality for the established parties, some interesting conclusions have been drawn. The importance of a country's history is important in both the Portuguese and German cases, and the possibility of perverse effects may be a significant issue. This section did not attempt to prove causality and the end of the chapter addresses the issue of the direction of causality in greater depth. Having considered the impact of high levels of electorate-orientated strategies on the fate of established parties, this chapter now turns to the assessment of the impact of low levels of electorate-orientated strategies. Established parties in Switzerland and Luxembourg have engaged in strategies that are unresponsive and relatively closed towards the electorate, so these parties should achieve only low levels of systemic centrality.

5.4 Switzerland

In Switzerland, two aspects of the institutional architecture exercise a major influence on the behaviour of political parties. The first is the nature of the Swiss federal system. Cantonal politics takes on a great importance within Swiss politics with Ladner (2001: 124) noting that '[t]he Swiss party system has ... to be regarded as one composed of 26 different party systems'. The importance of regionalism within Switzerland has hampered the creation of powerful national parties and has led to much stronger cantonal parties (Ladner 2001: 124). The second important feature of the Swiss political structure is the role played by direct democratic institutions. The people can challenge any parliamentary decision in a votation open to all citizens and popular initiatives allow the people to submit a proposition for constitutional change if 100,000 signatures are received (Linder 2000: 99). These two direct democratic avenues restrict political parties in their governing autonomy and strongly influence the composition of government. Swiss parties are considered to be weak (Ladner 2001: 132), and a weak party system (Lane 2001: 12) emerges because of the strategic reaction of the political parties to the institutional set-up: the presence of a permanent, oversized coalition of all four established parties.

Determining the established and non-established members of the Swiss party system appears to be relatively simple, as government in Switzerland is organised according to the 'magic formula'. This formula is an informal agreement between the four major parties to govern together and represents the distribution of Federal Council seats approximately in proportion to votes received.[5] The four parties featuring in the 'magic formula' are the CVP (Christian Democrats), the FDP (Free Thinking Democrats), the SPS (Social Democrats) and the SVP (Swiss People's Party). It appears that the governing parties should be established parties and all other parties classified as non-established. However, the issue is somewhat more complicated than it may first appear.

The SVP has traditionally been the junior member of the governing coalition, receiving only one seat in the Federal Council compared to the two seats received by the other three parties. Yet, the party has changed considerably and is now the largest of the four governing parties. The roots of the transformation in fortunes and substance of the party emerged from Christoph Blocher, who sought to represent the feelings of resentment within farmers and merchants, the SVP's traditional supporters (Ladner 2001: 130). Church (2000) notes that by 1995, Blocher had laid the foundations for a successful populist movement, and his wing of the party began to campaign for the protection of Swiss identity from new social pressures and campaigned against 'an incompetent, spendthrift and untrustworthy establishment' (2000: 217). The SVP effectively turned itself into an anti-political establishment party operating from within the establishment. Certainly, if the party were not a permanent feature of government, it would be an anti-political establishment party and a party that established parties would probably not consider a possible coalition partner. Therefore, in Switzerland, the curious situation emerges whereby the major anti-political establishment party within Switzerland has emerged from *within* the Federal Council itself and not from within the wider party system, highlighting the weakness of the party system and its inability to provide adequate opposition to the governing parties.

However, despite these recent ideological changes, the SVP is still an established party, as it was an established actor by the early 1970s. Table 5.7 presents the classification of established and non-established parties. The remainder of this section focuses on the centrality of the SVP, CVP, FDP and SPS within the Swiss party system and assesses the impact of any party system change on these four parties. Table 5.8 presents the centrality of the established parties within the Swiss party system.

Centrality of established parties

Within the electoral arena, Swiss established parties have generally experienced low levels of centrality, although levels of centrality appear to have declined since the late 1960s, but increased again since the mid-1990s. In 1991, the established four parties received a combined vote share of only 69.7 per cent, but at the three subsequent elections, the share of the vote received increased on each occasion, before falling back slightly in 2007. Ironically, this recent increase in the share of the vote for the established parties occurred because of the huge gains made by the SVP, employing strategies akin to those of an anti-political

Table 5.7 Established and non-established parties in Switzerland, 1951–2007

Established parties	*Non-established parties*
CVP/PDC (Christian Democratic People's Party) (1951–present)	FPS/APS (Freedom Party of Switzerland) (1987–2003)
FDP/PRD (Freethinking Democratic Party) (1951–present)	POCH (Progressive Organization Switzerland) (1971–91)
SVP/UDC (Swiss People's Party) (1951–present)	SD (Swiss Democrats) (includes Republican movement 1967–69) (1967–present)
SPS/PSS (Social Democratic Party of Switzerland) (1951–present)	GPS/PES (Green Party of Switzerland) (1975–present)
	EDU (Federal Democratic Union) (1975–present)
	LdU/AdI (Alliance of Independents) (1951–99)
	PdA/PdT (Labour Party of Switzerland) (1951–present)
	LdT (League of Ticinesians) (1991–present)
	S (Solidarités) (1999–present)
	LPS/PLS (Liberal Party of Switzerland) (1951–2009)
	EVP/PEP (Evangelical People's Party) (1951–present)
	GLP (Green Liberal Party Switzerland) (2007–present)
	CSP (Christian Social Party) (1997–present)

Table 5.8 Centrality of established parties in the Swiss party system, 1951–2007

	1951	1953	1955	1959	1963	1967	1971	1975
Percentage share of the vote	SPS: 26.0 FDP: 24.0 CVP: 22.5 SVP: 12.6 Total: 85.1%		SPS: 27.0 FDP: 23.3 CVP: 23.2 SVP: 12.1 Total: 85.6%	SPS: 26.4 FDP: 23.7 CVP: 23.3 SVP: 11.6 Total: 85.0%	SPS: 26.6 FDP: 24.0 CVP: 23.4 SVP: 11.4 Total: 85.4%	SPS: 23.5 FDP: 23.2 CVP: 22.1 SVP: 11.0 Total: 79.8%	SPS: 22.9 FDP: 21.7 CVP: 20.5 SVP: 11.1 Total: 76.2%	SPS: 24.6 FDP: 22.2 CVP: 20.6 SVP: 9.9 Total: 77.3%
Percentage share of seats	SPS: 25.3 FDP: 26.3 CVP: 24.7 SVP: 11.9 Total: 88.2%		SPS: 27.0 FDP: 25.5 CVP: 24.0 SVP: 11.2 Total: 87.7%	SPS: 26.0 FDP: 26.0 CVP: 24.5 SVP: 11.7 Total: 88.2%	SPS: 26.5 FDP: 25.5 CVP: 24.0 SVP: 11.0 Total: 87.0%	SPS: 25.5 FDP: 24.5 CVP: 22.5 SVP: 10.5 Total: 83.0%	SPS: 23.0 FDP: 24.5 CVP: 22.0 SVP: 11.5 Total: 81.0%	SPS: 27.5 FDP: 23.5 CVP: 23.0 SVP: 10.5 Total: 84.5%
Largest party within parliament (seats)	FDP	FDP	FDP	SPS and FDP	FDP	SPS	FDP	SPS
Time spent inside government								
SPS								
FDP								
CVP								
SVP								
Median legislator	CVP	CVP	CVP	CVP	CVP	CVP	CVP	CVP
Percentage share of government (Federal Council) positions	SPS: 14.3 FDP: 42.9 CVP: 28.6 SVP: 14.3	SPS: 14.3 FDP: 42.9 CVP: 28.6 SVP: 14.3	FDP: 42.9 CVP: 42.9 SVP: 14.3	SPS: 28.6 FDP: 28.6 CVP: 28.6 SVP: 14.3	SPS: 28.6 FDP: 28.6 CVP: 28.6 SVP: 14.3	SPS: 28.6 FDP: 28.6 CVP: 28.6 SVP: 14.3	SPS: 28.6 FDP: 28.6 CVP: 28.6 SVP: 14.3	SPS: 28.6 FDP: 28.6 CVP: 28.6 SVP: 14.3
Prime minister's party	FDP	FDP	SVP	FDP	CVP	SPS	FDP	SVP
Ratio of portfolios obtained to share of seats	SPS: 0.6:1 FDP: 1.6:1 CVP: 1.2:1 SVP: 1.2:1	SPS: 0.6:1 FDP: 1.6:1 CVP: 1.2:1 SVP: 1.2:1	FDP: 1.7:1 CVP: 1.8:1 SVP: 1.3:1	SPS: 1.1:1 FDP: 1.1:1 CVP: 1.2:1 SVP: 1.2:1	SPS: 1.1:1 FDP: 1.1:1 CVP: 1.2:1 SVP: 1.3:1	SPS: 1.1:1 FDP: 1.2:1 CVP: 1.3:1 SVP: 1.4:1	SPS: 1.2:1 FDP: 1.2:1 CVP: 1.3:1 SVP: 1.2:1	SPS: 1.0:1 FDP: 1.2:1 CVP: 1.2:1 SVP: 1.4:1

continued overleaf

Table 5.8 continued

	1979	1983	1987	1991	1995	1999	2003	2007
Percentage share of the vote	SPS: 24.4 FDP: 24.1 CVP: 21.5 SVP: 11.6 Total: 81.6%	SPS: 22.8 FDP: 23.3 CVP: 20.2 SVP: 11.1 Total: 77.4%	SPS: 18.4 FDP: 22.9 CVP: 19.7 SVP: 11.0 Total: 72.0%	SPS: 18.5 FDP: 21.0 CVP: 18.3 SVP: 11.9 Total: 69.7%	SPS: 21.8 FDP: 20.2 CVP: 16.8 SVP: 14.9 Total: 73.7%	SPS: 22.5 FDP: 19.9 CVP: 15.8 SVP: 22.5 Total: 80.7%	SPS: 23.3 FDP: 17.3 CVP: 14.4 SVP: 26.6 Total: 81.6%	SPS: 19.5 FDP: 15.6 CVP: 14.6 SVP: 29.0 Total: 78.7%
Percentage share of seats	SPS: 25.5 FDP: 25.5 CVP: 22.0 SVP: 11.5 Total: 84.5%	SPS: 23.5 FDP: 27.0 CVP: 21.0 SVP: 11.5 Total: 83.0%	SPS: 21.0 FDP: 25.5 CVP: 21.0 SVP: 12.5 Total: 80.0%	SPS: 21.5 FDP: 22.0 CVP: 18.0 SVP: 12.5 Total: 74.0%	SPS: 27.0 FDP: 22.5 CVP: 17.0 SVP: 14.5 Total: 81.0%	SPS: 25.5 FDP: 21.5 CVP: 17.5 SVP: 22.0 Total: 86.5%	SPS: 26.0 FDP: 18.0 CVP: 14.0 SVP: 27.5 Total: 85.5%	SPS: 21.5 FDP: 15.5 CVP: 15.5 SVP: 31.0 Total: 83.5%
Largest party within parliament (seats)	SPS and FDP	FDP	FDP	FDP	SPS	SPS	SVP	SVP
Time spent inside government SPS FDP CVP								

SVP								
Median legislator								
CVP	CVP	CVP	CVP	CVP	CVP	CVP	FDP	FDP
Percentage share of government (Federal Council) positions								
SPS: 28.6 FDP: 28.6 CVP: 28.6 SVP: 14.3	SPS: 28.6 FDP: 28.6 CVP: 28.6 SVP: 14.3	SPS: 28.6 FDP: 28.6 CVP: 28.6 SVP: 14.3	SPS: 28.6 FDP: 28.6 CVP: 28.6 SVP: 14.3	SPS: 28.6 FDP: 28.6 CVP: 28.6 SVP: 14.3	SPS: 28.6 FDP: 28.6 CVP: 28.6 SVP: 14.3	SPS: 28.6 FDP: 28.6 CVP: 14.3 SVP: 28.6	SPS: 28.6 FDP: 28.6 CVP: 14.3 SVP: 28.6	SPS: 28.6
FDP: 28.6 CVP: 14.3 SVP: 28.6								
Prime minister's party								
FDP	SVP	SPS	SPS	FDP	SVP	CVP	CVP	FDP
Ratio of portfolios obtained to share of seats								
SPS: 1.1:1 FDP: 1.1:1 CVP: 1.3:1 SVP: 1.2:1	SPS: 1.2:1 FDP: 1.1:1 CVP: 1.4:1 SVP: 1.2:1	SPS: 1.4:1 FDP: 1.1:1 CVP: 1.4:1 SVP: 1.1:1	SPS: 1.3:1 FDP: 1.3:1 CVP: 1.6:1 SVP: 1.1:1	SPS: 1.1:1 FDP: 1.3:1 CVP: 1.7:1 SVP: 1.0:1	SPS:1.1:1 FDP: 1.3:1 CVP: 1.6:1 SVP: 0.7:1	SPS: 1.1:1 FDP: 1.6:1 CVP: 1.0:1 SVP: 1.0:1		SPS: 1.3:1
FDP: 1.8:1 CVP: 0.9:1 SVP: 1.1:1								

Sources: Church (2004); Hardmeier (2004); Swiss Federal Statistics Office (2010); Woldendorp et al. (2000).

establishment party. In 1991, the SPS, FDP and CVP received 57.8 per cent of the vote, whereas in 2007, the combined share of the vote was just 49.7 per cent, indicating that although levels of electoral centrality for the four established parties have increased, this appears to be largely due to the increase in support for the SVP. The parliamentary arena data reinforces the findings within the electoral arena. Swiss established parties have achieved relatively low levels of centrality, but this centrality has been consistent over time. Due to the somewhat distorting impact of the electoral system favouring the larger parties through the system of *apparentement*, the decline in centrality in the electoral arena is less than in the parliamentary arena.

It is in the governmental arena that the established parties' centrality is most obvious. Since 1959, all governments have contained only the four established parties, governing together according to the 'magic formula', which was altered in 2003 to allow the SVP a second seat on the Federal Council at the expense of the CVP. The data relating to the ratio of positions obtained to share of seats emphasises why this change occurred. For much of the period covered, all parties received Federal Council seats approximately proportional to the number of parliamentary seats held. However, in 1999, the CVP ratio was 1.6:1, compared to 0.7:1 for the SVP. This inequality led to calls from the SVP for an extra Federal Council seat, with the change in the distribution of seats occurring in 2003. In 2003, the ratios were 1:1 for both the CVP and SVP, suggesting that proportionality had returned to the Swiss 'magic formula'. Overall, the data suggests that the Swiss established parties are dominant within the governmental arena because of the *Konkordanz* (Lehmbruch) or 'amicable agreement' (Steiner) (Lane 2001: 1).

Party system change

This chapter now moves on to an assessment of whether any changes have occurred in the party system. Table 5.9 presents a modified version of the typology of party system change outlined in the previous chapter. Whereas the German table took into account the particularly small number of parties within the party system, the Swiss case is characterised by a large number of parties. The effective number of parties boundary is set at six for the Swiss party system to assess if the format of the party system has changed.

There are three clear periods concerning the development of the format of the party system. The first, from 1951 to 1979, shows the average effective number of parties was 5.38. This increased between 1983 and 1995 to 6.79, perhaps indicating declining levels of centrality for the established parties as the party system began to fragment. However, this trend reversed in 1999 as the party system consolidated again, with the effective number of parties value returning to less than six. Yet, earlier in this section it was shown that although the party system consolidated and this should be beneficial for the established parties as it reconcentrated support in the hands of the four established parties, it could be argued that the party system consolidated principally because of the populist appeal of the SVP.

Table 5.9 Party system change in Switzerland, 1951–2007

	Effective number of parties	
Structure of competition	<6	≥6
Closed	1951–79, N_v: 5.38, N_s: 4.95 (n=8) 1999–2007, N_v: 5.65, N_s: 5.36 (n=2)	1983–95, N_v: 6.79, N_s: 5.77 (n=4)
Semi-closed		
Semi-open		
Open		

The average effective number of parties value of about six indicates the presence of multipartism and suggests the presence of either polarised or moderate pluralist mechanics operating within the system. However, although a Sartorian interpretation (1976) of the format of the party system suggests competitive, pluralist politics and crucially, alternation in government and the availability of alternative coalitions, the reality of the structure of competition proves to be somewhat different.

Table 5.9 shows that the structure of competition in Switzerland has not changed over the period covered. Swiss politics is characterised by non-alternation in governing formations, restricted access to government and familiar governing formulae since 1950. The only slight break from the closed nature of the party system occurred in the 1950s, when the SPS did not feature in government in 1953 or 1955. However, this is the only point at which the Swiss party system is not closed to all parties save the four established members that participate in the Federal Council. As the structure of competition remains the same, no party system change has taken place. The effective number of parties has fluctuated slightly over time, but this has not provoked any change in the structure of competition.

Switzerland stands out in western Europe as a country dominated by direct democracy where political parties and the party system are weak. Levels of centrality achieved by the established parties are relatively low in the parliamentary and electoral arenas, but complete in the governmental arena. Party system change has not occurred within Switzerland, as the party system has remained closed throughout the period covered. The overriding impression this data provides concerning the Swiss party system is one of stability only threatened within the past decade by the rise of the SVP, itself an established party. The use of electorate-orientated strategies has been exceptionally low and the data shows moderate levels of electoral and parliamentary arena centrality, but exceptional levels of governmental centrality. A comparative investigation into the centrality of established parties within Luxembourg should provide a useful insight into the impact of the low use of electorate-orientated strategies by established parties.

5.5 Luxembourg

Discussions concerning the party system and political parties of Luxembourg reflect on the context of the country's size and its position as a 'small democracy'. As one of the smallest nations in western Europe and the smallest country in this study, comparative European analysts often overlook Luxembourg. Dumont and De Winter lament that 'although often neglected, Luxembourg offers one of the best possible introductions to the world of coalition politics' (2000: 431) and to the world of party interactions and the operation of party systems.

The Socialists, Liberals and Catholics all became structured parties between 1902 and 1914 (Dumont and De Winter 2003: 477), with the Communist party founded in 1921 following a split from the Socialists (ibid.: 400). The modern-day incarnations of these historic parties are respectively the LSAP (Social Democrats), the DP (Democratic Party) and the CSV (Christian Social Party), with the KPL (Communists) historically the major non-established party to be found within the Luxembourg party system. The LSAP, DP and CSV are the established parties within the Luxembourg party system as they are the only three parties that have participated in government since 1950 and the established parties rejected the KPL as a coalition partner. Ian Budge *et al.* (1987: 256) describe the KPL as the 'most obscurantist in Western Europe' and 'a largely unreconstructed pro-Soviet party with very deep roots in the working class' and the party has shown few signs of willing to modernise in the same way as the former Communist parties in Italy and Germany.

Table 5.10 presents the full list of parties classified as established and non-established. The remainder of this section focuses on the centrality of the CSV, LSAP and DP within the Luxembourgish party system and assesses the impact of any party system change on these three parties. Table 5.11 presents the centrality data for the established parties within the Luxembourgish party system.

Centrality of established parties

The centrality of Luxembourgish parties within the electoral arena shows a relatively consistent pattern of decline since the early 1960s. The period between 1951

Table 5.10 Established and non-established parties in Luxembourg, 1951–2009

Established parties	Non-established parties
CSV (Christian Social People's Party) (1951–present)	GRÉNG (The Greens) (1984–present)
LSAP (Luxembourg Socialist Workers' Party) (1951–present)	ADR (Alternative Democratic Reform Party) (1989–present)
DP (Democratic Party) (1951–present)	LÉNK (The Left) (1994–present)
	KPL (Communist Party of Luxembourg) (1951–89)
	SDP (Social Democratic Party) (1974–9)

and 1959 demonstrates relatively high levels of electoral centrality for the established parties, with the peak of centrality occurring in 1959, when the three established parties received 90.3 per cent of the vote. However, since the 1960s, this centrality has declined to relatively low levels and since the mid-1980s, the three parties' share of the vote has fallen to around 75 per cent. The share of the vote has declined to approximately the same levels experienced by their Swiss counterparts, so in Luxembourg and Switzerland, established parties have achieved relatively low levels of centrality within the electoral arena. However, in Switzerland, recent trends suggest established party centrality may be rising, whereas in Luxembourg, the established parties have yet to reverse the trend in declining centrality.

The level of centrality within the parliamentary arena is slightly higher than the level found in the electoral arena due to the inbuilt tendency within most electoral systems to favour the large parties. However, the trend towards decline in centrality noted within the electoral arena is also present within the parliamentary arena, although the decline is less pronounced. Peak centrality occurs in the 1950s, with the established parties receiving 94.2 per cent of parliamentary seats in 1954 and 1959, compared to just 78.4 per cent achieved in 1999. The evidence suggests that the non-established parties are slowly eroding the centrality of the Luxembourgish established parties within the parliamentary arena as well as the electoral arena.

The governmental arena shows complete dominance for the three established parties, as these three parties are the only parties that have governed. The three established parties within Luxembourg have successfully formed governments throughout the period covered without recourse to the inclusion of non-established parties in coalitions, suggesting high levels of centrality. Overall, established parties within Luxembourg have demonstrated exceptionally high levels of governmental centrality, but only moderate levels of electoral and parliamentary centrality. This contrast between moderate levels of parliamentary and electoral centrality and high levels of governmental centrality reflects the findings produced by the Swiss case study. However, an important difference relates to recent trends. Trends in Luxembourg indicate a decline in established party centrality, whereas recent trends within Switzerland suggest rising levels of established party centrality. Government formation patterns differ in Luxembourg from those found within Switzerland, but high levels of governmental centrality occur in both countries. Although not all established parties govern together as is the case in Switzerland, in Luxembourg two out of the three established parties are permanent fixtures within government, generally with the CSV as the senior partner.

Party system change

For much of the period considered until the mid-1980s, the Luxembourgish party system was characterised by a four-party format, featuring the three established parties and the Communists. However, the entrance of the Greens into the electoral arena in 1984 and the ADR in 1989 has expanded the format somewhat and allied to the electoral decline of the KPL, Luxembourg now has a five-party format, although only three parties are governing parties. The effective number

Table 5.11 Centrality of established parties in the Luxembourgish party system, 1951–2009

	1951	1954	1959	1964	1969	1974
Percentage share of the vote	CSV: 33.3 LSAP: 41.4 DP: 8.4 Total: 83.1%	CSV: 42.4 LSAP: 35.1 DP: 10.8 Total: 88.3%	CSV: 36.9 LSAP: 34.9 DP: 18.5 Total: 90.3%	CSV: 33.3 LSAP: 37.7 DP: 10.6 Total: 81.6%	CSV: 35.3 LSAP: 32.3 DP: 16.6 Total: 84.2%	CSV: 27.6 LSAP: 29.2 DP: 22.2 Total: 79.0%
Percentage share of seats	CSV: 40.4 LSAP: 36.5 DP: 15.4 Total: 92.3%	CSV: 50.0 LSAP: 32.7 DP: 11.5 Total: 94.2%	CSV: 40.4 LSAP: 32.7 DP: 21.1 Total: 94.2%	CSV: 39.3 LSAP: 37.5 DP: 10.7 Total: 87.5%	CSV: 37.5 LSAP: 32.1 DP: 19.6 Total: 89.2%	CSV: 30.5 LSAP: 28.8 DP: 23.7 Total: 83.0%
Largest party within parliament (seats)	CSV	CSV	CSV	CSV	CSV	CSV
Time spent inside government						
CSV						
LSAP						
DP						
Median legislator	CSV	CSV	CSV	CSV	CSV	CSV
Percentage share of government positions	CSV: 60.0 LSAP: 40.0	CSV: 53.3 LSAP: 46.7	CSV: 57.1 LSAP: 42.9	CSV: 50.0 LSAP: 50.0	CSV: 42.9 DP: 57.1	LSAP: 46.7 DP: 53.3
Prime minister's party	CSV	CSV	CSV	CSV	CSV	DP
Ratio of portfolios obtained to share of seats	CSV: 1.5:1 LSAP: 1.1:1	CSV: 1.1:1 LSAP: 1.4:1	CSV: 1.4:1 LSAP: 1.3:1	CSV: 1.3:1 LSAP: 1.3:1	CSV: 1.1:1 DP: 2.9:1	LSAP: 1.6:1 DP: 2.2:1

	1979	1984	1989	1994	1999	2004	2009
Percentage share of the vote	CSV: 34.5 LSAP: 24.3 DP: 21.3 Total: 80.1%	CSV: 34.9 LSAP: 33.6 DP: 18.7 Total: 87.2%	CSV: 31.7 LSAP: 27.2 DP: 16.2 Total: 75.1%	CSV: 30.3 LSAP: 25.4 DP: 19.3 Total: 75.0%	CSV: 30.4 LSAP: 22.6 DP: 24.0 Total: 77.0%	CSV: 36.1 LSAP: 23.4 DP: 16.1 Total: 75.6%	CSV: 38.0 LSAP: 21.6 DP: 15.0 Total: 74.6%
Percentage share of seats	CSV: 40.7 LSAP: 23.7 DP: 25.4 Total: 89.8%	CSV: 39.1 LSAP: 32.8 DP: 21.9 Total: 93.8%	CSV: 36.7 LSAP: 30.0 DP: 18.3 Total: 85.0%	CSV: 35.0 LSAP: 28.3 DP: 20.0 Total: 83.3%	CSV: 31.7 LSAP: 21.7 DP: 25.0 Total: 78.4%	CSV: 40.0 LSAP: 23.3 DP: 16.7 Total: 80.0%	CSV: 43.4 LSAP: 21.7 DP: 15.0 Total: 80.1%
Largest party within parliament (seats)	CSV	CSV	CSV	CSV	CSV	CSV	CSV
Time spent inside government							
CSV							
LSAP							
DP							
Median legislator	CSV	CSV	CSV	CSV	CSV	CSV	CSV
Percentage share of government positions	CSV: 42.9 DP: 57.1	CSV: 57.9 LSAP: 42.1	CSV: 45.0 LSAP: 55.0	CSV: 52.4 LSAP: 47.6	CSV: 50.0 LSAP: 50.0	CSV: 60.0 LSAP: 40.0	CSV: 60.0 LSAP: 40.0
Prime minister's party	CSV	CSV	CSV	CSV	CSV	CSV	CSV
Ratio of portfolios obtained to share of seats	CSV: 1.5:1 DP: 2.2:1	CSV: 1.5:1 LSAP: 1.3:1	CSV: 1.2:1 LSAP: 1.8:1	CSV: 1.5:1 LSAP: 1.7:1	CSV: 1.6:1 LSAP: 2.3:1	CSV: 1.5:1 LSAP: 1.7:1	CSV: 1.4:1 LSAP: 1.8:1

Sources: Dumont and De Winter (2000); Luxembourg Government Homepage (2010); Woldendorp *et al.* (2000).

of parties figures produced for Luxembourg reflects this interpretation. Table 5.12 shows a steady rise in the effective number of parties from an average of 3.13 in the period between 1951 and 1954, to 4.29 between 1984 and the present day. The Luxembourgish party system has a more limited format than the Swiss, but recent trends suggest the Swiss format may be becoming more restricted whereas the Luxembourgish party system is expanding. This finding perhaps suggests declining centrality for the Luxembourgish established parties compared to increasing centrality for their Swiss counterparts.

The format of the Luxembourgish party system has gradually expanded over the period covered, but has this influenced the structure of competition within the party system? A Sartorian interpretation would suggest that an expanded format should alter the mechanics of the party system, leading to the greater presence of coalition alternatives and a more open system of governmental competition due to a rise in the number of 'streams of interaction' (Sjöblom 1968). However, the reverse appears to be true.

Table 5.12 depicts a structure of competition that has become more closed over the period covered. The Luxembourgish party system in the early post-war period was relatively open, and innovative governing patterns dominated until the mid-1950s. However, familiarity soon replaced innovative governing patterns as governing combinations became exhausted and the established parties permanently excluded the KPL from government. The system was not completely closed, as partial alternation dominated as generally, the CSV governed with either the LSAP or DP, a pattern that continues to the present day. The Greens and ADR are now the parties excluded from government, producing a restricted structure of party competition. Although the effective number of parties operating within the system has steadily increased over the period covered, the structure of competition has not changed since 1959. The Luxembourgish and Swiss party systems are both exceptionally stable, with neither party system experiencing any significant changes over the past 50 years.

In common with the Swiss example, participation in government is limited to a select few parties in terms of the structure of competition. However, the Luxembourgish party system is characterised by alternation in government, as opposed to

Table 5.12 Party system change in Luxembourg, 1951–2009

	Effective number of parties	
Structure of competition	<4	≥4
Closed		
Semi-closed	1959–79, N_v: 3.83, N_s: 3.45 (n=5)	1984–present, N_v: 4.29, N_s: 3.78 (n=6)
Semi-open	1951–54, N_v: 3.13, N_s: 2.88 (n=2)	
Open		

the lack of alternation found within the Swiss party system. Yet, the monopoly of the established parties over government is complete in both countries, with no party outside the group of established parties participating in government throughout the period covered. This governing monopoly explains to a large extent why the two party systems have remained so stable; however, the established parties within Luxembourg may find maintaining this governmental monopoly more problematic that their Swiss counterparts due to the increasing number of parties within the Luxembourgish party system. The next section explores further explanations for the similarities and differences found between the two party systems.

This section has shown that the established parties within Luxembourg have achieved only moderate levels of centrality within the electoral and parliamentary arenas, with centrality declining over recent years. This contrasts with levels of centrality within the governmental arena that have been consistently high over the period covered. The format of the Luxembourgish party system has expanded, but this expansion has resulted in a move towards a more closed structure of competition within the party system. The party system has changed very little and stability dominates within the Luxembourgish party system. Having assessed levels of established party centrality and the extent of party system change found within Luxembourg, while making comparisons with the Swiss example, this chapter now moves on to a more detailed analysis of the impact of the low use of electorate-orientated strategies on the fate of established parties within Luxembourg and Switzerland.

5.6 The infrequent use of electorate-orientated strategies and established parties' centrality

Chapter 2 showed that the established parties in Switzerland and Luxembourg engaged in the lowest levels of electorate-orientated strategies in western Europe. Established parties demonstrated low levels of ideological change, proved relatively unresponsive to the electorate in terms of government formation and engaged in a strategy of exclusion concerning anti-political establishment parties. Pre-electoral coalition agreements do not feature in either country; Switzerland does not produce coalition agreements whereas Luxembourg does not publish agreements, demonstrating a desire to keep the public unaware of coalition negotiations or policies. The findings suggest that established parties in Luxembourg and Switzerland have been unresponsive to the electorate and have conducted much of the affairs of the country behind closed doors, creating distance from the electorate.

This chapter has shown that there are many similarities between the impact that the use of these strategies have had on the established parties in Luxembourg and Switzerland. In both countries, established parties have experienced relatively low levels of centrality within the electoral and parliamentary arenas, but have monopolised the governmental arena. In neither country has any significant party system change taken place, resulting in two highly stable party systems. The only difference found in the studies of the two countries was in terms of recent trends in centrality. In Luxembourg, recent trends point to a decline in centrality for the established parties within the electoral and parliamentary arenas, whereas in Switzerland, established party centrality is increasing in these two arenas, albeit because of the increase in support for one party.

In line with a Downsian interpretation of party competition, engagement in low levels of electorate-orientated strategies by established parties should lead to low levels of systemic centrality. Established parties that demonstrate low levels of responsiveness towards the electorate in terms of government formation patterns and ideological change and keep coalition negotiations conducted behind closed doors should not achieve high levels of centrality within their respective national party systems. Part of this hypothesis appears to hold true for Switzerland and Luxembourg. Within the electoral and parliamentary arenas, established parties in both countries have only experienced relatively low levels of centrality, but within the governmental arena, levels of centrality have been exceptionally high. This apparent paradox is the focus of the rest of this section, as the chapter turns to the Swiss case to investigate why there is a contrast between the centrality of established parties within different arenas.

Established parties in Switzerland demonstrate one of the highest levels of governmental centrality in western Europe. All four established parties have governed together since 1959 despite relatively low levels of centrality within the parliamentary and electoral arenas. The dominance of consociational democracy in Switzerland (see Sciarini and Hug 1999 for more details) has produced a separation between the governing parties and the electorate and a divorce between electoral results and governmental outcomes. Despite the electorate voicing its dissatisfaction with the established parties through the act of voting, the lack of responsiveness of the established parties has ensured that the governmental level does not feel these ripples of discontent in terms of new parties entering government. However, the revision of the magic formula in 2003 took into account shifting popular support for the four established parties. Thus, a monopoly over governing opportunities by certain parties may be the natural manifestation of the engagement in strategies producing a closed and unresponsive relationship with the electorate.

The decision by the Swiss established parties to form a permanent, grand coalition of the four established parties is a decision strongly influenced by the institutional set-up in which they operate, highlighting the interplay of electorate-orientated strategies and institutional restrictions. Wolf Linder (2000: 102) confidently argues that 'the reason why there has been no change of government in the last 40 years is direct democracy'. He argues that an oversized coalition gives parliament a better chance to reach a sufficient majority that can avoid or win a referendum. Votations and popular initiatives allow the electorate to wield an enormous amount of power within the Swiss political system, thus the parties form oversized coalitions in order to protect their policies from the will of the electorate.

This argument challenges the earlier ideas presented about responsiveness. Instead of viewing the electorate as powerless and unable to influence the composition of government, in Switzerland the electorate wields power in other ways that can leave the established parties powerless. The established parties are *unresponsive* to the electorate in terms of government composition and ideological change, but the entire system of government formation in Switzerland exists *in response to* the potential power of the electorate granted through the institutional set-up. Linder (2000) argues that, in Switzerland, a trade-off between influence through election and referendum exists, therefore Switzerland represents an anomaly in terms of the assumptions concerning the relationship between voters and parties in democracies not strongly influenced by direct democratic methods. Direct democracy offers the people maximal influence and a direct influence over policy decisions, compared to the indirect impact on policy the act of voting produces.

Although the Swiss political system may not be as unresponsive as it first appears, the divorce of the relationship between voting and government formation opens the system up to allegations that the established parties engage in cartel-like behaviour. By engaging in low levels of electorate-orientated strategies, Swiss established parties are creating a cartel party system, preserving governmental entry for themselves. Linder argues 'certainly, one could take the view that Swiss democracy is a cartel, unresponsive to the will of the voters because they have no direct influence on the composition of government' (2000: 102). Of course, the absence of direct influence on the composition of government no longer holds because of the aftermath of the historic 2003 elections. For the first time in the period covered, election results influenced the composition of government, with the SVP receiving an extra seat in the Federal Council at the expense of the CVP. The SVP's share of the vote increased from 22.5 per cent to 26.6 per cent to become the largest party in terms of votes received and parliamentary seats held. The impact of the enormous electoral gains made by the SVP since the 1990s did eventually lead to a change in distribution of seats within government, suggesting the lack of responsiveness in the Swiss political system may be changing.

It can be seen that the Swiss party system represents an almost 'ideal type' interpretation of a cartel party system, with four parties monopolising government. The low level of use of electorate-orientated strategies by the established parties has strongly influenced the political system, which is unresponsive and closed towards the electorate. The distance created between the established parties and the electorate is further evidence of a cartel party system, where the relationship between the state and parties on the one hand and society on the other becomes bifurcated. This chapter now turns towards an analysis of the impact of the low use of electorate-orientated strategies in Luxembourg to determine similarities and differences between the two cases.

In Luxembourg, established parties are unresponsive to the views of the electorate and parties have created a closed political system. Dumont and De Winter (2000: 412) note that 'coalition agreements are and always remain top secret documents. Only the ministers and the parties' archives receive a copy'. This secrecy indicates a willingness to detach the electorate from the coalition process, in much the same way as has been observed in Switzerland. Whereas in Switzerland, four parties govern together in a permanent grand coalition, in Luxembourg, the CSV shapes coalitions. The CSV is regarded as the natural party of government in Luxembourg and on only one occasion since 1950 has the party been absent from government. The role of the CSV as the natural party of government partially explains why low levels of centrality in the electoral and parliamentary arenas do not produce low levels of governmental centrality. The choice of coalition partner made by the CSV dictates whether the established parties' governmental centrality remains, and thus far, the choice made has been restricted to the DP or LSAP.

Another point to consider regarding the Luxembourgish party system, which also has relevance for the Swiss example, is the importance of inputs and outputs within political systems. In Luxembourg and Switzerland, the influence of the electorate to alter the composition of government is lower than in many other western European countries. In Luxembourg, history suggests that the CSV is almost certain to be the largest party in parliament, hold the position of prime minister and choose with which party it wishes to govern. The input that the electorate can have in terms of influencing government composition is relatively limited. However, on the output side, there are some strong similarities between the Swiss and Luxembourgish examples. Both countries have high employment levels, strong economies and have the two highest GDPs per head in Europe (Smart 2000: 193). Although the voters may lack input into the political system, the outputs they receive in terms of their socio-economic standing are amongst the best in Europe.

As a result of the lack of input the electorate has into the political system, the privacy of established parties and the monopoly of government by the three established parties, the Luxembourgish party system, like the Swiss, has been strongly shaped by the low levels of electorate-orientated strategies employed by the established parties. The Luxembourgish party system resembles a cartel party system in much the same way as the Swiss one does, demonstrating a disjuncture between the established parties and society. These cartel strategies employed by the established parties impacts on the party system, which, in both countries, sees government monopolised by certain parties, with the terms for entry into the party system shaped by these parties. The low use of electorate-orientated strategies ensures that the established parties remain the only important governing actors in both countries, despite low levels of electoral and parliamentary centrality.

The Swiss and Luxembourgish case studies appear partially to support the hypothesis that low levels of engagement in electorate-orientated strategies should produce low levels of systemic centrality. In the electoral and parliamentary arenas in both countries, this hypothesis appears to hold true, as the levels of centrality found were relatively low. However, levels of centrality are exceptionally high within the governmental arena, suggesting that the hypothesis may only hold for the electoral and parliamentary arenas, as the governmental arena is protected. The use of electorate-orientated strategies by the established parties can help to explain this apparent paradox between high and low levels in different arenas. By engaging in strategies that are distant, closed and unresponsive towards the electorate, the relationship between centrality in the parliamentary and electoral arenas, and the governmental arena, should not be strong. Indeed, precisely because the parties have not engaged in responsive strategies towards the electorate and have instead engaged in cartel strategies, access to the governmental arena remains closed, but opposition to the cartel can be seen through low levels of parliamentary and electoral centrality.

5.7 Conclusion

This chapter has attempted to analyse to what extent the use of electorate-orientated strategies impacts on the fate of established parties. The high use of electorate-orientated strategies should produce high levels of systemic centrality for the established parties, whereas low levels of electorate-orientated strategies should produce low levels of centrality. The results of the study partially supported these hypotheses. In Germany, established parties have achieved exceptionally high levels of centrality, although these levels are declining in all three arenas, and in Portugal, centrality is increasing in the parliamentary and electoral arenas. In both countries, levels of centrality at present are approximately the same and are at moderately high levels. In Switzerland and Luxembourg, centrality is relatively low in the electoral and parliamentary arenas, but the established parties have monopolised the governmental arena. An analysis of the impact of electorate-orientated strategies explains many of the apparent contradictions in these findings.

The case studies of the four countries have revealed that strategies appear to have an important impact on the fate of established parties. Established parties that engage in high levels of electorate-orientated strategies and engage in an open and responsive relationship with the electorate are particularly successful within the electoral and parliamentary arenas. However, the German example raises the possibility of perverse effects, as the success of the established parties appears to have played a role in their recent decline in centrality. The converse appears to be the case where low levels of electorate-orientated strategies are used. In Switzerland and Luxembourg, centrality within the parliamentary and electoral arenas is low, but within the governmental arena, centrality is complete. The low use of electorate-orientated strategies implies the high use of cartel strategies, as by acting in an unresponsive and closed manner towards the electorate, the established parties are disengaging themselves from civil society. These parties can maintain dominance within the governmental arena, as, especially in Switzerland, the acts of voting and government formation are divorced.

This analysis suggests that both strategies have been successful for the established parties in different ways. The high use of electorate-orientated strategies appears to benefit established parties within the electoral and parliamentary arenas, whereas the high use of cartel strategies produces benefits within the governmental arena. One crucial point to highlight is the continuity demonstrated within each of the party systems covered – in all four countries, no major, established party has disappeared from the electoral scene over the period covered and only the Greens in Germany have emerged as a governing party. The use of high or low levels of electorate-orientated strategies may have produced some different outcomes over the four cases studied, but in all countries, the established parties have remained the dominant forces within their national party systems.

This chapter has assumed that the direction of causality flows from the actions of established parties to the centrality of the established parties. However, it is equally viable to suggest that the direction of causality operates in reverse; the centrality of the established parties may influence the use of strategies by the established parties. In Portugal, it could be argued that the high level of electorate-orientated strategies used is a result of the Portuguese established parties' low levels of centrality for much of the period covered and the experience of a rupture in democracy. Lacking the strong party organisations, mass membership and high levels of support of other western European parties, established parties in Portugal were not constrained by their organisations or by underlying cleavage structures in the early years of the post-Salazar regime and were free to engage in open and responsive strategies towards a wider section of the electorate. The alternative direction of causality may also exist in the German example. Secure in the their central position within the German system in the 1960s and 1970s, established parties were perhaps freer than established parties in other countries that did not enjoy the same levels of centrality, to engage in strategies that are responsive and open towards the electorate. In both the German and the Portuguese cases, the alternative direction of causality is a viable alternative.

The alternative direction of causality may also hold with reference to Luxembourg and Switzerland. The low levels of centrality experienced within the parliamentary and electoral arenas may have encouraged the parties to engage in cartel strategies to ensure that whatever the losses made within the electoral and parliamentary arenas, the governmental arena would remain relatively immune from electoral pressures and enable the established parties to continue to govern. Once the governing cartel is in place, it appears only natural that established parties are not responsive or open towards the electorate as their positions are secure and they are no longer reliant on the electorate for their central positions within the party system.

Although this revised direction of causality is a valid alternative interpretation, it is perhaps more valid to see both directions of causality working together. For example, in Germany, the strategies of the established parties *cannot* have been influenced by the high levels of centrality experienced by the established parties in the 1950s, as the German party system was consolidating and no parties had achieved high levels of centrality. Therefore, the use of strategies strongly influences levels of centrality during the consolidating period of a nation's party system. After this point, where the constellation of parties within the party system becomes more stable, the two directions of causality are both active. Strategies strongly influence the centrality of established parties, but equally high or low levels of centrality may influence the strategies used by the established parties following periods of party system consolidation. It is important to raise the issues concerning the alternative direction of causality, as the discussion highlights alternative hypotheses that the conclusion of the book addresses. Using empirical evidence, the conclusion suggests that impact of strategies on established party centrality is the more useful of the two interpretations of direction of causality.

This chapter has assessed the impact of the use of electorate-orientated strategies in four western European countries between 1950 and 2009, and suggested that parties may also seek to improve their systemic position through the development of their relationship with the state. Parties may engage in institutional strategies and, in line with the cartel thesis of Katz and Mair (1995), may seek to utilise the institutions of the state for their own means. The next chapter assesses the impact of the high and low use of institutional strategies. The high use of institutional strategies should produce high levels of centrality for the established parties, whereas the low use of strategies should produce low levels of centrality. The next chapter attempts to test the cartel thesis, by analysing whether an institutional set-up that strongly favours the established parties results in higher levels of centrality for the established parties than an institutional arrangement that favours non-established parties. Chapter 6 should shed more light on these issues.

6   The use of institutional strategies

Chapter 3 assessed established parties' use of institutional strategies and showed that the countries in which established parties engaged in the highest levels of institutional strategies were France and Greece and the lowest levels occur in Denmark and Ireland. Established parties in France and Greece engaged in 'cartel-like' behaviours, creating and presiding over institutional systems that favour the larger, established parties at the expense of smaller and newer parties. In contrast, the institutional arrangement in Denmark and Ireland favours smaller and newer parties. Established parties within France and Greece, because of their use of cartel strategies, should achieve high levels of centrality within their national party systems. Established parties in Denmark and Ireland should achieve only low levels of systemic centrality due to their lack of engagement in institutional strategies.

This chapter examines these four case studies to analyse whether the empirical evidence supports the hypotheses. The comparisons made during the course of this chapter will test the cartel thesis, and provide an assessment of the two divergent strategies, to determine the more effective strategy for established parties. The structure of this chapter is the same as that of the previous one. The chapter commences with the case study of France, followed by Greece and then a comparison of the impact of the high use of institutional strategies on the fate of the established parties in the two countries. The focus then shifts to Denmark and Ireland, studied as individual case studies, before analysing the impact on the fate of established parties of the engagement in low levels of institutional strategies.

6.1 France

France represents an ideal example of a country where history and institutions are of crucial importance. The creation of the Fifth Republic in 1958 ushered in a political system that would be distinct from the Third and Fourth Republics, where factionalism, governmental instability and policy immobilism dominated (Knapp 2002: 107). Charles De Gaulle blamed this fundamental instability on political parties; subsequently his vision for the Fifth Republic was for parties to play only a minor role within the French political system. The institution of the presidency was the main way in which parties were to be restricted in their actions. Parties would be subordinate organisations effecting presidential will, but not shaping politics itself (Bell 2000: 197) and the president would provide the principal source of policy.

The second institutional arrangement that has shaped the party system is the electoral system. Throughout the majority of the Fifth Republic, both presidential and legislative elections took place under a two-ballot electoral system. This electoral system encourages the formation of alliances but also factionalism within parliament, leading to bipolarisation and fractionalisation within the party system.

Political parties in France, as has already been shown, operate in a markedly different institutional environment from their west European counterparts, and party names have changed frequently during the Fifth Republic. It is therefore necessary to address French political parties as groups, using the framework proposed by Andrew Knapp (2004a). The most important political grouping on the right during the Fifth Republic has been the Gaullists, with the NGMR (Non-Gaullist Moderate Right) group acting as the Gaullists' main competitor (and ally) on the right. The Far Right group constitutes the non-established parties on the right of the spectrum, with the FN (Front National) the major far right party. The FN demonstrates an anti-immigrant policy, is highly critical of the political class and makes frequent attacks on both the left and the right, and subsequently the party has been 'shut out' by the mainstream parties (Knapp 2004a: 336) and must be considered a non-established party.

The situation on the left is more complex. The Socialists have proven to be the dominant force on the left and have constituted one of the three 'parties of government' along with the Gaullists and the NGMR. However, the other major actor on the left, the PCF (Communists), poses more problems. The PCF is a non-established party despite regularly receiving a higher vote share than the Socialists in the early years of the Fifth Republic and forming electoral alliances with the Socialists. The PCF had a strong pro-Soviet ideology, emphasised the organisational principle of democratic centralism and highlighted the desire for working class revolution (Bell 2000: 30). The party was politically isolated during the early years of the Fifth Republic (Wright 1989: 232) and the other parties have never accepted the PCF as a legitimate part of the party system.[1] The Greens only entered parliament and government in 1997 and it is not clear if they will endure.

The established and non-established parties within the French system and the first and most recent election in which they participated since 1958 are summarised in Table 6.1. The main groups of parties considered as established parties are the Gaullists, the NGMR and the Socialists; the three 'parties of government'. Table 6.2 summarises these parties' levels of centrality within the electoral, parliamentary and governmental arenas.

Centrality of established parties

Table 6.2 shows that the levels of electoral centrality for the established French parties have been consistently low and have declined over recent decades. The peak of centrality occurred in 1981, when the three parties received 83.1 per cent

Table 6.1 Established and non-established parties in France, 1958–2007

Established parties	Non-established parties
Gaullists: RPR (Rally for the Republic) (1976–2002, previously UDR, Union of Democrats for the Republic, 1968–76, previously UDVe, Union of Democrats for the 5th Republic, 1967–68, previously UNR, Union for the New Republic, 1958–67) Part of UMP (Union for a Popular Movement, 2002–present)	LO/LCR (Workers' Struggle/Revolutionary Communist Party) (1978–present)
Non-Gaullist Moderate Right: CDS (Democratic Social Centre) (1967–73, previously MRP, Republican People's Movement, 1958–67) RAD (Radical Party) (1958–62) CNIP/PR (National Centre of Independents and Peasants) (1958–62) DL (Liberal Democracy) (1997–2002, previously PR, Republican Party, 1967–97) UDF (Union for French Democracy) (included CDS, RAD, PR, 1973–2002) MPF (Movement for France) (1994–present) Part of UMP (Union for a Popular Movement) (2002–present) Also: MoDem (Democratic Movement) (2002–present) NC (New Centre) (2007–present)	FN (National Front) (1978–present)
Socialists: PS (Socialist Party) (1971–present, previously SFIO, French Section of the Workers International, 1958–71) PRG (Radical Party of the Left) (1972–present) MRC (Citizen and Republican Movement) (1993–present)	PCF (French Communist Party) (1958–present) Les Verts (The Greens) 1978–present) MNR (National Republican Movement) (1999–present)

Note
The complexity of the French party system renders the classification of every party competing in election since 1958 an impossible task. Only the most relevant and largest parties are included here.

of the vote, but over the past three elections the established parties have received a combined vote of less than 70 per cent. The data suggests that the three 'parties of government' have never achieved high levels of electoral arena centrality, but even the moderate levels of centrality achieved have declined over recent decades, before a slight revival in the 2000s.

The parliamentary arena paints a very different picture of centrality. The combined share of seats for the three established parties has only fallen below the 80 per cent mark once in 1979 and the parties received their highest share of the seats in 2002, securing 95.8 per cent of the seats in parliament. Established parties in France have achieved relatively high levels of centrality throughout most of the Fifth Republic, with recent trends pointing towards an increase in parliamentary centrality, with parliamentary centrality falling only slightly to 92.2 per cent in 2007. This contrasts markedly with the levels of centrality found within the electoral arena. The electoral system is clearly a major factor encouraging the difference between the levels of centrality found within the electoral and parliamentary arenas and the impact of the tension between the electoral and the parliamentary arenas is analysed in more detail later in this chapter.

The governmental arena reveals only moderate levels of centrality for the established parties. The data highlights two important points. The three established parties have been unable to monopolise the governmental arena, with the PCF entering a coalition with the Socialists in 1981 and the Greens and PCF participating in a broad left-wing coalition in 1997. The number of relevant actors within the governmental arena has increased over time and has not been restricted to the three 'parties of government'. Independent and non-party actors have also been prevalent within governments in the Fifth Republic, reinforcing the 'secondary' nature of parties within the political system. Established parties appear to have achieved only moderate levels of centrality within the governmental arena and this centrality has declined over time as new parties have entered the governing fold.

Party system change

The next question to consider is how the contrasts found between centrality within the different arenas and the recent trend towards declining centrality have manifested themselves within the party system as a whole. The party system of the Fifth Republic generally had a four party format until the emergence of the FN and the Greens as forces within the electoral arena in the mid-1980s and the mid-1990s respectively. References to competition within the French party system as *quadrille bipolaire*, to use Duverger's term, in particular during the late 1970s, highlight the presence of four evenly balanced competitors within the party system. Since the mid-1980s, the number of parties within the party system has increased at the electoral level, but has remained relatively static in the parliamentary arena primarily due to the impact of the electoral system. Table 6.3 highlights these trends in the effective number of parties. The table shows that there have been two periods where the average effective number of parties

Table 6.2 Centrality of established parties in the French party system, 1958–2007

	1958	1962	1967	1968	1969	1973	1974	1978	1981a
Percentage share of the vote	Gau: 20.6 NGMR: 31.1 Soc: 15.5 Total: 67.2%	Gau: 36.0 NGMR: 19.4 Soc: 12.4 Total: 67.8%	Gau: 38.5 NGMR: 17.4 Soc: 18.9 Total: 74.8%	Gau: 46.4 NGMR: 12.4 Soc: 16.5 Total: 75.3%		Gau: 37.0 NGMR: 16.7 Soc: 20.8 Total: 74.5%		Gau: 22.8 NGMR: 26.6 Soc: 25.0 Total: 74.4%	
Percentage share of seats	Gau: 39.1 NGMR: 38.6 Soc: 8.0 Total: 85.7%	Gau: 48.3 NGMR: 26.8 Soc: 13.7 Total: 88.8%	Gau: 41.1 NGMR: 17.0 Soc: 24.8 Total: 82.9%	Gau: 60.2 NGMR: 19.3 Soc: 11.7 Total: 91.2%		Gau: 37.3 NGMR: 24.3 Soc: 20.8 Total: 82.4%		Gau: 31.4 NGMR: 25.1 Soc: 23.4 Total: 79.9%	
Largest party within parliament (seats)	Gaullists	Gaullists	Gaullists	Gaullists	Gaullists	Gaullists	Gaullists	Gaullists	Gaullists
Time spent in government									
Gaullists									
NGMR									
Socialists									
Median legislator	Gaullists	Gaullists	NGMR	Gaullists	Gaullists	NGMR	NGMR	NGMR	NGMR
Percentage share of government positions	Gau: 30.0 NGMR: 35.0 Ind: 35.0	Gau: 61.9 NGMR: 14.3 Ind: 23.8	Gau: 73.9 NGMR: 8.7 Ind: 17.4	Gau: 73.7 NGMR: 15.8 Ind: 10.5	Gau: 66.7 NGMR: 33.3	Gau: 73.7 NGMR: 26.3	Gau: 37.5 NGMR: 43.8 Ind: 18.8	Gau: 28.6 NGMR: 52.4 Ind: 23.8	Soc: 89.5 NGMR: 10.5
Prime minister's party	Gaullists	Gaullists	Gaullists	Gaullists	Gaullists	Gaullists	Gaullists	Gaullists	Socialists
Ratio of portfolios obtained to share of seats	Gau: 0.8:1 NGMR: 0.9:1	Gau: 1.3:1 NGMR: 0.5:1	Gau: 1.8:1 NGMR: 0.5:1	Gau: 1.2:1 NGMR: 0.8:1	Gau: 1.1:1 NGMR: 1.7:1	Gau: 2.0:1 NGMR: 1.1:1	Gau: 1.0:1 NGMR: 1.8:1	Gau: 0.9:1 NGMR: 2.1:1	Soc: 3.6:1 NGMR: 0.4:1

	1981b	1984	1986	1988a	1988b	1993	1997	2002	2007
Percentage share of the vote	Gau: 21.2 NGMR: 22.4 Soc: 39.5 Total: 83.1%		Gau: 21.0 NGMR: 21.1 Soc: 31.6 Total: 73.7%		Gau: 19.2 NGMR: 18.5 Soc: 37.6 Total: 75.3%	Gau: 20.4 NGMR: 19.1 Soc: 20.3 Total: 59.8%	Gau: 15.6 NGMR: 14.3 Soc: 27.7 Total: 57.6%	Gau/NGMR: 45.0 Soc: 25.3 Total: 70.3%	Gau/NGMR: 49.5 Soc: 26.0 Total: 75.5%
Percentage share of seats	Gau: 17.9 NGMR: 12.8 Soc: 58.0 Total: 88.7%		Gau: 26.9 NGMR: 22.7 Soc: 36.7 Total: 86.3%		Gau: 22.7 NGMR: 22.9 Soc: 47.1 Total: 92.7%	Gau: 44.7 NGMR: 37.3 Soc: 9.9 Total: 91.9%	Gau: 24.3 NGMR: 19.6 Soc: 43.3 Total: 87.2%	Gau/ NGMR: 71.4 Soc: 24.4 Total: 95.8%	Gau/NGMR: 58.8 Soc: 33.4 Total: 92.2%
Largest party within parliament (seats)	Socialists	Socialists	Socialists	Socialists	NGMR	Gaullists	Socialists	Gaullists/ NGMR	Gaullists/ NGMR
Time spent in government									
Gaullists									
NGMR									
Socialists									
PCF									
Les Verts									
MPF									
NC									
Median legislator	Socialists	Socialists	NGMR	NGMR	Socialists	NGMR	Socialists	Gau/NGMR	Gau/NGMR
Percentage share of government positions	Soc: 75.8 PCF: 12.1 Ind: 12.1	Soc: 100	Gau: 56.5 NGMR: 30.4 Ind: 13.0	Soc: 83.3 NGMR: 16.7	Soc: 81.0 NGMR: 19.0	Gau: 43.3 NGMR: 46.7 Ind: 10.0	Soc: 70.6 PCF: 11.8 Verts: 17.6	Gau/NGMR: 81.0 Ind: 19.0	Gau/NGMR: 73.3 NC: 7.0 Ind: 20.0
Prime minister's party	Socialists	Socialists	Gaullists	Socialists	Socialists	Gaullists	Socialists	Gau/NGMR	Gau/NGMR
Ratio of portfolios obtained to share of seats	Soc: 1.3:1 PCF: 1.3:1	Soc: 1.7:1	Gau: 2.1:1 NGMR: 1.3:1	Soc: 2.3:1 NGMR: 0.7:1	Soc: 1.7:1 NGMR: 0.8:1	Gau: 1.0:1 NGMR: 1.3:1	Soc: 1.6:1 PCF: 1.9:1 Verts: 3.1:1	Gau/NGMR: 1.1:1	Gau/NGMR: 1.2:1 NC:1.8:1

Sources: Hanley (1999); Knapp (2002; 2004a); Ministère de L'intérieur (2010); Thiébault (2000); Woldendorp et al. (2000); Ysmal (2003).

has been greater than five. The first is in the period of transition during the early years of the Fifth Republic and the second is the most recent period since 1993. Both periods have been characterised by instability within the party system, the first because of the birth of the Fifth Republic and the inherent instability present within most new democracies and the second due to the policy failures of the established parties (Hanley 2002: 168) and the concomitant rise in support for the Greens and the FN.

Have these changes in format influenced the structure of competition within the French party system? Table 6.3 shows that the structure of competition within France has moved through five distinct stages. The first is the period of transition between 1958 and 1962, characterised by a semi-open structure of competition, the rise of a dominant Gaullist party (Hanley 2002: 148) and experimentation with coalition possibilities on the right of the political spectrum. The second period between 1967 and 1974 saw a more closed structure develop, as coalition patterns became more settled and the Gaullists monopolised government at the expense of the disunited left. The Fifth Republic's first left-wing government formed in 1981, opening up the structure of the French party system in the third period from 1978 to 1984 and breaking the hegemony of the Gaullists.

The fourth stage sees a closed party system in operation, as alternation between a centre-left and centre-right government structures competition, with the emerging FN rejected as a potential coalition ally. The final stage of the evo-lution of the party system sees competition opened up by the Socialists forming a coalition of the *gauche plurielle*. Changes have also occurred on the right, with the creation of the UMP (Union for a Popular Movement) as a single, relatively unified centre-right force.

The overall pattern provided by the study of the French party system is one of instability. Changes in the structure of competition have been numerous, but never durable. David Hanley describes the party system as demonstrating

Table 6.3 Party system change in France, 1958–2007

	Effective number of parties	
Structure of competition	<5	≥5
Closed	1986–88, N_v: 4.68, N_s: 3.69 (n=2)	
Semi-closed	1967–74, N_v: 3.97, N_s: 2.62 (n=3)	
Semi-open	1978–84, N_v: 4.38, N_s: 3.67 (n=2)	1958–62, N_v: 5.66, N_s: 3.54 (n=2) 1993–present, N_v: 6.03, N_s: 2.88 (n=4)
Open		

Note
The effective number of parties values relate to individual parties, as stated in the data presented by Parties and Elections in Europe (2010), as opposed to the party groupings used in Table 6.2.

'extraordinary dynamism' (2002: 150) and observes that the system's abiding characteristic is fluidity (1999: 48). Howard Machin echoes these sentiments, suggesting that 'change appears to be one of the few enduring characteristics of the party system' as 'the system as a whole remains intrinsically unstable' (1989: 59–60). The French party system has changed several times in the period covered, but the general pattern is of a party system continually in flux, with recent trends pointing towards a continuation of this instability and lack of systemic structure.

The French case study paints a picture of instability and flux, both in terms of the centrality of the French established parties and with reference to the party system as a whole. Established parties within France demonstrate low levels of centrality within the electoral arena, moderate levels within the governmental arena, but high levels within the parliamentary arena. The French party system has changed several times since 1958, but none of these changes has been permanent or durable. Having arrived at these findings based on the French case, this chapter now moves on to an examination of the Greek example to compare patterns regarding established party centrality and party system change.

6.2 Greece

In common with the other countries studied, the historical context from which the party system emerged is vital to understanding modern-day Greek politics. Greece has suffered enormous levels of regime instability since 1821 (Macridis and Lancaster 1987: 333) and since 1945 has fallen victim to a civil war from 1946 to 1949 and an authoritarian dictatorship from 1967 to 1974. This ruptured democratic history has strongly shaped the institutions and party system found within modern-day Greece. In contrast with the French case, in Greece, the political leaders did not blame political parties for the ruptures in democracy and, instead, parties were key features of the democratisation process. Konstantinos Karamanlis, one of the key actors in the democratisation of Greece after 1974, believed that an elected parliament would be the cornerstone in the consolidation of democracy (Spourdalakis 1996: 169). The impact of the democratic ruptures in Greece appears to have been to elevate the position of political parties within the Greek political system.

Karamanlis was the founder of a new centre-right political party in 1974, ND (New Democracy), described as a 'replica of de Gaulle's party' (Macridis and Lancaster 1987: 335) in France. The main party on the centre-left to emerge in 1974 was the PASOK (Pan Hellenic Socialist Movement), headed by Andreas Papandreou. Karamanlis and Papandreou proved to be the two key figures shaping Greece's democracy and recognised that democracy required parties organised on modern lines, with ideologies, programmes and mass organisations (Close 2002: 151). ND and PASOK have been the major political forces over the past 30 years and constitute the group of established parties within the Greek party system. Indeed, Spourdalakis notes that 'ND and PASOK have determined the direction of the party system' (1996: 173), highlighting the importance of these two established political parties in the process of democratic consolidation. The two Communist parties on the far left of the spectrum, the KKE (Communist Party of Greece) and the SYN (Left Coalition) have been important actors, but cannot be considered as established parties, as neither party has achieved democratic legitimacy within the system and has not been able to shape the terms of party competition. Table 6.4 presents the summary of the established and non-established parties found within the Greek party system, with the two parties considered in terms of systemic centrality ND and PASOK.

Centrality of established parties

Table 6.5 summarises the levels of centrality within the electoral, parliamentary and governmental arenas for the two established parties. Within the electoral arena, the two established parties have achieved very high levels of centrality. Since 1981, the combined share of the vote for the two parties has only fallen below 80 per cent on three occasions, with the two parties consistently receiving around 86 per cent of the vote. These figures reveal strong levels of centrality in a democratic system only founded in 1975. In common with the Portuguese case, these high levels of centrality reflect the vital role that ND and PASOK played in the process of democratic consolidation within Greece, with the two parties establishing themselves as enduring and consistently important parts of the party system.

The parliamentary arena reflects the high levels of centrality found for the two established parties within the electoral arena. Since 1981, the two established parties have received consistently over 90 per cent of the seats in parliament, with the exception of the two most recent elections in 2007 and 2009. Although the Greek electoral system is one of the most disproportional in western Europe, high levels of centrality for ND and SYN occur within both the electoral and parliamentary arenas and there is less tension between these two arenas than found in France.

Table 6.4 Established and non-established parties in Greece, 1975–2009

Established	Non-established
PASOK (Panhellenic Socialist Movement) (1975–present)	EPEN (National Political Union) (1975–85)
ND (New Democracy) (1975–present)	POLA (Political Spring) (1993–96)
	DIKKI (Democratic Social Movement) (1996–present)
	KKE (Communist Party of Greece) (1975–present, part of SYN from 1989–90)
	SYRIZA (Coalition of the Radical Left) (2004–present, previously SYN, Left Coalition 1975–2004)
	LAOS (Popular Orthodox Rally) (2000–present)
	OP (Ecologist Greens) (2002–present)

The governmental arena demonstrates slightly lower levels of centrality for the established parties than the other arenas. In 1989, two governments were formed which contained the SYN (at the time, a merger between SYN and the KKE). The second of these governments was a grand coalition, featuring PASOK, ND and SYN, the three major parties within the Greek political system. These incidences of non-established parties becoming part of government indicate that the two established parties have not held a total monopoly over the governmental arena over the period covered. However, the two parties have still achieved relatively high levels of centrality within the party system. Except for the two coalition governments in 1989, all other governments have been comprised of a single party, either the ND or PASOK. Each party governs alone and is able to wield an enormous amount of legislative power, especially as parliament is weak in Greece, with less than 0.1 per cent of legislation in the period 1974–87 initiated by opposition parties and passed (Close 2002: 145).

Overall, Greek established parties have obtained consistently high levels of centrality within all three arenas throughout most of the period covered, except for the first democratic election held in Greece after 1975, and with a slight decrease in centrality evident in the 2000s. These levels of centrality are even more exceptional when Greece's ruptured democratic history is taken into account. Karamanlis was able to lay the foundations for a liberal political system and to hold free elections within a year of the fall of the military dictatorship (Trantas *et al.* 2003: 376) and the party system appears to have consolidated exceptionally quickly based around ND and PASOK, the major centre-right and centre-left parties within Greece. The high levels of centrality experienced by the established parties are all the more extraordinary as the parties retained high levels of centrality throughout all stages of the consolidation of the Greek party system and, through the strategies adopted, have helped to shape and secure a stable party system for Greece.

Party system change

The Greek party system is a 'two-and-a-half' party system, with ND and PASOK constituting the major parties and the KKE the third 'half' force (Trantas *et al.* 2003: 381). The system has been noted as 'quasi-perfect bipartyism' (Magone 1998: 235), acknowledging the presence of two major parties and a smaller party. Table 6.6 reinforces this description of the party system. The effective number of parties within the Greek party system is under three for the period covered, suggesting a very limited, but consistent party system format. Recent trends point towards a slight decrease in the effective number of parties, principally because of the decline in support for the far left in the 1990s, indicating that the Greek party system format may be becoming more limited.

The structure of competition has proved to be equally consistent. Greece demonstrates a semi-closed structure of competition throughout the whole period, except for the brief period of coalition governments in 1989 and 1990. The Greek structure of competition is characterised by wholesale or non-alternation in government, as

Table 6.5 Centrality of established parties in the Greek party system, 1975–2009

	1977	1981	1985	1989a	1989b	1990	1993
Percentage share of the vote	PASOK: 25.3 ND: 41.9 Total: 67.2%	PASOK: 48.1 ND: 35.9 Total: 84.0%	PASOK: 45.8 ND: 40.8 Total: 86.6%	PASOK: 39.1 ND: 44.3 Total: 83.4%	PASOK: 40.7 ND: 46.2 Total: 86.9%	PASOK: 38.6 ND: 46.9 Total: 85.5%	PASOK: 46.9 ND: 39.3 Total: 86.2%
Percentage share of seats	PASOK: 31.0 ND: 57.0 Total: 88.0%	PASOK: 57.3 ND: 38.3 Total: 95.6%	PASOK: 53.7 ND: 42.0 Total: 95.7%	PASOK: 41.7 ND: 48.3 Total: 90.0%	PASOK: 42.7 ND: 49.3 Total: 92.0%	PASOK: 41.7 ND: 50.0 Total: 91.7%	PASOK: 56.7 ND: 37.0 Total: 93.7%
Largest party within parliament (seats)	ND	PASOK	PASOK	ND	ND	ND	PASOK
Time spent in government PASOK ND SYN							
Median legislator	ND	PASOK	PASOK	PASOK	PASOK	ND	PASOK
Percentage share of government positions	ND: 100.0	PASOK: 100.0	PASOK: 100.0	ND: 89.5 SYN: 10.5	PASOK: 31.6 ND: 31.6 SYN: 5.3 Ind: 31.6	ND: 100.0	PASOK: 100.0
Prime minister's party	ND	PASOK	PASOK	ND	Ind	ND	PASOK
Ratio of positions obtained to share of seats	ND: 1.8:1	PASOwK: 1.7:1	PASOK: 1.9:1	ND: 1.9:1 SYN: 1.1:1	PASOK: 0.7:1 ND: 0.6:1 SYN: 0.8:1	ND: 2.0:1	PASOK: 1.8:1

	1996	2000	2004	2007	2009
Percentage share of the vote	PASOK: 41.5 ND: 38.1 Total: 79.6%	PASOK: 43.8 ND: 42.7 Total: 86.5%	PASOK: 45.4 ND:40.6 Total: 86.0%	PASOK: 38.1 ND:41.8 Total: 79.9%	PASOK: 43.9 ND:33.5 Total: 77.4%
Percentage share of seats	PASOK: 54.0 ND: 36.0 Total: 90.0%	PASOK: 52.7 ND: 41.7 Total: 94.3%	PASOK: 39.0 ND: 55.0 Total: 94.0%	PASOK: 34.0 ND:50.7 Total: 84.7%	PASOK: 53.3 ND:30.3 Total: 83.6%
Largest party within parliament (seats)	PASOK	PASOK	ND	ND	PASOK
Time spent in government PASOK ND					
Median legislator	PASOK	PASOK	ND	ND	PASOK
Percentage share of government positions	PASOK: 100.0	PASOK: 100.0	ND: 100.0	ND: 100.0	PASOK: 100.0
Prime minister's party	PASOK	PASOK	ND	ND	PASOK
Ratio of positions obtained to share of seats	PASOK: 1.9:1	PASOK: 1.9:1	ND: 1.8:1	ND: 2.0:1	PASOK: 1.9:1

Sources: Mavrogordatos (2005); Greek Ministry of Internal Affairs (2010); Woldendorp *et al.* (2000).

Table 6.6 Party system change in Greece, 1975–2009

	Effective number of parties	
Structure of competition	<3	≥3
Closed		
Semi-closed	1974–85, N_v: 2.94, N_s: 2.08 (n=3) 1993–present, N_v: 2.86, N_s: 2.36 (n=6)	
Semi-open	1989–90, N_v: 2.64, N_s: 2.35 (n=3)	
Open		

ND and PASOK generally govern alone and alternately. Government formation patterns are familiar, as single-party governments of ND or PASOK are the norm, but governing opportunities are open to all parties within the system, as ND and PASOK have both governed with the far left in 1989 and 1990.

Except for the brief period of uncertainty in the late 1980s and early 1990s, the Greek party system has established a stable structure of competition, not threatened by emerging parties (Pappas 2003: 111). David Close argues that this period of instability had no lasting effect on the party system as the development of a stable pattern of party competition in the 1970s and 1980s became embedded in the voters' minds and the preceding stability explains why no lasting change occurred in the party system in the 1990s (2002: 160). A two-party system has developed, coinciding with the consolidation of the young democratic regime, reflecting ND and PASOK's exceptional levels of centrality within all three arenas, especially the electoral and parliamentary arenas. The strategies employed by ND and PASOK had a major impact on the development and consolidation of the Greek party system and played a leading role in creating a stable structure of competition.

This section has highlighted the high levels of centrality demonstrated by the established parties within Greece. ND and PASOK have experienced high levels of centrality within the parliamentary and electoral arenas and relatively high levels of centrality within the governmental arena. This two-party dominance of the party system is reflected in the findings concerning overall systemic stability. The Greek party system is remarkably stable and this stability may be a result of the strategies employed by ND and PASOK, an argument pursued in more detail in the next section of this chapter. Greece's ruptured democratic history makes the speed of the transition from authoritarian dictatorship to a stable, two-party system all the more remarkable and the actions of ND and PASOK assisted this transformation.

6.3 The frequent use of institutional strategies and established parties' centrality

Chapter 3 showed that France and Greece engaged in the highest levels of institutional strategies in western Europe. Established parties created or presided

over electoral systems that were restrictive for non-established parties and electoral laws were somewhat restrictive. Television advertising and state subsidies
were weighted in favour of the established parties in Greece, with television
advertising somewhat favouring the established parties in France. The institutional arrangements in the two countries are generally restrictive for new and
smaller parties, yet despite the similarities in the strategies employed by the
established parties, the outcomes in terms of the centrality of the established parties and systemic stability have been very different.

Levels of centrality for the established parties in France and Greece have been
moderate within the governmental arena and high within the parliamentary
arena, yet real differences emerge in the electoral arena. In Greece, levels of centrality for the established parties have been consistently high throughout the
period covered, whereas in France, levels of centrality are low and have been
declining over recent years. There is also a contrast between the levels of party
system change found in the two countries. In France, the system has changed
several times and appears to be in a permanent state of flux, whereas in Greece
the party system is exceptionally stable and has experienced only one brief
period of instability in 1989 and 1990. How can the differences found in terms
of electoral arena centrality and overall systemic stability be explained?

Before this chapter embarks on the study into the impact of the high use of
institutional strategies on French established parties, this section addresses the
importance of institutional factors. In each of the other countries in this study,
parties are the principal legislators and the impact of strategies that *the established parties themselves* have initiated is analysed. However, in France, Hanley
(2002: 167) argues that the French president often imposes institutional changes
on parties, with the president playing a leading role in initiating legislation.
Parties must often react to the institutional changes made, as opposed to initiating changes themselves. It is important to note that when the impact of institutional strategies in the French case is discussed, parties are often only acting as
passive receivers of the president's will and are more reactive than proactive in
terms of shaping the institutional system.

The presidency has played a vital role in the development of the French party
system. De Gaulle's vision for the Fifth Republic was to restrict the role of parties to 'contributing to the expression of suffrage' (Thiébault 2003: 327) and to
play only a minimal role in legislation. There was no place for the 'normal'
activity of parties in western Europe and parties were pushed to the sidelines
with the intention of excluding them (Bell 2000: 198). It is unsurprising that the
levels of centrality experienced by the established parties under the Fifth Republic are low, simply because the centrality of *all* parties within the political process *as a whole* is low. The institution of the presidency also encourages
systemic instability, as parties are viewed as 'rallies' around their presidential
leader (Cole 1990: 4) and presidential elections often lead to a recomposition of
the party political landscape (Knapp 2004a: 233), resulting in frequent splits
within parties, changing of party names and identities and party mergers, producing instability and systemic discontinuity.

The lowly status of political parties in France contrasts with the status of parties in other countries, in particular in Germany. In Germany, political parties hold an important constitutional position, whereas in France, the status of parties is much lower. The French perception of democracy is less 'party-centric' than in Germany and the party-centric nature of democracy may be an important influence on the levels of systemic centrality found within the countries in this study.

The second institutional feature that has a major impact on the fate of established parties is the electoral system. The French two-ballot electoral system is the most disproportional in western Europe (see section 3.2) and, as such, has important implications for established party centrality and systemic stability. The distorting impact of the electoral system helps to explain the dominance of the French established parties within the parliamentary arena, but the low levels of centrality found within the electoral arena are also a by-product of the electoral system. The electoral system encourages alliances to be formed between parties as the centre-left and centre-right groupings enter deals to commit to a 'mutual withdrawal' on the first or second ballot (Thiébault 2000: 501), but the side-effect of the electoral system is to foster divisions within blocs and create tension between the electoral and parliamentary arenas.

The electoral system fosters multipartism within the electoral arena, by allowing voters to select the candidate of their choice at the first ballot, but 'forced bipolarity' within the parliamentary arena, as options are restricted on the second ballot, with voters often faced with a choice between only two parties. The tension between the multipartism that emerges from the first ballot and the bipolarity present within the second ballot has important implications for the party system and the fate of the established parties. One of the major reasons for the decline in established party support since the 1980s has been 'dissatisfaction with the bipolar basis of competition, which no longer corresponds to the electors' aspirations' (Wilson 1988: 19). Alistair Cole (2003: 20) echoes this sentiment, highlighting the 'ever increasing gap between formal bipolarity and the underlying fragmentation of electoral choice'.

The low levels of centrality for the established parties within the electoral arena and general systemic instability has emerged in France as a result of the institution of the presidency, the concomitant low importance of parties institutionally and also the unwanted effects of a disproportional electoral system that fosters alliances, but also encourages divisions. In other western European nations, it is generally the parties themselves that shape the institutions that govern the country, but in France, largely, the president puts these institutions in place, restricting the role that political parties can play. France stands out as something of an anomaly compared to the rest of western Europe in terms of the ability of political parties to control their own fate within party systems.

In common with the formation of the French Fifth Republic, one man with a democratic vision for his country founded the restoration of Greek democracy after 1975. The vision of Karamanlis was very different to the vision of de Gaulle. De Gaulle sought to reduce the role of political parties within the new system, but

Karamanlis argued that 'it is political parties rather than governments to which peoples attach themselves and … a regime's fortune is more affected by the number and behaviour of political parties than by its formal framework' (Spourdalakis 1996: 169). The difference in attitude towards the role played by political parties within France and Greece is obvious and partially explains why the Greek established parties have been able to achieve higher levels of centrality than their French counterparts have, simply because political parties have an institutionally important role to play in Greece as opposed to France. Political parties were key factors in the democratisation and consolidation processes (Spourdalakis 1996: 167), further increasing their important position within Greek politics.

The institution of the presidency is one of the most important features encouraging systemic instability and low levels of established party centrality in France. In Greece, the 1975 constitution created a similar semi-presidential system giving the Greek president important powers such at the right to dissolve parliament and to call a national referendum without the counter-signatures of the cabinet. However, a constitutional revision in 1986 distributed most of these rights between the prime minister, cabinet and parliament (Trantas *et al.* 2003: 376), downgrading the role of the president in favour of political parties. A different relationship exists between political parties and the president in Greece compared to France, and the important position of political parties vis-à-vis the presidency within Greece is an important reason for systemic stability and the consistently high levels of systemic centrality experienced by ND and PASOK.

The second important institutional feature noted in the French case was the electoral system. This feature in Greece can help indicate why the party system is stable and levels of centrality for established parties are high. In both countries, electoral systems are highly disproportional, explaining the high levels of parliamentary centrality achieved in both countries. Yet, despite the high levels of disproportionality found in both electoral systems, the systems operate in very different ways. The Greek electoral system of 'reinforced proportional representation', a variant of which has been used for most elections during the period covered, was designed to produce a stable, one-party government and to penalise either the third party or the second party depending on the variant of formula used (Dimitras 1994: 172). The Greek electoral system has played a major role in shaping the party system, providing a two-party structure of competition with strong single-party government and high levels of centrality for the established parties.

The institutional strategies employed by the established parties can explain the stability and high levels of systemic centrality for the established parties found in Greece. Political parties were the key factors in the democratisation and consolidation processes since the fall of the military dictatorship in 1974, and thus hold an important position in Greek politics. The constitutional revision of 1986 further strengthened the position of political parties vis-à-vis the president. The electoral system has shaped the party system and provided Greece with a stable party system dominated by two strong parties. The actions of ND and

PASOK have proven to be vital for the consolidation of democracy in Greece and the subsequent establishment of a stable structure of competition producing high levels of centrality for the two established parties.

This first half of this chapter has shown that the high use of institutional strategies has had a markedly different impact on the established parties of Greece and France. In France, an unstable party system exists, with centrality within the electoral, parliamentary and governmental arenas low, high and medium respectively, painting a conflicting picture of centrality. The institution of the presidency and the electoral system help to explain the instability within the party system and low levels of systemic centrality for the established parties. In contrast, in Greece, established parties experience high levels of centrality within the electoral and parliamentary arenas and moderate levels within the governmental arena and the party system was exceptionally stable. The importance of the role of political parties within the two systems is as a vital reason explaining why the two party systems have developed in contrasting ways. Having analysed the impact of the high use of institutional strategies on the fate of established parties, this chapter now moves on to an assessment of the impact of the low use of strategies in Ireland and Denmark.

6.4 Denmark

The Danish party system, in common with its Scandinavian counterparts, has been dominated by a strong Social Democratic party since the 1920s, and the Social Democrats has been the largest party in parliament between 1924 (Damgaard 2000: 233) and 2001. Between 1950 and 2001, the party often received twice as many votes as its nearest competitor (most often the Liberals) and was the natural party of government in Denmark. The impact of the dominance of one party shapes much of the Danish political system and facilitates the bloc structure of competition found within Danish politics. Another major feature of the Danish political system is the prevalence of minority governments and this marks Denmark out as something of an anomaly when compared to the other seven case studies. Since 1950, parties have formed only one majority government, so in contrast with the other countries covered in these two chapters, parties outside government can also wield enormous legislative influence.[2]

The dominance of social democracy and the prevalence of minority governments strongly influences the way in which the Danish party system has developed. As has already been stated, the supremacy of social democracy is a Scandinavian phenomenon and comprises an important part of the 'traditional' five-party model of party competition dominant in Scandinavia, advanced by Sten Berglund and Ulf Lindström (1978). David Arter (1999a) argues that a four party model is perhaps more applicable in the Danish case due to the weakness of the DKP (Communist Party) and it is these four 'old' parties that comprise the established group of parties for this study. The SD (Social Democrats), V (the Liberal Party), KF (the Conservative People's Party) and the

RV (Radical Liberals) are the core parties that came to dominate the Danish party system around Lipset and Rokkan's crucial period of the 1920s and have continued to structure the pattern of Danish party competition ever since, justifying their positions as established parties. The status of the Radical Liberals is perhaps somewhat controversial, as the party is the smallest of the established parties, but the party's classification as one of the 'historic' parties by Berglund and Lindström (1978) and their presence within governing coalitions in 1957, 1960 and 1968, suggests the party is an established party.

Notable omissions from the group of established parties may arguably be the KD (Christian Democrats) and CD (Centre Democrats). Both parties gained parliamentary representation in 1973 and remained in parliament until 2001 and 1998 respectively. During this period, the parties often received a similar share of the vote to the Radical Liberals, participated in several governments, and were crucial supporting parties to many minority governments. However, these parties have proved to be ephemeral in nature; they lack historic grounding and have achieved weak electoral scores (the CD received an electoral high of just 8.3 per cent in 1981). The parties were also not important actors before the early 1970s, so are not established parties. Other parties such as the DKP, FRP (Progress Party) and DF (Danish People's Party) must clearly belong in the non-established group as, although the DF is currently supporting the minority V/KF government, all three parties have been treated with suspicion by academics and other Danish parties alike regarding their democratic credentials.[3] Table 6.7 presents the established and non-established parties within the Danish party system. The four parties considered in terms of systemic centrality are the Social Democrats, Conservatives, Liberals and Radical Liberals.

Table 6.7 Established and non-established parties in Denmark, 1950–2007

Established	Non-established
SD (Social Democracy) (1950–present)	DF (Danish People's Party) (1998–present)
V (Left – Denmark's Liberal Party) (1950–present)	SF (Socialist People's Party) (1960–present)
KF (Conservative People's Party) (1950–present)	EL (Unity List – The Red-Greens) (1994–present)
RV (Radical Left) (1950–present)	KD (Christian Democrats) (previously KRF Christian People's Party, 1973–2001) CD (Centre Democrats) (1973–98) FRP (Progress Party) (1973–98) VS (Left Socialists) (1968–84) DKP (Communist Party) (1950–77) GB (Justice League) (1950–79) I (Liberal Alliance) (2008–present, previously Y, New Alliance, 2007–8)

Centrality of established parties

Table 6.8 summarises the levels of centrality within the electoral, parliamentary and governmental arenas for the four established parties. It shows that the centrality of Danish established parties within the electoral arena has progressed through three distinct stages. Between 1950 and 1971, centrality levels within the electoral arena were high, as the four established parties regularly polled over 85 per cent of the vote. However, the data clearly shows the impact of the earthquake election of 1973, as centrality within the electoral arena fell drastically for the established parties. In 1973, the four established parties received a combined vote share of just 58.3 per cent of the vote, a loss of 25.7 per cent compared to the 1971 election. Levels of centrality remained low for the next decade, but since the 1980s, the established parties have gradually regained some of the losses and current levels of centrality are moderate, as the established parties have received an average of over 70 per cent of the vote in the 2000s.

Due to the proportional nature of the Danish electoral system, levels of centrality within the parliamentary arena strongly mirror the patterns found within the electoral arena. The same three periods can be seen within the parliamentary arena, as levels of centrality from 1950 to 1971 were high, averaging around 90 per cent of parliamentary seats between the four established parties. Again, 1973 marks a sharp drop in levels of centrality as the combined share of seats fell from 90.2 per cent in 1971 to 59.4 per cent in 1973, an even more significant decline in centrality than was seen within the electoral arena. As in the electoral arena, centrality in the parliamentary arena increased after 1973, although levels are still well below those found before 1973.

Levels of centrality within the governmental arena have progressed through different stages from the other arenas. Between 1950 and 1981, levels of centrality appear to be relatively high, as on only one occasion a non-established party (the Justice Party in 1957) entered government. However, most Danish governments are minority administrations, so although governmental centrality was relatively high until 1981, these governments would often rely on non-established parties for parliamentary support. Between 1982 and 1994, five out of the seven governments formed contained non-established parties, indicating low levels of centrality for the established parties, but since 1996, only established parties have taken part in government. Centrality was low between 1982 and 1994, but the prime minister belonged to an established party on every occasion, suggesting that although non-established parties have taken part in governments, the established parties have still led all governments since 1950 and have been able to wield the most governmental influence.

Party system change

The Danish party system forms part of the traditional Scandinavian 'five-party' model, emphasising the historic strength of the Liberals, Social Democrats, Radical Liberals, Communists and Conservatives, although as has already been

Table 6.8 Centrality of established parties in the Danish party system, 1950–2007

	1950a	1950b	1953a	1953b	1957	1960	1964	1966	1968
Percentage share of the vote	SD: 39.6 V: 21.3 KF: 17.8 RV: 8.2 Total: 86.9%		SD: 40.4 V: 22.1 KF: 17.3 RV: 8.6 Total: 88.4%	SD: 41.3 V: 23.1 KF: 16.8 RV: 7.8 Total: 89.0%	SD: 39.4 V: 25.1 KF: 16.6 RV: 7.8 Total: 88.9%	SD: 42.1 V: 21.1 KF: 17.9 RV: 5.8 Total: 86.9%	SD: 41.9 V: 20.8 KF: 20.1 RV: 5.3 Total: 88.1%	SD: 38.2 V: 19.3 KF: 20.1 RV: 5.3 Total: 82.9%	SD: 34.2 V: 18.6 KF: 20.4 RV: 15.0 Total: 88.2%
Percentage share of seats	SD: 39.6 V: 21.5 KF: 18.1 RV: 8.1 Total: 87.3%		SD: 40.9 V: 22.1 KF: 17.4 RV: 8.7 Total: 89.1%	SD: 42.2 V: 24.0 KF: 17.1 RV: 8.0 Total: 91.3%	SD: 40.0 V: 25.7 KF: 17.1 RV: 8.0 Total: 90.8%	SD: 43.4 V: 21.7 KF: 18.3 RV: 6.3 Total: 89.7%	SD: 43.4 V: 21.7 KF: 20.6 RV: 5.7 Total: 91.4%	SD: 39.4 V: 20.0 KF: 19.4 RV: 7.4 Total: 86.2%	SD: 35.4 V: 19.4 KF: 21.1 RV: 15.4 Total: 91.3%
Largest party within parliament (seats)	SD	SD	SD	SD	SD	SD	SD	SD	SD
Time spent in government									
SD									
V									
KF									
RV									
JP									
Median legislator	RV	RV	RV	RV	RV	RV	RV	RV	RV
Percentage share of government positions	SD: 92.3 Ind: 7.7	KF: 61.5 V: 38.5	KF: 61.5 V: 38.5	SD: 100	SD: 58.8 RV: 29.4 JP: 11.8	SD: 66.7 RV: 26.7 Ind: 6.7	SD: 100	SD: 100	V: 29.4 KF: 47.1 RV: 23.5
Prime minister's party	SD	V	V	SD	SD	SD	SD	SD	RV
Ratio of positions obtained to share of seats	SD: 2.3:1	KF: 3.4:1 V: 1.8:1	KF: 3.5:1 V: 1.7:1	SD: 2.4:1	SD: 1.5:1 RV: 3.7:1 JP: 2.3:1	SD: 1.5:1 RV: 4.2:1	SD: 2.3:1	SD: 2.5:1	V: 1.5:1 KF: 2.2:1 RV: 1.5:1

continued overleaf

Table 6.8 continued

	1971	1973	1975	1977	1978	1979	1981	1982	1984	1987
Percentage share of the vote	SD: 37.3 V: 15.6 KF: 16.7 RV: 14.4 Total: 84.0%	SD: 25.6 V: 12.3 KF: 9.2 RV: 11.2 Total: 58.3%	SD: 29.9 V: 23.3 KF: 5.5 RV: 7.1 Total: 65.8%	SD: 37.0 V: 12.0 KF: 8.5 RV: 3.6 Total: 61.1%		SD: 38.3 V: 12.5 KF: 12.5 RV: 5.4 Total: 68.7%	SD: 32.9 V: 11.3 KF: 14.5 RV: 5.1 Total: 63.8%		SD: 31.6 V: 12.1 KF: 23.4 RV: 5.5 Total: 72.6%	SD: 29.3 V: 10.5 KF: 20.8 RV: 6.2 Total: 66.8%
Percentage share of seats	SD: 40.0 V: 17.1 KF: 17.7 RV: 15.4 Total: 90.2%	SD: 26.3 V: 12.6 KF: 9.1 RV: 11.4 Tota: 59.4%	SD: 30.3 V: 24.0 KF: 5.7 RV: 7.4 Total: 67.4%	SD: 37.1 V: 12.0 KF: 8.6 RV: 3.4 Total: 61.1%		SD: 38.9 V: 12.6 KF: 12.6 RV: 5.7 Total: 69.8%	SD: 33.7 V: 11.4 KF: 14.9 RV: 5.1 Total: 65.1%		SD: 32.0 V: 12.6 KF: 24.0 RV: 5.7 Total: 74.3%	SD: 30.9 V: 10.9 KF: 21.7 RV: 6.3 Total: 69.8%
Largest party within parliament (seats)	SD	SD	SD	SD	SD	SD	SD	SD	SD	SD
Time spent in government SD V KF CD CPP										
Median legislator	RV	RV	RV	CD	CD	CD	CD	CD	CD	CD
Percentage share of government positions	SD: 94.1 Ind: 5.9	V: 100	SD: 100	SD: 100	SD: 63.2 V: 36.8	SD: 100	SD: 100	KF: 26.3 V: 42.1 CD: 21.1 CPP: 10.5	KF: 26.3 V: 42.1 CD: 21.1 CPP: 10.5	V: 26.3 KF: 52.6 CD: 15.8 CPP: 5.3
Prime minister's party	SD	V	SD	SD	SD	SD	SD	KF	KF	KF
Ratio of positions obtained to share of seats	SD: 2.4:1	V: 7.9:1	SD: 3.3:1	SD: 2.7:1	SD: 1.7:1 V: 3.1:1	SD: 2.6:1	SD: 3.0:1	KF: 1.8:1 V: 3.7:1 CD: 2.5:1 CPP: 4.6:1	KF: 1.1:1 V: 3.3:1 CD: 4.6:1 CPP: 3.6:1	V: 2.4:1 KF: 2.4:1 CD: 3.1:1 CPP: 2.3:1

	1988	1990	1993	1994	1996	1998	2001	2005	2007
Percentage share of the vote	SD: 29.8 V: 11.8 KF: 19.3 RV: 5.6 Total: 66.5%	SD: 37.4 V: 15.8 KF: 16.0 RV: 3.5 Total: 72.7%		SD: 34.6 V: 23.3 KF: 15.0 RV: 4.6 Total: 77.5%		SD: 36.0 V: 24.0 KF: 8.9 RV: 3.9 Total: 72.8%	SD: 29.1 V: 31.3 KF: 9.1 RV: 5.2 Total: 74.7%	SD: 25.8 V: 29.0 KF: 10.3 RV: 9.2 Total: 74.3%	SD: 25.5 V: 26.3 KF: 10.4 RV: 5.1 Total: 67.3%
Percentage share of seats	SD: 31.4 V: 12.6 KF: 20.0 RV: 5.7 Total: 69.7%	SD: 39.4 V: 16.6 KF: 17.1 RV: 4.0 Total: 77.1%		SD: 35.4 V: 24.0 KF: 4.6 RV: 4.6 Total: 68.6%		SD: 36.0 V: 24.0 KF: 9.1 RV: 4.0 Total: 73.1%	SD: 29.7 V: 32.0 KF: 9.1 RV: 5.1 Total: 75.9%	SD: 26.9 V: 29.7 KF: 10.1 RV: 9.1 Total: 75.8%	SD: 25.1 V: 25.7 KF: 10.1 RV: 5.0 Total: 65.9%
Largest party within parliament (seats)	SD	SD	SD	SD	SD	SD	V	V	V
Time spent in government									
SD									
V									
KF									
RV									
CD									
CPP									
Median legislator	CD	CD	CD	RV	RV	CD	KF	KF	KF
Percentage share of government positions	V: 29.4 KF: 41.2 RV: 29.4	V: 55.6 KF: 44.4	SD: 63.2 RV: 15.8 CD: 10.5 CPP: 10.5	SD: 73.7 RV: 15.8 CD: 10.5	SD: 75.0 RV: 25.0	SD: 75.0 RV: 25.0	V: 67.0 KF: 33.0	V: 61.1 KF: 38.9	V: 62.5 KF: 37.5
Prime minister's party	KF	KF	SD	SD	SD	SD	V	V	V
Ratio of positions obtained to share of seats	V: 2.3:1 KF: 2.1:1 RV: 5.2:1	V: 3.3:1 KF: 2.6:1	SD: 1.6:1 RV: 4.0:1 CD: 2.1:1 CPP: 4.6:1	SD: 2.1:1 RV: 3.4:1 CD: 3.6:1	SD: 2.1:1 RV: 5.4:1	SD: 2.1:1 RV: 6.3:1	V: 2.1:1 KF: 3.6:1	V: 2.1:1 KF: 3.6:1	V: 2.4:1 KF: 3.7:1

Sources: Bille (2002); Damgaard (2000); Official Website of Denmark (2010); Woldendorp et al. (2000).

stated, the Communists are historically weaker in Denmark than in the other Scandinavian nations. Table 6.9 reflects the strength of the four established parties, as the average effective number of parties present within the electoral party system between 1950 and 1968 is about four. The trends in the effective number of parties reflect the findings concerning established party centrality within the electoral and parliamentary arenas, as the effective number of parties increases considerably between 1971 and 1988, but then decreases in the most recent period, but remain higher than the levels found between 1950 and 1968.

The earthquake election of 1973 is important in terms of electoral and parliamentary arena centrality and the average effective number of parties. However, the 1973 electoral earthquake appears to have had less impact on the structure of competition than these other measures. Table 6.9 indicates that no change in the structure of competition occurred in 1973, as the system was semi-closed before and after the 1973 election and was characterised by restricted access to government, some innovation in government formulae and generally wholesale or no alternation. Indeed, there is only one period where the Danish party system had not been characterised by a semi-closed structure of competition, when the Radical Liberals and Justice Party entered government for the first time in 1957.

There is much debate in the literature concerning the extent of party system change following the 1973 election. Smith (1989b: 167) argues that there is more evidence of continuity than change within the Danish party system: 'the Social Democrats ... have stabilised their vote at around 30 per cent during the 1980s. Taking that continuity into account, the Danish party system appears to have undergone no more than a restricted change.' Lars Bille argues that the change was more significant, and suggests that the Danish party system moved from moderate to polarised pluralism after 1973 as the process of government formation became much more complex and bilateral oppositions were present (1989: 50). Yet the four established parties have remained the core parties within the party system and, as Table 6.9 shows, patterns of government formation and the structure of competition within the party system did not change after 1973.[4]

Table 6.9 Party system change in Denmark, 1950–2007

Structure of competition	Effective number of parties	
	<5	≥5
Closed		
Semi-closed	1950–53, N_v: 3.92, N_s: 3.82 (n=3) 1964–71, N_v: 4.44, N_s: 4.05 (n=3) 1990–present, N_v: 4.94, N_s: 4.77 (n=6)	1973–88, N_v: 5.71, N_s: 5.42 (n=8)
Semi-open	1957–64, N_v: 3.83, N_s: 3.64 (n=3)	
Open		

This section has uncovered a mixed pattern of centrality for the established parties within the Danish party system. The 1973 electoral earthquake drastically reduced the previously high levels of centrality for the established parties within the electoral and parliamentary arenas and increased the effective number of parties found within the party system. However, the established parties have regained moderate levels of centrality within the electoral and parliamentary arenas, but have yet to return to their pre-1973 levels of dominance. In contrast to the patterns found at the electoral level, the impact on the governmental arena and the structure of competition has been far weaker and does not appear to have changed dramatically after 1973. Section 6.6 discusses in more detail the reasons for the reduced impact of the electoral earthquake, with the impact of the low use of institutional strategies on the established parties also discussed. This chapter now moves on to the Irish example to determine similarities and differences between the cases.

6.5 Ireland

Several unique features have strongly shaped the operation of Irish party politics and the Irish party system. The first unique feature of the Irish political system is the STV (Single Transferable Vote) electoral system for elections to the lower house. STV is a preferential system that allows voters to rank candidates in order of preference within a given constituency. The electoral system encourages candidates to compete with other candidates from other parties, but also with candidates from within their own party. Voters under the STV system cast a vote for individual candidates as opposed to a party, so the system is individualistic and highlights the importance of personalistic rather than partisan links between voters and politicians (Mair 1987: 61–2).

The second notable feature of the Irish political system is the absence of a class basis to political competition. At the time when the Irish party system crystallised in the 1920s, the major issue on the political agenda was the Anglo-Irish Treaty, with political forces divided between those in favour and those against the Treaty. The class party of the day, the Labour party, did not present any candidates in the crucial 1918 election (Mair 1987: 45) and instead the nationalist debate decided the election. The United Kingdom introduced universal suffrage at this election and according to the work of Lipset and Rokkan (1967), it is for this reason that the parties that emerged from pro-treaty (Fine Gael) and anti-treaty (Fianna Fáil) forces formed the basis of the new party system. Although some political scientists have argued against this deterministic approach to the development of the Irish party system (see Mair 1987 and 1999), the absence of a class basis to political competition ensures that the main parties stand on their records rather than position on the political spectrum (Collins and Cradden 1997: 24). The relative absence of ideological division has led to the system becoming a 'prototypic catch-all system', dominated by centrist parties competing on the issue of economic management (Carty 1988: 225).

From the previous discussion, it should be clear which parties are the established parties within the Irish system. Fianna Fáil and Fine Gael emerged as the two principal Irish parties during the 1920s and remain the two most important parties in terms of share of the vote today, with either party having held the position of prime minister in all governments in the period covered. The Labour party has also been a crucial part of the Irish party system since the 1920s and is included in the group of established parties although its vote share has consistently been lower than that of Fianna Fáil or Fine Gael. These three parties are the established parties within the Irish party system; they were the dominant parties at the time of systemic crystallisation in the 1920s and continue to be the leading parties today. Other small parties such as the CnT (Children of the Country) and the PD (Progressive Democrats) have taken part in government during the period covered, but their share of the vote, limited governmental participation, short periods spent in parliament and recent entrance into the party system do not justify established party status. The list of established and non-established parties are summarised in Table 6.10.

Centrality of established parties

As shown in Table 6.11, levels of centrality for the established Irish parties within the electoral arena have been exceptionally high throughout much of the period covered. In common with the Danish example, one crucial election stands out as the point at which centrality for the established parties dropped dramatically. Between 1965 and 1982, the established parties received consistently over 90 per cent of the vote, with their share of the vote gradually increasing during the period between 1950 and 1965. However, the 1987 election marks the turning point for levels of centrality within the electoral arena, as the combined share of the vote for the three parties fell to just 77.6 per cent, a decline of 16.2 percentage points from the previous election. Since this dramatic election, levels

Table 6.10 Established and non-established parties in Ireland, 1951–2007

Established	Non-established
FF (Fianna Fáil: Soldiers of Destiny – The Republican Party) (1951–present)	PD (Progressive Democrats) (1987–2009)
FG (Fine Gael: Family of the Irish – The United Ireland Party) (1951–present)	SF (Sinn Féin: We Ourselves) (1954–present)
Lab (Labour Party) (1951–present)	GP (Green Party) (1987–present) SP (Socialist Party) (1997–present) WP (Workers' Party) (1981–present) DL (Democratic Left) (1992–97) CnP (Clann na Poblachta: Republican Family) (1951–65) CnT (Clann na Talmhan: Children of the Country) (1951–61)w

of centrality have remained at a moderate level, with the 2002 election marking the lowest combined share of the vote for the three parties since 1951, before levels increased again in 2007.

The relatively proportional nature of the Irish electoral system ensures that patterns of centrality within the parliamentary arena generally mirror those found within the electoral arena, although the impact of the 1987 election is not as dramatic within the parliamentary arena as the electoral arena. Levels of centrality within the parliamentary arena increased steadily between 1951 and 1965 and remained consistently at exceptional levels until 1987, when the percentage of seats gained by the three parties decreased from 92.8 per cent to 86.7 per cent, a reduction of just 6.1 percentage points compared to the 16.2 point loss in electoral support. This data appears to show that the electoral system does favour the established parties, especially Fianna Fáil, which lost 1.1 per cent of the vote, but gained 3.6 per cent of seats between the 1982 and 1987 elections. Recent trends match those found within the electoral arena and show that the established parties have yet to regain their previous dominance.

Within the governmental arena, patterns of centrality reflect those found within the other two arenas. The CnT was involved in government in 1954 but between 1957 and 1987, only established parties took part in government. However, following the election of 1987, government formation patterns have become unpredictable and open and the established parties no longer dominate the governmental arena in the way they were able to until 1987. Since 1989, the Progressive Democrats, Workers' Party, Democratic Left and the Greens have all taken part in governments and, although the prime minister continues to emerge from either Fianna Fáil or Fine Gael, there has been a significant decrease in the levels of centrality achieved by the established parties within the governmental arena since the 1987 election.

Levels of centrality for the established parties were high in all three arenas until the 1987 election, which significantly affected levels of centrality within all three arenas, especially the electoral and governmental arenas. This contrasts with the Danish case, where the 1973 election did not appear to alter significantly the levels of centrality experienced by the established parties within the governmental arena, but made a considerable impact within the electoral and parliamentary arenas. Section 6.6 discusses the reasons for the particularly significant impact of the 1987 election on the established parties within Ireland and discusses the potential reasons for the differing impact on the governmental arena found within the two countries.

Party system change

The Irish party system has often been described as 'Fianna Fáil versus the rest' (for example, by Mair 1979: 459), highlighting the predominance of Fianna Fáil and the alliance of Fine Gael and Labour (since the mid-1950s) as the only governing alternative. However, this 'traditional' image of the Irish party system altered in 1987 and the system is now a more 'normal' western European party

Table 6.11 Centrality of established parties in the Irish party system, 1951–2007

	1951	1954	1957	1961	1965	1969	1973	1977	1981
Percentage share of the vote	FF: 46.3 FG: 25.8 Lab: 11.4 Total: 83.5%	FF: 43.4 FG: 32.0 Lab: 12.1 Total: 87.5%	FF: 48.3 FG: 26.6 Lab: 9.1 Total: 84.0%	FF: 43.8 FG: 32.0 Lab: 11.6 Total: 87.4%	FF: 47.7 FG: 34.1 Lab: 15.4 Total: 97.2%	FF: 45.7 FG: 34.1 Lab: 17.0 Total: 96.8%	FF: 46.2 FG: 35.1 Lab: 13.7 Total: 95.0%	FF: 50.6 FG: 30.5 Lab: 11.6 Total: 92.7%	FF: 45.3 FG: 36.5 Lab: 9.9 Total: 91.7%
Percentage share of seats	FF: 46.9 FG: 27.2 Lab: 10.9 Total: 85.0%	FF: 44.2 FG: 34.0 Lab: 12.9 Total: 91.1%	FF: 53.1 FG: 27.2 Lab: 8.2 Total: 88.5%	FF: 48.6 FG: 32.6 Lab: 11.1 Total: 92.3%	FF: 50.0 FG: 32.6 Lab: 15.3 Total: 97.9%	FF: 52.1 FG: 34.7 Lab: 12.5 Total: 99.3%	FF: 47.9 FG: 37.5 Lab: 13.2 Total: 98.6%	FF: 56.8 FG: 29.1 Lab: 11.5 Total: 97.4%	FF: 47.0 FG: 39.2 Lab: 9.0 Total: 95.2%
Largest party within parliament (seats)	FF	FF	FF	FF	FF	FF	FF	FF	FF
Time spent in government									
FF									
FG									
Lab									
CnT									
Median legislator	FF	FF	FF	FF	FF	FF	FF	FF	FF
Percentage share of government positions	FF: 100	FG: 60.0 Lab: 33.3 CnT: 6.7	FF: 100	FF: 100	FF: 100	FF: 100	FG: 56.3 Lab: 43.7	FF: 100	FG: 64.7 Lab: 35.3
Prime minister's party	FF	FG	FF	FF	FF	FF	FG	FF	FG
Ratio of positions obtained to share of seats	FF: 2.1:1	FG: 1.8:1 Lab: 2.6:1 CnT: 2.0:1	FF: 1.9:1	FF: 2.1:1	FF: 2.0:1	FF: 1.9:1	FG: 1.5:1 Lab: 3.3:1	FF: 1.8:1	FG: 1.7:1 Lab: 3.9:1

	1982a	1982b	1987	1989	1992	1994	1997	2002	2007	2008
Percentage share of the vote	FF: 47.3 FG: 37.3 Lab: 9.1 Total: 93.7%	FF: 45.2 FG: 39.2 Lab: 9.4 Total: 93.8%	FF: 44.1 FG: 27.1 Lab: 6.4 Total: 77.6%	FF: 44.1 FG: 29.3 Lab: 9.5 Total: 82.9%	FF: 39.1 FG: 24.5 Lab: 19.3 Total: 82.9%		FF: 39.3 FG: 27.9 Lab: 10.4 Total: 77.6%	FF: 41.5 FG: 22.5 Lab: 10.8 Total: 74.8%	FF: 41.6 FG: 27.3 Lab: 10.1 Total: 79.0%	FF: 41.6 FG: 27.3 Lab: 10.1 Total: 79.0%
Percentage share of seats	FF: 48.8 FG: 38.0 Lab: 9.0 Total: 95.8%	FF: 45.2 FG: 38.0 Lab: 9.6 Total: 92.8%	FF: 48.8 FG: 30.7 Lab: 7.2 Total: 86.7%	FF: 46.4 FG: 33.1 Lab: 9.0 Total: 88.5%	FF: 41.0 FG: 27.1 Lab: 19.9 Total: 88.0%		FF: 46.4 FG: 32.5 Lab: 10.2 Total: 89.1%	FF: 48.8 FG: 18.7 Lab: 12.7 Total: 80.2%	FF: 47.0 FG: 30.7 Lab: 12.0 Total: 89.7%	FF: 47.0 FG: 30.7 Lab: 12.0 Total: 89.7%
Largest party within parliament (seats)	FF	FF	FF	FF	FF	FF	FF	FF	FF	FF
Time spent in government										
FF										
FG										
Lab										
PD										
DL										
GP										
Median legislator	FF	FF	FF	FF	FF	FF	FF	FF	FF	FF
Percentage share of government positions	FF: 100	FG: 60.0 Lab: 40.0	FF: 100	FF: 83.3 PD: 16.7	FF: 61.1 Lab: 38.9	FG: 47.1 Lab: 52.9	FF: 83.3 PD: 16.7	FF: 86.7 PD: 13.3	FF: 81.2 PD:6.3 GP: 12.5	FF: 81.2 GP: 12.5 Ind:6.3
Prime minister's party	FF	FG	FF	FF	FF	FG	FF	FF	FF	FF
Ratio of positions obtained to share of seats	FF: 2.0:1	FG: 1.6:1 Lab: 4.2:1	FF: 2.0:1	FF: 1.8:1 PD: 1.7:1	FF: 1.5:1 Lab: 2.0:1	FG: 1.7:1 Lab: 2.7:1	FF: 1.8:1 PD: 7.0:1	FF: 1.8:1 PD: 2.8:1	FF: 1.7:1 PD: 5.3:1 GP: 3.5:1	FF: 1.7:1 GP: 3.5:1

Sources: Irish Government Homepage (2010); Mitchell (2000); O'Malley and Marsh (2003); Woldendorp et al. (2000).

Note
The composition of the Irish government changed in 2008 following the dissolution of the Progressive Democrat party. The PD's cabinet minister, Mary Harney, remained in cabinet as an Independent.

system, characterised by moderate pluralism and coalition politics. The effective number of parties present within the system reflects these patterns. Table 6.12 shows that the effective number of parties value was relatively static until the 1987 election, when the number of parties increased substantially, indicating an increasingly fragmented party system.

In the Danish case, the electoral earthquake and the large increase in the effective number of parties that took place in 1973 did not have a significant impact on the structure of competition. However, this is not the case with the Irish party system. Table 6.12 shows that the structure of competition changed in 1957 and in 1989. The move in the late 1980s of the party system from a semi-closed system with a limited format to an open system with an enlarged format constitutes a party system change. The elections of the late 1980s proved notable for several reasons. The election of 1987 saw the Progressive Democrats enter parliament with 11.8 per cent of the vote and saw a dramatic decline in the vote share of the established parties, as demonstrated in Table 6.11. In 1989, following another strong showing for the non-established parties, Fianna Fáil formed a coalition for the first time in the history of the party and in doing so, opened up the political market (Mair 1999: 142). Until this point, Fianna Fáil had dismissed coalitions as inherently divisive, incoherent and unstable (Carty 1988: 229), but the decision of Fianna Fáil in 1989 changed the structure of competition within the Irish party system from a semi-closed, predictable structure to a 'free-for-all', open structure where the previous structural certainties had been destroyed.

The Irish party system has changed in many ways and the change in the structure of competition has challenged the established parties, but according to Mair and Michael Marsh, the established parties have demonstrated their 'extraordinary adaptive capacity' despite 'operating in an unfamiliar and potentially inhospitable political landscape' (2004: 256–7). The Irish party system appears to stand out as the system that has experienced the most permanent party system change in the eight case studies considered, to the extent that Mair argues 'there is … nothing which remains of the old order' (1993c: 172).

This section has highlighted the importance of the 1987 election for the development of the Irish party system. At this election, established party

Table 6.12 Party system change in Ireland, 1951–2007

	Effective number of parties	
Structure of competition	<3	≥3
Closed		
Semi-closed	1957–87, N_v: 2.93, N_s: 2.64 (n=10)	
Semi-open		1951–4, N_v: 3.11, N_s: 3.15 (n=2)
Open		1989–present, N_v: 3.86, N_s: 3.20 (n=5)

centrality within the electoral and parliamentary arenas fell dramatically and shortly after, governmental centrality fell to moderate levels. The 1987 election significantly affected the structure of competition within the Irish party system and party system change occurred following the important decision of Fianna Fáil in 1989 to enter a coalition for the first time. The effective number of parties within the party system increased in the period since the late 1980s and the structure of competition changed from semi-closed to open.

6.6 The infrequent use of institutional strategies and established parties' centrality

Chapter 3 demonstrated that the established parties in Denmark and Ireland engaged in the lowest levels of institutional strategies within western Europe. In both countries, laws concerning the electoral system, television advertising regime and state subsidies either favour the non-established parties (in the case of Denmark), or were neutral for non-established parties (in the case of Ireland). Additionally, the Irish system of electoral laws is the most permissive in western Europe. The low use of these strategies should have a significant impact on the party systems in question. Permissive institutions for non-established parties should produce party systems that contain a large number of parties (and where established party centrality should be relatively low), with party system instability the norm due to the difficult and complex nature of coalition formation.

However, despite the use of similar strategies in Ireland and Denmark, the results of the study in this chapter have produced contrasting results regarding the impact of the low use of institutional strategies. Some features are similar in both countries; established parties experienced high levels of centrality within all three arenas for a period, until an earthquake election challenged the traditional structure of competition within both countries. In Denmark, governmental centrality and the structure of competition remained unaffected after the 1973 earthquake election, whereas in Ireland, the party system changed after the 1987 election and produced a fundamental shift in both levels of governmental centrality for the established parties, and the structure of competition within the party system. It is the principal task of this section to assess why the 1987 Irish election had a more significant impact on the party system than the 1973 election in Denmark.

In the late 1970s, Berglund and Lindström argued that the Danish party system was 'ultra stable' (1978: 74) and that deep social cleavages and a commitment to national unity and democratic principles were the principal reasons for this stability (Sundberg 2002: 181). The underlying class basis for competition, combined with the dominance of the Social Democrats shaping the structure of competition in Denmark, helps to explain why, until 1973, established parties enjoyed high levels of centrality in all three arenas and the party system demonstrated a remarkable degree of consensus and stability (Bille 1989: 42). However, the 1973 election showed the importance of low levels of engagement by the established parties in institutional strategies, as the party system was accessible. Unprecedented levels of volatility occurred at the 1973 election, with the Christian Democrats and Progress Party gaining a combined 23.7 per cent of the vote at their first elections. Factors such as structural dealignment, a decline in class loyalties, the rapid expansion of the public sector and economic recession (Bille and Pedersen 2004: 211) are reasons why the earthquake election occurred in 1973, but the Danish institutional setting played a role in assisting these parties. A permissive electoral system, equitable distribution of television advertising airtime and a generous state subsidy regime for new and smaller parties ensured that new parties had a relatively easy passage into parliament and would receive support to remain in parliament. Although the institutional setting cannot fully explain why the electoral earthquake occurred in 1973, it can help to explain why the new parties were able to achieve almost instantaneous success.

The most interesting point to consider as far as the impact of the low use of institutional strategies is concerned is to assess why the 1973 earthquake election had a major impact on the parliamentary and electoral arenas, but did not dramatically affect the governmental arena or the structure of competition. The low use of institutional strategies applies predominantly to the electoral and parliamentary arenas; electorate-orientated strategies are more likely to control what occurs in the governmental arena. The electoral system, electoral laws, state subsidies and television advertising assist smaller and newer parties *to enter the electoral and parliamentary arenas*, as the regimes in place are relatively permissive, but cannot assist the parties to gain access to the governmental arena. The entry of the new parties in these two arenas was not enough in the Danish example to force a change in the structure of competition or change in the centrality of established parties in the governmental arena. Why was this the case?

The combination of two features of the Danish party system helps to explain the continued dominance of the established parties in the governmental arena and the stability found in the structure of competition. The first is the prevalence of minority governments. In the post-war period, all but one Danish government has relied on the support of non-governmental parties to pass legislation. The enormous decline in the share of the vote received by the established parties in 1973 did not alter the structure of competition because government formation in Denmark was not based on the achievement of a parliamentary majority by one party or parties. The shift in electoral preferences seen in 1973 influenced the governmental structure far less than would have been expected in a country where majority governments were the norm. If majority governments had been the norm, an electoral shift of this magnitude may have eroded the parliamentary majority enjoyed by a party or parties, forcing a change in the structure of competition. However, minority governments containing the same established parties could continue, albeit perhaps with slightly more of a 'minority' status than before, particularly the 1973 Liberal minority government controlling only 22 out of the 179 seats in parliament.

The second important factor is the distribution of seats between the left and right blocs. Berglund and Lindström (1978: 174) argue that the 'two main blocs ... did remain pretty stable during the 1970s', but acknowledge a slight shift to the right following the 1973 election. Bille (1989: 55) comments on 'the remarkable stability of the distribution of seats in parliament between the bourgeois bloc ... and the non-bourgeois bloc ... and the delicate balance which existed between the two blocs' and observes that most electoral volatility takes place *within* blocs and not *between* blocs. The 1973 election did not affect the balance between the blocs and the high levels of intra-bloc volatility did not have a major impact on the structure of competition within the party system.

This section has argued that the minimal impact on the structure of competition of the 1973 Danish election is largely due to the prevalence of minority governments and the equitable and stable distribution of seats between the two blocs. The importance of the interplay of electorate-orientated and institutional strategies is also significant. Although the institutional environment has been shown to be permissive for smaller and newer parties, the strategies of the established parties concerning the structure of competition and government formation has produced a loss of connection between the will of the people and the composition of government (Arter 1999a: 157). This disconnectedness has allowed the structure of competition to remain stable and the established parties to continue to achieve high levels of centrality in the governmental arena.

The Irish case resembles the Danish in important ways, as outlined earlier, but the Irish earthquake election of 1987 had a greater impact on the governmental arena and the structure of competition than in the Danish example. In both countries, the party systems before the electoral earthquakes were very stable with one party dominating. Until 1987, there was a lack of competition in Ireland as Fianna Fáil held the key to alternation in government. If Fianna Fáil achieved a parliamentary majority, the party would govern alone. If the party failed to achieve a majority, the 'rest' of the parties would form a coalition government, with divisions between the parties comprising the 'rest' sometimes leading to the formation of a Fianna Fáil minority government. Mair (1987: 60) highlights the crucial importance for the stability of the party system of the choices made by Fianna Fáil: 'the potential for major post-war change was frustrated by the strategic decisions of the parties themselves and as a consequence of the logistics of government formation'. The STV electoral system further reinforced the lack of competition present in the pre-1987 Irish party system, as often candidates from the same party contested the final seat in a constituency (Mair 1987: 64). The dominance of Fianna Fáil and the party's decision to eschew coalitions, effectively closing competition in the party system, combined with the STV electoral system strongly contributed to the stability found in the pre-1987 party system.

The 1987 election was notable for the entrance of the Progressive Democrats onto the electoral scene, achieving 11.8 per cent of the vote at the party's first election. As with the Danish example, the Irish institutional set-up and the low levels of institutional strategies in which the established parties engaged facilitated the entrance of this new party. However, the electoral shock of 1987 in Ireland had a more profound and enduring impact on the governmental arena and the structure of competition than in Denmark. In Denmark, the bloc structure of competition and the prevalence of minority governments were factors that prevented electoral arena changes from influencing the governmental arena. In Ireland, majority governments are the norm and although Ireland has experienced several minority administrations, majority governments have been more common and there was no bloc system in operation. The electoral changes that occurred in 1987 introduced new actors into the electoral market and raised the possibility the Fianna Fáil may never again achieve a majority in parliament due to the new crowding of the electoral market.

Following the 1989 election, Fianna Fáil entered a coalition for the first time, destroying the previously stable structure of competition in the Irish party system. The entrance of a new actor had forced Fianna Fáil to reconsider its place within the party system. It could either continue to govern alone, almost certainly only as a minority administration or it could form a coalition and potentially (as the largest party) remain permanently in government (Mair 1999: 145). Fianna Fáil chose the latter option, opening up the governmental arena and the structure of government in Ireland in a way that never occurred in Denmark following the 1973 election. Since Fianna Fáil's radical strategic change of 1989, the Irish party system has been in flux, with its previous structural certainties removed. Fine Gael has suffered a drastic loss in its share of the vote, yet still formed a coalition in 1994, whereas Fianna Fáil's share of the vote has remained remarkably stable,[5] with the Greens emerging as a coalition partner for Fianna Fáil from 2007–11.

The electoral shock of 1987, assisted by the permissive institutional setting for new and smaller parties, had a dramatic impact on the Irish party system. The importance of the strategies engaged in by Fianna Fáil has also been highlighted, with the decision to open up the Irish party system following decades of a lack of competition brought about by the dominance of Fianna Fáil single-party rule. The actions of the established parties mediated the impact of the two electoral earthquakes in Denmark and Ireland, highlighting the vital importance of acknowledging the interplay between institutional and electorate-oriented strategies. The conclusion of this chapter pursues this point further.

This section has highlighted the contrasting impact of the two earthquake elections in Denmark in 1973 and in Ireland in 1987. In Denmark, the structure of competition was unaffected due to the dominance of minority governments and the bloc structure of the party system. In Ireland, the party system transformed due to the decision of Fianna Fáil to change the structure of competition in 1989 that has left the Irish party system in a state of flux. Having examined the four cases in this, this chapter now concludes by analysing the central hypotheses, assessing the relevance of the cartel thesis for these four countries and finally examining the importance of the interplay between institutional and electorate-oriented strategies.

6.7 Conclusion

This chapter has assessed the impact of the high and low use of institutional strategies on the established parties of Greece and France, and Ireland and Denmark. In line with the cartel thesis, established parties that engaged in the highest levels of institutional strategies were moving themselves closer to the state and attempting to restrict competition within the party system. Established parties engaging in high levels of these strategies should achieve high levels of centrality within their national party systems.

In France and Greece, the countries in which established parties engaged in the highest levels of institutional strategies, established parties should achieve high levels of centrality in all three arenas and the party system should be extremely stable due to the institutional set-up restricting opportunities for non-established parties. In Denmark and Ireland, the countries in which the lowest levels of engagement in institutional strategies occurred, established parties should achieve low levels of centrality in all three arenas and the party system should be relatively unstable due to the presence of a multitude of small parties, assisted by the favourable institutional setting. These hypotheses were only partially borne out by this study. In the Greek party system, the two established parties achieve high levels of centrality in all three arenas and the party system is extremely stable, supporting the hypothesis. However, the situation in France is somewhat different. Low levels of centrality occurred within the electoral arena, moderate levels within the governmental arena and high levels within the parliamentary arenas. The party system was in a permanent state of flux, challenging the hypothesis.

The Danish case partly supports the hypothesis. The party system was stable and established party centrality high until 1973, when centrality within the electoral and parliamentary arenas fell dramatically and the effective number of parties within parliament increased significantly. However, the structure of competition did not change and centrality within the governmental arena remained moderate, which implies that the Danish system appears to be far more stable than predicted. The Irish party system was also very stable until 1987, but since then, Ireland appears to support the hypothesis and is characterised by moderate levels of centrality within the electoral and parliamentary arenas and low levels within the governmental arena. Additionally, the party system has become unstable and is characterised by an increasing number of parties. It appears that half of the cases support the hypotheses and half do not. How can these findings be explained?

The importance of the interplay of institutional and electorate-orientated strategies is an explanation for the minimal impact of the 1973 Danish election on the governmental arena and the structure of competition. Although the institutional setting may be favourable for the smaller parties, this would only allow these parties opportunities to enter the electoral and parliamentary arenas; entry to the governmental arena remained controlled by the electorate-orientated strategies of the established parties. Although institutions can help to shape a country's political system, the strategic actions of political parties are crucially important. Electorate-orientated strategies solidified the pre-1987 Irish party system, as Fianna Fáil governed alone or not at all. Similarly, it was the change in strategy of Fianna Fáil in 1989 that opened up the Irish party system, suggesting that although institutions have proved to be permissive for non-established parties in both Denmark and Ireland, established parties can still shape the party system by controlling the structure of competition and access to the governmental arena.

Acknowledging the interplay of electorate-orientated and institutional strategies explains many of the anomalies found in the results, but cannot explain the French established parties' moderate levels of centrality, despite high levels of institutional strategies. France is a unique case in this study as in the other 16 countries studied, political parties shape institutions, make legislation and the prime minister is the most important political figure in the country. This is not the case in France, as the institution of the presidency ensures that party politics is of secondary importance compared to presidential politics. France is an outlier in this study, but the case study did produce many interesting findings, especially when compared to the Greek case.

This chapter also aimed to test the relevance of the cartel thesis and to assess the extent to which the four party systems resemble cartel party systems. The work of Katz and Mair (1995) argues that parties put restrictive institutional settings in place in order to maintain the cartel and prevent entry into the system of outsider parties. The systems of Greece and France should most strongly resemble cartel party systems, whereas the Danish and Irish party systems should have few features in common with a cartel party system. The party system of Greece appears to fit the model the closest. ND and PASOK have monopolised government except for a brief period in 1989 and 1990, and have achieved exceptionally high levels of centrality within all three arenas, and the party system has proved to be exceptionally stable. None of the other three countries considered fit the cartel model as well as the Greek case. In France, the system is in flux and the established parties have achieved only moderate levels of systemic centrality within the three arenas. In Denmark, the structure of competition has always been relatively open and fluid, in contrast to the structure of competition expected within a cartel party system. The present day Irish system does not conform to the cartel system model, as although the established parties have adjusted well to the new electoral distribution and their new competitors, established parties have not closed entry to the system to non-established parties. The cartel thesis does seem to find some support within this chapter, as Greece conforms closely to cartel party system and Denmark and Ireland do not, in line with the hypotheses generated.

This chapter has attempted to analyse the impact of the high and low use of institutional strategies on the fate of established parties. The findings of this chapter somewhat validate the hypotheses and appear to lend a certain degree of support to the cartel thesis, but these issues will be assessed in greater depth in the concluding chapter. The focus of the concluding chapter is on the hypotheses generated throughout this book, the potential for perverse effects to emerge from the engagement in strategies and issues of causality.

7 Party strategies in western Europe

Party competition and electoral outcomes

The preceding chapters examined the extent to which established parties engaged in strategies in the period 1950–2009, as well as the impact of these strategies upon those parties' centrality in their respective national party systems. This final chapter brings together the results of the study and broadens out the analysis of the impact of strategies to all 17 countries under consideration. Strategies can explain, to a certain extent, the success of established parties across western Europe, but this chapter addresses a number of caveats to provide a more complete overview of the impact of strategies on the fate of established parties.

This chapter begins with an overview of the extent to which data from all 17 countries supports the hypotheses generated in Chapters 2 and 3, acknowledging that the impact of strategies varies according to the arena in which parties compete. Intervening regime and systemic factors are important considerations, as the French, Danish and Swiss examples in particular showed that the semi-presidential nature of the system, the prevalence of minority governments and direct democracy, respectively, can shape party strategies and mitigate their impact. The study has assumed that the established parties influence their systemic position, but this chapter assesses the chain of causality in greater depth, with a particular focus on the 'newer' western European democracies. Finally, the chapter explores the relationship between electoral change and party system change to reflect further on the party-centric perspective on party system change advanced in Chapter 1.

7.1 The impact of party strategies

Chapters 2 and 3 suggested that differences in the extent to which parties engage in strategies should produce varied levels of systemic centrality for established parties, with high levels of engagement in electorate-orientated strategies producing high levels of systemic centrality, and low levels of electorate-orientated strategies producing low levels of systemic centrality. High levels of institutional strategies should produce high levels of systemic centrality, whilst low levels should produce only low levels of centrality. Chapters 5 and 6 addressed these hypotheses with reference to the selected eight countries, but this chapter considers these hypotheses in more comparative detail for all 17 countries.

Electorate-orientated strategies

Table 7.1 presents the criteria for assessing whether strategies have produced low, moderate or high levels of systemic centrality for established parties. Table 7.2 ranks all 17 countries from the highest use of electorate-oriented strategies to the lowest, with the countries towards the top of the table expected to achieve higher levels of systemic centrality than those at the bottom.

Table 7.2 shows that where parties have engaged in electorate-orientated strategies to attract the highest number of votes possible, they achieve high levels of electoral centrality within the electoral arena. This finding supports a Downsian interpretation of party competition, as his essential argument is that '[parties] formulate whatever policies they believe will gain the most votes' (1957: 295), that is, their prime goal is vote-seeking. In contrast, where low levels of electorate-orientated strategies are present, only moderate levels of electoral centrality are present. Again, this finding supports the Downsian concept of party competition. Where parties do not act in a rational, vote-seeking manner, as was found in the strategies employed in Switzerland and Luxembourg, established parties have achieved only moderate levels of electoral centrality. Three out of the highest-ranking seven countries have achieved high levels of electoral centrality (Portugal, Germany and Greece) and the ten highest-ranking countries achieve only low or moderate levels of centrality within the governmental arena, demonstrating a relatively strong association between high levels of electorate-orientated strategies and high levels of electoral centrality, but low levels of governmental centrality.

Table 7.1 Criteria to determine levels of centrality for established parties, 1950–2009

Level of centrality	Arena in which centrality is measured		
	Electoral	*Parliamentary*	*Governmental*
High	More than 80% of the vote	More than 90% of seats	Only established parties have governed
Moderate	Between 70% and 80% of the vote	Between 80% and 90% of seats	Non-established parties have taken part in fewer than four governments, or only established parties have governed but with high numbers of non-party actors involved in government
Low	Less than 70% of the vote	Less than 80% of seats	Non-established parties have taken part in four or more governments

Note
The last five elections determine levels of centrality within the electoral and parliamentary arenas to see the impact that strategies have had on levels of centrality taking into account most recent trends. Average scores are calculated and the criteria applied to this average figure. Within the governmental arena, all governments determine levels of centrality.

Table 7.2 Levels of systemic centrality in 17 western European countries, 1950–2009, ranked by electorate-orientated strategies

	Arena in which centrality is measured		
	Electoral	Parliamentary	Governmental
Portugal	High (83.0%)	High (91.1%)	Moderate
Germany	High (80.4%)	Moderate (85.2%)	Moderate
Ireland	Moderate (79.4%)	Moderate (87.1%)	Low
Finland	Moderate (72.1%)	Low (78.2%)	Low
France	Low (67.7%)	High (92.0%)	Moderate
The Netherlands	Low (66.5%)	Low (68.5%)	Low
Austria	Low (66.1%)	Low (69.0%)	Low
Norway	Moderate (71.8%)	Low (74.4%)	Moderate
Greece	High (81.9%)	Moderate (89.3%)	Moderate
Italy	Low (3.2%)	Low (5.5%)	Low
Belgium	Moderate (70.1%)	Low (77.2%)	Low
Sweden	Moderate (76.0%)	Low (78.9%)	Moderate
Denmark	Moderate (73.3%)	Low (71.9%)	Low
United Kingdom	Moderate (72.6%)	Moderate (89.7%)	High
Spain	Moderate (78.6%)	Moderate (88.0%)	High
Luxembourg	Moderate (75.5%)	Moderate (81.4%)	High
Switzerland	Moderate (76.9%)	Moderate (82.1%)	High

Likewise, four out of the seven lowest ranking countries achieve high levels of governmental centrality (United Kingdom, Spain, Luxembourg and Switzerland). Furthermore, the lowest ranking ten countries achieve only low or moderate levels of centrality within the electoral arena, reinforcing the association between electorate-orientated strategies and levels of centrality within the electoral and governmental arenas. The data reported for the parliamentary arena in Table 7.2 shows that there is a strong similarity in most countries between levels of centrality within the electoral arena and the parliamentary arena. The arguments linking electorate-orientated strategies with the electoral arena also apply to the parliamentary arena, and only in the French example is there a clear difference between the levels of centrality within the electoral and parliamentary arenas.

Perhaps the most intriguing pattern found in Table 7.2 is the contrast between the levels of centrality found within the electoral and governmental arenas. Within the governmental arena, the levels of centrality generally differ from those found within the electoral arena, particularly when focusing on the countries at the top and bottom of the table. Moderate levels of governmental centrality are present in Portugal and Germany, whereas in Luxembourg and Switzerland, high levels are present. This contrast suggests that where parties employ vote-seeking strategies, they achieve high levels of *electoral* centrality, but where parties do not employ vote-seeking strategies, they achieve high levels of *governmental* centrality. This finding further supports the work of Downs and supports the arguments of Müller and Strøm (1999b), who argue that rational behaviour in political parties is not purely about vote-seeking and instead posit that parties can act in a rational manner by prioritising other goals. Whereas established parties in Germany and Portugal have engaged in high levels of electorate-orientated strategies and have appeared to favour vote-seeking goals, in Switzerland and Luxembourg, parties have pursued office-seeking goals. By engaging in a closed and unresponsive relationship with the electorate, established parties in Luxembourg and Switzerland are clearly not prioritising votes, but instead, 'seek to maximise [votes] only up to the point of subjective certainty of winning [control of the executive branch]' (Riker 1962: 33).

Engagement in strategies creating distance from the electorate and focusing on office-seeking goals is a core element of the cartel thesis. Katz and Mair argue that there has been a movement of parties away from civil society towards the state and that this movement 'could continue to such an extent that parties become part of the state apparatus itself' (1995: 14). The definition of parties as 'groups of leaders who compete for the opportunity to occupy government offices and to take responsibility at the next election for government performance' (Katz and Mair 1995: 21) strongly suggests that the pursuit of office is a prime goal of parties engaging in cartel behaviours.

The findings suggest that *party strategies do matter*. Although, as argued by Downs, parties operate in situations of uncertainty, the evidence presented appears to suggest, in line with the work of Müller and Strøm (1999b), that parties prioritise certain goals. Parties within their 'target' arena then achieve high levels of centrality. The evidence suggests that if parties engage in high levels of electorate-orientated and vote-seeking strategies, they should achieve high levels of electoral centrality. In contrast, if parties engage in low levels of electorate-orientated strategies and instead pursue office-related goals, they should achieve high levels of governmental centrality.

Institutional strategies

Table 7.3 shows whether the same logic also applies to institutional strategies. High levels of engagement in institutional strategies should produce high levels of systemic centrality, particularly within the parliamentary and governmental arenas. By contrast, high levels of institutional strategies should accompany low levels of electoral centrality. This is because such strategies' prime focus is on achieving systemic dominance via the state as opposed to currying favour with the electorate. Established parties' focus upon their proximity to the state creates a perception within the electorate that they are remote and should result in low levels of electoral centrality.

The evidence from Table 7.3 partially supports the hypotheses. The four countries in which the highest levels of institutional strategies are present have all recorded moderate or high levels of centrality within the parliamentary and governmental arenas, whereas the six countries in which the lowest levels of institutional strategies are present all demonstrate low or moderate levels of centrality within the governmental arena.

Table 7.3 Levels of systemic centrality in 17 western European countries, 1950–2009, ranked by institutional strategies

	Arena in which centrality is measured		
	Electoral	*Parliamentary*	*Governmental*
France	Low (67.7%)	High (92.0%)	Moderate
Greece	High (81.9%)	Moderate (89.3%)	Moderate
Luxembourg	Moderate (75.5%)	Moderate (81.4%)	High
United Kingdom	Moderate (72.6%)	Moderate (89.7%)	High
Austria	Low (66.1%)	Low (69.0%)	Low
Finland	Moderate (72.1%)	Low (78.2%)	Low
Sweden	Moderate (76.0%)	Low (78.9%)	Moderate
Spain	Moderate (78.6%)	Moderate (88.0%)	High
Belgium	Moderate (70.1%)	Low (77.2%)	Low
Italy	Low (3.2%)	Low (5.5%)	Low
Switzerland	Moderate (76.9%)	Moderate (82.1%)	High
Germany	High (80.4%)	Moderate (85.2%)	Moderate
The Netherlands	Low (66.5%)	Low (68.5%)	Low
Norway	Moderate (71.8%)	Low (74.4%)	Moderate
Portugal	High (83.0%)	High (91.1%)	Moderate
Ireland	Moderate (79.4%)	Moderate (87.1%)	Low
Denmark	Moderate (73.3%)	Low (71.9%)	Low

Focusing on the top and bottom of the table, electoral centrality is low in France as predicted, and moderate in Ireland in Denmark. Yet in Greece, levels of electoral centrality are high, which runs counter to the hypothesis, perhaps due to Greece's history, raising the importance of intervening factors to be discussed in the following section. In the parliamentary and governmental arenas, the hypotheses appear to hold more strongly. France and Greece, the countries in which established parties engaged in the highest levels of institutional strategies, demonstrate high levels of parliamentary centrality. In Ireland and Denmark, where established parties engaged in only low levels of institutional strategies, moderate and low levels of parliamentary centrality are present. Moderate levels of governmental centrality are present in France and Greece, compared to low levels in Ireland and Denmark.

The results of this empirical study have partially supported the cartel thesis. Higher levels of governmental centrality generally occur in those countries where established parties have engaged in high levels of institutional strategies than in those countries where engagement has been at low levels. This finding suggests that some established parties do engage in cartel strategies and that, where established parties engage in these strategies, the strategies appear to be associated with success within the governmental arena. There is a caveat, however. Katz and Mair argue that cartel party systems and the use of cartel strategies should be most prevalent in countries such as Austria, Denmark and Germany where 'a tradition of inter-party cooperation combines with a contemporary abundance of state support for parties' (1995: 17). In contrast, countries in which 'a tradition of adversarial politics' is present, such as the United Kingdom, should be less likely to cartelise (1995: 17). However, the evidence found in this study appears to show that two-party systems such as Greece, or two-bloc systems such as France, are those in which a cartel party system is more likely to emerge; an argument supported by Mark Blyth and Katz (2005: 46–53), who argue that cartelisation has taken place in the United Kingdom. Evidence in support of the process of cartelisation is clear, but not in the countries that Katz and Mair initially predicted to be the most receptive to cartel strategies.

The evidence presented in this section reinforces the conclusion that party strategies do matter. Where established parties have pursued an office-seeking policy and have engaged in high levels of institutional strategies, they have experienced high levels of governmental centrality. Parties can attempt to control their own fate and, in line with the work of Katz and Mair (1995), can attempt to preserve their systemic positions through the creation of a cartel where competition is managed and the spoils of the state are shared between the 'insiders'.

Overall, established parties in some countries do engage in certain strategies and prioritise office or vote-seeking goals. Where established parties have engaged in high levels of these strategies, parties have generally achieved moderate or high levels of centrality within their 'target' arena. These findings suggest that established parties can control their own fate and, through engagement in strategies, can secure their positions at the heart of their national party systems and act as independent actors in the process of party system change.

Voter backlash and perverse effects

Yet, the hypotheses did not hold for all 17 countries, perhaps because of 'perverse effects'. In other words, the strategies employed by the established parties may not result in high levels of systemic centrality within national party systems because of a number of different factors related to the response of voters. For example, high levels of electorate-orientated strategies might produce low levels of centrality. Engagement in strategies that are open and responsive to all voters may alienate the parties' existing voters and may promote a transient image in which policies are changed frequently on the basis of public opinion, rather than pursued for the 'greater good'. Furthermore, a high level of electoral responsiveness may also produce a backlash, as the people may view the established parties as populist, seeking only to follow the whims of the electorate and not taking a long-term perspective.

An interesting example of the role of perverse effects is apparent in Austria, which recorded the fifth highest levels of institutional strategies but where established parties have recently achieved only low levels of centrality in all three arenas. The electorate has rejected these parties and has turned towards populism in the form of the FPÖ (Freedom Party of Austria), perhaps because of the cartel-like behaviours in which they have engaged. The formation of grand coalitions in Austria between the ÖVP (Austrian People's Party) and SPÖ (Social

Democratic Party of Austria) between 1947 and 1966 and the subsequent continuing dominance of the governmental arena by these two parties 'allowed the FPÖ to harvest frustrated voters' (Müller *et al.* 2004: 175). The SPÖ and ÖVP did not only monopolise the electoral, parliamentary and governmental arenas, but also the neo-corporatist arena. Luther argues that 'the domain of the elite cartel ranged from virtual monopoly of federal and regional government, to duopolistic control over the neo-corporatist system, as well as over large parts of the civil service and public sector enterprises' (1999: 70). Austria may be a good example where perverse effects have been in operation, supporting the Katz and Mair argument that 'the cartel inevitably generates its own opposition' (1995: 24). The Austrian established parties engaged in strategies in order to dominate the Austrian political system, yet this dominance provided a fertile environment in which the populist FPÖ could harvest voters who were frustrated by the lack of alternatives.

Intervening systemic and regime factors

A second principal reason why established parties' levels of engagement in utility maximising strategies on the one hand and systemic centrality on the other is not deterministic are systemic and regime factors, and Chapters 5 and 6 considered the institutional and historical factors that influenced the shape of each party system. One of the most obvious countries in which these institutional and historical factors are present is in France, and established parties experienced lower levels of centrality than would have been expected given their engagement in high levels of institutional strategies. The presidency has played a major role in restricting the levels of centrality that established parties could achieve within the French party system, as party politics in France is of secondary importance compared to presidential politics. Since the first presidential election in 1965, the directly elected president could 'claim that their mandate came directly from the people, that the source of their authority was impeccable and that their democratic legitimacy was at least equal to that of the National Assembly' (Wright 1989: 13). Where most political parties in western Europe claim democratic legitimacy because of their direct election by the people, in France, the president can claim equal, if not greater, levels of legitimacy.

This institutional arrangement has strongly influenced the levels of systemic centrality that French political parties are able to achieve, which stands in contrast to the German example. Despite engagement in high levels of institutional strategies, established parties have achieved only low or moderate levels of electoral and governmental centrality within the French party system. Comparisons are relevant with the German case, as 'the 1949 constitution gave democratic parties the status of semi-constitutional organs, giving them some legal privileges as a result of their mandated role of helping to shape the public will' (Scarrow 2002: 78). The contrast between the roles prescribed to political parties within these two countries is obvious and the contrast in levels of centrality achieved is striking, especially within the electoral arena.

Another interesting institutional feature that has strongly influenced the levels of centrality of established parties in some of the countries covered in this study is the prominence of minority administrations. Within Denmark, the enormous legislative influence wielded by parties outside government strongly affected the levels of centrality achieved by established parties. Minority governments are particularly prevalent amongst the Scandinavian nations, and the dominance of minority governments ensures that multiple actors are able to take part in legislative decisions; indeed, Pedersen (1967: 14) argues that 'to say when the government leaves off and the opposition begins is an exercise in metaphysics'. All parliamentary actors have an opportunity to influence legislation, whether they are formally part of the government or not.

The dominance of minority governments has important implications for the levels of centrality that established parties can achieve in the Scandinavian democracies. First, the prevalence of minority governments in Denmark can help to explain why Danish established parties engaged in the fourth lowest levels of electorate-orientated strategies and the lowest levels of institutional strategies in the study. Although it may be counter-intuitive to find that established parties engage in low levels of strategies, this strategy appears to be logical when considering the levels of political cooperation needed within a regime where minority governments dominate. Government legislation requires the support of non-governing parties and so it makes sense for established parties to refrain from engaging in strategies that may weaken potentially vital parliamentary allies. This line of argument refers back to the discussion in Chapter 1 about 'nested games', where Tsebelis argues that 'actors do not choose the apparently optimal alternative because they are involved in nested games, that is, contextual or institutional factors have an overriding importance' (1990: 11). It is clear that within the Danish system, the dominance of minority governments restricts the strategies that established parties engage in and limits the levels of centrality parties can achieve. This is also obvious in the other Scandinavian democracies, where established parties do not achieve high levels of centrality in any of the three arenas.

A further interesting point relates to the interplay between institutional and electorate-orientated factors. Chapter 5 highlighted the Swiss case as an example where electorate-orientated strategies are strongly restricted by the institutional environment in which political parties operate. In the Swiss case, the regime of direct democracy in which political parties must operate shapes the strategies of the established parties and influences the levels of systemic centrality these parties can achieve, reinforcing the importance of approaching the relationship between strategies and levels of centrality from a 'nested games' perspective.

7.2 The chain of causality

This study assumes a chain of causality that moves from party strategies to systemic centrality, and established parties engage in differing levels of strategies because they believe that high levels of engagement in electorate-orientated or institutional strategies may have a beneficial impact on their systemic positions. However, the chain of causality may also operate in the opposite direction. If, as has been shown, there were an association between high levels of engagement in strategies and high levels of systemic centrality, the opposite chain of causality would operate as follows. Established parties that achieve high levels of systemic centrality within their party systems would be able to engage in high levels of electorate-orientated and institutional strategies because the costs of the failure of the strategies may be less than for other parties with lower levels of systemic centrality. Conversely, established parties that have achieved only low levels of systemic centrality may feel less able to engage in high levels of strategies due to the costs involved should these strategies fail. An ill-conceived strategic move for a party with high levels of systemic centrality may be far less costly than an ill-conceived strategic choice made by a party with already low levels of centrality.

At first glance, it may appear that the issue of causality is a mutually reinforcing argument, as parties in most of the countries in this study achieved high levels of centrality before 1950, so it is problematic to differentiate between the two directions of causality for countries with long democratic histories. However, in Spain, Greece and Portugal, democratic revolutions took place in the 1970s, and the main parties that emerged at this time had no history of high levels of centrality within the party system, providing an opportunity to explore the direction of the chain of causality.[1]

Table 7.4 shows that in all three countries parties have engaged in relatively high levels of strategies. Moderate or high levels of engagement in both strategies are present in Greece, whereas Portuguese established parties engaged in the highest levels of electorate-orientated strategies, but only low levels of institutional strategies. In Spain, low levels of electorate-orientated strategies predominated and only moderate levels of institutional strategies were present. However, low levels of engagement in electorate-orientated strategies imply a distancing from the electorate and a desire for parties to remove themselves from civil society in line with the cartel thesis.

In Spain, Greece and Portugal, established parties have engaged in strategies in order to consolidate their positions within their party systems, and from the electoral centrality data, these attempts have proved to be relatively successful. Figure 7.1 shows the pattern of electoral centrality in Portugal, Spain and

Table 7.4 Levels of engagement in strategies in Greece, Spain and Portugal, 1975–2009

	Electorate-orientated strategies	*Institutional strategies*
Greece	9	2
Spain	15	8
Portugal	1	15

Note
The figures in the table reflect the ranking of each country in Chapter 4.

Greece. In all three countries, the vote share for the established parties began at between approximately 65 per cent and 75 per cent and has increased until the present day, with the established parties receiving over 75 per cent of the vote at the most recent election in all three countries.

There appears to be a relationship between high levels of engagement in strategies and high levels of electoral centrality in Portugal, Greece and Spain. Table 7.5 shows further evidence that supports the assumed direction of causality from party strategies to systemic centrality. High levels of centrality are present in two out of the five arenas in which high levels of centrality are expected, based on the hypotheses put forward, with a further three cases showing moderate levels of centrality.

This section has examined the three countries with the shortest democratic histories in western Europe, where, in general, the established parties have formed within the past 50 years. This analysis challenges the alternative direction of causality, as high levels of systemic centrality could not have influenced party strategies, as the parties did not exist before 1975. In the countries considered, the established parties have engaged in high levels of strategies and have achieved high levels of centrality. These levels have increased since the mid-1970s in the cases of Greece, Spain and Portugal. These findings appear to provide support for the argument that high levels of party strategies *do lead to* high levels of systemic centrality.

This is not to dismiss the alternative direction of causality, as this may certainly also be in operation. It is possible that in these three countries, the chain of causality operates in both directions simultaneously. High levels of centrality achieved because of the high levels of engagement in strategies may then allow established parties to continue to engage in these strategies, safe in the

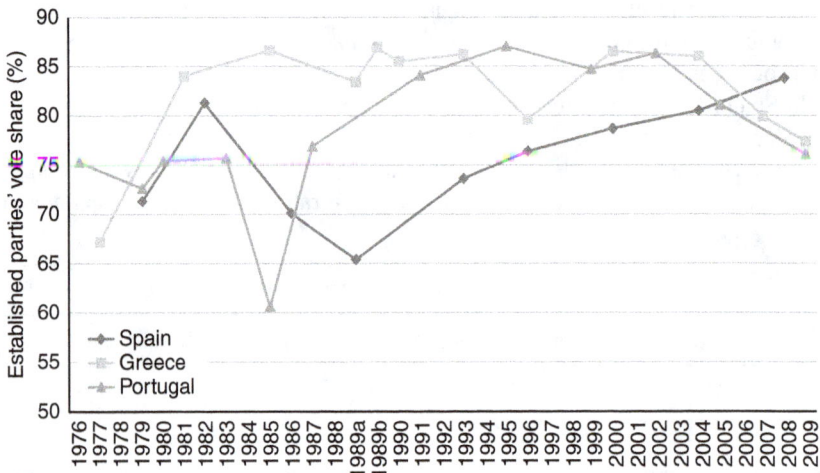

Figure 7.1 Levels of electoral centrality in Greece, Spain and Portugal, 1976–2009.

Table 7.5 Levels of electoral, parliamentary and governmental centrality for established parties in Greece, Spain and Portugal, 1975–2009

	Electoral arena	*Parliamentary arena*	*Governmental arena*
Greece	High	**Moderate**	**Moderate**
Spain	Moderate	**Moderate**	**High**
Portugal	**High**	High	Moderate

Note
Text in bold denotes where high levels of centrality are expected.

knowledge that their systemic positions are now secure. The two chains of causality may also work simultaneously in the other 14 countries in this study that have longer democratic histories and more historic established parties. The findings of this section suggest that parties can attempt to control their own fate and provides further evidence in support of the view of political parties as independent actors. To expand on this idea further, the final section of this chapter expands on the independent role that parties can play in the process of party system change.

7.3 Electoral change and party system change

A core assumption of this study is that political parties act as intervening factors in the relationship between electoral change and party system change. Electoral change may not necessarily produce party system change and equally, party system change may occur without any significant preceding electoral change. This section explores this relationship by comparing the levels of electoral change and party system change found in the eight case study countries.

The table produces results that challenge the assumption that electoral change always produces party system change. Twelve instances of electoral change occur (as shown in column 2) and on only half of those occasions did the party system change (as noted in the final column). Furthermore, thirteen instances of party system change occur, of which only six are associated with electoral change. In sum, the relationship between electoral change and party system is certainly related, but is not deterministic.

In Switzerland, the effective number of electoral parties figure has changed twice (in 1983 and 1999), yet the structure of competition has not changed, suggesting the party system has remained immune from electoral pressures. Conversely, in Greece, the party system changed on two occasions (in 1989 and 1993), yet there was no electoral change. The Danish party system is perhaps one of the most-cited examples of a party system that has undergone substantial change in western Europe. The 1973 election brought extraordinary levels of electoral volatility, interpreted as a sign of the dealignment process in action. Table 7.6 highlights an increase in the effective number of parties in 1973 and a decrease in 1990, as the party system began to recover from the

Table 7.6 Electoral change and party system change in western Europe, 1950–2009[a]

	Electoral change (N_v)[b]	Party system change[c]				Relationship between electoral and party system change?
		Open	Semi-open	Semi-closed	Closed	
Portugal	Decrease (1987)		X ⟶		X (1987)	Yes (1987)
Germany	Decrease (1965)		X ⟶	X (1965)		Yes (1965)
	Increase (1987)					No (1987)
Switzerland	Increase (1983)					No (1983)
	Decrease (1999)					No (1999)
Luxembourg	Increase (1984)		X ⟶	X (1959)		No (1959)
						No (1984)
France	Decrease (1967)		X ↕	X (1967)		Yes (1967)
	Increase (1993)		X ↓	X (1978)		No (1978)
			X ↕		X (1986)	No (1986)
			X ↓		X (1993)	Yes (1993)
Greece	N/A		X ↕	X (1989)		No (1989)
			X ↕	X (1993)		No (1993)
Denmark	Increase (1973)		X	X (1957)		No (1957)
	Decrease (1990)		X ↑	X (1964)		No (1964)
						No (1973)
						No (1990)
Ireland	Decrease (1957)		X ⟶	X (1957)		Yes (1957)
	Increase (1989)	X ↓		X (1989)		Yes (1989)

Notes

a The table reads as follows, using the Danish example. In 1973, there was an increase in the effective number of electoral parties, as shown in column 2, but no change in the party system in 1973, as shown by the next column. There was a decrease in the effective number of electoral parties in 1990, but again, no change in the party system. Regarding the party system, a change from a semi-closed to a semi-open system is recorded in 1957, and a change from a semi-open to a semi-closed system is recorded in 1964. Yet, on neither of these occasions did a change in the effective number of electoral parties occur, as shown by column 2. The final column shows that there was no association between electoral change and party system change in 1957, 1964, 1973 and 1990, as on all four instances, only one process of change occurred.

b Electoral change occurs when the effective number of electoral parties figure moves between the categories stated in each country study. For example, in Portugal, four was the dividing value between the categories. The move from fewer than four effective electoral parties to greater than four would constitute an electoral change, or a change in the electoral arena.

c Party system change is assessed with reference to the typology of competition structure developed by Mair, used in Chapters 5 and 6.

shock of 1973. Yet *the party system did not change* at these times. The structure of competition within the Danish party system changed slightly in 1957 and 1964, *but not in 1973*. The established parties continued with a semi-closed structure of competition that rejected many of the new parties that entered parliament in 1973. The Danish example suggests that electoral change does not always produce party system change, even when massive levels of electoral change are present.

At first glance, the Irish case appears to support the deterministic relationship between electoral change and party system change. In the late 1980s, the Progressive Democrats entered parliament and created a strategic dilemma for the 'natural party of government' in Ireland, Fianna Fáil. This electoral shock raised questions about Fianna Fáil's ability to continue to govern alone and the party entered a coalition with the Progressive Democrats in 1989, thereby transforming the structure of competition within Ireland. Yet the change in the structure of competition was not an automatic response to the electoral change. Rather, the *strategic choice* made by Fianna Fáil opened up the party system and encouraged competitive party politics. By forming a coalition, Fianna Fáil could remain permanently in government (Mair 1999: 145). Furthermore, the opening of the structure of competition by Fianna Fáil saw the effective number of parties remain high. Volatility levels also increased, particularly at the 1993 election, where the Labour party doubled its vote to the highest level ever recorded. The Irish case raises the possibility that parties' decisions to bring about a change in the party system can produce electoral change.

The Danish and Irish cases demonstrate that electoral change does not always lead to party system change. The Danish example shows that the strategic options pursued by the established parties can mediate the impact of electoral change. The Irish case suggests that sometimes a change in the party system can lead to electoral change. The evidence in this section suggests that parties have the potential to be independent actors within the process of party system change. They have the potential to make choices and engage in strategies that reinforce their systemic positions and they are not merely subservient to the whims of the electorate.

7.4 Conclusion

This chapter has shown that the hypotheses put forward in Chapters 2 and 3 have partially been borne out. High levels of engagement in strategies are associated with high levels of systemic centrality for the established parties, and where the hypothesised relationship does not hold, perverse effects may be at work, or intervening institutional or historical factors may be important. In relation to the chain of causality, the Spanish, Greek and Portuguese examples provide evidence that engagement in high levels of strategies produces high levels of systemic centrality, and political parties can act as important intervening factors influencing the impact of electoral change on the party system, as demonstrated by section 7.3.

This study has shown that established parties engage in a range of strategies and use them to various extents, and that engagement in these strategies has had significant implications for the systemic positions of the established parties. Party strategies do matter and where established parties have engaged in high levels of strategies, high levels of systemic centrality have followed. Political parties can operate as independent actors within the political systems of western Europe and can engage in strategies to attempt to control their own fate. Although environmental factors play a role in shaping party competition, this study has shown that political parties can and do shape their own environment, with established parties able to secure their dominant systemic positions through strategic choices.

The relationship between the electorate and political parties is central to the analysis. A number of parties engage in high levels of strategies that have a successful impact on levels of systemic centrality, appearing to show that political parties have agency and can act to influence their own fate. Parties are not solely reliant on the electorate for their systemic positions, but can take action to protect their own interests. In line with the cartel thesis of Katz and Mair (1995), this finding appears to suggest that some political parties are distancing themselves from the electorate, as the relationship between civil society and parties weakens.

Although parties can attempt to control their own fate, this is not to suggest that political parties can at all times counter electoral change and that they can indefinitely ignore voter preferences. Elections do matter, but parties matter as well and have the power to shape the political system in which they compete. Instead of asking *whether* parties can act as independent actors shaping the environment in which they operate, a more interesting question is *how* parties shape their environment and with what consequences.

Appendix 1

Established parties in western Europe, 1950–2009

Austria

ÖVP	Österreichische Volkspartei	Austrian People's Party
SPÖ	Sozialdemokratische Partei Österreichs	Social Democratic Party of Austria

Belgium

BSP	Belgische Socialistische Partij	Socialist Party of Belgium
CDH	Centre Démocrate Humaniste	Democratic Humanist Centre
CD&V	Christen-Democratisch en Vlaams	Christian Democratic and Flemish
CVP	Christelijke Volkspartij	Christian People's Party
MR	Mouvement Réformateur	Reform Movement
PS	Parti Socialiste	Socialist Party
PVV	Partij voor Vrijheid en Vooruitgang	Party for Freedom and Progress
SPA	Socialistische Partij-Anders	Socialist Party Different
VLD	Vlaamse Liberalen en Democraten	Flemish Liberals and Democrats

Denmark

KF	Det Konservative Folkeparti	Conservative People's Party
RV	Det Radikale Venstre	Radical Left
SD	Socialdemokratiet	Social Democracy
V	Venstre – Danmarks Liberale Parti	Left – Denmark's Liberal Party

Finland

SDP	Suomen Sosialidemokraattinen Puolue	Finnish Social Democratic Party
KESK	Suomen Keskusta	Finnish Centre
KOK	Kansallinen Kokoomus	National Coalition Party
Lib (1965–2000: LKP)	Liberaalit (1965–2000: Liberaalinen Kansanpuolue)	Liberals (1965–2000: Liberal People's Party)
SFP	Svenska Folkpartiet i Finland	Swedish People's Party in Finland

France

MoDEM	Mouvement Démocrate	Democratic Movement
MRC	Mouvement des Citoyens	Citizen and Republican Movement
		(1993–2002: Citizen's Movement)
NC	Nouveau Centre	New Centre
PS	Parti Socialiste	Socialist Party
(1958–71: SFIO)	(1958–71: Section Française de l'Internationale Ouvrière)	(1958–71: French Section of the Workers International)
PRG	Parti Radical de Gauche	Radical Party of the Left
UMP	Union pour un Mouvement Populaire	Union for a Popular Movement
(1976–2002: RPR)	(1976–2002: Rassemblement pour la République)	(1976–2002: Rally for the Republic)
(1968–76: UDR)	(1968–76: Union des Démocrates pour la République)	(1968–76: Union of Democrats for the Republic)
(1967–68: UDVe)	(1967–68: Union des Démocrates pour la Ve République)	(1967–68: Union of Democrats for the 5th Republic)
(1958–67: UNR)	(1958–67: Union pour la Nouvelle République)	(1958–67: Union for the New Republic)
Also:	(1973–2002: Union pour la Démocratie Française)	(1973–2002: Union for French Democracy)
(1973–2002: UDF)	(1967–73: Centre des Démocrates Sociaux)	(1967–73: Democratic Social Centre)
(1967–73: CDS)	(1958–67: Mouvement Républicain Populaire)	(1958–67: Republican People's Movement)
(1958–67: MRP)	(1958–62: Parti Radical)	(1958–62: Radical Party)
(1958–62: RAD)	(1958–62: Centre National des Indépendants et des Paysans)	(1958–62: National Centre of Independents and Peasants)
(1958–62: CNIP)	(1997–2002: Démocratie Libérale)	(1997–2002: Liberal Democracy)
(1997–2002: DL)	(1994–2002: Mouvement pour la France)	(1994–2002: Movement for France)
(1994–2002: MPF)	(1967–97: Parti Républicain)	(1967–97: Republican Party)
(1967–97: PR)		

Germany

CDU/CSU	Christlich Demokratische Union Deutschlands/Christlich-Soziale Union	Christian Democratic Union/ Christian Social Union
FDP	Freie Demokratische Partei	Free Democratic Party
SPD	Sozialdemokratische Partei Deutschlands	Social Democratic Party

Greece

ND	Nea Dhimokratia	New Democracy
PASOK	Panellinio Sosialistiko Kinima	Panhellenic Socialist Movement

Ireland

FF	Fianna Fáil	Soldiers of Destiny – The Republican Party
FG	Fine Gael	Family of the Irish – The United Ireland Party
Lab	Labour Party	Labour Party

Italy

DC	Democrazia Cristiana	Christian Democracy
PLI	Partito Liberale Italiano	Italian Liberal Party
PRI	Partito Repubblicano Italiano	Italian Republican Party
PSDI	Partito Socialista Democratico Italiano	Italian Democratic Socialist Party
PSI	Partito Socialista Italiano	Italian Socialist Party

Luxembourg

CSV	Chrëschtlech Sozial Vollekspartei	Christian Social People's Party
DP	Demokratesch Partei	Democratic Party
LSAP	Lëtzebuerger Sozialistesch Arbechterpartei	Luxembourg Socialist Workers' Party

The Netherlands

ARP	Anti-Revolutionaire Partij	Anti-Revolution Party
CDA	Christen-Democratisch Appèl	Christian Democratic Appeal
CHU	Christelijk Historische Unie	Christian Historic Union
KVP	Katholieke Volkspartij	Catholic Peoples' Party
PvdA	Partij van de Arbeid	Labour Party
VVD	Volkspartij voor Vrijheid en Democratie	People's Party for Freedom and Democracy

Norway

A	Det Norske Arbeiderparti	Norwegian Labour Party
H	Høyre	Right
KRF	Kristelig Folkeparti	Christian People's Party
SP	Senterpartiet	Centre Party
V	Venstre	Left

Portugal

AD	Aliança Democrática	Democratic Alliance
PP-CDS	Centro Democrático e Social – Partido Popular	People's Party
PS	Partido Socialista	Socialist Party
PSD	Partido Social Democrata	Social Democratic Party

Spain

PP	Partido Popular	People's Party
PSOE	Partido Socialista Obrero Español	Spanish Socialist Workers' Party
UCD	Unión de Centro Democrático	Democratic Centre Union

Sweden

C	Centerpartiet	Centre Party
FP	Folkpartiet Liberalerna	Liberal People's Party
M	Moderata Samlingspartiet	Moderate Rally Party
SAP	Socialdemokratiska Arbetarepartiet	Social Democratic Workers' Party

Switzerland

CVP	Christlich Demokratische Volkspartei	Catholic Conservatives
FDP	Freisinnig-Demokratische Partei der Schweiz	Free-Thinking Democrats
SPS	Sozialdemokratische Partei der Schweiz	Social Democratic Party of Switzerland
SVP	Schweizerische Volkspartei	Swiss People's Party

United Kingdom

Con	Conservative Party
Lab	Labour Party

Appendix 2
Anti-political establishment parties in western Europe, 1950–2009

Source: Based on Abedi (2004: 147–50).

Austria

BZÖ	Bündnis Zukunft Österreich	Alliance for the Future of Austria
FPÖ	Freiheitliche Partei Österreichs	Freedom Party of Austria
GRÜNE	Die Grünen – Die Grüne Alternative	The Greens – The Green Alternative
KPÖ	Kommunistische Partei Österreichs	Communist Party of Austria

Belgium

ECOLO	Écologistes	Ecologists
FN	Front National	National Front
Groen	De Flaamse Groenen	The Flemish Greens
(1981–2003: AGALEV)	(1981–2003: Anders Gaan Leven)	(1981–2003: Live in Another Way)
N-VA	Nieuw-Vlaamse Alliantie	New Flemish Alliance
(1954–99: VU)	(1954–99: Volksunie)	(1954–99: Flemish People's Union)
PC	Kommunistische Partij van België/ Parti Communiste de Belgique	Communist Party
VB	Vlaams Belang	Flemish Interest
	(1981–2004: Vlaams Bloc)	(1981–2004: Flemish Bloc)

Denmark

DF	Dansk Folkeparti	Danish People's Party
DKP	Kommunistisk Parti i Danmark	Communist Party
EL	Enhedslisten – De Rød-Grønne	Unity List – The Red-Greens
FRP	Fremskridtspartiet	Progress Party
SF	Socialistisk Folkeparti	Socialist People's Party
VS	Venstresocialisterne	Left-Socialists

Finland

PS (1962–95: SMP)	Perussuomalaiset (1962–95: Suomen Maaseudun Puolue)	True Finns (1962–95: Finnish Rural Party)
VAS (1944–90: SKDL)	Vasemmistoliitto (1944–90: Suomen Kansan Demokraattinen Liitto)	Left Alliance (1944–90: Finnish People's Democratic League)
VIHR	Vihreä Liitto	Green Alliance

France

FN	Front National	National Front
Les Verts	Les Verts	The Greens
LO/LCR	Lutte Ouvrière/Ligue Communiste Révolutionnaire	Workers' Struggle/Revolutionary Communist Party
MNR	Mouvement National Républicain	National Republican Movement
PCF	Parti Communiste Français	French Communist Party

Germany

BP	Bayernpartei	Bavarian Party
Die Linke (1987–2002: PDS) (1961–83: DKP) (1950–53: KPD)	Die Linkspartei Partei des Demokratischen Sozialismus Deutsche Kommunistische Partei Kommunistische Partei Deutschlands	Left Party (1987–2002: Party of Democratic Socialism) (1961–83: German Communist Party) (1950–53: Communist Party of Germany)
NPD (1950–61: DRP)	Nationaldemokratische Partei Deutschlands (1950–61: Deutsche Reichspartei)	National Democratic Party (1950–61: German Reich Party)
REP	Die Republikaner	Republicans
The Greens	Die Grünen	Federation 90/The Greens

Greece

EPEN	Ethniki Politiki Enosis	National Political Union
KKE	Kommunistiko Komma Elladas	Communist Party of Greece
LAOS	Laikos Orthodoxos Sunagermos	Popular Orthodox Rally
OP	Oikologoi Prasinoi	Ecologist Greens
SYRIZA (1975–2004: SYN)	Synaspismos tis Rizospastikis Aristeras Synaspismos	Coalition of the Radical Left Left Coalition

Ireland

CnP	Clann na Poblachta	Republican Family
CnT	Clann na Talmhan	Children of the Country
DL	Democratic Left	Democratic Left
GP	Green Party	Green Party
SF	Sinn Fein	We Ourselves
WP	Workers' Party	Workers' Party

Italy

AN	Alleanza Nazionale	National Alliance
(1950–95: MSI-DN)	Movimento Sociale Italiano-Destra Nazionale	Italian Social Movement – National Right
DS	Democratici di Sinistra	Left Democrats
(1991–98: PDS)	Partito democratico della Sinistra	Democratic Party of the Left
(1950–91: PCI)	Partito Comunista Italiano	Italian Communist Party
FI	Forza Italia	Forward Italy
LL	Lega Lombarda	Lombard League
LN	Lega Nord	League North
MPA	Movimento per le Autonomie	Movement for Autonomies
PDCI	Partito dei Comunisti Italiani	Party of Italian Communists
PNM	Partito Nazionale Monarchico	National Monarchist Party
PR	Partito Radicale	Radical Party
PRC	Partito della Rifondazione Comunista	Communist Refoundation Party
RETE	Movimento per la Democrazia – La Rete	Movement for Democracy – The Net
RI	Rinnovamento Italiano	Italian Renewal Movement
SD	Sinistra Democratica	Democratic Left
SVP	Südtiroler Volkspartei	South Tyrolean People's Party
Verdi	Federazione dei Verdi	Federation of the Greens

Note
Due to the complex nature of the Italian party system after 1994, only the most significant anti-political establishment parties are noted here.

Luxembourg

ADR	Alternativ Demokratesch Reformpartei	Alternative Democratic Reform Party
GRÉNG	Déi Gréng	The Greens
KPL	Kommunistesch Partei Lëtzebuerg	Communist Party of Luxembourg
LÉNK	Déi Lénk	The Left

The Netherlands

BP	Boerenpartij	Rural Party
CPN	Communistische Partij Nederland	Communist Party
D66	Democraten 66	Democrats 66
EVP	Evangelische Volkspartij	Evangelical People's Party
GL	Groen Links	Green Left
GPV	Gereformeerd Politiek Verbond	Reformed Political League
LPF	Lijst Pim Fortuyn	List Pim Fortuyn
PPR	Politieke Partij Radicalen	Radical Party
PSP	Pacifistisch Socialistische Partij	Pacifist Socialist Party
PvdD	Partij voor de Dieren	Party for the Animals
PVV	Partij voor de Vrijheid	Freedom Party
RPF	Reformatorisch Politieke Federatie	Reformed Political Federation
SGP	Staatskundig Gereformeerde Partij	Reformed Political Party
SP	Socialistische Partij	Socialist Party

Norway

FRP	Fremskrittspartiet	Progress Party
NKP	Norges Kommunistiske Parti	Norwegian Communist Party
RV	Rød Valgallianse	Red Electoral Alliance

Portugal

BE (1974–2005: UDP)	Bloco de Esquerda (1974–2005: União Democrática Popular)	Left Bloc (1974–2005: Democratic People's Union)
PCP	Partido Comunista Português	Communist Party

Spain

BNG	Bloque Nacionalista Galego	Galician Nationalist Bloc
CC	Coalición Canaria	Canarian Coalition
CHA	Chunta Aragonesista	Aragonese Council
CiU	Convergència i Unió	Convergence and Union
EA	Eusko Alkartasuna	Basque Solidarity
EAJ-PNV	Eusko Alderdi Jeltzalea – Partido Nacionalista Vasco	Basque National Party
ERC	Esquerra Republicana de Catalunya	Republican Left of Catalonia
ICV	Iniciativa per Catalunya Verds	Initiative for Catalonia Greens
IU	Izquierda Unida	United Left
NA-BAI	Nafarroa Bai	Navarre Yes
UPD	Progreso y Democracia	Union, Progress and Democracy

Sweden

MP	Miljöpartiet de Gröna	Environment Party The Greens
ND	Ny Demokrati	New Democracy
SD	Sverigedemokraterna	Sweden Democrats
V	Vänsterpartiet	Left Party

Switzerland

EDU	Eidgenössisch-Demokratische Union	Federal Democratic Union
FPS	Freiheits-Partei der Schweiz	Freedom Party of Switzerland
LdT	Lega dei Ticinesi	League of Ticinesians
PdA	Partei der Arbeit der Schweiz	Labour Party
SD	Schweizer Demokraten	Swiss Democrats

United Kingdom

GP	Green Party
NF	National Front
PC	Plaid Cymru
SNP	Scottish National Party
SF	Sinn Féin

Appendix 3

Centrality data for countries not the subject of case studies, 1950–2009[a]

Centrality of established parties in the Austrian party system, 1953–2008

	1953	1956	1959	1963	1966	1970	1971	1975	1979
Percentage share of the vote	ÖVP: 41.3 SPÖ: 42.1 Total: 83.4%	ÖVP: 46.0 SPÖ: 43.0 Total: 89.0%	ÖVP: 44.2 SPÖ: 44.8 Total: 89.0%	ÖVP: 45.4 SPÖ: 44.0 Total: 89.4%	ÖVP: 48.4 SPÖ: 42.6 Total: 91.0%	ÖVP: 44.7 SPÖ: 48.4 Total: 93.1%	ÖVP: 43.1 SPÖ: 50.0 Total: 93.1%	ÖVP: 43.0 SPÖ: 50.4 Total: 93.4%	ÖVP: 41.9 SPÖ: 51.0 Total: 92.9%
Percentage share of seats	ÖVP: 44.8 SPÖ: 44.2 Total: 89.0%	ÖVP: 49.7 SPÖ: 44.8 Total: 94.5%	ÖVP: 47.9 SPÖ: 47.3 Total: 95.2%	ÖVP: 49.1 SPÖ: 46.1 Total: 95.2%	ÖVP: 51.5 SPÖ: 44.8 Total: 96.3%	ÖVP: 47.9 SPÖ: 49.1 Total: 97.0%	ÖVP: 43.7 SPÖ: 50.8 Total: 94.5%	ÖVP: 43.7 SPÖ: 50.8 Total: 94.5%	ÖVP: 42.1 SPÖ: 51.9 Total: 94.0%
Largest party within parliament (seats)	ÖVP	ÖVP	ÖVP	ÖVP	ÖVP	ÖVP	SPÖ	SPÖ	SPÖ
Time spent in government ÖVP SPÖ									
Prime minister's party	ÖVP	ÖVP	ÖVP	ÖVP	ÖVP	SPÖ	SPÖ	SPÖ	SPÖ

continued overleaf

Note

Tables do not include factors concerning median legislator, percentage share of government positions or the ratio of positions obtained to share of seats.

Centrality of established parties in the Austrian party system, 1953–2008 continued

	1983	1987	1990	1994	1996	2000	2003	2007	2008
Percentage share of the vote	ÖVP: 43.2 SPÖ: 47.7 Total: 90.9%	ÖVP: 41.3 SPÖ: 43.1 Total: 84.4%	ÖVP: 32.1 SPÖ: 42.8 Total: 74.9%	ÖVP: 27.7 SPÖ: 34.9 Total: 62.6%	ÖVP: 28.3 SPÖ: 38.1 Total: 66.4%	ÖVP: 26.9 SPÖ: 33.2 Total: 60.1%	ÖVP: 42.3 SPÖ: 36.5 Total: 78.9%	ÖVP: 35.3 SPÖ: 34.3 Total: 69.6%	ÖVP: 26.0 SPÖ: 29.3 Total: 55.3%
Percentage share of seats	ÖVP: 44.3 SPÖ: 49.2 Total: 93.5%	ÖVP: 42.1 SPÖ: 43.7 Total: 85.8%	ÖVP: 32.8 SPÖ: 43.7 Total: 76.5%	ÖVP: 28.4 SPÖ: 35.5 Total: 63.9%	ÖVP: 29.0 SPÖ: 38.8 Total: 67.8%	ÖVP: 28.4 SPÖ: 35.5 Total: 63.9%	ÖVP: 43.2 SPÖ: 37.7 Total: 80.9%	ÖVP: 36.1 SPÖ: 37.2 Total: 73.3%	ÖVP: 27.9 SPÖ: 31.1 Total: 59.0%
Largest party within parliament (seats)	SPÖ	SPÖ	SPÖ	SPÖ	SPÖ	SPÖ	ÖVP	SPÖ	SPÖ
Time spent in government ÖVP SPÖ FPÖ									
Prime minister's party	SPÖ	SPÖ	SPÖ	SPÖ	SPÖ	ÖVP	ÖVP	SPÖ	SPÖ

Party abbreviations: SPÖ (Social Democratic Party of Austria); ÖVP (Austrian People's Party); FPÖ (Freedom Party of Austria).

Sources: Bundesministerium für Inneres (2010); Fallend (2001, 2004); Müller (2000b); Woldendorp et al. (2000).

Note
The SPÖ/FPÖ coalition governed Austria between 2003 and April 2005, when a split in the FPÖ resulted in the SPÖ continuing its coalition with the BZÖ (the Alliance for the future of Austria).

Centrality of established parties in the Belgian party system, 1950–2008

	1950	1954	1958a	1958b	1961	1965	1966	1968	1971	1973
Percentage share of the vote	CVP: 47.7 BSP: 34.5 PVV: 11.3 Total: 93.5%	CVP: 41.2 BSP: 37.3 PVV: 12.2 Total: 90.7%	CVP: 46.5 BSP: 35.8 PVV: 11.1 Total: 93.4%		CVP: 41.5 BSP: 36.7 PVV: 12.3 Total: 90.5%	CVP: 34.5 BSP: 28.3 PVV: 21.6 Total: 84.4%		CVP: 31.7 BSP: 28.0 PVV: 20.9 Total: 80.6%	CVP: 30.0 BSP: 27.2 PVV: 16.7 Total: 73.9%	
Percentage share of seats	CVP: 50.9 BSP: 36.3 PVV: 9.4 Total: 96.6%	CVP: 44.8 BSP: 40.6 PVV: 11.8 Total: 97.2%	CVP: 49.1 BSP: 39.7 PVV: 9.9 Total: 98.7%		CVP: 49.1 BSP: 39.7 PVV: 9.4 Total: 98.2%	CVP: 36.3 BSP: 30.2 PVV: 22.6 Total: 89.1%		CVP: 32.5 BSP: 27.8 PVV: 22.2 Total: 82.5%	CVP: 31.6 BSP: 28.8 PVV: 16.0 Total: 76.4%	
Largest party within parliament (seats)	CVP	CVP	CVP	CVP	CVP	CVP	CVP	CVP	CVP	CVP
Time spent in government										
CVP										
BSP										
PVV										
Prime minister's party	CVP	BSP	CVP	CVP	CVP	CVP	CVP	CVP	CVP	BSP

	1974a	1974b	1977a	1977b	1978	1980a	1980b	1980c
Percentage share of the vote	CVP: 32.3 BSP: 26.7 PVV: 15.2 Total: 74.2%			CVP: 36.0 BSP: 27.0 PVV: 15.5 Total: 78.5%	CVP: 36.3 BSP: 25.4 PVV: 15.5 Total: 77.2%			
Percentage share of seats	CVP: 34.0 BSP: 27.8 PVV: 14.2 Total: 76.0%			CVP: 37.7 BSP: 29.2 PVV: 15.6 Total: 82.5%	CVP: 38.7 BSP: 27.4 PVV: 17.5 Total: 83.6%			

continued overleaf

Centrality of established parties in the Belgian party system, 1950–2008 continued

	1974a	1974b	1977a	1977b	1978	1980a	1980b	1980c
Largest party within parliament (seats)	CVP	CVP	CVP	CVP	CVP	CVP	CVP	CVP
Time spent in government								
CVP								
BSP								
PVV								
RW								
FDF								
VU								
Prime minister's party	CVP	CVP	CVP	CVP	CVP	CVP	CVP	CVP

	1981	1985	1987	1991	1995	1999	2003	2008
Percentage share of the vote	VLD: 12.9 CD&V: 19.3 PS: 12.7 MR: 8.6 SPA: 12.4 CDH: 7.2 Total: 73.1%	VLD: 10.7 CD&V: 21.3 PS: 13.8 MR: 10.2 SPA: 14.5 CDH: 8.0 Total: 78.5%	VLD: 11.5 CD&V: 19.5 PS: 15.6 MR: 9.4 SPA: 14.9 CDH: 8.0 Total: 78.9%	VLD: 12.0 CD&V: 16.8 PS: 13.5 MR: 8.1 SPA: 12.0 CDH: 7.7 Total: 70.1%	VLD: 13.1 CD&V: 17.2 PS: 11.9 MR: 10.3 SPA: 12.6 CDH: 7.7 Total: 72.8%	VLD: 14.3 CD&V: 14.1 PS: 10.2 MR: 10.1 SPA: 9.5 CDH: 5.9 Total: 64.1%	VLD: 15.5 CD&V: 13.3 PS: 13.0 MR: 11.4 SPA: 14.9 CDH: 5.5 Total: 73.6%	VLD: 11.8 CD&V: 18.5 PS: 10.9 MR: 12.5 SPA: 10.3 CDH: 6.1 Total: 70.1%
Percentage share of seats	VLD: 13.2 CD&V: 20.3 PS: 16.5 MR: 11.3 SPA: 12.3 CDH: 8.5 Total: 82.1%	VLD: 10.4 CD&V: 23.1 PS: 16.5 MR: 11.3 SPA: 15.1 CDH: 9.4 Total: 85.8%	VLD: 11.8 CD&V: 20.3 PS: 18.9 MR: 10.8 SPA: 15.1 CDH: 9.0 Total: 85.9%	VLD: 12.3 CD&V: 18.4 PS: 16.5 MR: 9.4 SPA: 13.2 CDH: 8.5 Total: 78.3%	VLD: 14.0 CD&V: 19.3 PS: 14.0 MR: 12.0 SPA: 13.3 CDH: 6.7 Total: 80.6%	VLD: 15.3 CD&V: 14.0 PS: 12.7 MR: 12.0 SPA: 9.3 CDH: 6.7 Total: 70.0%	VLD: 16.7 CD&V: 14.0 PS: 16.7 MR: 16.0 SPA: 15.3 CDH: 5.3 Total: 84.0%	VLD: 12.0 CD&V: 16.7 PS: 13.3 MR: 15.3 SPA: 9.3 CDH: 6.7 Total: 73.3%

Largest party within parliament (seats)	CD&V	CD&V	CD&V	CD&V	CD&V	CD&V	VLD	VLD/CD&V	CD&V
Time spent in government									
VLD									
CD&V									
PS									
MR									
SPA									
CDH									
VU									
ECOLO									
GROEN									
Prime minister's party	CD&V	CD&V	CD&V	CD&V	CD&V	CD&V	VLD	VLD	CD&V

Party abbreviations: CVP (Christian People's Party); BSP (Socialist Party of Belgium); PVV (Party for Freedom and Progress); PC (Communist Party); RW (Walloon Rally); FDF (Democratic Front of Francophones); VU (People's Union); VLD (Flemish Liberals and Democrats); CD&V (Christian Democratic and Flemish); PS (Socialist Party); MR (Reform Movement); SPA (Socialist Party Different); CDH (Democratic Humanist Centre); ECOLO (Ecologists); GROEN (The Flemish Greens); NVA (New Flemish Alliance)

Sources: De Winter (2002); Direction des Elections (2010); Rihoux (2000); Rihoux *et al.* (2004); Timmermans and Andeweg (2000); Woldendorp *et al.* (2000)

Centrality of established parties in the Finnish party system, 1951–2007

	1951	1953	1954a	1954b	1956	1957a	1957b	1957c
Percentage share of the vote	SDP: 26.5 KESK: 23.2 KOK: 14.6 SFP: 7.3 Lib: 5.7 Total: 77.3%		SDP: 26.2 KESK: 24.1 KOK: 12.8 SFP: 6.8 Lib: 7.9 Total: 77.8%					
Percentage share of seats	SDP: 26.5 KESK: 25.5 KOK: 14.0 SFP: 7.5 Lib: 5.0 Total: 78.5%		SDP: 27.0 KESK: 26.5 KOK: 12.0 SFP: 6.5 Lib: 6.5 Total: 78.5%					
Largest party within parliament (seats)	SDP	SDP	SDP	SDP	SDP	SDP	SDP	SDP
Time spent in government								
SDP								
KESK								
SFP								
Lib								
SDL								
Prime minister's party	KESK	KESK	SFP	KESK	SDP	KESK	KESK	KESK

	1958	1959	1962	1966	1968	1970	1971	1972a	1972b	1975
Percentage share of the vote	SDP: 23.2 KESK: 23.1 KOK: 15.3 SFP: 6.5 Lib: 5.9 Total: 74.0%		SDP: 19.5 KESK: 23.0 KOK: 15.0 SFP: 6.1 Lib: 6.3 Total: 69.9%	SDP: 27.2 KESK: 21.2 KOK: 13.8 SFP: 5.7 Lib: 6.5 Total: 74.4%		SDP: 23.4 KESK: 17.1 KOK: 18.0 SFP: 5.3 Lib: 6.0 Total: 69.8%		SDP: 25.8 KESK: 16.4 KOK: 17.6 SFP: 5.1 Lib: 5.2 Total: 70.1%		SDP: 24.9 KESK: 17.6 KOK: 18.4 SFP: 4.7 Lib: 4.3 Total: 69.9%
Percentage share of seats	SDP: 24.0 KESK: 24.0 KOK: 14.5 SFP: 7.0 Lib: 4.0 Total: 73.5%		SDP: 19.0 KESK: 26.5 KOK: 16.0 SFP: 7.0 Lib: 6.5 Total: 75.0%	SDP: 27.5 KESK: 24.5 KOK: 13.0 SFP: 6.0 Lib: 4.5 Total: 75.5%		SDP: 26.0 KESK: 18.0 KOK: 18.5 SFP: 6.0 Lib: 4.0 Total: 72.5%		SDP: 27.5 KESK: 17.5 KOK: 17.0 SFP: 5.0 Lib: 3.5 Total: 70.5%		SDP: 27.0 KESK: 19.5 KOK: 17.5 SFP: 5.0 Lib: 4.5 Total: 73.5%
Largest party within parliament (seats)	SDP/KESK	SDP/KESK	KESK	SDP	SDP	SDP	SDP	SDP	SDP	SDP
Time spent in government										
SDP										
KESK										
KOK										
VAS										
SFP										
Lib										
TPSL										
Prime minister's party	SDP	KESK	KESK	SDP	SDP	KESK	KESK	SDP	SDP	KESK

continued overleaf

Centrality of established parties in the Finnish party system, 1951–2007 continued

	1976	1977	1978	1979	1982	1983	1987	1990	1991	1994
Percentage share of the vote				SDP: 23.9 KESK: 17.3 KOK: 21.7 SFP: 4.3 Lib: 3.7 Total: 70.9%		SDP: 26.7 KESK: 17.6 KOK: 22.1 SFP: 4.9 Lib: 0.0 Total: 71.3%	SDP: 24.1 KESK: 17.6 KOK: 23.1 SFP: 5.6 Lib: 1.0 Total: 71.4%		SDP: 22.1 KESK: 24.8 KOK: 19.3 SFP: 5.5 Lib: 0.8 Total: 72.5%	
Percentage share of seats				SDP: 26.0 KESK: 18.0 KOK: 23.5 SFP: 5.0 Lib: 2.0 Total: 74.5%		SDP: 28.5 KESK: 19.0 KOK: 22.0 SFP: 5.5 Lib: 0.0 Total: 75.0%	SDP: 28.0 KESK: 20.0 KOK: 26.5 SFP: 6.5 Lib: 0.0 Total: 81.0%		SDP: 24.0 KESK: 27.5 KOK: 20.0 SFP: 6.0 Lib: 0.5 Total: 78.0%	
Largest party within parliament (seats)	SDP	SDP	SDP	SDP	SDP	SDP	SDP	SDP	KESK	KESK
Time spent in government										
SDP										
KESK										
KOK										
VAS										
SFP										
PS										
KD										
Lib										
Prime minister's party	KESK	SDP	SDP	SDP	SDP	SDP	KOK	KOK	KESK	KESK

	1995	1999	2002	2003	2007
Percentage share of the vote	SDP: 28.3 KESK: 19.4 KOK: 17.9 SFP: 5.1 Lib: 0.6 Total: 71.3%	SDP: 22.9 KESK: 22.4 KOK: 21.0 SFP: 5.1 Lib: 0.2 Total: 71.6%		SDP: 24.5 KESK: 24.7 KOK: 18.5 SFP: 4.6 Lib: 0.3 Total: 72.6%	SDP: 21.4 KESK: 23.1 KOK: 22.3 SFP: 4.5 Lib: 0.1 Total: 72.4%
Percentage share of seats	SDP: 31.5 KESK: 22.0 KOK: 19.5 SFP: 6.0 Lib: 0.0 Total: 79.0%	SDP: 25.5 KESK: 24.0 KOK: 23.0 SFP: 6.0 Lib: 0.0 Total: 78.5%		SDP: 26.5 KESK: 27.5 KOK: 20.0 SFP: 4.0 Lib: 0.0 Total: 78.0%	SDP: 22.5 KESK: 25.5 KOK: 25.0 SFP: 4.5 Lib: 0.0 Total: 77.5%
Largest party within parliament (seats)	SDP	SDP	SDP	KESK	KESK
Time spent in government					
SDP					
KESK					
KOK					
VAS					
SFP					
VIHR					
Prime minister's party	SDP	SDP	SDP	KESK	KESK

Party abbreviations: SDP (Social Democratic Party); KESK (Centre Party); VAS (Left Alliance); SFP (Swedish People's Party); Lib (Liberals); TPSL (Workers' and Smallholders Social Democratic Party); KOK (National Coalition League); PS (True Finns); KD (Christian Democrats); VIHR (Green League)

Sources: Ministry of Justice (2010); Nousiainen (2000); Sundberg (2003, 2004); Woldendorp *et al.* (2000)

Centrality of established parties in the Italian party system, 1953–2008

	1953	1954	1957	1958	1959	1962	1963a	1963b	1968a	1968b	1969
Percentage share of the vote	DC: 40.1 PSI: 12.8 PSDI: 4.5 PRI: 1.6 PLI: 3.0 Total: 62.0%			DC: 42.4 PSI: 14.2 PSDI: 4.5 PRI: 1.4 PLI: 3.5 Total: 66.0%			DC: 38.3 PSI: 13.8 PSDI: 6.1 PRI: 1.4 PLI: 7.0 Total: 66.6%		DC: 39.1 PSI/PSDI: 14.5 PRI: 2.0 PLI: 5.8 Total: 61.4%		
Percentage share of seats	DC: 44.6 PSI: 12.7 PSDI: 3.2 PRI: 0.8 PLI: 2.2 Total: 63.5%			DC: 45.8 PSI: 14.1 PSDI: 3.7 PRI: 1.0 PLI: 2.9 Total: 67.5%			DC: 41.3 PSI: 13.8 PSDI: 5.2 PRI: 1.0 PLI: 6.2 Total: 67.5%		DC: 42.2 PSI/PSDI: 14.4 PRI: 1.4 PLI: 4.9 Total: 62.9%		
Largest party within parliament (seats)	DC	DC	DC	DC	DC	DC	DC	DC	DC	DC	DC
Time spent in government											
DC											
PSI											
PSDI											
PRI											
PLI											
Prime minister's party	DC	DC	DC	DC	DC	DC	DC	DC	DC	DC	DC

	1970	1972a	1972b	1973	1974a	1974b	1976a	1976b	1979a	1979b	1980a	1980b
Percentage share of the vote			DC: 38.7 PSI: 9.6 PSDI: 5.1 PRI: 2.9 PLI: 3.9 Total: 60.2%					DC: 38.7 PSI: 9.6 PSDI: 3.4 PRI: 3.1 PLI: 1.3 Total: 56.1%		DC: 38.3 PSI: 9.8 PSDI: 3.8 PRI: 3.0 PLI: 1.9 Total: 56.8%		
Percentage share of seats			DC: 42.2 PSI: 9.7 PSDI: 4.6 PRI: 2.4 PLI: 3.2 Total: 62.1%					DC: 41.7 PSI: 9.0 PSDI: 2.4 PRI: 2.2 PLI: 0.8 Total: 56.1%		DC: 41.6 PSI: 9.8 PSDI: 3.2 PRI: 2.5 PLI: 1.4 Total: 58.5%		
Largest party within parliament (seats)	DC	DC	DC	DC	DC	DC	DC	DC	DC	DC	DC	
Time spent in government												
DC												
PSI												
PSDI												
PRI												
PLI												
Prime minister's party	DC	DC	DC	DC	DC	DC	DC	DC	DC	DC	DC	

continued overleaf

Centrality of established parties in the Italian party system, 1953–2008 continued

	1981	1982	1983	1987a	1987b	1991	1992	1993
Percentage share of the vote			DC: 32.9 PSI: 11.4 PSDI: 4.1 PRI: 5.1 PLI: 2.9 Total: 56.4%		DC: 34.3 PSI: 14.3 PSDI: 2.9 PRI: 3.7 PLI: 2.1 Total: 57.3%		DC: 29.7 PSI: 13.6 PSDI: 2.7 PRI: 4.4 PLI: 2.8 Total: 53.2%	
Percentage share of seats			DC: 35.7 PSI: 11.6 PSDI: 3.7 PRI: 4.6 PLI: 2.5 Total: 58.1%		DC: 37.1 PSI: 14.9 PSDI: 2.7 PRI: 3.3 PLI: 1.7 Total: 59.7%		DC: 32.7 PSI: 14.6 PSDI: 2.5 PRI: 4.3 PLI: 2.7 Total: 56.8%	
Largest party within parliament (seats)	DC	DC	DC	DC	DC	DC	DC	DC
Time spent in government								
DC								
PSI								
PSDI								
PRI								
PLI								
Prime minister's party	PRI	DC	PSI	DC	DC	DC	PSI	Ind

	1994	1996	1998	2001	2006	2008
Percentage share of the vote	Total: 0.0%	DC: 5.8 Total: 5.8%		DC: 3.2 Total: 3.2%	DC: 6.8 Total: 6.8%	Total: 0.0%
Percentage share of seats	DC: 4.8[a] Total: 4.8%	DC: 4.8 Total: 4.8%		DC: 6.3 Total: 6.3%	DC: 6.2 Total: 6.2%	DC: 5.2 Total: 5.2%
Largest party within parliament (seats)	DS	DS	DS	FI	DS	PDL[b]
Time spent in government						
LN						
FI						
AN						
PRC						
DS						
DL						
RI						
CCD						
VERDI						
PDCI						
SDI						
UDR						
UDC						
NPSI						
MpA						
Prime minister's party	FI	PPI	DS	FI	L'Ulivo[c]	PDL

Party abbreviations: DC (Christian Democracy); DS (Italian Democratic Socialist Party); PSI (Italian Socialist Party); PSDI (Italian Democratic Socialist Party); PRI (Italian Republican Party); PLI (Italian Liberal Party); LN (League North); FI (Forward Italy); AN (National Alliance); PRC (Communist Refoundation Party); DS (Left Democrats); DL (Democracy is Freedom); RI (Italian Renewal Movement); CCD (Christian Democratic Centre/Christian Democratic Union); VERDI (Green Federation); PDCI (Party of Italian Communists); SDI (Italian Democratic Socialists); UDR (Democratic Union for the Republic); UDC (Union of Christian and Centre Democrats); NPSI (New Italian Socialist Party); MpA (Movement for Autonomies)

Sources: Ignazi (2002, 2006); Ministero dell'Interno (2010); Verzichelli and Cotta (2000); Woldendorp et al. (2000)

Notes
a Post-1992, remnants of the former DC stood for election as the Christian Democratic Centre/Christian Democratic Union (CDC/CDU), also known as CCD.
b The PDL (People of Freedom) emerged in 2007 and is a broad centre-right political grouping, comprising the FI and AN, along with dozens of smaller parties and groupings. The PDL became Italy's largest party in 2008, with party officially founded in 2009, signalling the dissolution of a number of its smaller, previously affiliated parties.
c L'Ulivo is an Italian centre-left political party coalition, comprising, amongst others, the parties stated.

Centrality of established parties in the Dutch party system, 1952–2006

	1952	1956	1958	1959	1963	1965	1966	1967	1971
Percentage share of the vote	PvdA: 29.0 VVD: 8.8 KVP: 28.7 ARP: 11.3 CHU: 8.9 Total: 86.7%	PvdA: 32.7 VVD: 8.8 KVP: 31.7 ARP: 9.9 CHU: 8.4 Total: 91.5%		PvdA: 30.4 VVD: 12.2 KVP: 31.6 ARP: 9.4 CHU: 8.1 Total: 91.7%	PvdA: 28.0 VVD: 10.3 KVP: 31.9 ARP: 8.7 CHU: 8.6 Total: 87.5%			PvdA: 23.6 VVD: 10.7 KVP: 26.5 ARP: 9.9 CHU: 8.1 Total: 78.8%	PvdA: 24.6 VVD: 10.3 KVP: 21.9 ARP: 8.6 CHU: 6.3 Total: 71.7%
Percentage share of seats	PvdA: 30.0 VVD: 9.0 KVP: 30.0 ARP: 12.0 CHU: 9.0 Total: 90.0%	PvdA: 34.0 VVD: 9.0 KVP: 33.0 ARP: 10.0 CHU: 8.0 Total: 94.0%		PvdA: 32.0 VVD: 12.7 KVP: 32.7 ARP: 9.3 CHU: 8.0 Total: 94.7%	PvdA: 28.7 VVD: 10.7 KVP: 33.3 ARP: 8.7 CHU: 8.7 Total: 90.1%			PvdA: 24.7 VVD: 11.3 KVP: 28.0 ARP: 10.0 CHU: 8.0 Total: 82.0%	PvdA: 26.0 VVD: 10.7 KVP: 23.3 ARP: 8.7 CHU: 6.7 Total: 75.4%
Largest party within parliament (seats)	PvdA/KVP	PvdA	PvdA	KVP	KVP	KVP	KVP	KVP	PvdA
Time spent in government									
PvdA									
VVD									
KVP									
ARP									
CHU									
Prime minister's party	PvdA	PvdA	KVP	KVP		KVP	ARP	KVP	ARP

	1972	1973	1977	1981	1982a	1982b	1986	1989
Percentage share of the vote	PvdA: 27.4 VVD: 14.4 KVP: 17.7 ARP: 8.8 CHU: 4.8 Total: 73.1%		PvdA: 33.8 VVD: 18.0 CDA: 31.9 Total: 83.7%	PvdA: 28.3 VVD: 17.3 CDA: 30.8 Total: 76.4%		PvdA: 30.4 VVD: 23.1 CDA: 29.3 Total: 82.8%	PvdA: 33.3 VVD: 17.4 CDA: 34.6 Total: 85.3%	PvdA: 31.9 VVD: 14.6 CDA: 35.3 Total: 81.8%
Percentage share of seats	PvdA: 28.7 VVD: 14.7 KVP: 18.0 ARP: 9.3 CHU: 4.7 Total: 75.4%		PvdA: 35.3 VVD: 18.7 CDA: 32.7 Total: 86.7%	PvdA: 29.3 VVD: 17.3 CDA: 32.0 Total: 78.6%		PvdA: 31.3 VVD: 24.0 CDA: 30.0 Total: 85.3%	PvdA: 34.7 VVD: 18.0 CDA: 36.0 Total: 88.7%	PvdA: 32.7 VVD: 14.7 CDA: 36.0 Total: 83.4%
Largest party within parliament (seats)	PvdA	PvdA	PvdA	CDA	CDA	PvdA	CDA	CDA
Time spent in government								
PvdA								
VVD								
KVP								
ARP								
CHU								
DS70								
CDA								
PPR								
D66								
Prime minister's party	ARP	PvdA	CDA	CDA	CDA	CDA	CDA	CDA

continued overleaf

Centrality of established parties in the Dutch party system, 1952–2006 continued

	1994	1998	2002	2003	2006	2007
Percentage share of the vote	PvdA: 24.0 VVD: 19.9 CDA: 22.2 Total: 66.1%	PvdA: 29.0 VVD: 24.7 CDA: 18.4 Total: 72.1%	PvdA: 15.1 VVD: 15.4 CDA: 27.9 Total: 58.4%	PvdA: 27.3 VVD: 17.9 CDA: 28.6 Total: 73.8%		PvdA: 21.2 VVD: 14.6 CDA: 26.5 Total: 62.3%
Percentage share of seats	PvdA: 24.7 VVD: 20.7 CDA: 22.7 Total: 68.1%	PvdA: 30.0 VVD: 25.3 CDA: 19.3 Total: 74.6%	PvdA: 15.3 VVD: 16.0 CDA: 28.7 Total: 60.0%	PvdA: 28.0 VVD: 18.7 CDA: 29.3 Total: 76.0%		PvdA: 22.0 VVD: 14.7 CDA: 27.3 Total: 64.0%
Largest party within parliament (seats)	PvdA	PvdA	CDA	CDA		CDA
Time spent in government						
PvdA	▓	▓	▓			
VVD	▓	▓	▓	▓	▓	
CDA			▓	▓	▓	▓
D66	▓	▓		▓		
LPF			▓			
CU						▓
Prime minister's party	PvdA	PvdA	CDA	CDA	CDA	CDA

Party abbreviations: PvdA (Labour Party); VVD (People's Party for Freedom and Democracy); KVP (Catholic Peoples' Party); ARP (Anti-Revolution Party); CHU (Christian Historic Union); DS70 (Democratic Socialists '70); CDA (Christian Democratic Appeal); PPR (Radical Party); D66 (Democrats 66); LPF (List Pim Fortuyn); CU (Christian Union)

Sources: Dutch Government Homepage (2010); Lucardie (2003); Lucardie and Voerman (2004); Woldendorp et al. (2000)

Centrality of established parties in the Norwegian party system, 1953–2009

	1953	1957	1961	1963a	1963b	1965	1969	1971	1972	1973	1977	1981
Percentage share of the vote	A: 46.7 H: 18.6 SP: 9.1 KRF: 10.5 V: 10.0 Total: 94.9%	A: 48.3 H: 18.9 SP: 9.3 KRF: 10.2 V: 9.7 Total: 96.4%	A: 46.8 H: 20.0 SP: 9.4 KRF: 9.6 V: 8.8 Total: 94.6%			A: 43.1 H: 21.1 SP: 9.9 KRF: 8.1 V: 10.4 Total: 92.6%	A: 46.6 H: 19.7 SP: 10.3 KRF: 9.4 V: 9.4 Total: 95.4%			A: 35.4 H: 17.4 SP: 11.0 KRF: 12.2 V: 3.5 Total: 79.5%	A: 42.2 H: 24.8 SP: 8.6 KRF:12.4 V: 3.2 Total: 91.2%	A: 37.1 H: 31.7 SP: 6.7 KRF: 9.4 V: 3.9 Total: 88.8%
Percentage share of seats	A: 51.3 H: 18.0 SP: 9.3 KRF: 9.3 V: 10.0 Total: 97.9%	A: 52.0 H: 19.3 SP: 10.0 KRF: 8.0 V: 10.0 Total: 99.3%	A: 49.3 H: 19.3 SP: 10.7 KRF: 10.0 V: 9.3 Total: 98.6%			A: 45.3 H: 20.7 SP: 12.0 KRF: 8.7 V: 12.0 Total: 98.7%	A: 49.3 H: 19.3 SP: 13.3 KRF: 9.3 V: 8.7 Total: 100.0%			A: 41.3 H: 19.3 SP: 14.0 KRF: 13.3 V: 1.3 Total: 89.2%	A: 49.0 H: 26.5 SP: 7.7 KRF: 14.2 V: 1.3 Total: 98.7%	A: 42.6 H: 34.2 SP: 7.1 KRF: 9.7 V: 1.3 Total: 94.9%
Largest party within parliament (seats)	A	A	A	A	A	A	A	A	A	A	A	A
Time spent in government												
A												
H												
SP												
KRF												
V												
Prime minister's party	A	A	A	H	A	SP	SP	A	KRF	A	A	A

continued overleaf

Centrality of established parties in the Norwegian party system, 1953–2009 continued

	1983	1985	1986	1989	1990	1993	1997	2000	2001	2005	2009
Percentage share of the vote		A: 40.7 H: 30.4 SP: 6.6 KRF: 8.3 V: 3.1 Total: 89.1%		A: 34.4 H: 22.1 SP: 6.5 KRF: 8.5 V: 3.2 Total: 74.7%		A: 36.9 H: 17.0 SP: 16.7 KRF: 7.9 V: 3.6 Total: 82.1%	A: 35.1 H: 14.3 SP: 8.0 KRF: 13.7 V: 4.4 Total: 75.5%		A: 24.3 H: 21.2 SP: 5.6 KRF: 12.4 V: 3.9 Total: 67.4%	A: 32.7 H: 14.1 SP: 6.5 KRF: 6.8 V: 5.9 Total: 66.0%	A: 35.4 H: 17.2 SP: 6.2 KRF: 5.5 V: 3.9 Total: 68.2%
Percentage share of seats		A: 45.2 H: 31.8 SP: 7.6 KRF: 13.2 V: 0.0 Total: 54.8%		A: 38.2 H: 22.4 SP: 6.7 KRF: 8.5 V: 0.0 Total: 75.8%		A: 40.6 H: 17.0 SP: 19.4 KRF: 7.9 V: 0.6 Total: 85.5%	A: 39.4 H: 13.9 SP: 6.7 KRF: 15.2 V: 3.6 Total: 78.8%		A: 26.1 H: 23.0 SP: 6.1 KRF: 13.3 V: 1.2 Total: 69.7%	A: 36.1 H: 13.6 SP: 6.5 KRF: 6.5 V: 5.9 Total: 68.6%	A: 37.9 H: 17.8 SP:6.5 KRF: 5.9 V: 1.2 Total: 69.3%
Largest party within parliament (seats)	A	A	A	A	A	A	A	A	A	A	A
Time spent in government											
A											
H											
SP											
KRF											
V											
SV											
Prime minister's party	H	H	A	H	A	A	KRF	A	KRF	A	A

Party abbreviations: A (Norwegian Labour Party); H (Right); SP (Centre Party); KRF (Christian People's Party); V (Left); SV (Socialist Left Party)

Sources: Aalberg (2001, 2002); Aalberg and Brekken (2006); Ministry of Local Government and Regional Development (2010); Narud and Strøm (2000); Wolden-dorp et al. (2000)

Centrality of established parties in the Spanish party system, 1979–2008

	1979	1982	1986	1989	1993	1996	2000	2004	2008
Percentage share of the vote	PSOE: 30.4 PP: 6.1 UCD: 34.8 Total: 71.3%	PSOE: 48.1 PP: 26.4 UCD: 6.8 Total: 81.3%	PSOE: 44.1 PP: 26.0 Total: 70.1%	PSOE: 39.6 PP: 25.8 Total: 65.4%	PSOE: 38.8 PP: 34.8 Total: 73.6%	PSOE: 37.6 PP: 38.8 Total: 76.4%	PSOE: 34.2 PP: 44.5 Total: 78.7%	PSOE: 42.6 PP: 37.7 Total: 80.5%	PSOE: 43.9 PP: 39.9 Total: 83.8%
Percentage share of seats	PSOE: 34.6 PP: 2.6 UCD: 39.4 Total: 76.6%	PSOE: 57.7 PP: 30.2 UCD: 3.4 Total: 91.3%	PSOE: 52.6 PP: 30.0 Total: 82.6%	PSOE: 50.0 PP: 30.3 Total: 80.3%	PSOE: 45.4 PP: 40.3 Total: 85.7%	PSOE: 40.3 PP: 44.6 Total: 84.9%	PSOE: 35.7 PP: 52.3 Total: 88.0%	PSOE: 46.9 PP: 42.3 Total: 89.2%	PSOE: 48.3 PP: 44.0 Total: 92.3%
Largest party within parliament (seats)	UCD	PSOE	PSOE	PSOE	PSOE	PP	PP	PSOE	PSOE
Time spent in government									
PSOE									
PP									
UCD									
Prime minister's party	UCD	PSOE	PSOE	PSOE	PSOE	PP	PP	PSOE	PSOE

Party abbreviations: PSOE (Spanish Socialist Workers' Party); PP (People's Party); UCD (Democratic Centre Union)

Sources: Delgado and López Nieto (2001, 2005); Ministerio del Interior (2010); Woldendorp et al. (2000)

Centrality of established parties in the Swedish party system, 1952–2006

	1952	1956	1957	1958	1960	1964	1968	1970	1973	1976
Percentage share of the vote	SAP: 46.1 M: 14.4 C: 10.7 FP: 24.4 Total: 95.6%	SAP: 44.6 M: 17.1 C: 9.4 FP: 23.8 Total: 94.9%		SAP: 46.2 M: 19.5 C: 12.7 FP: 18.2 Total: 96.6%	SAP: 47.8 M: 16.5 C: 13.6 FP: 17.5 Total: 95.4%	SAP: 47.3 M: 13.7 C: 13.2 FP: 17.0 Total: 91.2%	SAP: 50.1 M: 12.9 C: 15.7 FP: 14.3 Total: 93.0%	SAP: 45.3 M: 11.5 C: 19.9 FP: 16.2 Total: 92.9%	SAP: 43.6 M: 14.3 C: 25.1 FP: 9.4 Total: 92.4%	SAP: 42.7 M: 15.6 C: 24.1 FP: 11.1 Total: 93.5%
Percentage share of seats	SAP: 47.8 M: 13.5 C: 11.3 FP: 25.2 Total: 97.8%	SAP: 45.9 M: 18.2 C: 8.2 FP: 25.1 Total: 97.4%		SAP: 48.1 M: 19.5 C: 13.9 FP: 16.5 Total: 98.0%	SAP: 49.1 M: 16.8 C: 14.7 FP: 17.2 Total: 97.8%	SAP: 48.5 M: 14.2 C: 15.5 FP: 18.5 Total: 96.7%	SAP: 53.6 M: 13.7 C: 16.7 FP: 14.6 Total: 98.6%	SAP: 46.6 M: 11.7 C: 20.3 FP: 16.6 Total: 95.2%	SAP: 44.6 M: 14.6 C: 25.7 FP: 9.7 Total: 94.6%	SAP: 43.6 M: 15.8 C: 24.6 FP: 11.2 Total: 95.2%
Largest party within parliament (seats)	SAP	SAP		SAP	SAP	SAP	SAP	SAP	SAP	SAP
Time spent in government										
SAP										
M										
C										
FP										
Prime minister's party	SDA	SLA	SDA	SDA	SDA	SDA	SDA	SDA	SDA	C

	1978	1979	1981	1982	1985	1988	1991	1994	1998	2002	2006
Percentage share of the vote		SAP: 43.2 M: 20.3 C: 18.1 FP: 10.6 Total: 92.2%		SAP: 45.6 M: 23.6 C: 15.5 FP: 5.9 Total: 90.6%	SAP: 44.7 M: 21.3 C: 9.9 FP: 14.2 Total: 90.1%	SAP: 43.2 M: 18.3 C: 11.3 FP: 12.2 Total: 85.0%	SAP: 37.7 M: 21.9 C: 8.5 FP: 9.1 Total: 77.2%	SAP: 45.4 M: 22.2 C: 7.7 FP: 7.2 Total: 82.5%	SAP: 36.6 M: 22.7 C: 5.1 FP: 4.7 Total: 69.1%	SAP: 39.9 M: 15.1 C: 6.2 FP: 13.3 Total: 74.5%	SAP: 35.0 M: 26.2 C: 7.9 FP: 7.5 Total: 76.6%
Percentage share of seats		SAP: 42.9 M: 20.9 C: 18.3 FP: 10.9 Total: 93.0%		SAP: 47.6 M: 24.6 C: 16.0 FP: 6.0 Total: 94.2%	SAP: 45.6 M: 21.8 C: 12.6 FP: 14.6 Total: 94.6%	SAP: 44.7 M: 18.9 C: 12.0 FP: 12.6 Total: 88.2%	SAP: 39.5 M: 22.9 C: 8.9 FP: 9.5 Total: 80.8%	SAP: 46.1 M: 22.9 C: 7.7 FP: 7.4 Total: 84.1%	SAP: 37.5 M: 23.5 C: 5.2 FP: 4.9 Total: 71.1%	SAP: 41.3 M: 15.8 C: 6.3 FP: 13.8 Total: 77.2%	SAP: 37.2 M: 27.8 C: 8.3 FP: 8.0 Total: 81.3%
Largest party within parliament (seats)	SAP	SAP	SAP	SAP	SAP	SAP	SAP	SAP	SAP	SAP	SAP
Time spent in government — SAP											
M											
C											
FP											
KD											
Prime minister's party	FP	C	C	SDA	SDA	SDA	M	SDA	SDA	SDA	M

Party abbreviations: SAP (Social Democratic Workers' Party); M (Moderate Rally Party); C (Centre Party); FP (Liberal People's Party); KD (Christian Democrats)

Sources: Bergman (2000); Pierre and Widfeldt (1999); Swedish Government Homepage (2010); Widfeldt (2003); Woldendorp et al. (2000)

Centrality of established parties in the United Kingdom party system, 1950–2005

	1950	1951	1955	1959	1964	1966	1970	1974a
Percentage share of the vote	Con: 43.5 Lab: 46.1 Total: 89.6%	Con: 48.0 Lab: 48.8 Total: 96.8%	Con: 49.7 Lab: 46.4 Total: 96.1	Con: 49.4 Lab: 43.8 Total: 93.2%	Con: 43.3 Lab: 44.1 Total: 87.4%	Con: 41.9 Lab: 47.9 Total: 89.8%	Con: 46.4 Lab: 43.0 Total: 89.4%	Con: 37.8 Lab: 37.1 Total: 74.9%
Percentage share of seats	Con: 47.8 Lab: 50.4 Total: 98.2%	Con: 51.4 Lab: 47.2 Total: 98.6%	Con: 54.8 Lab: 44.0 Total: 98.8%	Con: 57.9 Lab: 41.0 Total: 98.9%	Con: 48.3 Lab: 50.3 Total: 98.6%	Con: 40.2 Lab: 57.6 Total: 97.8%	Con: 52.4 Lab: 45.7 Total: 98.1%	Con: 46.8 Lab: 47.4 Total: 94.2%
Largest party within parliament (seats)	Lab	Con	Con	Con	Lab	Lab	Con	Lab
Time spent in government Con Lab								
Prime minister's party	Lab	Con	Con	Con	Lab	Lab	Con	Lab

	1974b	1979	1983	1987	1992	1997	2001	2005
Percentage share of the vote	Con: 35.8 Lab: 39.2 Total: 75.0%	Con: 43.9 Lab: 37.0 Total: 80.9%	Con: 42.4 Lab: 27.6 Total: 70.0%	Con: 42.3 Lab: 30.8 Total: 73.1%	Con: 41.9 Lab: 34.4 Total: 76.3%	Con: 30.6 Lab: 43.2 Total: 73.8%	Con: 31.7 Lab: 40.7 Total: 72.4%	Con: 32.3 Lab: 35.2 Total: 67.5%
Percentage share of seats	Con: 43.6 Lab: 50.2 Total: 93.8%	Con: 53.4 Lab: 42.4 Total: 95.8%	Con: 61.1 Lab: 32.2 Total: 93.3%	Con: 57.7 Lab: 35.2 Total: 92.9%	Con: 51.6 Lab: 41.6 Total: 93.2%	Con: 25.0 Lab: 63.6 Total: 88.6%	Con: 25.2 Lab: 62.7 Total: 87.9%	Con: 30.5 Lab: 55.2 Total: 85.7%
Largest party within parliament (seats)	Lab	Con	Con	Con	Con	Lab	Lab	Lab
Time spent in government								
Con								
Lab								
Prime minister's party	Lab	Con	Con	Con	Con	Lab	Lab	Lab

Party abbreviations: Con (Conservatives Party; Lab (Labour Party)

Sources: Electoral Commission Homepage (2010); Fisher, J. (2002); Fisher, S. (2006); Woldendorp *et al.* (2000)

Notes

1 A party-centric approach to party system change

1 Many of the major Social Democratic and Christian Democratic or Conservative parties across Europe remain key systemic actors. For example, the Labour and Conservative parties in Britain, the CDU and SPD in Germany, the SPO and OVP in Austria, and the Social Democratic/Labour parties of the Scandinavian nations. However, an obvious exception is the Italian Christian Democratic party, which had been the key actor in Italian post-war politics until its collapse in the early 1990s.
2 Figure calculated in accordance with the Pedersen index of volatility (1979).
3 More recently, the rational choice literature has identified more differentiated party goals (see Müller and Strøm, 1999b, discussed in more detail in section 1.3).
4 The study examines parties' strategies in France from 1958 when the Fifth Republic was established. The establishment of democratic constitutions in Spain, Portugal and Greece in 1978, 1976 and 1975 respectively means that the studies of these countries commence in these years.
5 See Appendices 1 and 2 for parties considered as established and anti-political establishment parties.

2 Electorate-orientated strategies

1 The unit of a 'government' is central to this analysis, alongside an understanding of when a change in government occurs. Müller and Strøm (2000a: 12) argue that a change in government occurs when there is a change in party or set of parties holding cabinet posts or any general election. In line with Müller and Strøm's definition, no new government is noted when a party changes name or splits.
2 The number of countries covered increased to 51 from 1990 onwards.
3 For a detailed analysis of the validity and reliability of the CMP data see Hearl 2001; McDonald and Mendes 2001 and Klingemann *et al.* 2006.
4 To name but a few, neo-populist parties (Betz 1994), protest parties (Smith 1987), discontent parties (Lane and Ersson 1994) or anti-party parties (Poguntke 1996).
5 Appendix 2 provides a full list of anti-political establishment parties according to Abedi (2004) updated by applying the same criteria to anti-political establishment parties that emerged after 1999.
6 The study concludes in 2009, and therefore does not take into account the Conservative/Liberal Democrat coalition formed in the United Kingdom following the 2010 general election.

3 Institutional strategies

1 This is dependent upon the wealth of parties. Where parties are wealthy, deposit requirements may not pose a barrier. In contrast, for a less wealthy party, any deposit requirement may be highly restrictive.

2 When assessing this aspect, a qualitative judgment, based on the qualitative data available and the populations of districts and countries, allows the classification of a country's signature requirements effectively. One solution to this problem may be to construct a figure that corresponds to the proportion of voters' signatures required. However, this figure would fluctuate at every election due to changes in the number of registered voters and the data may not easily be available where a different number of signatures are required according to district size.

3 However, some established parties fund smaller parties and independent candidates to undermine oppositions.

4 An obvious exception to this rule is Forza Italia, the party financed and headed by media magnate Silvio Berlusconi that swept to power in Italy in 1994, only a few months after its formation.

5 Although restrictive electoral systems will generally disfavour smaller parties, non-established parties will also be penalised, as, in general, non-established parties are the smaller parties to be found within a party system.

6 Carter (2005) discusses 14 of the 17 countries under consideration. Luxembourg, Finland and Ireland do not feature, but all have single-tier systems. Similarly, Carter's data does not incorporate the changes made in 2003 to the Belgian system and the 2006 change to the Italian system, but these two changes resulted in a single tier of districting.

7 Applying this index, the lower the value obtained, the more proportional a system. The value can approach 0 at its base point and 100 at its peak, although this is almost impossible practically. A problem emerges with the measure, as with many other similar measures such as Mogens Pedersen's (1979) volatility measure and Laakso and Taagepera's (1979) effective number of parties index, regarding how to treat small parties, which may only receive one seat or less than 1 per cent of the vote. This issue is dealt with thoroughly by Gallagher and Mitchell (2005c), who conclude that excluding the category of 'others' completely produces accurate results comparable with a number of other methods used (such as Taagepera's least squares approach, see Gallagher and Mitchell 2005c for more details), so 'others' are disregarded in order to calculate disproportionality values.

8 The section on free airtime is narrowly focused and does not include free advertising time that is available to governing parties for the purposes of giving government statements, which are often used for free campaigning (see Plasser and Plasser 2002 for more details).

4 Selection of cases and measurements

1 Where an odd number of countries do not score on a factor, the middle values can be removed, but when an even number of countries do not score, the middle values and the higher of the two values remaining are removed.

2 Presenting a cumulative score favours those countries that receive a score on every dimension, but by providing an average score, no country is penalised.

3 However, 1998 marked the first election at which a new government wholly replaced an outgoing government in the post-war period.

4 The growth in electoral support for the SVP led to a change in the magic formula in 2003. Previously, the Federal Council contained two ministers each from the CVP (Christian Democrats), the SPS (Social Democrats) and the FDP (Free Democrats) and one from the SVP. Under the new magic formula starting from 1 January 2004, the party composition of the cabinet changed to the following: 1 CVP, 2 SP, 2 FDP and 2 representatives from the SVP (Detterbeck 2005: 189).

5 Additionally, governing parties in France have used their incumbency status to use government information broadcasting spots for free partisan advertising.
6 Party splits and mergers are problematic, but parties are treated as continuous entities, as innovation in government formation occurs when wholly new parties enter government for the first time. A party has governed before if the party had previously governed under a different name or as part of a larger party.
7 Pedersen's (1979) index of electoral volatility is also widely used as an indicator of electoral change, although the effective number of parties index is the more intuitively useful of the two measures for assessing party system, rather than purely electoral, change.
8 The concept of 'systemic centrality' differs from Smith's (1976) concept of 'the politics of centrality', applied to the German party system.
9 Clearly, the measure of the largest party in parliament is also an indicator of parliamentary strength. The measure of *number* of seats in parliament and *largest* party in parliament have been separated out as it is the number of seats which is relevant for a party's *parliamentary* strength, but the party which receives the highest number of seats is relevant for studying the formation of *government* formation patterns.

5 The use of electorate-orientated strategies

1 Section 1.3 outlined the criteria for established or non-established status. At the risk of over-simplification, an established party was in a leading position within its national party system by the early 1970s whereas a non-established party was not.
2 Some of the parties considered have histories which date back to before 1976, yet as the democratic period in Portugal's political history is the main focus of this enquiry, it is only the periods in which the parties obtained parliamentary representation since 1976 that are of concern.
3 West Germany between 1949 and 1990 and unified Germany post-1990.
4 Formal agreements in the case of Portugal and informal agreements in the case of Germany.
5 The distribution of Federal Council seats changed in 2003, a point fully addressed later in this section.

6 The use of institutional strategies

1 The definition of established parties proposed in section 1.3 suggests that influence in terms of the governmental arena is a defining property of an established party. The PCF has not 'proved to be especially influential for the functioning of the system' (Smith 1989b: 161) and has governed infrequently during the period covered. The party has had a strong systemic impact since 1958, but in terms of the importance of the party as an actor, particularly in terms of the governing arena, the party is not an established party as it was not a significant actor before the early 1970s. If the governing arena is especially influential for determining the established or non-established nature of parties, it appears sensible only to consider the three 'parties of government' as established parties and exclude the PCF from this group. Conversely, the Socialists entered government for the first time only in 1981, but as a 'party of government', must be considered an established party.
2 The importance of parties acting in a regime that encourages minority governments raises further issues concerning regime and systemic level influences acting as independent factors, able to influence the levels of centrality established parties can achieve. In the French case, presidentialism played an important role in influencing levels of centrality and with the Danish case, minority governance is crucial. The concluding chapter of the book discusses these issues in detail.

3 For more details on the extreme right-wing party presence in Denmark, see Rydgren (2004) and Widfeldt (2000).

4 This section strongly supports the perspective presented in Chapter 1, which highlighted the possibility of electoral change not automatically leading to party system change. In the Danish case, this indeed was the case, as the electoral upheaval of 1973 did not translate into party system change. The concluding chapter explores the relationship between electoral change and party system change in more detail.

5 As the analysis concludes in 2009, the study does not include the dramatic election of 2011, which saw Fianna Fáil's share of the vote decimated.

7 Party strategies in western Europe: party competition and electoral outcomes

1 The one exception is the PSOE (Spanish Socialist Workers Party), formed in 1879 (see Share 1999).

Bibliography

Aalberg, T. (2001) 'Norway', *European Journal of Political Research*, 40: 375–82.

Aalberg, T. (2002) 'Norway', *European Journal of Political Research*, 41: 1047–56.

Aalberg, T. and Brekken, T. (2006) 'Norway', *European Journal of Political Research*, 45: 1221–30.

Abedi, A. (2004) *Anti-Political Establishment Parties: a comparative analysis*, London: Routledge.

Administration and Cost of Elections (2010) www.aceproject.org, accessed 6 June.

Allern, E. and Aylott, N. (2009) 'Overcoming the fear of commitment: pre-electoral coalitions in Norway and Sweden', *Acta Politica*, 44: 259–85.

Alliance for Sweden Homepage (2010) www.alliansforverige.se/, accessed 1 June.

Andeweg, R. (1996) 'The Netherlands', in J. Blondel and M. Cotta (eds) *Party and Government: an inquiry into the relationships between governments and supporting parties in liberal democracies*, Basingstoke: Macmillan.

Andeweg, R. (2005) 'The Netherlands: the sanctity of proportionality', in M. Gallagher and P. Mitchell (eds) *The Politics of Electoral Systems*, Oxford: Oxford University Press.

Ansolabehere, S., Behr, R. and Iyengar, S. (1993) *The Media Game: American politics in the television age*, New York: Macmillan.

Appleton, A. (1995) 'Parties under pressure: challenges to 'established' French parties' *West European Politics*, 18: 52–77.

Arter, D. (1999a) 'Party system change in Scandinavia since 1970: 'restricted change' or 'general change'?' *West European Politics*, 22: 139–58.

Arter, D. (1999b) *Scandinavian Politics Today*, Manchester and New York: Manchester University Press.

Austin, R. and Tjernström, M. (2003) *Funding of Political Parties and Election Campaigns*, Stockholm: International Institute for Democracy and Electoral Assistance.

Austrian Federal Chancellery (2010) www.bka.gv.at/site/3327/Default.aspx, accessed 5 June.

Bartolini, S. (1984) 'Institutional constraints and party competition in the French party system', *West European Politics*, 7: 103–27.

Bartolini, S. (2002) 'Electoral and party competition: analytical dimensions and empirical problems', in R. Gunther, J. Montero and J. Linz (eds) *Political Parties: old concepts and new challenges*, Oxford: Oxford University Press.

Bartolini, S. and Mair, P. (1990) *Identity, Competition and Electoral Availability the Stabilisation of European Electorates, 1885–1985*, Cambridge: Cambridge University Press.

Baum, M. and Freire, A. (2002) 'Second-order elections in democratic Portugal, 1975–2001', paper presented at the Conference on Portugal and Southern European Politics, University of California at Berkeley, October/November 2002.

Belgian Federal E-Portal (2010) www.belgium.be/eportal/index.jsp, accessed 17 February.

Bell, D. (1973) *The Coming of Post-Industrial Society*, New York: Basic Books.

Bell, D. (2000) *Parties and Democracy in France: parties under presidentialism*, Aldershot: Ashgate.

Bennett, A. (1997) 'Party system change in redemocratizing countries', in P. Pennings and J. E. Lane (eds) *Comparing Party System Change*, London and New York: Routledge.

Benoit, K. (2004) 'Electoral reform: models of electoral system change', *Electoral Studies*, 23: 363–89.

Berelson, B. (1952) *Content Analysis in Communication Research*, New York: Free Press.

Berglund, S. and Lindström, U. (1978) *The Scandinavian Party System(s)*, Sweden: Studentlitteratur.

Bergman, T. (2000) 'Sweden: when minority cabinets are the rule and majority coalitions the exception', in W. Müller and K. Strøm (eds) *Coalition Governments in Western Europe*, Oxford: Oxford University Press.

Bergman, T., Müller, W., Strøm, K. and Blomgren, M. (2003) 'Democratic delegation and accountability: cross-national patterns', in K. Strøm, W. Müller and T. Bergman (eds), *Delegation and Accountability in Parliamentary Democracies*, Oxford: Oxford University Press.

Betz, H. (1994) *Radical Right-Wing Populism in Western Europe*, New York: St Martins Press.

Betz, H. and Welsh, H. (1995) 'The PDS in the new German party system', *German Politics*, 4: 92–111.

Bille, L. (1989) 'Denmark: the oscillating party system', *West European Politics*, 12: 42–58.

Bille, L. (2002) 'Denmark', *European Journal of Political Research*, 41: 941–46.

Bille, L. and Pedersen, K. (2004) 'Electoral fortune and responses of the Social Democratic Party and Liberal Party in Denmark: ups and downs', in P. Mair, W. Müller and F. Plasser (eds) *Political Parties and Electoral Change: party responses to electoral markets*, London: Sage.

Blais, A. and Massicotte, L. (2002) 'Electoral systems' in L. LeDuc, R. Niemi and P. Norris (eds) *Comparing Democracies 2: new challenges in the study of elections and voting*, London: Sage.

Blondel, J. (1968) 'Party systems and patterns of government in western democracies', *Canadian Journal of Political Science*, 1: 180–203.

Blondel, J. (1996) 'Britain', in J. Blondel and M. Cotta (eds) *Party and Government: an inquiry into the relationships between governments and supporting parties in liberal democracies*, Basingstoke: Macmillan.

Blondel, J. and Cotta, M. (1996) *Party and Government: an inquiry into the relationships between governments and supporting parties in liberal democracies*, Basingstoke: Macmillan.

Blyth, M. and Katz, R. (2005) 'From catch-all politics to cartelisation: the political economy of the cartel party', *West European Politics*, 28: 33–60.

Bottom, K. (2003) 'The changing fortunes of parties without establishment status: new-populism in the cartel?', paper presented at the Conference of the Annual Elections,

Public Opinion and Parties Specialist Group of the Political Studies Association, Cardiff, September 2003.

Boucek, F. (1998) 'Electoral and parliamentary aspects of dominant party systems', in P. Pennings and J. E. Lane (eds) *Comparing Party System Change*, London: Routledge.

Bowler, S. and Farrell, D. (1992) *Electoral Strategies and Political Marketing*, Basingstoke: Palgrave Macmillan.

Bowler, S., Carter, E. and Farrell, D. (2003) 'Changing party access to elections', in B. Cain, R. Dalton and S. Scarrow (eds) *Democracy Transformed? Expanding political opportunities in advanced industrial democracies*, Oxford: Oxford University Press.

Bruneau, T. (1984) 'Continuity and change in Portuguese politics: ten years after the revolution of 25 April 1974', *West European Politics*, 7: 72–83.

Bruneau, T. (1997) *Political Parties and Democracy in Portugal: organizations, elections and public opinion*, Boulder: Westview Press.

Bryman, A. (2001) *Social Research Methods*, Oxford: Oxford University Press.

Budge, I. and Bara, J. (2001) 'Introduction: content analysis and political texts', in I. Budge *et al.* (eds) *Mapping Policy Preferences: estimates for parties, electors and governments, 1945–1998*, Oxford: Oxford University Press.

Budge, I., Robertson, D. and Hearl, D. (eds) (1987) *Ideology, Strategy and Party Change: spatial analyses of post-war election programmes in 19 democracies*, Cambridge: Cambridge University Press.

Budge, I., Klingemann, H. D., Volkens, A., Bara, J. and Tanenbaum, E. (2001) *Mapping Policy Preferences: estimates for parties, electors and governments, 1945–1998*, Oxford: Oxford University Press.

Bundesministerium für Inneres (Austria) (2010) www.bmi.gv.at/cms/bmi/_news/bmi.aspx, accessed 29 January.

Carter, E. (2005) *The Extreme Right in Western Europe: success or failure?*, Manchester: Manchester University Press.

Carty, R. (1988) 'Ireland: from predominance to competition', in S. Wolinetz (ed.) *Parties and Party Systems in Liberal Democracies*, London and New York: Routledge.

Casas-Zamora, K. (2005) *Paying for Democracy: political finance and state funding for parties*, Colchester: ECPR Press.

Centre for European Constitutional Law – Themistokles and Dimitris Tsatsos Foundation, (2009) www.cecl.gr, accessed 17 July.

Chandler, W. (1988) 'Party system transformation in the Federal Republic of Germany', in S. Wolinetz (ed.) *Parties and Party Systems in Liberal Democracies*, London and New York: Routledge.

Chandler, W. and Siaroff, A. (1986) 'Postindustrial politics in Germany and the origins of the Greens', *Comparative Politics*, 18: 303–24.

Church, C. (2000) 'The Swiss elections of October 1999: learning to live in more interesting times', *West European Politics*, 23: 215–30.

Church, C. (2004) 'The Swiss elections of October 2003: two steps to system change', *West European Politics*, 27: 518–34.

Clift, B. (2003) 'PS intra-party politics and party system change', in J. Evans (ed.) *The French Party System*, Manchester: Manchester University Press.

Clift, B. and Fisher, J. (2004) 'Comparative political finance reform: the cases of France and Britain', *Party Politics*, 10: 677–99.

Close, D. (2002) *Greece Since 1945*, London: Longman.

Cole, A. (1990) 'The evolution of the party system, 1974–1990', in A. Cole (ed.) *French Political Parties in Transition*, Aldershot: Dartmouth.

Cole, A. (2003), 'Stress, strain and stability in the French party system', in J. Evans (ed.) *The French Party System*, Manchester: Manchester University Press.

Collins, N. and Cradden, T. (1997) *Irish Politics Today*, 3rd edn, Manchester: Manchester University Press.

Colomer, J. (2005), 'It's parties that choose electoral systems (or, Duverger's law upside down)', *Political Studies*, 53: 1–21.

Comissão Nacional de Eleições (Portugal) (2010) www.legislativas2009.mj.pt/, accessed 8 April.

Cotta, M. and Verzichelli, L. (1996) 'Italy', in J. Blondel and M. Cotta (eds) *Party and Government: an inquiry into the relationships between governments and supporting parties in liberal democracies*, Basingstoke: Macmillan.

Crewe, I. (1985) 'Introduction: electoral change in western democracies: a framework for analysis', in I. Crewe and D. Denver (eds) *Electoral Change in Western Democracies*, London: Croon Helm.

Crewe, I. and Denver, D. (1985) *Electoral Change in Western Democracies*, London: Croon Helm.

D'Alimonte, R. (2005) 'Italy: a case of fragmented bipolarism', in M. Gallagher and P. Mitchell (eds) *The Politics of Electoral Systems*, Oxford: Oxford University Press.

Dahl, R. (1966) 'Patterns of opposition', in R. Dahl (ed.) *Political Oppositions in Western Democracies*, New Haven and London: Yale University Press.

Dahl, R. and Tufte, E. (1973) *Size and Democracy*, Stanford, CA: Stanford University Press.

Dalton, R. (1996) *Citizen Politics: public opinion and political parties in advanced western democracies*, 2nd edn, Chatham, NJ: Chatham House.

Dalton, R. and Wattenberg, M. (2000a) 'Partisan change and the democratic process', in R. Dalton and M. Wattenberg (eds) *Parties Without Partisans: political change in advanced industrial democracies*, Oxford: Oxford University Press.

Dalton, R., and Wattenberg, M. (2000b) *Parties without Partisans: political change in advanced industrial democracies*, Oxford: Oxford University Press.

Dalton, R. Beck, P. and Flanagan, S. (1984) 'Electoral change in advanced industrial democracies', in R. Dalton, S. Flanagan and P. Beck (eds) *Electoral Change in Advanced Industrial Democracies: realignment or dealignment?*, Princeton: Princeton University Press.

Damgaard, E. (2000) 'Denmark: the life and death of government coalitions', in W. Müller and K. Strøm (eds) *Coalition Governments in Western Europe*, Oxford: Oxford University Press.

Damgaard, E. (2003) 'Denmark: delegation and accountability in minority situations', in K. Strøm, W. Müller and T. Bergman (eds) *Delegation and Accountability in Parliamentary Democracies*, Oxford: Oxford University Press.

De Sousa, L. (2001) 'Political parties and corruption in Portugal', *West European Politics*, 24: 157–80.

De Swaan, A. (1973) *Coalition Theory and Cabinet Government*, Amsterdam: Elsevier.

De Winter, L. (2002) 'Parties and government formation, portfolio allocation and policy definition', in K. R. Luther and F. Müller-Rommel (eds) *Political Parties in the New Europe: political and analytical challenges*, Oxford: Oxford University Press.

De Winter, L. (2005), 'Belgium: empowering voters or party elites?', in M. Gallagher and P. Mitchell (eds) *The Politics of Electoral Systems*, Oxford: Oxford University Press.

De Winter, L., Frognier, A. P. and Rihoux, B. (1996) 'Belgium', in J. Blondel and M. Cotta (eds) *Party and Government: an inquiry into the relationships between governments and supporting parties in liberal democracies*, Basingstoke: Macmillan.

De Winter, L., Timmermans, A. and Dumont, P. (2000) 'Belgium: on government agreements, evangelists, followers and heretics', in W. Müller and K. Strøm (eds) *Coalition Governments in Western Europe*, Oxford: Oxford University Press.

Delgado, I. and López Nieto, L. (2001) 'Spain', European Journal of Political Research, 40: 413–20.

Delgado, I. and López Nieto, L. (2005) 'Spain', *European Journal of Political Research*, 44: 1188–94.

Department of the Taoiseach (2010) www.taoiseach.gov.ie, accessed 21 February.

Deschouwer, K. (1994) 'The decline of consociationalism and the reluctant modernization of Belgian mass parties', in R. Katz and P. Mair (eds) *How Parties Organize: change and adaptation in party organizations in western democracies*, London: Sage.

Deschouwer, K. (2002) 'The colour purple: the end of predictable politics in the Low Countries', in P. Webb, D. Farrell and I. Holliday (eds) *Political Parties in Advanced Industrial Democracies*, Oxford: Oxford University Press.

Detterbeck, K. (2005) 'Cartel parties in western Europe?', *Party Politics*, 11: 173–91.

Deutsch, K. and Smith, D. (1987) 'The Federal Republic of Germany: West Germany', in R. Macridis (ed.) *Modern Political Systems: Europe*, 6th edn, London: Prentice-Hall.

Diamandouros, P. (1998) 'The political system in post-authoritarian Greece (1974–1996): outline and interpretations', in P. Ignazi and C. Ysmal (eds) *The Organization of Political Parties in Southern Europe*, Westport: Praeger.

Dimitras, P. (1994) 'Electoral systems in Greece', in S. Nagel and V. Rukavishnikov (eds) *Eastern European Development and Public Policy*, Basingstoke: Macmillan.

Direction des Elections Belgium (2010) www.ibz.rrn.fgov.be/index.php?id=33&L=0, accessed 2 September.

Downs, A. (1957) *An Economic Theory of Democracy*, New York: Harper and Row Publishers.

Dumont, P. and Caulier, J. (2005) 'The "effective" number of relevant parties: how voting power improves Laakso-Taagepera's index', Cahier du CEREC, FUSL.

Dumont, P. and De Winter, L. (2000) 'Luxembourg: stable coalitions in a pivotal party system', in W. Müller and K. Strøm (eds) *Coalition Governments in Western Europe*, Oxford: Oxford University Press.

Dumont, P. and De Winter, L. (2003) 'Luxembourg: a case of more 'direct' delegation and accountability', in K. Strøm, W. Müller and T. Bergman (eds) *Delegation and Accountability in Parliamentary Democracies*, Oxford: Oxford University Press.

Dunleavy, P. and Boucek, F. (2003) 'Constructing the number of parties', *Party Politics*, 9: 291–315.

Dutch Government Homepage (2010) www.government.nl, accessed 16 April.

Dutch Government Portal (2010) www.regering.nl/index.jsp, accessed 24 February.

Duverger, M. (1954) *Political Parties: their organization and activity in the modern state*, London: Metheun and Co. Ltd.

Einhorn, E. and Logue, J. (1988) 'Continuity and change in the Scandinavian party systems', in S. Wolinetz (ed.) *Parties and Party Systems in Liberal Democracies*, London and New York: Routledge.

Eldersveld, S. (1964) *Political Parties: a behavioral analysis*, Chicago: Rand McNally.

Election World (2010) www.electionworld.org, accessed 24 April.

Electoral Commission Homepage (UK) (2010) www.electoralcommission.org.uk, accessed 24 June.

Elgie, R. (1999) 'The changing French political system: introduction', *West European Politics*, 22: 1–19.

Elgie, R. (2005) 'France: stacking the deck', in M. Gallagher and P. Mitchell (eds) *The Politics of Electoral Systems*, Oxford: Oxford University Press.

Elklit, J. (2005) 'Denmark: simplicity embedded in complexity (or is it the other way round?)', in M. Gallagher and P. Mitchell (eds) *The Politics of Electoral Systems*, Oxford: Oxford University Press.

Epstein, L. (1967) *Political Parties in Western Democracies*, London: Pall Mall Press.

Evans, J. (2003a) 'Introduction', in J. Evans (ed.) *The French Party System*, Manchester: Manchester University Press.

Evans, J. (2003b) *The French Party System*, Manchester: Manchester University Press.

Fallend, F. (2001) 'Austria', *European Journal of Political Research*, 40: 238–53.

Fallend, F. (2004) 'Austria', *European Journal of Political Research*, 43: 934–49.

Farrell, D. (1999) 'Ireland: a party system transformed?', in D. Broughton and M. Donovan (eds) *Changing Party Systems in Western Europe*, London and New York: Pinter.

Farrell, D. (2002), 'Campaign modernization and the west European party', in K. R. Luther and F. Müller-Rommel (eds) *Political Parties in the New Europe: political and analytical challenges*, Oxford: Oxford University Press.

Farrell, D. and Webb, P. (2000) 'Political parties as campaign organizations', in R. Dalton and M. Wattenberg (eds) *Parties Without Partisans: political change in advanced industrial democracies*, Oxford: Oxford University Press.

Finnish Government Homepage (2010) www.government.fi, accessed 18 February.

Fisher, J. (2002) 'United Kingdom', *European Journal of Political Research*, 41: 1101–10.

Fisher, S. (2006) 'United Kingdom', *European Journal of Political Research*, 45: 1282–91.

Franklin, M. (2004) *Voter Turnout and the Dynamics of Electoral Competition in Established Democracies since 1945*, Cambridge: Cambridge University Press.

Franklin, M., Mackie, T. and Valen, H. (1992) *Electoral Change: responses to evolving social and attitudinal structures in western countries*, Cambridge: Cambridge University Press.

Franzmann, S. and Kaiser, A. (2006) 'Locating political parties in policy space: a reanalysis of party manifesto data, *Party Politics*, 12: 163–88.

Gallagher, M. (1991) 'Proportionality, disproportionality and electoral systems', *Electoral Studies*, 10: 33–51.

Gallagher, M. (2005a) 'Conclusion', in M. Gallagher and P. Mitchell (eds), *The Politics of Electoral Systems*, Oxford: Oxford University Press.

Gallagher, M. (2005b) 'Ireland: the discreet charm of PR-STV', in M. Gallagher and P. Mitchell (eds) *The Politics of Electoral Systems*, Oxford: Oxford University Press.

Gallagher, M. and Mitchell, P. (2005a) 'Introduction to electoral systems', in M. Gallagher and P. Mitchell (eds) *The Politics of Electoral Systems*, Oxford: Oxford University Press.

Gallagher, M. and Mitchell, P. (2005b) *The Politics of Electoral Systems*, Oxford: Oxford University Press.

Gallagher, M. and Mitchell, P. (2005c) 'Appendix B', in M. Gallagher and P. Mitchell (eds) *The Politics of Electoral Systems*, Oxford: Oxford University Press.

Gallagher, M., Laver, M. and Mair, P. (2005) *Representative Government in Modern Europe: institutions, parties and governments*, 3rd edn, Boston: McGraw-Hill.

Gallagher, T. (1996) 'The emergence of new party systems and transitions to democracy: Romania and Portugal compared', in G. Pridham and P. Lewis (eds) *Stabilising Fragile*

Democracies: comparing new party systems in southern and eastern Europe, London and New York: Routledge.

German Christian Democratic Union Homepage (2010) www.cdu.de/, accessed 2 April.

German Government Homepage (2010) www.bundesregierung.de, accessed 6 January.

German Green Party Homepage (2010) www.gruene.de/index.htm, accessed 20 February.

Gidlund, G. and Koole, R. (2001) 'Political finance in the north of Europe: the Netherlands and Sweden', in K. H. Nassmacher (ed.) *Foundations for Democracy: approaches to comparative political finance*, Baden-Baden: Nomos Verlagsgesellschaft.

Golder, S. (2006) 'Pre-electoral coalition formation in parliamentary democracies', *British Journal of Political Science*, 36: 193–212.

Greek Ministry of Internal Affairs (2010) www.ypes.gr/en/Elections, accessed 16 March.

Grofman, B. and Lijphart, A. (1986) *Electoral Laws and their Political Consequences*, New York: Agathon Press.

Gunther, R. and Mughan, A. (2000) *Democracy and the Media*, Cambridge: Cambridge University Press.

Hancock, M. (1992) 'The SPD seeks a new identity: party modernization and prospects in the 1990s', in R. Dalton (ed.) *The New Germany Votes: unification and the creation of the new German party system*, Oxford: Berg-Providence.

Hanley, D. (1999) 'France: living with instability' in D. Broughton and M. Donovan (eds) *Changing Party Systems in Western Europe*, London and New York: Pinter.

Hanley, D. (2002) *Party, Society and Government: republican democracy in France*, New York: Berghahn Books.

Hardmeier, S. (2004) 'Switzerland', *European Journal of Political Research*, 43: 1151–9.

Harmel, R. and Janda, K. (1994) 'An integrated theory of party goals and party change', *Journal of Theoretical Politics*, 6: 259–87.

Hearl, D. (2001) 'Checking the party policy estimates: reliability', in I. Budge, H. Klingemann, A. Volkens, J. Bara and E. Tanenbaum (eds) *Mapping Policy Preferences: estimates for parties, electors and governments, 1945–1998*, Oxford: Oxford University Press.

Hooghe, M., Maddens, B. and Noppe, J. (2006) 'Why parties adapt: electoral reform, party finance and party strategy in Belgium', *Electoral Studies*, 25: 351–68.

Holliday, I. (2002) 'Spain: building a parties state in a new democracy', in P. Webb, D. Farrell and I. Holliday (eds) *Political Parties in Advanced Industrial Democracies*, Oxford: Oxford University Press.

Hopkin, J. (2003) 'The emergence and convergence of the cartel party: parties, state and economy in western Europe', paper presented at the London School of Economics Conference, London, January 2003.

Hopkin, J. (2005) 'Spain: proportional representation with majoritarian outcomes', in M Gallagher and P. Mitchell (eds) *The Politics of Electoral Systems*, Oxford: Oxford University Press.

Ignazi, P. (1992) 'The silent counter-revolution: hypotheses on the emergence of extreme right-wing parties in Europe', *European Journal of Political Research*, 22: 3–34.

Ignazi, P. (2002) 'Italy', *European Journal of Political Research*, 41: 992–1000.

Ignazi, P. (2006) 'Italy', *European Journal of Political Research*, 43: 1143–51.

Inglehart, R. (1977) *The Silent Revolution: changing values and political styles among western publics*, Princeton: Princeton University Press.

Inter-Parliamentary Union Parline Database (2010) www.ipu.org/parline-e/parlinesearch.asp, accessed 5 July.

Irish Government Homepage (2010) www.gov.ie/en, accessed 1 December.

Isaksson, G. E. (2001) 'Parliamentary government in different shapes', *West European Politics*, 24: 40–54.

Ivaldi, G. (2003) 'The FN split: party system change and electoral prospects', in J. Evans (ed.) *The French Party System*, Manchester: Manchester University Press.

Janda, K. (1990) 'Towards a performance theory of change in political parties', paper presented as the World Congress of the International Sociological Association, Madrid, July 1990.

Jeffery, C. (1999) 'Germany: from hyperstability to change?', in D. Broughton and M. Donovan (eds) *Changing Party Systems in Western Europe*, London and New York: Pinter.

Kaid, L. and Holtz-Bacha, C. (1995) *Political Advertising in Western Democracies: parties and candidates on television*, Thousand Oaks, CA: Sage.

Katz, R. (2002) 'The internal life of parties', in K. R. Luther and F. Müller-Rommel (eds) *Political Parties in the New Europe: political and analytical challenges*, Oxford: Oxford University Press.

Katz, R. (2003) 'Reforming the Italian electoral law, 1993', in M. Shugart and M. Wattenberg (eds) *Mixed-Member Electoral Systems: the best of both worlds?*, Oxford: Oxford University Press.

Katz, R. (2005) 'Why are there so many (or so few) electoral reforms?', in M. Gallagher and P. Mitchell (eds) *The Politics of Electoral Systems*, Oxford: Oxford University Press.

Katz, R. and Mair, P. (1992) *Party Organizations: a data handbook on party organizations in western democracies, 1960–1990*, London: Sage.

Katz, R. and Mair, P. (1994) *How Parties Organize: change and adaptation in party organizations in western democracies*, London: Sage.

Katz, R. and Mair, P. (1995) 'Changing models of party organization and party democracy: the emergence of the cartel party', *Party Politics*, 1: 5–28.

Katz, R. and Mair, P. (1996) 'Cadre, catch-all or cartel?: a rejoinder', *Party Politics*, 2: 525–34.

Katzenstein, P. (1985) *Small States in World Markets: industrial policy in Europe*, Ithaca and London: Cornell University Press.

Kim, H. and Fording, R. (2001) 'Extending party estimates to governments and electors', in I. Budge, H. Klingemann, A. Volkens, J. Bara and E. Tanenbaum (eds) *Mapping Policy Preferences: estimates for parties, electors and governments, 1945–1998*, Oxford: Oxford University Press.

Kirchheimer, O. (1966) 'The transformation of western European party systems', in J. LaPalombara and M. Weiner (eds) *Political Parties and Political Development*, Princeton: Princeton University Press.

Klapper, J. (1960) *The Effects of Mass Communication*, New York: Free Press.

Klingemann, H. D., Hofferbert, R. and Budge, I. (1994) *Parties, Policy and Democracy*, Boulder, CO: Westview.

Klingemann, H. D., Volkens, A., Bara, J., Budge, I. and McDonald, M. (2006) *Mapping Policy Preferences II: estimates for parties, electors, and governments in eastern Europe, European Union and OECD 1990–2003*, Oxford: Oxford University Press.

Knapp, A. (2002) 'France: never a golden age', in P. Webb, D. Farrell and I. Holliday (eds) *Political Parties in Advanced Industrial Democracies*, Oxford: Oxford University Press.

Knapp, A. (2003) 'From the Gaullist movement to the president's party' in J. Evans (ed.) *The French Party System*, Manchester: Manchester University Press.

Knapp, A. (2004a) *Parties and the Party System in France: a disconnected democracy?*, Basingstoke: Macmillan.

Knapp, A. (2004b) 'Ephemeral victories? France's governing parties, the ecologists and the far right', in P. Mair, W. Müller and F. Plasser (eds) *Political Parties and Electoral Change: party responses to electoral markets*, London: Sage.

König, T. and Liebert, U. (1996) 'Germany', in J. Blondel and M. Cotta (eds) *Party and Government: an inquiry into the relationships between governments and supporting parties in liberal democracies*, Basingstoke: Macmillan.

Koole, R. (2001) 'Political finance in western Europe: Britain and France', in K. H. Nassmacher (ed.) *Foundations for Democracy: approaches to comparative political finance*, Baden-Baden: Nomos Verlagsgesellschaft.

Koss, M. (2010) *The Politics of Party Funding: state funding to political parties and party competition in western Europe*, Oxford: Oxford University Press.

Laakso, M. and Taagepera, R. (1979) '"Effective" number of parties: a measure with application to west Europe', *Comparative Political Studies*, 12: 3–27.

Ladner, A. (2001) 'Swiss political parties: between persistence and change', *West European Politics*, 24: 123–45.

Lane, J. E. (2001) 'Introduction: Switzerland: key institutions and electorate-orientated outcomes', *West European Politics*, 24: 1–18.

Lane, J. E. and Ersson, S. (1994) *Politics and Society in Western Europe*, 3rd edn, London: Sage.

Laver, M. (1989) 'Party competition and party system change: the interaction of coalition bargaining and electoral competition', *Journal of Theoretical Politics*, 1: 301–24.

Laver, M. (1999) 'The Irish party system approaching the millennium', in M. Marsh and P. Mitchell (eds) *How Ireland Voted 1997*, Boulder, CO: Westview.

Laver, M. and Budge, I. (1992) *Party Policy and Government Coalitions*, London: Macmillan.

Laver, M. and Hunt, W. (1992) *Policy and Party Competition*, New York: Routledge.

Laver, M. and Marsh, M. (1999) 'Parties and voters', in J. Coakley and M. Gallagher (eds) *Politics in the Republic of Ireland*, 3rd edn, London and New York: Routledge.

Laver, M. and Schofield, N. (1990) *Multiparty Government: the politics of coalition in Europe*, Oxford: Oxford University Press.

Lees, C. (2002) 'Coalitions: beyond the politics of centrality?', in S. Padgett and T. Poguntke (eds) *Continuity and Change in German Politics: beyond the politics of centrality? A festschrift for Gordon Smith*, London: Frank Cass.

Leonard, D. (1983) 'Benelux', in V. Bogdanor and D. Butler (eds) *Democracy and Elections: electoral systems and their political consequences*, Cambridge: Cambridge University Press.

Lewis, J. and Williams, A. (1984) 'Social cleavages and electoral performance: the social basis of Portuguese political parties, 1976–1983', *West European Politics*, 7: 119–37.

Lijphart, A. (1968) 'Typologies of democratic systems', *Comparative Political Studies*, 1: 3–44.

Lijphart, A. (1984) *Democracies: patterns of majoritarian and consensus government in twenty-one countries*, New Haven: Yale University Press.

Lijphart, A. (1994) *Electoral Systems and Party Systems: a study of twenty-seven democracies, 1945–1990*, Oxford: Oxford University Press.

Linder, W. (2000) 'Swiss politics today', in M. Butler, M. Pender and J. Charnley (eds) *The Making of Modern Switzerland*, Basingstoke: Macmillan.

Lipset, S. M. and Rokkan, S. (1967) *Party Systems and Voter Alignments: cross-national perspectives*, London and New York: The Free Press.

Lucardie, P. (2003) 'The Netherlands', *European Journal of Political Research*, 42: 1029–36.

Lucardie, P. and Voerman, G. (2004) 'The Netherlands', *European Journal of Political Research*, 43: 1084–92.

Luther, K. R. (1989) 'Dimensions of party system change: the case of Austria', *West European Politics*, 12: 3–27.

Luther, K. R. (1999), 'Must what goes up always come down?', in K. R. Luther and K. Deschouwer (eds) *Party Elites in Divided Societies*, London and New York: Routledge.

Luther, K. R. (2003a) 'The self-destruction of a right-wing populist party? The Austrian parliamentary election of 2002', *West European* Politics, 26: 136–52.

Luther, K. R. (2003b) 'The FPÖ: from populist protest to incumbency', in P. Merkl and L. Weinberg (eds) *Right-Wing Extremism in the Twenty-First Century*, London: Frank Cass.

Luther, K. R. and Deschouwer, K. (1999) *Party Elites in Divided Societies: political parties in consociational democracies*, London: Routledge.

Luther, K. R. and Müller, W. (1992) *Politics in Austria: still a case of consociationalism?*, London: Frank Cass.

Luxembourg Government Homepage (2010) www.gouvernement.lu, accessed 15 January.

Lyrintzis, C. (2005) 'The changing party system: stable democracy, contested modernisation', *West European Politics*, 28: 242–59.

McDonald, M. and Mendes, S. (2001) 'Checking the party policy estimates: convergent validity', in I. Budge *et al.* (eds) *Mapping Policy Preferences: estimates for parties, electors and governments, 1945–1998*, Oxford: Oxford University Press.

MacKenzie, W. J. M. (1958) *Free Elections*, London: Allen and Unwin.

Machin, H. (1989) 'Stages and dynamics in the evolution of the French party system', *West European Politics*, 12: 59–81.

Mackie, T. and Rose, R. (1991) *The International Alamanac of Electoral History*, 3rd edn, Basingstoke: Macmillan.

Macridis, R. (1987) 'Politics of France', in R. Macridis (ed.) *Modern Political Systems: Europe*, 6th edn, London: Prentice-Hall.

Macridis, R. and Lancaster, T. (1987) 'Mediterranean Europe: toward an end to instability?', in R. Macridis (ed.) *Modern Political Systems: Europe*, 6th edn, London: Prentice-Hall.

Magone, J. (1998) 'The logics of party system change in southern Europe', in P. Pennings and J. E. Lane (eds) *Comparing Party System Change*, London: Routledge.

Magone, J. (1999) 'Portugal: party system installation and consolidation', in D. Broughton and M. Donovan (eds) *Changing Party Systems in Western Europe*, London and New York: Pinter.

Magone, J. (2000), 'Portugal: the rationale of democratic regime building', in W. Müller and K. Strøm (eds) *Coalition Governments in Western Europe*, Oxford: Oxford University Press.

Magone, J. (2002) 'Portugal', *European Journal of Political Research*, 41: 1068–74.

Magone, J. (2003) 'Portugal', *European Journal of Political Research*, 42: 1058–66.

Magone, J. (2004) 'Portugal', *European Journal of Political Research*, 43: 1116–20.

Magone, J. (2005) 'Portugal', *European Journal of Political Research*, 44: 1158–66.

Magone, J. (2006) 'Portugal', *European Journal of Political Research*, 45: 1247–53.

Magone, J. (2010) 'Portugal', *European Journal of Political Research*, 49: 1130–8.

Mair, P. (1979) 'The autonomy of the political: the development of the Irish party system', *Comparative Politics*, 11: 445–66.

Mair, P. (1987) *The Changing Irish Party System*, London: Pinter.

Mair, P. (1989a) 'The problem of party system change', *Journal of Theoretical Politics*, 1: 251–76.

Mair, P. (1989b) 'Ireland: from predominance to moderate pluralism and back again?', *West European Politics*, 12: 129–42.

Mair, P. (1993a) 'Myths of electoral change and the survival of traditional parties', *European Journal of Political Research*, 24: 121–33.

Mair, P. (1993b) 'How and why, newly-emerging party systems may differ from established party systems', paper presented at the Conference on the Emergence of New Party Systems and Transitions to Democracy, Bristol, September 1993.

Mair, P. (1993c) 'Fianna Fáil, Labour and the Irish party system', in M. Gallagher and M. Laver (eds) *How Ireland Voted 1992*, Dublin: Folens and PSAI Press.

Mair, P. (1997) *Party System Change: approaches and interpretations*, London: Clarendon.

Mair, P. (1999) 'Party competition and the changing party system', in J. Coakley and M. Gallagher (eds) *Politics in the Republic of Ireland*, 3rd edn, London and New York: Routledge.

Mair, P. (2002) 'Comparing party systems', in L. LeDuc, R. Niemi and P. Norris (eds) *Comparing Democracies 2: new challenges in the study of elections and voting*, London: Sage.

Mair, P. and Marsh, M. (2004) 'Political parties in electoral markets in postwar Ireland', in P. Mair, W. Müller and F. Plasser (eds) *Political Parties and Electoral Change: party responses to electoral markets*, London: Sage.

Mair, P. and Van Biezen, I. (2001) 'Party membership in twenty European democracies', *Party Politics*, 7: 5–21.

Mattila, M. and Raunio, T. (2004) 'Does winning pay? Electoral success and government formation in 15 west European countries', *European Journal of Political Research*, 43: 263–85.

Mavrogordatos, G. (2005) 'Greece', *European Journal of Political Research*, 44: 1025–32.

Mayer, L. (1980) 'A note on the aggregation of party systems', in P. Merkl (ed.), *Western European Party Systems: trends and prospects*, New York: The Free Press.

Ministère de L'intérieur (France) (2010) www.interieur.gouv.fr/, accessed 23 June.

Ministerio del Interior (Spain) (2010) www.mir.es/, accessed 23 April.

Ministero dell'Interno (Italy) (2010) www.elezioni.interno.it/, accessed 2 May.

Ministry of Justice (Finland) (2010) www.vaalit.fi/15499.htm, accessed 26 October.

Ministry of Local Government and Regional Development (Norway), (2010) www.regjeringen. no/nb.html?id=4, accessed 26 May.

Mitchell, P. (2000) 'Ireland: from single-party to coalition rule', in W. Müller and K. Strøm (eds) *Coalition Governments in Western Europe*, Oxford: Oxford University Press.

Mitchell, P. (2003a) ' "O what a tangled web..." – delegation, accountability and executive power', in K. Strøm, W. Müller and T. Bergman (eds) *Delegation and Accountability in Parliamentary Democracies*, Oxford: Oxford University Press.

Mitchell, P. (2003b) 'Fianna Fáil: still dominant in the coalition era: the Irish general election of May 2002', *West European Politics*, 26: 174–83.

Mitchell, P. (2005) 'The United Kingdom: plurality rule under siege', in M. Gallagher and P. Mitchell (eds) *The Politics of Electoral Systems*, Oxford: Oxford University Press.

Molinar, J. (1991) 'Counting the number of parties: an alternative index', *The American Political Science Review*, 85: 1383–91.

Morel, L. (1996) 'France', in J. Blondel and M. Cotta (eds), *Party and Government: an inquiry into the relationships between governments and supporting parties in liberal democracies*, Basingstoke: Macmillan.

Mudde, C. (1996) 'The paradox of the anti-party party: insights from the extreme right', *Party Politics*, 2: 265–76.

Mughan, A. and Gunther, R. (2000) 'The media in democratic and non-democratic regimes: a multilevel perspective', in R. Gunther and A. Mughan (eds) *Democracy and the Media: a comparative perspective*, Cambridge: Cambridge University Press.

Müller, W. (1993) 'The relevance of the state for party system change', *Journal of Theoretical Politics*, 5: 419–54.

Müller, W. (2000a) 'Patronage by national governments', in J. Blondel and M. Cotta (eds) *The Nature of Party Government: a comparative European perspective*, Basingstoke: Macmillan.

Müller, W. (2000b) 'Austria: tight coalitions and stable government', in W. Müller and K. Strøm (eds) *Coalition Governments in Western Europe*, Oxford: Oxford University Press.

Müller, W. (2002) 'Parties and the institutional framework', in K. R. Luther and F. Müller-Rommel (eds) *Political Parties in the New Europe: political and analytical challenges*, Oxford: Oxford University Press.

Müller, W. (2005) 'Austria: a complex electoral system with subtle effects', in M. Gallagher and P. Mitchell (eds) *The Politics of Electoral Systems*, Oxford: Oxford University Press.

Müller, W. (2006) 'Party patronage and party colonization of the state', in R. Katz and W. Crotty (eds) *Handbook of Party Politics*, London: Sage.

Müller, W. and Sieberer, U. (2006) 'Party law', in R. Katz and W. Crotty (eds) *Handbook of Party Politics*, London: Sage.

Müller, W. and Strøm, K. (1999a) 'Conclusions: party behaviour and representative democracy', in W. Müller and K. Strøm (eds) *Policy, Office, or Votes?: how political parties in western Europe make hard decisions*, Cambridge: Cambridge University Press.

Müller, W. and Strøm, K. (1999b) *Policy, Office, or Votes? How political parties in western Europe make hard decisions*, Cambridge: Cambridge University Press.

Müller, W. and Strøm, K. (1999c) 'Political parties and hard choices', in W. Müller and K. Strøm (eds) *Policy, Office, or Votes? How political parties in western Europe make hard decisions*, Cambridge: Cambridge University Press.

Müller, W. and Strøm, K. (2000a) 'Coalition governance in western Europe – an introduction', in W. Müller and K. Strøm (eds) *Coalition Governments in Western Europe*, Oxford: Oxford University Press.

Müller, W. and Strøm, K. (2000b) *Coalition Governments in Western Europe*, Oxford: Oxford University Press.

Müller, W. and Strøm, K. (2000c), 'Conclusion – coalition governance in western Europe', in W. Müller and K. Strøm (eds) *Coalition Governments in Western Europe*, Oxford: Oxford University Press.

Müller, W., Philipp, W. and Steiniger, B. (1996) 'Austria', in J. Blondel and M. Cotta (eds) *Party and Government: an inquiry into the relationships between governments and supporting parties in liberal democracies*, Basingstoke: Macmillan.

Müller, W., Plasser, F. and Ulram, P. (2004) 'Party responses to the erosion of voter loyalties in Austria: weakness as an advantage and strength as a handicap', in P. Mair,

W. Müller and F. Plasser (eds) *Political Parties and Electoral Change: Party Responses to Electoral Markets*, London: Sage.

Murphy, R. and Farrell, D. (2002) 'Party politics in Ireland: regularizing a volatile system', in P. Webb, D. Farrell and I. Holliday (eds) *Political Parties in Advanced Industrial Democracies*, Oxford: Oxford University Press.

Narud, H. and Strøm, K. (2000) 'Norway: a fragile coalitional order', in W. Müller and K. Strøm (eds) *Coalition Governments in Western Europe*, Oxford: Oxford University Press.

Nassmacher, K. H. (2001a) 'Political finance in west central Europe: Austria, Germany and Switzerland', in K. H. Nassmacher (ed.) *Foundations for Democracy: approaches to comparative political finance*, Baden-Baden: Nomos Verlagsgesellschaft.

Nassmacher, K. H. (2001b), 'Comparative political finance in established democracies (introduction)', in K. H. Nassmacher (ed.), *Foundations for Democracy: approaches to comparative political finance*, Baden-Baden: Nomos Verlagsgesellschaft.

Nassmacher, K. H. (2001c) *Foundations for Democracy*, Baden-Baden: Nomos Verlagsgesellschaft.

Nassmacher, K. H. (2003) 'Party funding in continental western Europe', in R. Austin and M. Tjernström (eds) *Funding of Political Parties and Election Campaigns*, Stockholm: International Institute for Democracy and Electoral Assistance.

Nassmacher, K. H. (2006), 'Regulation of party finance', in R. Katz and W. Crotty (eds) *Handbook of Party Politics*, London: Sage.

Neto, O. (2003) 'Portugal: changing patterns of delegation and accountability under the president's watchful eyes', in K. Strøm, W. Müller and T. Bergman (eds), *Delegation and Accountability in Parliamentary Democracies*, Oxford: Oxford University Press.

Nicolacopoulos, I. (2005) 'Elections and voters, 1974–2004', *West European Politics*, 28: 260–78.

Niedermayer, O. (1997) 'German unification and party system change', in P. Pennings and J. E. Lane (eds) *Comparing Party System Change*, London and New York: Routledge.

Norris, P. (2000) *A Virtuous Circle: political communications in post-Industrial societies*, New York: Cambridge University Press.

Norris, P. (2005) *Radical Right: voters and parties in the regulated market*, New York: Cambridge University Press.

Norwegian Centre Party Homepage (2010) www.senterpartiet.no/index.htm, accessed 25 February.

Norwegian Venstre Party Homepage (2010) www.venstre.no/vev/hovedsiden/, accessed 25 February.

Nousiainen, J. (1996) 'Finland', in J. Blondel and M. Cotta (eds), *Party and Government: an inquiry into the relationships between governments and supporting parties in liberal democracies*, Basingstoke: Macmillan.

Nousiainen, J. (2000), 'Finland: the consolidation of parliamentary governance', in W. Müller and K. Strøm (eds) *Coalition Governments in Western Europe*, Oxford: Oxford University Press.

O'Malley, E. and Marsh, M. (2003) 'Ireland', *European Journal of Political Research*, 42: 979–85.

Official Website of Denmark (2010) www.denmark.dk, accessed 21 January.

Padgett, S. (2000) 'The boundaries of stability: the party system before and after the 1998 Bundestagwahl', in S. Padgett and T. Saalfeld (eds) *Bundestagwahl '98: end of an era?*, London: Frank Cass.

Padgett, S. (2001) 'The German volkspartei and the career of the catch-all concept', *German Politics*, 10: 51–72.

Padgett, S. and Poguntke, P. (2002) 'Introduction: beyond the politics of centrality?', in S. Padgett and T. Poguntke (eds) *Continuity and Change in German Politics: beyond the politics of centrality? A festschrift for Gordon Smith*, London: Frank Cass.

Panebianco, A. (1988) *Political Parties: organization and power*, Cambridge: Cambridge University Press.

Papathanassopoulos, S. (2000) 'Election campaigning in the television age: the case of contemporary Greece', *Political Communication*, 17: 57–60.

Pappas, T. (2003) 'The transformation of the Greek party system since 1951', *West European Politics*, 26: 90–114.

Parties and Elections in Europe (2010) www.parties-and-elections.de, accessed 7 November.

Pedersen, K. (2005) 'The 2005 Danish general election', *West European Politics*, 28: 1101–8.

Pedersen, M. (1967) 'Consensus and conflict in the Danish folketing, 1945–1965', *Scandinavian Political Studies*, 2: 143–66.

Pedersen, M. (1979) 'The dynamics of European party systems: changing patterns of electoral volatility', *European Journal of Political Research*, 7: 1–26.

Pennings, P., Keman, H. and Kleinnijenhuis, J. (2006) *Doing Research in Political Science*, 2nd edn, London: Sage.

Pierre, J. and Widfeldt, A. (1999) 'Sweden', *European Journal of Political Research*, 36: 511–18.

Pierre, J., Svåsand, L. and Widfeldt, A. (2000), 'State subsidies to political parties: confronting rhetoric with reality', *West European Politics*, 23: 1–24.

Plasser, F. and Plasser, G. (2002), *Global Political Campaigning: a worldwide analysis of campaign professionals and their practices*, Westport, CT: Praeger.

Poguntke, T. (1987) 'New politics and party systems: the emergence of a new type of party?', *West European Politics*, 10: 76–88.

Poguntke, T. (1993) *Alternative politics: the German Green Party*, Edinburgh: Edinburgh University Press.

Poguntke, T. (1996) 'Anti-party sentiment: conceptual thoughts and empirical evidence: explorations into a minefield', *European Journal of Political Research*, 29: 319–44.

Poguntke, T. (2001) 'The German party system: eternal crisis?', *German Politics*, 10: 37–50.

Poguntke, T. (2003) 'Germany', *European Journal of Political Research*, 42: 957–63.

Portuguese Government Portal (2010) www.portugal.gov.pt/Portal/PT, accessed 22 February.

Pridham, G. and Lewis, P. (1996) 'Introduction: stabilising fragile democracies and party system development', in G. Pridham and P. Lewis (eds) *Stabilising Fragile Democracies: comparing new party systems in southern and eastern Europe*, London and New York: Routledge.

Prime Minister's Office Homepage (Denmark) (2010) www.statsministeriet.dk, 19 February.

Rae, D. (1967) *The Political Consequences of Electoral Laws*, New Haven and London: Yale University Press.

Raunio, T. (2005) 'Finland: one hundred years of quietude', in M. Gallagher and P. Mitchell (eds) *The Politics of Electoral Systems*, Oxford: Oxford University Press.

Rihoux, B. (2000) 'Belgium', *European Journal of Political Research*, 38: 338–47.

Rihoux, B., I. De Winter, P. Dumont and R. Dandoy (2004) 'Belgium', *European Journal of Political Research*, 43: 950–62.

Riker, W. (1962) *The Theory of Political Coalitions*, New Haven and London: Yale University Press.

Riker, W. (1980) 'Implications from the disequilibrium of majority rule for the study of institutions', *American Political Science Review*, 74: 432–46.

Roberts, G. (1989) 'Party system change in West Germany: land-federal linkages', *West European Politics*, 12: 98–113.

Rokkan, S. (1968) 'The structuring of mass politics in the smaller European democracies: a developmental typology', *Comparative Studies in Society and History*, 10: 173–210.

Rose, R. and Urwin, D. (1970) 'Persistence and change in western party systems since 1945', *Political Studies*, 18: 287–319.

Ross, G. (1992) 'Party decline and changing party systems: France and the French Communist Party', *Comparative Politics*, 25: 43–62.

Ruin, O. (1996) 'Sweden', in J. Blondel and M. Cotta (eds), *Party and Government: an inquiry into the relationships between governments and supporting parties in liberal democracies*, Basingstoke: Macmillan.

Rydgren, J. (2004) 'Explaining the emergence of the radical right-wing populist parties: the case of Denmark', *West European Politics*, 27: 474–502.

Saalfeld, T. (2000) 'Germany: stable parties, chancellor democracy and the art of informal settlement', in W. Müller and K. Strøm (eds), *Coalition Governments in Western Europe*, Oxford: Oxford University Press.

Saalfeld, T. (2002) 'The German party system: continuity and change', *German Politics*, 11: 99–130.

Saalfeld, T. (2003), 'Germany: multiple veto points, informal coordination and problems of hidden action', in K. Strøm, W. Müller and T. Bergman (eds), *Delegation and Accountability in Parliamentary Democracies*, Oxford: Oxford University Press.

Saalfeld, T. (2005) 'Germany: stability and strategy in a mixed-member proportional system', in M. Gallagher and P. Mitchell (eds) *The Politics of Electoral Systems*, Oxford: Oxford University Press.

Sainsbury, D. (1984) 'Scandinavian party politics re-examined: social democracy in decline?', *West European Politics*, 7: 67–102.

Sartori, G. (1966) 'European political parties: the case of polarised pluralism', in J. LaPalombara and M. Weiner (eds) *Political Parties and Political Development*, Princeton, New Jersey: Princeton University Press.

Sartori, G. (1968), 'Political development and political engineering', in J. Montgomery and A. Hirschmann (eds), *Public Policy XVII*, Cambridge: Harvard University Press.

Sartori, G. (1976) *Parties and Party Systems: a framework for analysis*, Cambridge: Cambridge University Press.

Sauger, N. (2004) 'Reaggregating interests? How the break-up of the Union for French Democracy has changed the response of the French moderate right', in K. Lawson and T. Poguntke (eds) *How Political Parties Respond: interest aggregation revisited*, London: Routledge.

Scarrow, S. (2002) 'Party decline in the parties state? The changing environment of German politics', in P. Webb, D. Farrell and I. Holliday (eds) *Political Parties in Advanced Industrial Democracies*, Oxford: Oxford University Press.

Scarrow, S. (2004) 'Embracing dealignment, combating realignment: German parties respond', in P. Mair, W. Müller and F. Plasser (eds) *Political Parties and Electoral Change: party responses to electoral markets*, London: Sage.

Scarrow, S. (2006) 'Party subsidies and the freezing of party competition: do cartel mechanisms work?', *West European Politics*, 29: 619–39.

Schedler, A. (1996) 'Anti-political establishment parties', *Party Politics*, 2: 291–312.

Sciarini, P. and Hug, S. (1999) 'The odd fellow: parties and consociationalism in Switzerland', in K. R. Luther and K. Deschouwer (eds) *Party Elites in Divided Societies: political parties in consociational democracies*, London and New York: Routledge.

Seferiades, S. (1986), 'Polarization and nonproportionality: the Greek party system in the postwar era', *Comparative Politics*, 19: 69–93.

Share, D. (1999) 'From policy-seeking to office-seeking: the metamorphosis of the Spanish Socialist Workers' Party', in W. Müller and K. Strøm (eds), *Policy, Office, or Votes? How political parties in western Europe make hard decisions*, Cambridge: Cambridge University Press.

Shugart, M. (1992) 'Electoral reform in systems of proportional representation', *European Journal of Political Research*, 21: 207–24.

Sinnott, R. (1999) 'The electoral system', in J. Coakley and M. Gallagher (eds) *Politics in the Republic of Ireland*, 3rd edn, London and New York: Routledge.

Sjöblom, G. (1968) *Party Strategies in a Multi-Party System*, Lund: Studentlitteratur.

Smart, M. (2000) 'Luxembourg: the national elections of 13 June 1999', *West European Politics*, 23: 193–4.

Smith, G. (1976) 'The politics of centrality in West Germany', *Government and Opposition*, 11: 387–407.

Smith, G. (1982), 'The German volkspartei and the career of the catch-all concept', in H. Döring and G. Smith (eds) *Party Government and Political Culture in Western Germany*, London: Macmillan.

Smith, G. (1987) 'Party and protest: the two faces of opposition in western Europe', in E. Kolinsky (ed.) *Opposition in Western Europe*, London and Sydney: Croon Helm.

Smith, G. (1989a) 'A system perspective on party system change', *Journal of Theoretical Politics*, 1: 349–63.

Smith, G. (1989b) 'Core persistence: change and the "People's Party"', *West European Politics*, 12: 157–68.

Smith, G. (1993) 'Dimensions of change in the German party system', in S. Padgett (ed.) *Parties and Party Systems in the New Germany*, Aldershot: Dartmouth.

Spourdalakis, M. (1996) 'Securing democracy in post-authoritarian Greece: the role of political parties', in G. Pridham and P. Lewis (eds) *Stabilising Fragile Democracies: comparing new party systems in southern and eastern Europe*, London and New York: Routledge.

Steiner, J. (1974) *Amicable Agreement Versus Majority Rule: conflict resolution in Switzerland*, Chapel Hill: University of North Carolina Press.

Strøm, K. (1984) 'Minority governments in parliamentary democracies: the rationality of non-winning cabinet solutions', *Comparative Political Studies*, 17: 199–227.

Strøm, K. (1990) *Minority Government and Majority Rule*, Cambridge: Cambridge University Press.

Sundberg, J. (1999) 'The enduring Scandinavian party system', *Scandinavian Political Studies*, 22: 221–39.

Sundberg, J. (2002) 'The Scandinavian party model at the crossroads', in P. Webb, D. Farrell and I. Holliday (eds) *Political Parties in Advanced Industrial Democracies*, Oxford: Oxford University Press.

Sundberg, J. (2003) 'Finland', *European Journal of Political Research*, 42: 940–2.

Sundberg, J. (2004) 'Finland', *European Journal of Political Research*, 43: 1000–5.

Swedish Government Homepage (2010) www.sweden.gov.se, accessed 25 April.

Swiss Federal Statistics Office (2010) www.bfs.admin.ch, accessed 28 May.

Szarka, J. (1999) 'The parties of the French "plural left": an uneasy complementarity', *West European Politics*, 22: 20–37.

Taagepera, R. (1984) 'The effect of district magnitude and properties of two-seat districts', in A. Lijphart and B. Grofman (eds) *Choosing an Electoral System: issues and alternatives*, Westport, CT: Praeger).

Taagepera, R. (1999) 'Supplementing the effective number of parties', *Electoral Studies*, 18: 497–504.

Thiébault, J. (2000) 'France: forming and maintaining government coalitions in the Fifth Republic', in W. Müller and K. Strøm (eds) *Coalition Governments in Western Europe*, Oxford: Oxford University Press.

Thiébault, J. (2003) 'France: delegation and accountability in the Fifth Republic', in K. Strøm, W. Müller and T. Bergman (eds) *Delegation and Accountability in Parliamentary Democracies*, Oxford: Oxford University Press.

Timmermans, A. and Andeweg, R. (2000) 'The Netherlands: still the politics of accommodation?', in W. Müller and K. Strøm (eds) *Coalition Governments in Western Europe* Oxford: Oxford University Press.

Trantas, G., Zagoriti, P., Bergman, T., Müller, W. and Strøm, K. (2003) 'Greece: "rationalizing" constitutional powers in a post-dictatorial country', in K. Strøm, W. Müller and T. Bergman (eds) *Delegation and Accountability in Parliamentary Democracies*, Oxford: Oxford University Press.

Tsebelis, G. (1990) *Nested Games: rational choice in comparative politics*, Berkeley: University of California Press.

Van Biezen, I. (2000) 'Party financing in new democracies: Spain and Portugal', *Party Politics*, 6: 329–42.

Van Biezen, I. (2003) 'The place of parties in contemporary democracies', *West European Politics*, 26: 171–84.

Van Biezen, I. (2004) 'Political parties as public utilities', *Party Politics*, 10: 701–22.

Van Biezen, I. and Nassmacher, K. H. (2001) 'Political finance in southern Europe: Italy, Portugal and Spain', in K. H. Nassmacher (ed.) *Foundations for Democracy: approaches to comparative political finance*, Baden-Baden: Nomos Verlagsgesellschaft.

Villalba, B. and Vieillard-Coffre, S. (2003) 'The Greens: from idealism to pragmatism (1984–2002)', in J. Evans (ed.) *The French Party System*, Manchester: Manchester University Press.

Verzichelli, L. and Cotta, M. (2000) 'Italy: from "constrained" coalitions to alternating governments?', in W. Müller and K. Strøm (eds) *Coalition Governments in Western Europe*, Oxford: Oxford University Press.

Volkens, A. (2001) 'Quantifying the election programmes: coding procedures and controls', in I. Budge, H. Klingemann, A. Volkens, J. Bara and E. Tanenbaum (eds) *Mapping Policy Preferences: estimates for parties, electors and governments, 1945–1998*, Oxford: Oxford University Press.

Volkens, A. and Klingemann, H. D. (2002), 'Parties, ideologies, and issues: stability and change in 15 European party systems, 1945–1998', in K. R. Luther and F. Müller-Rommel (eds) *Parties in the New Europe: political and analytical challenges*, Oxford: Oxford University Press.

Webb, P. (2002) 'Party systems, electoral cleavages and government stability', in P. Heywood, E. Jones and M. Rhodes (eds) *Developments in West European Politics 2*, London: Macmillan.

Webb, P., Farrell, D. and Holliday, I. (2002) *Political Parties in Advanced Industrial Democracies*, Oxford: Oxford University Press.

Widfeldt, A. (2000) 'Scandinavia: mixed success for the populist right', *Parliamentary Affairs*, 53: 486–501.

Widfeldt, A. (2003) 'Sweden', *European Journal of Political Research*, 42: 1091–1101.

Wilson, F. (1988) 'The French party system in the 1980s', in S. Wolinetz (ed.) *Parties and Party Systems in Liberal Democracies*, London and New York: Routledge.

Wolinetz, S. (1979) 'The Transformation of Western European Party Systems Revisited', *West European Politics*, 4–28.

Wright, V. (1989) *The Government and Politics of France*, London: Routledge.

Woldendorp, J., Keman, H. and Budge, I. (2000) *Party Government in 48 Democracies*, Dordrecht: Kluwer.

Wolinetz, S. (1999) 'The consociational party system', in K. R. Luther and K. Deschouwer (eds) *Party Elites in Divided Societies: political parties in consociational democracies*, London and New York: Routledge.

Wolinetz, S. (2004) 'Classifying party systems: where have all the typologies gone?', paper presented at the Annual Meeting of the Canadian Political Science Association, Winnipeg, Manitoba, June 2004.

xe.com, www.xe.com (2009) accessed 25 July.

Ysmal, C. (2003) 'France', *European Journal of Political Research*, 42: 943–56.

Index

Note: Page numbers in *italics* denote tables, those in **bold** denote figures.

Abedi, A. 31

alternation in government, conceivable patterns 99

Anglo-Irish Treaty 171

anti-political establishment parties: Abedi's list 31; countries' exclusion strategies 90; criteria 31; definition 9; electorate-orientated strategies 30–3; established parties' strategies towards 32, *33*; Germany 9, 92; and the governing threshold 100; Luxembourg 93; Portugal 90; Switzerland 92–3, 129–30; threshold of systemic relevance 32; in western Europe 201

Arter, D. 164

Austria: average length of coalition agreements *38*; cartel party system 54; cartel strategies 54; coalition formation 188–9; coalition governments based on pre-electoral coalition agreements *36*; electoral laws *48*; electoral laws and non-established parties *48*; electoral responsiveness 28, *29*, 30; electorate-orientated strategies *91*; electorate-orientated strategies and systemic centrality levels *185*; established parties 197; established parties' centrality 40, *205*; ideological change and party incumbency *24*; ideological change in governing parties 20; institutional strategies *95*; institutional strategies and systemic centrality levels *187*; party system 101; role of perverse effects 188–9; state subsidy system 77, *82*; strategy towards anti-establishment parties *33*; television campaigning regimes *70*

Belgium: coalition agreements 36, *38*;

electoral laws *52*, 54; electoral responsiveness 28, *29*, 30; electorate-orientated strategies *91*; electorate-orientated strategies and systemic centrality levels *185*; established parties 197; established parties' centrality *207*; ideological change and party incumbency *25*; ideological change in governing parties 20; institutional strategies *95*; institutional strategies and systemic centrality levels *187*; strategy towards anti-establishment parties 32, *33*; television campaigning regimes *72*

Berglund, S. 164–5

Berlusconi, Silvio 67

Blocher, Christoph 129

Blyth, Mark 188

Bottom, K. 8

Boucek, F. 107

Bowler, S. 43–5

Bruneau, T. 126

campaign subsidies: in electoral law 45–6; French experience 94; role of eligibility thresholds 45–6

cantonal politics, Switzerland 129

cartel behaviours, prime goal of parties engaging in 186

cartel party system: concept analysis 8; conditions for 187–8; Denmark and Austria 54; exclusion strategies 32; key features 45, 74; literature review 8; Luxembourg 144; major features 74; and media access 74; and state subsidies 74; Switzerland 93, 143

cartel strategies, countries engaged in 54

cartel thesis: basis 42; and centrality levels 187; core elements 186; and electoral responsiveness 30; Katz and Mair's arguments 11; and state subsidy systems 77

Carter, E. 43, 45, 56

causality chains 183, 190–3

centrality: assessment criteria *184*; and electorate-orientated strategies 125–8, 141–5, 184–6, 188; of established parties, *see* established parties' centrality; impact of party strategies on 183; Luxembourg–Switzerland comparison 137, 142

civil society, movement of parties away from 186

CMP (Comparative Manifesto Project) 18

coalition agreements: average document length *38*, 40; consequences of lengthy 37; definitions 34; Dumont and De Winter on the secrecy of 40; and electoral responsiveness 34, 37; German experience 92; Golders' arguments 34; Luxembourger experience 93; Luxembourg–Switzerland comparison 141; Portuguese experience 90, 92; secrecy 143–4; Swiss experience 93

coalition make-up, relationship between vote share and 27

coalitions: and electoral responsiveness 34; Irish experience 177

consociational democracies, Swiss dominance 142

core parties 8, 45, 128, 165, 170

Crewe, I. 3

Dalton, R. 3, 13

De Swaan, A. 109

De Winter, L. 40, 136, 143

declining party membership 1

definitions: anti-political establishment parties 9; coalition agreements 34; electoral laws 43; electoral systems 54; electorate-orientated strategies 7; established parties 7–9, 106; institutional strategies 7; party system 12; party system change 13; political party 6–8, 186

democratic legitimacy 27, 113, 189

democratic revolutions 191

Denmark: average length of coalition agreements *38*; cartel party system 54; cartel strategies 54; centrality 66; centrality levels 187; coalition governments based on pre-electoral

coalition agreements *36*; dominant parties 164; electoral earthquakes 171, 176; electoral responsiveness *29*; electoral system 166; electoral systems *64*; electorate-orientated strategies *91*; electorate-orientated strategies and systemic centrality levels *185*; established and non-established parties *165*; established parties 197; established parties' centrality 166, 190; free airtime allocation methods 96; ideological change and party incumbency *24*; ideological change in governing parties *20*; institutional strategies *95*, 96–7; institutional strategies and systemic centrality levels *187*; natural party of government 164; party system change 166–71; state subsidy system 77; strategy levels 190–1; strategy towards anti-establishment parties 32, *33*

Denmark–Ireland comparisons: institutional strategies 177–80; party system change 176

deposit requirements, in electoral law 44

DF (Danish People's Party) 165

Dimitras, P. 96

direct democracy 129, 135, 142–3, 183, 190

disproportionality: Danish experience 96; French experience 94–5; Greek experience 96; Irish experience 97

Downs, A. 6, 10, 185–6

Dumont, P. 40, 136, 143

Duverger, M. 54–5

'earthquake' elections 2, 28

effective number of parties index 105–6

electoral campaigns, increase in costs 46

electoral centrality: and high levels of strategy engagement 192; levels of in Greece, Spain and Portugal *192*

electoral earthquakes: Denmark 171, 176

electoral laws: adoption of permissive systems 54; campaign expenditure limits 46; campaign subsidies 45–6; coding categories *47*; definitions 43; deposit requirements 44; independent candidates 45; literature review 43–4; and non-established parties in western Europe *48*; signature requirements 44–5

electoral performance of governments, Müller and Strøm's work 19

electoral responsiveness: German
experience 92; Luxembourg–
Switzerland comparison 143–4;
Switzerland 28, *29*, 30, 143; and voter
backlash 188
electoral shocks 28, 180
electoral systems: ballot structure 55;
definition 54; district magnitude 55–6;
impact on party systems 54–5; legal
thresholds 56–7; and non-established
parties in western Europe *58*; number of
tiers 56; scholarly attention 4; Single
Transferable Vote 171
electoral turnout, decreasing 1
electoral volatility 1–3, 17, 28, 193
electorate-orientated strategies 89, 112;
and centrality of established parties
125–8, 141–5, 184–5, 188; definition 7;
electoral responsiveness 26–30 (*see also*
electoral responsiveness); findings
summarisation problems 89–90;
Germany 92, 119–25; Germany–
Portugal comparison 125–8; ideological
change 16–26; impacts 184–6; length of
coalition agreements 37, 40;
Luxembourg 93, 136–41; Luxembourg–
Switzerland comparison 143–4; in the
parliamentary arena 185; Portugal
112–19; pre-election coalition
agreements 34–7; relations with anti-
political establishment parties 30–3;
Switzerland 93, 129–35; and systemic
centrality levels *185*; use of by country
91
electronic media 11, 68
Elgie, R. 94
established parties: assessing the fate of
106; definition 7–9, 106
established parties assessment: government
positions measures 109–10; 'king
maker' measure 109; share of
parliamentary seats 108; share of the
vote 107–8; time spent in government
109
established parties' centrality: Austria *205*;
Belgium *207*; Finland *210*; frequent use
of electorate-orientated strategies and
125–8; Italy *214*; measuring 106–10;
Netherlands *218*; Norway *221*; Spain
223; Sweden *225*; United Kingdom *227*

Fifth Republic: creation 148; electoral
system 149; party system format 151
Finland *29*; alternation in government

patterns 101; average length of coalition
agreements *38*; coalition governments
based on pre-electoral coalition
agreements 36; electoral responsiveness
29; electorate-orientated strategies *91*;
electorate-orientated strategies and
systemic centrality levels *185*;
established parties 197; established
parties' centrality *210*; ideological
change and party incumbency *24*;
ideological change in governing parties
20; institutional strategies *95*;
institutional strategies and systemic
centrality levels *187*; state subsidy
system 77, *78*; strategy towards anti-
establishment parties 32, *33*
Fording, R. 18
formula, for calculating effective number
of parties 105
fractionalisation index, Rae's 105–6
France: alternation in government issues
99; average length of coalition
agreements *38*; centrality 66; centrality
levels 187; coalition governments based
on pre-electoral coalition agreements
36; competition structure stages 154;
electoral responsiveness 28, *29*;
electoral system 149; electoral system
changes 57; electoral systems *58*;
electorate-orientated strategies *91*;
electorate-orientated strategies and
systemic centrality levels *185*;
established and non-established parties
150; established parties 198; established
parties' centrality 149–51, *152*; free
airtime allocation criteria 94–5;
ideological change and party
incumbency *25*; ideological change in
governing parties 20; institutional
strategies 94, *95*, 148–55; institutional
strategies and systemic centrality levels
187; party ideologies 149; party system
change 151–5; presidential politics 189;
quadrille bipolaire 151; strategy
towards anti-establishment parties *33*;
systemic centrality 189
Franklin, M. 2
'freezing hypothesis' 2

Gaulle, Charles De 148
German–Portuguese comparisons:
electorate-orientated strategies 125–8;
party system change 125; party systems
124

Germany: anti-political establishment parties 9, 92; average length of coalition agreements *38*, 92; electoral laws *50*; electoral responsiveness *29*; electoral systems *62*; electorate-orientated strategies and systemic centrality levels *91*, 92, 119–25, *185*; established and non-established parties 9, 119, *120*, 199; established parties' centrality 119–20, *121*, 126–8; established parties' strategies 186; governmental centrality levels 185; governments based on pre-electoral coalition agreements *36*; Greens' entrance into parliament 124; ideological change and party incumbency *24*; ideological change in governing parties 20; institutional strategies 95; institutional strategies and systemic centrality levels *187*; *Parteieinverdrossenheit* 128; party system change *124*, 125; post-war democratic era 119; principal feature of the coalition system 35; responsiveness in 92; state subsidy system 77, *84*; strategy towards anti-establishment parties *33*; television campaigning regimes *70*
Golder, S. 34–5
government access, Mair vs Sartori 100
Greece: adoption of proportional representation system 96; average length of coalition agreements *38*; centrality 66; centrality levels 187; coalition governments based on pre-electoral coalition agreements *36*; democratic revolution 191; electoral responsiveness *29*; electoral system changes 57; electorate-orientated strategies *91*; electorate-orientated strategies and systemic centrality levels *185*; free airtime allocation method 96; ideological change and party incumbency *24*; ideological change in governing parties 20; institutional strategies *95*; institutional strategies and systemic centrality levels *187*; proportional representation in 57; public availability of coalition agreements 40; state subsidy system *82*; strategy engagement levels *191*; strategy towards anti-establishment parties *33*; television campaigning regimes *70*
Grofman, B. 43
Gunther, R. 67

Hanley, D. 154

Holtz-Bacha, C. 66

ideological change 26; assessing 18–19; concept analysis 16–17; Downsian argument 22; following an electoral defeat 17; German experience 20, *24*, 92; and government status *26*; incumbency effects 19–23, *24*; Kim and Fording formula 19; levels of and party responsiveness 17; long-term perspective 17–18; optimal strategy 23; Portuguese experience 90; positive associations of high levels 23; Swiss experience 130; two hypotheses 26; in western European governing parties 20
impacts: of electorate-orientated strategies 184–6; of institutional strategies 186–8; intervening systemic and regime factors 189–90; of social change 2–5; voter backlash and perverse effects 188–9
incumbency, effects of ideological change on 19–23, *24*
independent candidates, in electoral law 45
independent candidates, Irish example 45
industrialisation 3
instability: French experience 154–5, 164; Greek experience 161
institutional arrangements, role in the process of party system change 4
institutional manipulation 11
institutional strategies: and centrality of established parties 160–4, 177–80; definition 7; Denmark 164–71; Denmark–Ireland comparison 177–80; electoral laws, *see* electoral laws; electoral systems, *see* electoral systems; established parties' engagement and systemic dominance 98; France 94–5, 148–55; and governmental centrality 188; Greece 155–60; Greece–France comparison 164; impacts of 186–8; Ireland 171–7; and parliamentary centrality 187; prime focus 186; state subsidies, *see* state subsidies; and systemic centrality levels *187*; television campaigning, *see* television campaigning; use of by country 95
Ireland: average length of coalition agreements *38*; centrality levels 187; coalition governments based on pre-electoral coalition agreements *36*; electoral laws 54; electoral responsiveness *29*; electoral shock 180;

Ireland *continued*
electoral system 97, 171; electorate-orientated strategies *91*; electorate-orientated strategies and systemic centrality levels *185*; established and non-established parties *172*; established parties' centrality 172–3, *174*; free airtime allocation methods 97; ideological change and party incumbency *24*; ideological change in governing parties 20; institutional strategies *95*, 97; institutional strategies and systemic centrality levels *187*; leading parties 172; party system change 173–7; strategy towards anti-establishment parties 32, *33*; television campaigning regimes *72*; unique features 171
Italy: average length of coalition agreements *38*; coalition governments based on pre-electoral coalition agreements 36; electoral laws *48*; electoral responsiveness *29*; electoral systems *60*; electorate-orientated strategies *91*; electorate-orientated strategies and systemic centrality levels *185*; established parties' centrality *214*; ideological change and party incumbency *25*; ideological change in governing parties 20; institutional strategies *95*; institutional strategies and systemic centrality levels *187*; state subsidy system *80*; strategy towards anti-establishment parties *33*

Janda, K. 17

Kaid, L. 66
Katz, R. 6–8, 11, 27, 32, 42, 45, 74, 188
Katz and Mair 98, 186–7
Kim, H. 18
Kirchheimer, O. 13
Knapp, A. 149

Laakso, M. 105–6
Ladner, A. 129
Laver, M. 13
Lijphart, A. 43, 101
Linder, W. 142–3
Lindström, U. 164–5
Lipset, S.M. 2, 171
Luther, K.R. 14, 107, 189
Luxembourg: anti-political establishment parties 93; average length of coalition agreements *38*; cartel party system 144; categorisation of party system 102; coalition agreements 144; coalition governments based on pre-electoral coalition agreements *36*; electoral laws *50*; electoral responsiveness *29*, 143–4; electoral systems *60*; electorate-orientated strategies *91*, 92–3; electorate-orientated strategies and systemic centrality levels *185*; established and non-established parties in *136*; established parties' centrality 136–7; established parties' strategies 186; governmental centrality levels 185; ideological change and party incumbency *25*; ideological change in governing parties 20; institutional strategies *95*; institutional strategies and systemic centrality levels *187*; party system change 137, *140*, 141; public availability of coalition agreements 40; state subsidy system *86*; strategy towards anti-establishment parties 32, *33*
Luxembourg–Switzerland comparisons: centrality 137, 142; coalition agreements 141; electoral responsiveness 143–4; electorate-orientated strategies 143–4; party system change 141

Magone, J. 118
Mair, P. 1, 3–4, 7–8, 11, 13–14, 27, 32, 45, 74
Mair typology 14, *99*; access to government component 100–1; alternation in government component 99; benefits of the revised 104–5; components 99; focus 102, 104; innovative or familiar governing formulae component 100; introduction of a numerical aspect *104*; major advantage over other party system typologies 98; missing element 102; overview 101–6; principal advantage 14; problems with 100–1; revised 102, *103*, 106; value 14
manifestos 18
Mughan, A. 67
Müller, W. 1, 4–5, 10–11, 13, 19, 34, 42, 185–6

nested games 12, 190
Netherlands: average length of coalition agreements *38*; centrality 66; coalition governments based on pre-electoral

coalition agreements 36; earthquake election 28; electoral responsiveness *29*; electoral systems *64*; electorate-orientated strategies *91*; electorate-orientated strategies and systemic centrality levels *185*; established parties' centrality *218*; ideological change and party incumbency *25*; ideological change in governing parties 20; institutional strategies *95*; institutional strategies and systemic centrality levels *187*; state subsidy system 77; strategy towards anti-establishment parties 32, *33*; television campaigning regimes *70*

non-established parties: Danish experience 96–7; French systems' restrictiveness 94; Greek institutions' restrictiveness 96; Irish experience 97

Norway: average length of coalition agreements *38*; coalition governments based on pre-electoral coalition agreements *36*; electoral responsiveness *29*; electorate-orientated strategies *91*; electorate-orientated strategies and systemic centrality levels *185*; established parties' centrality 40, *221*; ideological change and party incumbency *25*; ideological change in governing parties 20; institutional strategies *95*; institutional strategies and systemic centrality levels *187*; party system 104; state subsidy system 77; strategy towards anti-establishment parties 32, *33*

office-seeking model 10

parties: basic motive underlying the behaviour of 10; defining established and non-established *9*; definition 186

partisan dealignment 1

party competition, Downsian model 10, 16–17, 126, 142, 184

party funding, Katz and Mair's conclusion 74

party membership, declining 1

party system, classic definition 12

party system change: defining 13; Denmark–Ireland comparison 176; electoral change and 193–5; France 151–5; Germany–Portugal comparison 125; important factors in 11; Ireland 173–7; Luxembourg–Switzerland comparison 141; Mair's unique measure

of 98 (*see also* Mair typology); Portugal 117–18, 126; role of state institutions in the relationship between electoral and 4; Switzerland 134–5

party systems: Austria–Finland–Netherlands comparisons 104; characteristics of closed 100, 102, 104–5; Germany–Portugal comparison 124; innovation vs familiarity 100; open vs closed 14 (*see also* Mair typology); role of numbers in the assessment of 102; Sartorian interpretation 13–14, 135; two vital elements 105

payout thresholds, of state subsidies 76, *77*

perverse effects 188–9

Pierre, J. 45, 74

polarised pluralism, Sartori's concept 100

Political Consequences of Electoral Laws, The (Rae) 43

political parties, role of 5–6

political party, definitions of a 6–7

Portugal: anti-political establishment parties 90; average length of coalition agreements *38*; coalition governments based on pre-electoral coalition agreements *36*; democratic revolution 191; electoral responsiveness 28, *29*; electoral systems *60*; electorate-orientated strategies *91*, 92; electorate-orientated strategies and systemic centrality levels *185*; established and non-established parties in *113*; established parties' centrality 40, *114*, 116, 118–19, 126–7; established parties' strategies 186; governing parties 118; governmental centrality levels 185; ideological change and party incumbency *24*; ideological change in governing parties 20; institutional strategies *95*; institutional strategies and systemic centrality levels *187*; levels of electorate-orientated strategies 90; parties' role in democracy 126; party system change 117–18, 126; party system destabilisation 118; post-war democratic era 112–13; state subsidy system 77; strategy engagement levels *191*; strategy towards anti-establishment parties 32, *33*; television campaigning regimes *72*

proportional representation: Greek adoption 96

Rae, D. 55, 105

Rokkan, S. 2, 171

Saalfeld, T. 35, 37
Salazar, António de Oliveira 113
Sartori, G. 12–14, 100, 102
Scandinavia: dominant model of party
    competition 164; minority governments'
    prevalence 190
Scarrow, S. 45, 75, 128
Schedler, A. 30–1
Smith, G. 3–4, 7–8, 13, 107
social change, impact on modern-day party
    systems 2–5
social democracy, Danish experience 164
Spain: average length of coalition
    agreements *38*; coalition governments
    based on pre-electoral coalition
    agreements 36; democratic revolution
    191; electoral laws *52*, *54*; electoral
    responsiveness 28, *29*; electorate-
    orientated strategies *91*; electorate-
    orientated strategies and systemic
    centrality levels *185*; established parties'
    centrality *223*; ideological change and
    party incumbency *25*; ideological
    change in governing parties 20;
    institutional strategies *95*; institutional
    strategies and systemic centrality levels
    187; state subsidy system *80*; strategy
    engagement levels *191*; strategy towards
    anti-establishment parties 32, *33*;
    television campaigning regimes *70*
state institutions, and party system change
    4, 11
state subsidies: allocation methods 76;
    coding categories *77*; French experience
    95; funded institutions 75; Irish
    experience 97; Katz and Mair's
    conclusion 74; levels 75; literature
    review 74–5; payout thresholds 76
strategies: prime motivation for engaging
    in 10; two types of 10
strategies and systems: concept analysis 9,
    12; established parties 7–9; party system
    change 12–14
strategy engagement levels, in Greece,
    Spain and Portugal *191*
Strøm, K. 1, 10, 19, 26–7, 34, 185–6
STV (Single Transferable Vote) 171
subsidies, balance of power impact 45
Sundberg, J. 96
Sweden: average length of coalition
    agreements *38*; centrality 66; coalition
    governments based on pre-electoral

coalition agreements *36*; electoral
    responsiveness 28, *29*, 30; electorate-
    orientated strategies *91*; electorate-
    orientated strategies and systemic
    centrality levels *185*; established parties'
    centrality *225*; ideological change and
    party incumbency *24*; ideological
    change in governing parties 20;
    institutional strategies *95*; institutional
    strategies and systemic centrality levels
    187; strategy towards anti-establishment
    parties 32, *33*
Switzerland: anti-political establishment
    parties 92–3, 129–30; average length of
    coalition agreements *38*; cartel party
    system 93, 143; coalition agreements
    144; coalition governments based on
    pre-electoral coalition agreements 36;
    electoral laws *50*; electoral
    responsiveness 28, *29*, 30, 143; electoral
    systems *62*; electorate-orientated
    strategies *91*, 92; electorate-orientated
    strategies and systemic centrality levels
    185; established and non-established
    parties 129, *130*; established parties'
    centrality 130–4; established parties'
    strategies 186; federal system 129;
    governmental centrality levels 185;
    ideological change and party
    incumbency *24*; ideological change in
    governing parties 20; important features
    of the political structure 129;
    institutional strategies *95*; institutional
    strategies and systemic centrality levels
    187; 'magic formula' 93, 129, 134, 142;
    party system change 134–5; political
    characteristics 135; power of the
    electorate 142–3; public availability of
    coalition agreements 40; state subsidy
    system *78*; strategy towards anti-
    establishment parties 32, *33*; television
    campaigning regimes *72*

Taagepera, R. 105–6
television campaigning: airtime 42, 66;
    'American style' 66–7; coding
    categories *69*; Danish experience 96–7;
    eligibility for and allocation of free
    airtime 68; French system 94; Greek
    system 96; impact on voters 67; Irish
    experience 97; literature review 66–7;
    paid vs free airtime 67–8; penetration in
    western Europe 66; regimes and non-
    established parties in western Europe *70*

traditional cleavages, decline of the importance of 11
traditional parties, Mair's definition 8
Tsebelis, G. 12, 190

United Kingdom: alternation in government 101; average length of coalition agreements *38*; cartelisation argument 188; centrality *66*; coalition governments based on pre-electoral coalition agreements 36; electoral laws *52*; electoral responsiveness *29*; electoral systems *58*; electorate-orientated strategies *91*; electorate-orientated strategies and systemic centrality levels *185*; established parties' centrality *227*; ideological change and party incumbency *25*; ideological change in governing parties 20; institutional strategies *95*; institutional strategies and systemic centrality levels *187*; introduction of universal suffrage 171; state subsidy system 77, *78*; strategy towards anti-establishment parties *33*

volatility, electoral 1–3, 17, 28, 193
vote share, Mair's argument 108
vote-seeking 6, 10–12, 184–6, 188
voter backlash 188–9

Wattenberg, M. 3

For Product Safety Concerns and Information please contact our EU
representative GPSR@taylorandfrancis.com
Taylor & Francis Verlag GmbH, Kaufingerstraße 24, 80331 München, Germany

www.ingramcontent.com/pod-product-compliance
Lightning Source LLC
Chambersburg PA
CBHW071221290326
41931CB00037B/1597